LIBRARY OF
RELIGIOUS AND PHILOSOPHICAL THOUGHT

PRIMITIVE CHRISTIANITY

VOL. I

PRIMITIVE CHRISTIANITY

ITS WRITINGS AND TEACHINGS IN THEIR HISTORICAL CONNECTIONS

BY

OTTO PFLEIDERER, D.D.

PROFESSOR OF PRACTICAL THEOLOGY IN THE UNIVERSITY OF BERLIN

TRANSLATED BY

W. MONTGOMERY, B.D.

AND EDITED BY

THE REV. W. D. MORRISON, LL.D.

VOL. I

REFERENCE BOOK PUBLISHERS, INC.
CLIFTON, NEW JERSEY
1965

Published 1965 by
Reference Book Publishers, Inc.

Library of Congress Catalog Card Number: 65-22085

Printed in the United States of America

PREFACE

In the present edition the work appears in a thoroughly revised and greatly extended form. The progress which the last decade has witnessed in exegetical and critical studies, and in the historical investigation of religion, has throughout been turned to account. Among theologians of the present day, I am indebted above all others to my honoured friend Dr Heinrich Holtzmann, whose works on New Testament Introduction, Theology, and Exegesis are so notably distinguished by complete mastery of the material, by absence of prejudice, and by critical acumen, that they will doubtless long rank as standard authorities. But I have carefully studied also the work of other theologians of the most diverse tendencies; and where I have learned anything from them, or have had the satisfaction of finding myself in agreement with their results, I have indicated of the fact by quotations or references. On the other hand, I have on principle refrained from polemics, in order, for one thing, not to extend my book beyond due limits, but also because, in my belief, polemics are of little value. Those who are directly attacked seldom allow themselves to be moved from their opinions; while for others, the only effect of polemical digressions is to increase the difficulty of gaining a general impression of the view which the writer desires to set forth. Consequently, the power of the argument to produce conviction is weakened; since that depends in no small measure on the consonance of its several parts. I have therefore to ask the reader to be kind enough not to conclude from my not mentioning opinions which diverge from mine, that I am unacquainted with them; I ventured to hope that the most convincing method of refuting them would be to set forth plainly the grounds on which my own opinions were based. Next to the labours of my fellow-workers in theology, that which has proved of most service to me in working over the material again, has been my own continued study of the history of religion. I have become more and more strongly convinced in the course of these studies how much that is helpful for the understanding of primitive Christianity is to be learned from the comparison with extra-Biblical Jewish, and heathen, religious history; how indispensable, indeed, such comparison is for the elucidation of some of the most important questions. I am well aware that, to many, my practice of drawing parallels from the sphere of heathen religion will appear superfluous, while to some it will even be a ground of offence. In Germany, even more than elsewhere, it is still customary to take up a shy and suspicious attitude towards the application of the Science of Comparative Religion within the domain of Biblical Theology. The few who venture to make use of it draw on themselves, as I know from my own experience, the reproach of " paganising." That, however, has never made me waver in my conviction, which has remained unshaken ever since I studied under my revered teacher, Ferdinand Christian Baur, that Christianity as a historical phenomenon is to be investigated by the same methods as all other history, and that, in particular, its origin is to be understood by being studied as the normal outcome of the manifold factors in the religious and ethical life of the time. Even though the way in which Baur conceived this development was not, as we all know now, quite accurate in detail, yet the principle of development, which he introduced into the historical study of theology, retains its position by an incontestable right—a position which the temporary reactionary tendency of traditionalism and dogmatic positivism will not ultimately affect in the slightest degree. I believe, moreover, that this tendency is already on the wane, and that the time is not far distant when the application to Biblical Theology of the historical and comparative methods of the Science of Religion will be generally welcomed.

When that takes place, people will be able to convince themselves that this scientific investigation of its history in no way endangers the stability of the Christian religion. Quite the contrary. So long as Christianity is conceived of as a miracle, whether unique or repeated, its truth is, for the men of our critical age, always more or less problematical. But when it is recognised as the necessary outcome of the development of the religious spirit of our race, towards the production of which the whole history of the ancient world was moving onward, in the furnishing forth of which the mental and spiritual acquisitions of the East and West have found their application, their enhancement, and their higher unity —when this is recognised, it becomes, in my opinion, the most solid and imposing Apology for Christianity which it is possible to conceive. Of course, the historical investigator ought not to allow himself to be guided in the treatment of particulars by an apologetic purpose, but should seek to discover, with the utmost possible precision, exactly how things were. The more loyally he strives after the attainment of objective truth in his exposition of the manifold con-current causes, the more certainly will the general result shape itself into a defence of essential Christianity. The whole wealth of religious ideas and ethical motives which the Christian principle includes within itself cannot be rightly grasped by any method of studying its history which is fettered by dogmatic prejudices, or is held in leading-strings by subjective or Confessional prepossessions. Only a science which is free from the fetters of dogma, and which seeks to understand the origin and growth of Christianity with reference to conditions of period and environment, will succeed in obtaining full recognition for the surpassing greatness of its principle, which unites within itself the most various aspects and the most opposite tendencies. Free historical inquiry is therefore no enemy to the most pious reverence for Christianity; it opposes only the dogmatic narrow-ness and exclusiveness which can allow value only to one form of Truth, while it has no comprehension for the revelation of Truth in other forms. Holding this opinion, I desire that this book, while designed in the first place to serve the interests of scientific knowledge, may at the same time contribute to the furtherance of the great practical task of our time—the task of reconciling the just claims of modern scientific thought, and the critical testing of all tradition, with the reverent recognition of the abiding truth and of the unique value of Christianity as the basis of our common ethical education.

CONTENTS

CHAP.   PAGES
I. THE FIRST CHRISTIAN COMMUNITY 1–32

THE APOSTLE PAUL.

II. PERSONALITY 33–39

III. EDUCATION: GREEK INFLUENCE 40–63

IV. EDUCATION: JEWISH INFLUENCE 64–83

V. CONVERSION AND CALL 84–106

VI. PAUL AND THE FIRST APOSTLES 107–124

THE WRITINGS OF PAUL.

VII. THE LETTERS TO THE THESSALONIANS . . . 125–143

VIII. THE LETTERS TO THE CORINTHIANS . . . 144–190

IX. THE LETTER TO THE GALATIANS . . . 191–210

X. THE LETTER TO THE ROMANS . . . 211–247

XI. THE LETTER TO THE PHILIPPIANS . . . 248–257

XII. THE LETTERS TO PHILEMON AND THE COLOSSIANS . 258–269

CONTENTS

THE THEOLOGY OF PAUL.

CHAP.		PAGES
XIII.	THE NATURAL MAN	270–292
XIV.	HEATHENISM AND JUDAISM	293–314
XV.	REDEMPTION THROUGH JESUS CHRIST	315–343
XVI.	JUSTIFICATION BY FAITH	344–368
XVII.	LIFE IN THE SPIRIT	369–410
XVIII.	CHURCH AND WORLD	411–434
XIX.	THE METHODS AND AIMS OF THE PLAN OF SALVATION	435–471

PRIMITIVE CHRISTIANITY

CHAPTER I

THE FIRST CHRISTIAN COMMUNITY

HOWEVER much we may regret that we have so little certain knowledge regarding the first beginnings of Christianity, the fact itself can hardly be disputed. Not until the appearance of the Apostle Paul, in whose letters authentic information lies before us, is the historical darkness in some measure lightened. But of the manner in which the Church arose, Paul gives us only a few scanty indications (1 Cor. xv. 3 ff.) from which it is not possible to draw a clear picture of the course of events. This *lacuna* the Gospels, written at a later period, and the Acts of the Apostles, do not completely fill. It is true these various witnesses are in general agreement that the Christian community arose in consequence of the wonderful experiences of the first disciples of Jesus, through which they came to be convinced that their crucified Master had risen again and was alive. But so soon as we inquire concerning the how and where of these experiences, we encounter the gravest difficulties: The oldest Gospel, from which we might

1

fairly expect the earliest clear historical tradition, is mutilated at the decisive passage, and the genuine conclusion, now lost, has been replaced by an abstract from the later Gospels (Mark xvi. 9 ff.); while the reports of the other Gospels are so contradictory that it is not possible to gain from them a clear mental picture. It is impossible completely to realise the representation of a body of the risen Jesus which is at one time wholly material, and, like an ordinary earthly body, can be handled and can take food, but at another time seems to be of supernatural character, since it passes through closed doors, suddenly appears and disappears, and is taken up into heaven. Again, the Evangelists contradict one another as regards the place of the appearances. In Mark, the disciples are directed to go to Galilee in order to see the risen Jesus there; similarly in Matthew, who, further, gives an account of the appearance on a mountain in Galilee, but places it after another appearance to the women as they were returning from the grave; Luke, on the other hand, tells only of appearances on the road to Emmaus in the neighbourhood of Jerusalem, and in Jerusalem itself, and completely excludes the Galilæan appearances by indicating that the disciples were charged to remain in Jerusalem; John, again, recounts, like Luke, the appearances to the disciples in Jerusalem, but at the same time reports, like Matthew, the previous appearance to Mary at the grave, and a last appearance to the disciples in Galilee, at the Lake of Gennesareth. Finally, Paul knows nothing of that which the Evangelists place in the forefront of their account—how the women found the grave empty, and witnessed an appearance of an angel, or of Christ; instead he mentions a series of appearances which do not agree with the report of any of the Evangelists (1 Cor. xv. 5 ff.). Thus we are confronted with a multitude of problems, from which the only thing that clearly appears, is, how very little certain knowledge even the earliest Christian tradition preserved in regard to these events.

In these circumstances we are thrown back upon conjectures of more or less probability. Fixed points of attachment for these are commonly found in Mark as regards the place, and in Paul and the Acts as regards the character, of the events in question. In Mark xiv. 27 f. Jesus says to the disciples on the way to the Mount of Olives: "Ye shall all be offended (*i.e.* stumble and fall), for it is written, I will smite the shepherd, and the sheep shall be scattered (Zech. xiii. 7). But after that I am risen I will go before you into Galilee." To this promise there is a further reference in the charge given by the angel to the women (Mark xvi. 7): "Go tell his disciples and Peter (in particular) that Jesus goeth before you into Galilee; there shall ye see him as he said unto you before." There can be no doubt that we have in these words a *vaticinium post eventum* from which, therefore, conclusions may be drawn as to the actual course of events in the time immediately following the death of Jesus. In fact, we draw the twofold conclusion: (1) that under the shattering blow of the death of Jesus the disciples lost all self-command, wavered in their faith, scattered and fled to their Galilæan homes; (2) that they, and most of all Peter, believed that they saw the crucified Jesus alive again in Galilee, and that in consequence the

scattered flock gathered together once more.   This inference, drawn from the oldest Gospel, gains the more
in probability the less it agrees with the later tradition
concerning the events of the Easter-tide at Jerusalem.
For if the later tradition, based upon Luke's representation, according to which the disciples as a body
saw Jesus again on the very day of the resurrection,
and never dispersed, but remained together waiting
for the descent of the Spirit at Pentecost, had been
historically correct, it would be simply inconceivable
how the oldest Gospel came to speak, in words
expressly ascribed to Jesus, and alluding to a passage
from the ancient prophets, of a stumbling and dispersion of the disciples, and to represent them as
expecting the first meeting with the crucified Master
to take place in Galilee.   But, on the other hand, it
is easy to understand why this situation disappeared
from the later legend and gave place to a different
view.   In later times people could not reconcile
themselves to the thought that the Apostles, those
honoured heroes of the Faith, had once, on the death
of the Lord, become so weak as to scatter like the
sheep of a flock left without a shepherd.   In addition to this, Christians felt the need of having the
reality of the Resurrection of Jesus, of which they
were firmly convinced, confirmed by unmistakable
tokens at the place of His death and burial.   Alongside of this motive, however, remembrance of Galilee
as the scene of the first appearance of Christ to the
Apostles exercised sufficient influence to cause the
appearance at the grave to be represented as not
occurring to Peter or any other of the Apostles, but
only to a few women, as to whose names the tradi-

tion was uncertain because there was here no basis
of definite recollection.   It is quite clearly recognisable, especially from Matthew's version of the story,
that the appearance of Christ to the women in the
neighbourhood of the grave is simply a doublet of
the appearance of the angel in the same place,
which is the only one mentioned by Mark.   I
believe, therefore, that in the appearances of Christ
at the grave we have only a more developed form
of the legend, which in its earlier stage told only of
an appearance of an angel at the grave, as a preparation for the subsequent appearance of Christ in Galilee.
If we take into consideration, further, that this preparation consists of nothing more than a repetition of
the charge already given by Christ Himself (Mark xiv.
28), and that its aim becomes nugatory if the disciples
immediately after the death of Jesus (indeed immediately upon his arrest) scattered at once, the conclusion
becomes inevitable that even this oldest form of the
legend of miraculous events at the grave has no historical foundation.   As, however, the discovery of
the empty grave is so inseparably connected with
these events that they stand or fall together, it
follows, finally, that along with the appearances at
the sepulchre, the opened grave itself is to be credited
to the legend, which has been freely moulded by
an apologetic interest; and this is also probable on
the further ground that the accounts of the solemn
interment of Jesus are subject to the gravest
doubt.

We find ourselves, therefore, in the position of
being obliged to deny all historical foundation to
the group of narratives of the Easter appearances at

Jerusalem. Not at Jerusalem, but in Galilee, have we to seek the facts which lie at the basis of the belief of the Christian community in the resurrection of Jesus. Any connection of this belief with convincing experiences of Peter or of the other disciples at the sepulchre is excluded in advance. It is clear that a strong presumption is thereby established regarding the further question as to the content of these miraculous experiences.

If Jesus was seen by His disciples only in Galilee, far from the spot where His body was buried, then the same body which was buried at Jerusalem cannot have been alive in Galilee; it cannot in my judgment be a question of the appearance of the risen Christ in bodily form. But in that case, what was it? For the answering of this question Paul has given us a hint in placing the earlier appearances of Christ in line with that which he himself had witnessed (1 Cor. xv. 8), and therefore manifestly explaining them as of a similar character. Now as regards this appearance to Paul, we have not only the secondary testimony of Acts, but the first-hand references of the Apostle himself, from which we can recognise with a high degree of probability the character of the revelation of Christ which was made to him. In order not to anticipate too completely what must be later set forth in detail, we recall here only the following facts. Paul says that God had revealed His Son in him, that He had made the light to shine in his heart, to give the illumination of the knowledge of the glory of God in the face of Jesus Christ; he thinks of the risen Christ as the Spirit, the Heavenly Man, the Lord of Glory, who has not the flesh and blood of earthly men, but a glorified body, such as is proper to spiritual beings in heaven.[1] A supersensuous being of this kind cannot have been apprehended by the bodily senses, and conversely what is revealed and recognised inwardly and spiritually in the heart cannot have been a corporeal person. The mode of the revelation and the character of the object revealed correspond to one another, and agree in pointing to an inward and spiritual or visionary experience, in which the Apostle was convinced that he received, under the form of an appearance of light, a revelation of the heavenly spiritual existence of Christ. His conviction of the reality of that which he beheld is by no means excluded by the visionary character of the experience; Paul elsewhere speaks of " visions and revelations of the Lord," in which he apprehended that which was ineffable without the mediation of the bodily senses (2 Cor. xii. 1 ff.). What is certainly excluded is the sensuous reality, the corporeity, of that which he saw, and accordingly, any kind of relation of the heavenly life of Christ which was thus revealed to the body of Jesus which was laid in the grave.

Such a relation Paul cannot well, in view of all the above considerations, have had in mind. Since, however, as was remarked above, he places the appearance of Christ to him on the same footing as that to the other disciples, the conclusion lies near at hand that he thought of these, not as appearances of the reanimated earthly body, but of the heavenly spirit of Christ to the spiritual vision of the disciples. This is precisely the conclusion which we drew from

[1] Gal. i. 16; 2 Cor. iv. 6, iii. 17; 1 Cor. xv. 47; Phil. iii. 21.

the locality of the appearances according to the testimony of Mark.

Thus the two oldest witnesses whom we can consult upon the point are essentially agreed in pointing to a view of the experiences of the disciples after the death of Jesus which differs widely from the later legendary representation, but which is all the more favourable to the psychological explanation of the belief in the Resurrection, so far as the explanation can be given on historical grounds.

In order to consider without prejudice the possibility of such an explanation, we must make clear to ourselves what is actually meant by it. Obviously the meaning cannot be that what the Evangelists narrate concerning the prolonged intercourse of the disciples with the risen Jesus, concerning His being handled, eating, and the like, could be explained, just as it stands, as purely psychical experiences. But the mere examination of the witnesses shows that their narrative cannot be taken as a literal transcript of the facts; they give merely a transmutation of what actually occurred under the influence of the growth of legend, of apologetic reflection, and of allegorising imagination. The problem with which we are here concerned can be analysed into two easily separable questions: (1) How are we to conceive the fact which lies at the basis of the legend as a psychical experience of the disciples? (2) On the assumption of this psychical basis, how are we to explain its transmutation into the outward supernatural facts of the legend? Here, as elsewhere, a problem which, looked at as a single whole, would be insoluble, becomes in a measure soluble by means of an analysis into its simpler elements.

In this connection we have more especially to take into account that the belief in a resurrection played a large part in the Jewish thought of the time. It was not merely, as one might almost say it is in our Christian society, a doctrine which is held to be theoretically true, but of which no use is made in practical life. The period was marked by strong religious excitement. For the imagination of the Palestinian Jews—at all times prone to exaggeration—the bounds between the natural and spiritual worlds had become so fluctuating that they found no difficulty in seeing in a mighty personality like Jesus an ancient prophet returned to Earth, and therefore risen from the dead, an Elias, a Jeremiah, or even the lately-beheaded John the Baptist. Popular conceptions of this kind, such as the Evangelists record for us, are a clear proof how natural the thought of the resurrection of a good man was to the Jewish people. That, too, explains the numerous legends of raising of the dead by Jesus and His disciples, and the statement of Matt. xxvii. 52, that at the death of Jesus the rock-hewn graves were opened and many bodies of the saints arose and, after the resurrection of Jesus, appeared to many in Jerusalem. In a period and environment in which a mental tendency of this kind ruled, in which men stood in such close relations with the other world, and were constantly, indeed, in a state of strained expectation as to whether its gates would not open, whether some communication, some messenger, would not come forth from it —is it any wonder if something which all held to be possible, and even probable, and which was expected by many, should once, under exceptional circumstances, be actually experienced by a few?

These exceptional causes are, in the case of the disciples of Jesus immediately after the shock of His death, by no means difficult to recognise. Stunned by a catastrophe for which they were wholly unprepared, they had, it is true, lost for the moment all self-command and power of deliberate thought, and had fled to their Galilæan homes. Here, however, in the very scenes where they had lingered, so short a time before, in the company of Jesus, and received the deepest impressions from Him, their power of reflection returned. They felt what a barren desert their life would become if all was over with the Cause of Jesus, to which they had given themselves so joyfully and confidently. They recalled now many of the words which Jesus had spoken to them, before the journey to Jerusalem, concerning the necessity of suffering for the Kingdom of God, and the certainty of its ultimate victory. Could, then, these promises of a faith which could remove mountains be mere delusion? And yet, how could they be true, if He in whom they recognised the Messiah sent by God, the founder of the Kingdom of God, remained in the power of death? But must He remain in the power of death, or should not that prove true in Him to which so many texts of Scripture witnessed, that God delivered His saints from death? They could recall several sayings which Jesus Himself had uttered, and passages of Scripture which He had quoted, of which the pictorial phraseology could now, after His death had actually happened, no longer be understood in reference to miraculous deliverance from death, but only to a release from the bonds of death by being miraculously awakened from death and raised to a heavenly life.[1] When memories of this kind began to revive the fallen courage of the disciples, when their hearts burned within them in the hot strife between doubt and hope (Luke xxiv. 32), when yearning love steeped itself in the memory of the Lord's appearance as He used to open up to them the Scriptures; all the psychic conditions were present in which a visionary experience, such as that of which Paul was at a later time the subject, becomes completely explicable. What was the exact content of this experience, whether a form was seen in which their memory-picture portrayed itself circumstantially upon the field of vision, or whether, perhaps, only a shining appearance and a voice were apprehended, as is related of Paul in Acts—as to all this, not only is no exact knowledge possible for us, but even the consciousness of those who actually experienced the vision can hardly have been perfectly clear. That, however, does not affect the question. Enough that Peter, and after him the others, became convinced, on the ground of such experiences, that they had seen their crucified Master as the living and ascended Messiah.

That Peter was the first who saw such an appearance of Christ is not only attested by Paul and

[1] We may recall in this connection such passages as Ps. xvi. 10, "Thou wilt not leave my soul in Sheol, nor let thy holy one see the grave"; Ps. lxxxvi. 13, "Great is thy mercy towards me; thou deliverest my soul from the depths of Sheol"; Hos. vi. 2, "After two days will he revive us: in the third day he will raise us up, and we shall live in his sight."

confirmed by a hint in Mark (xvi. 7), but has also all
intrinsic probability in its favour. It is completely
in harmony with the character of his temperament—
easily excited, and hastily moved, by momentary
impulses of feeling, to conviction and resolve—as it
expressed itself in the Messianic confession (Mark
viii. 29). Just as he was, on that occasion, the first of
the disciples in whose mind the overmastering impression of the personal dignity and significance of Jesus
crystallised into the conviction of His Messianic
vocation, so he was now again the first to rescue from
the shipwreck of his earthly Messianic hopes a belief
in the person and divine vocation of Jesus, by means
of the conviction of the new life and heavenly
Messiahship of the risen Lord. There, as here, it was
a revelation, an immediate certainty and irresistible
impression of the divine truth ; a revelation which is
not indeed purely supernatural, inasmuch as we can
understand how it was psychologically mediated, but
which, nevertheless, has its source in those depths of
the soul in which it is in touch with the Spirit of
God, and feels itself taken hold of by His power.
And therefore the belief of the disciples in this
resurrection of Jesus is, in its essence, Truth, even
if the form in which this truth entered into their
consciousness was determined by the conditions of
human psychology and their situation at the time,
and, accordingly, is only of historical significance.

It was a proof of the essential truth of the revelation of Christ to Peter, that, like every genuine
revelation, it did not remain isolated, but at once
extended a kindling and inspiring influence to others,
and became the source of a mighty stream of spiritual

life. His newly-won certainty of Christ's life and lordship became a foundation for that of others, his enthusiasm, strong in the courage of faith, worked magnetically, and soon all the disciples experienced moments of enthusiastic vision, which served them as confirmatory evidence of Peter's words. That such appearances took place in the presence of several persons and even of large assemblies, is so far from being opposed to the psychological explanation given above that it rather serves as a support for it. For it is a well-known matter of experience that conditions of strong mental excitement, such as religious enthusiasm and ecstasy, have in them something infectious, and lay hold, with elemental power, of whole assemblies. Abundant examples of this are furnished by the religious history of all times, from the " Schools of the Prophets," among the ancient Hebrews, down to the American " Revivals " of our own time. Something of this sort is what we have to suppose in the case of the manifestation of Christ, which Paul records in 1 Cor. xv. 6, to more than five hundred brethren at once. As this event must in any case have been of exceptional significance for the progress of the belief in Christ and for the formation of the Christian community, it would be very remarkable, and, indeed, scarcely comprehensible, if there had been no trace of it elsewhere in the tradition. The conjecture, therefore, has much in its favour which makes the same event the foundation of the narrative in Acts of the outpouring of the Spirit at Pentecost. No doubt in this narrative, as will be shown in a later connection, legend and allegory play a considerable part ; yet it seems possible, by the separation of these legendary elements, to extract a sound kernel of history which would harmonise well enough with our conception of the appearances of Christ. If in that instance the being filled with the Holy Spirit is accompanied by a noise from heaven and appearances of flame (Acts ii. 2 f.), we may well recognise in this an exaggerated version of the same phenomenon which has met us before in the appearances of Christ as the beholding in vision of a marvellous light, and the hearing of heavenly voices. And if, as a consequence, the men thus inspired begin to speak in strange tongues, so that many hearers suppose them to be intoxicated, while Peter finds in their conduct the fulfilment of the prediction of Joel, there is clearly here a basis of recollection that the enthusiasm of the early Christian assemblies expressed itself especially in ecstatic utterances and in prophetic predictions. It is true the writer of Acts has changed the actual "speaking with tongues"—which according to 1 Cor. xiv. was nothing else than an inarticulate outpouring of the overflow of ecstatic feeling—into a speaking in other tongues in which the hearers thought they recognised their own several languages. This is a mythico-allegorical trait, by means of which this decisive event in the history of the Christian community is made a counterpart of the giving of the law at Sinai; at which, according to Jewish legend, the voice of God, in making known the law, divided itself into seventy languages, representing all the peoples of the earth. But that the writer, in spite of this unhistorical transformation of the "speaking with tongues," had before him a sound historical tradition, is unmistakably apparent in the course of his narrative. When he records that some of the hearers mocked, being under the impression that the enthusiasm which inspired the speech of the disciples was drawn from "new wine," it is evident that a suspicion of this kind is not reconcilable with the foregoing account of their speaking in foreign, but genuine and intelligible, languages. On the other hand, it agrees well with the conception which we are led to form of the actual speaking with tongues—that unintelligible mouthing and stammering of ecstasy, which, as we gather from 1 Cor. xiv. 23 f. also, sometimes made the impression of madness on those standing at a distance. Further, the speech which according to Acts, Peter, on the occasion of these events, addressed to the people, makes no reference whatever to the alleged miracle of the gift of speaking in foreign languages, but explains the surprising conduct of the disciples as the fulfilment of the prophecy of Joel, that all men should be filled with the Holy Spirit and thereby enabled to see visions and to prophesy. Obviously, therefore, what on that occasion attracted the attention of the crowd, must have consisted in the enthusiastic state of mind and the ecstatic utterances of the disciples, in which they were able to recognise the signs of prophetic inspiration as Joel had described them; but these have no connection with a speaking in foreign languages. There can accordingly, for the attentive reader, be no doubt that two different conceptions of the character of those marvellous events are found in the description of what took place at Pentecost. (1) The unhistorical representation of a speaking in various languages, founded on an allegorical imitation of a Jewish legend, and, accordingly, to be ascribed to the reflection of the narrator. (2) A representation answering to the analogies which we find elsewhere in historical accounts of "speaking with tongues" and prophesying, and of ecstatic and visionary appearances. The fact that the latter does not fit in with the author's individual conception of the matter (as a gift of languages) makes it the more certain that it rests on a basis of historical tradition. Accordingly we are to find the historical kernel of the Pentecost-narrative in the fact that the enthusiastic seeing and speaking, which was received as a revelation of the living Christ, and which had hitherto been confined to individuals or to the inner circle of the disciples, was now for the first time extended to a great multitude; and carried them away so irresistibly, that several hundreds were suddenly converted to believe in Christ. That this epoch-making event took place in Jerusalem at the Feast of Pentecost, not many weeks, therefore, after the death of Jesus—and that it gave the impulse to the migration of the Galilæan believers to Jerusalem and their permanent settlement there, and consequently to the real foundation of the Church at Jerusalem—of these facts there can be no reasonable doubt.

If we accept this conception of the events of Pentecost, identifying it with the manifestation of Christ to five hundred brethren in 1 Cor. xv. 6, there results further confirmatory evidence of our explanation of the appearances of Christ. The stories of Easter and of Pentecost seem no doubt different enough if we look at both in the later

legendary transformation and embellishment embodied in Luke's account. But when we reduce them
both to their substratum of historical fact, they fall
into line, and mutually explain one another, like the
different manifestations of Christ recounted by Paul
in 1 Cor. xv. 5 ff. In all these instances the explanation lies in a condition of strong religious enthusiasm,
rising into ecstatic visions and exclamations. What
filled the consciousness might take different forms in
different individuals ; in all cases it was apprehended
as a spiritual influence from above, in which the life
of the exalted Messiah Jesus truly revealed itself
in the believer, and in which therefore the commencement of the time of Messianic salvation promised by
the prophets became a reality. But for all the extraordinary character of these experiences of the earliest
company of the disciples, into which the Christian
Spirit entered in its creative originality and overmastering power, they have nevertheless manifold
analogies in all those conditions of more or less
strong religious excitement, in which a congregation
assembled in prayer feels itself seized by the movement of the Spirit. Something wonderful and
mysterious takes place in all cases where the souls
of men feel themselves raised to a higher world of
inspiring truth and moved to world-renewing deeds
of faith and love. The forms of consciousness may
be as different as you please in different individuals,
natures, and times ; it is never mere human caprice or
poetic imagination, but the unfathomable working of
that Divine Spirit, of which it is said " It bloweth
whither it listeth and thou hearest the sound thereof,
but canst not tell whence it cometh nor whither it

2

goeth." The revelations of the Spirit of God may take different forms in the primitive Christian community from that which they take in present-day Christians, yet it is the same Spirit of Christ, whose operation is in truth mysterious, and yet is no purely supernatural miracle.

In addition to the speaking with tongues, "prophesying," the prophetic enunciation of deeper truths, was held from the first to be an especial sign of the Christian's reception of the Spirit. That is implied not only by the Pentecost-narrative and its interpretation of the passage in Joel, but also by other passages in the Acts of the Apostles and the Pauline Epistles. A prophetic insight into the future was a natural consequence of faith in the risen Jesus. In the closest connection with the certainty that He was the Messiah, exalted to the right hand of God, there went the expectation that He would soon come again upon the clouds of heaven, as Daniel had predicted of the Son of Man, to reveal Himself as the Messiah of the whole world and to establish His Kingdom upon Earth. Towards this approaching return all the hope and desire of the Christian community was, from the time of Christ's appearances, unceasingly directed. That the Lord was nigh, and with Him the great day of judgment and deliverance, of world-renewal and the commencement of a new order of things, of the Kingdom of God instead of the Kingdom of the World: that was the constantly recurring watchword in which the whole confession of the first Christians was summed up. It was in the light of this glowing hope that they regarded and interpreted every event of the present—the sufferings

and the successes of the community, the confusion
and storm of the political world, even the calamities
of Nature such as earthquake, famine, and pestilence—
in all these they saw the tokens and pledges of the
speedy coming of Christ and of His Kingdom.   From
this it may easily be gathered that they had not yet
formed any precisely defined views as to the nature
of the Kingdom of Christ, but that very various views
were confusedly blended together.   So far as it is a
Kingdom which comes from heaven, forms of life
higher than those of Earth seem to be appropriate to
it ; its members will, either by a resurrection or by
means of some change, receive a new body, and will
no longer marry nor be given in marriage.[1]   Then,
on the other hand, it is represented that the members
of the Kingdom sit at meat with Abraham, Isaac,
and Jacob, drink again of the fruit of the vine, receive
an hundredfold for all their sacrifices and losses of
domestic happiness and possessions, and sit on thrones
beside the Messiah judging the Twelve Tribes of
Israel.[2]   It is no doubt difficult to say in particular
cases how much is meant literally and in sober
earnest, and how much is pictorial metaphor ; it is in
any case certain that the Kingdom of Christ was not
thought of purely as heavenly felicity in the other
world, nor, on the other hand, purely as an entirely
inward condition of religious and moral perfection.
Piety and morality were no doubt held to be the
necessary condition of having part in the Kingdom
of God, but not as its sole content; they are the seed
sown in the present life, the future harvest and

[1] Mark xii. 25 ; 1 Cor. xv. 50 ff. ; 1 Thess. iv. 17 ; Phil. iii. 21.
[2] Matt. viii. 11, xix. 27 ff., xxvi. 29.

reward are associated with the Kingdom. Those
who now sow with tears, will then reap with joy ;
those who now mourn, who are hungry, oppressed,
or persecuted, will then laugh, be filled, judge the
world. Thus Christ, on His return in heavenly power,
will establish an entirely new order of things upon
Earth,[1] will judge the proud, self-satisfied world,
which is at enmity with God, and bring deliverance,
consolation, refreshing, to the poor, the sad, the
suffering, who have put their trust in Him, and have
suffered and fought for Him.[2]

But it was not only towards the future, and the
hoped-for manifestation of God in deliverance and
judgment, that the Seer's glance of the early Christian
prophets was directed ; the earlier Revelation also
was placed by the Christ-faith in a new light. It
was now of importance to draw a proof for the
Messiahship of Jesus from the types and prophecies
of the Old Testament. For the disciples themselves,
faith in Jesus' Messiahship rested on their confident
belief in His resurrection ; but this had arisen from
experiences of a subjective character, which could not
be assumed in the case of others, and did not admit
of direct proof. Now, the offence which the Jews
found in the Cross of Jesus could be diminished by
the Messianic interpretation of those passages which
spoke of the sufferings of the righteous one, by which
the fate of Jesus was proved to have been foretold
in the Holy Scriptures, and, therefore, to have been

---

[1] παλινγενεσία, Matt. xix. 28 ; καιροὶ αναψύξεως . . . . ἀποκατά-
στασις πάντων, Acts iii. 19, 21.

[2] Luke vi. 20 ff., i. 51 ff. ; Jas. iv. 9, v. 1–11 ; 1 Pet. iii. 13–19 ;
Apoc. xix.–xxi.

foreordained in the Divine counsel. This, accordingly, was the central point in early Christian Apologetics; this was the essential, indeed properly speaking the only, subject of what we may call the earliest Apostolic Theology. The primary interest in this proof from Scripture was not the dogmatic question, Why, on what grounds, or with what aim, had Christ to suffer? The primary interest was to prove simply that the sufferings of Christ were a divinely ordained necessity, founded in the will and predetermined counsel of God, and therefore not a thwarting of it, not in contradiction with the revealed vocation of the Messiah.

Many passages were of value for this purpose; above all, the passage in Isaiah about the Servant of God (lii., liii.), the Man of Sorrows, who bore our sicknesses and was wounded for our transgressions, that we might obtain peace and be healed through His wounds. It is true the Prophet doubtless understood by the " Servant," not so much a single person, as the ideal Israel, the sound kernel of the people, which by its innocent suffering should make atonement for the guilt of the rest. Jewish Exegesis, too, for the most part remained constant to this interpretation, and when it did understand the Servant of God Messianically, it sought, by explaining away in an allegorical fashion the features which suggested suffering, to hold aloof from the thought of a suffering Messiah. Against this, it was easy for the Christians to make good their position—how much more natural, how much clearer, it was, to the popular comprehension, to understand this graphically drawn picture of the righteous Sufferer as

portraying a definite person, and how extremely
natural was the application to the sufferings and
death of Jesus! To whom better than to Him did
the words apply: " As a lamb that is led to the
slaughter, as a sheep before her shearers, is dumb, so
he opened not his mouth. Through oppression and
judgment was he cut off, but, of the men of his time,
who reflected that he was stricken for the transgressions of my people? They made his grave with
the wicked and with the godless in his death,
although he had done no evil, neither was guile
found in his mouth. Yet it pleased Jahwe to wound
him. But when his soul has offered the guilt-offering
he shall see his posterity, he shall prolong his days, and
the cause of Jahwe shall prosper in his hand. His
portion shall be with the mighty, and with heroes
shall he share the spoil; because he poured out his
soul unto death and was reckoned with the transgressors." We may well suppose that the appeal of
the Christians to this prophetic passage, as having
foretold the sufferings and resurrection of Christ,
must have made on many a similar impression to
that which it made on the chamberlain of the Queen
of Æthiopia, to whom Philip explained it (Acts viii.
30 ff.). If perchance the objection was raised that
Jesus could not be the Messiah because He had been
rejected by His own people and their rulers, a saying
of Jesus at once suggested the reply that it was the
stone which the builders rejected which was made by
God the headstone of the corner (Mark xii. 10). As
a proof of the resurrection of Jesus they offered
passages like Ps. xvi. 10, lxxxvi. 13, Hos. vi. 2;
especially upon the first of these does the early

Christian Apologetic appear to have laid stress, since in two passages in Acts it forms the foundation of the argument (ii. 27, xiii. 35). The expectation of His speedy return from heaven, and His revelation to the whole people, could claim support from Daniel's prophecy about the Son of Man appearing upon the clouds of heaven (Dan. vii. 13), and from the word of Zechariah, " They shall look upon him (properly "thee ") whom they have pierced " (Zech. xii. 10 ; Apoc. i. 7). Thus, once they entered upon the search they could easily discover in the Scriptures a word or type for every trait in the life of Jesus, and in fact find the whole Christ Jesus in the Old Testament. But once the principle was established that the picture of the Messiah was portrayed in the Old Testament, the further step followed inevitably that the traits which were thought to be found in the sacred archives were introduced into the life of Jesus, and that, consequently, the record of Jesus' life and work was modified in conformity with the standard of the Messianically interpreted passages of the Old Testament. In this way the necessity for the apologetic use of the Old Testament, and along with that, the natural impulse to illustrate symboli- cally the Messianic salvation by typical miraculous events in the life of the Saviour, became fertile sources for the production of legends, which, as time went on, embellished and elaborated more and more the picture of Jesus which survived in memory. As we shall have to examine them more closely later, when we come to analyse the Gospels, this is not the place to go into particulars, especially as the most significant of the legends have been moulded by the influence of Pauline ideas. Nevertheless, it is certainly the case that the roots from which spring the legends which find place in the Gospels, reach back to the first beginnings of the Church and stand in the closest relations with the peculiar experiences of its members. After they had beheld Jesus in glory as the Heavenly Messiah, it came to pass inevitably that His heavenly splendour was reflected back upon His earthly life, and the latter, under this illumination, acquired more and more supernatural colouring and content. In the Apostles' visions of Christ lay the seed of the whole Church dogma of Christ's person. The higher world, whose wonderful powers were felt in the ecstatic "speaking with tongues," and towards the marvellous revelation of which the prophetic vision of the Christian seers was directed, must, it was felt, have allowed men to see pledges, in typical miracles during Christ's earthly life, of its future full manifestation in the Kingdom of Christ. It was therefore substantially one and the same prophetic intuition which, when directed to the future, created the symbolic pictures of the Apocalypse, and which, when directed backwards, altered the history into poetry as a symbol of the glorious hopes for the future, the fulfilment of which should accompany the return of Christ.

If, as we have seen, the doctrinal impulse in early Christianity expressed itself more in the prophetic creation of sensuous pictures than in dogmatic reflection and the formation of intellectual conceptions, yet incentives to the latter were even then not wholly wanting. If according to the testimony of Scripture the suffering of Jesus the Messiah was predetermined

in the Divine counsel, then the question lay too near
at hand to escape notice and consideration : To what
end did God surrender His Ambassador to death?
To this question also the classical passage in Isaiah
contained the answer, since there the suffering of the
righteous servant of God is represented as a vicarious
bearing of the penalty in the place of sinners, to pro-
cure for them peace, that is, the forgiveness of sin.
That the original community of disciples regarded
the death of Christ from this point of view, namely,
as a means of expiation, for the forgiveness of sins,
and did so on the ground of such passages as the one
just mentioned, is expressly testified by Paul, when
in 1 Cor. xv. 3, among the few things which he "had
received," he mentions this: that Christ "died for
our sins according to the Scriptures." But if Christ
won forgiveness of sins for His people through His
atoning death, it follows that the forgiveness of sins
is the first gift which God bestows upon those who
believe in Him, receive Him as Messiah, and attach
themselves to Him as His disciples and as members
of His brotherhood. When, therefore, in Acts the
prospect of the forgiveness of sins is always offered
as the first consequence of conversion to Jesus and
acceptance of Him as the Christ, it is not to be doubted
that this really corresponds to the belief of the
primitive Christian community. At the same time we
must avoid exaggerating the scope of this belief in the
mind of the primitive community, and we must not
fail to recognise the width of the differences which,
in spite of all resemblances, still separated it from
the Pauline doctrine. According to Paul the death
of Christ, while expiating the curse of the law, at the

same time annuls the law and opens up a new way
of salvation in place of that which the old legal
religion provided. The original Christian community
was far from drawing this inference. Even though
they saw in the death of Christ a means for the
forgiveness of sins, yet this was only meant in the
same sense in which the Jewish theology of the day
attributed to the martyrdom of any righteous man
an atoning merit, which benefited his people by
cancelling their sins, without on that account dis-
pensing them from the obligation of keeping the
Jewish law. Nay more, this saving power of atonement in the sufferings of the righteous, benefited
only those who stood on a legal footing and by their
own deeds made themselves worthy of having the
merit of the other's achievements and expiatory
suffering attributed to them. In other words, the
effect of the sufferings of the righteous in cancelling
the sins of their people did not, so to speak, take the
place of their own legal righteousness, but rather, on
the assumption that the latter was in some measure
present, it came in only in a supplementary way to
cover deficiencies and imperfections. It was just in
the same fashion that the primitive Christian community thought of the saving power of the death of
Christ. The thought of an expiatory cancellation
of sin through the suffering of a righteous man was
nothing new to them; they were by no means likely
therefore to draw new inferences from it, of the
far-reaching character of the Pauline doctrine of
atonement and justification. We can recognise quite
distinctly the point where the two ways divide from
the argument of Paul in the controversy about the

law at Antioch. According to Galatians ii. 16, he was able to assume, as recognised by both in common, that we became believers in Christ in the conviction that the works of the law were not an adequate ground for a man's justification; but that this justification' could only be attained by means of faith in Christ. But the inference that the works of the law had now no more significance as a means to justification, that they were set aside by faith and had become, from the religious point of view, worthless, was drawn from the common premises by Paul alone, whereas his Jewish-Christian opponents could see in it only a blasphemous degradation of Christ to be the patron of the sinful heathen life (17). We can accordingly summarise what was common and what was different as follows: the original Christian community, like Paul, ascribed to the death of Christ a saving power which brought forgiveness of sin, but it valued this only as a supplementary means of salvation, inside the permanent boundaries of the legal religion; for Paul, on the contrary, it was a new and sole means of salvation, which made the old superfluous and thereby abolished Legalism.

That through the belief in Jesus as Messiah the value of the Jewish law was done away with, and that a new religious fellowship had been founded on a basis external to Judaism, is a conception which, prior to the appearance of Paul, did not enter into the mind of the early Christian community, even as a bare possibility. Just as the advent of the Kingdom of the Messiah, with its blessings, was regarded as the fulfilment of the promises given to the Fathers, so it was self-evident that the Messianic

community should build itself up upon the firm
foundation of the Law given by God to the Fathers.
No doubt they had learned from Jesus that mercy
was more important than sacrifice and the keeping
of the Sabbath, purity of heart better than the
washing of hands and the straining out of gnats;
but from this recognition of the higher value of the
moral as compared with the ceremonial it is still
a very long step to the perception of the religious
indifference and the non-binding character of the
ceremonial law.   Moreover, the first disciples had
not received any impulse or direction towards the
making of this step from Jesus Himself; for, despite
the freedom and elevation of His judgment in these
matters, He had not, so far as we can see, disregarded
in His actual conduct the laws which regulated the
life of His nation.   It is therefore by no means
likely that the early Christian community, in which
we cannot of course assume the same degree
of freedom and clarity of ethical judgment, would
form the conclusion that the abandonment of the
Jewish law was incumbent upon it.   It is possible
that the picture of the manner in which the believers
in Christ surpassed even the other Jews in their
conscientious fulfilment of all the legal ordinances
and usages of worship, and of the reputation which
they held for especial zeal towards the law, is to be
ascribed in part to the idealising purpose of the
Acts of the Apostles, but in essentials it no doubt
represents correctly the real historical position.   The
best proof of this is the later attitude of the church
at Jerusalem towards the question of the Law, when
this had become a practical, and even a burning,

question in consequence of the Pauline mission to the Gentiles. Even at the Apostolic Council, when it was conceded to Paul that the Gentile converts might be exempted from the claims of the Law, the Jewish Christians were still far from thinking that for them there was to be any alteration in the existing obligation to full observance of the Law. And when the circumstances in Antioch led to the limits of Jewish liberality, as contemplated in the Apostolic compact, being exceeded, the only consequence of this was that henceforward the Jewish churches stiffened in their zeal for the Law, and also began to work actively in the Gentile churches against the Apostolic compact. All those long and fierce struggles which Paul was subsequently obliged to wage with the Jewish Christians over the question of the Law, would become unintelligible if we had to assume that the primitive community took from the first the same view of the freedom of Christians from the Law as was taken by Paul. They form therefore an irrefutable proof that the primitive community held itself to be permanently bound by the obligations of the Jewish Law.

From what has been said it follows self-evidently that the first Christians cannot have intended to constitute themselves as a new and peculiar community, separate from Judaism. They desired to be nothing else than the faithful "remnant" of the People spoken of by the prophets, and they expected the fulfilment of the promises in the speedy establishment of the Messianic Kingdom through the Second Coming of Jesus; how then could they contemplate setting up special organisations and usages for this

short period ? Even Baptism and the Lord's Supper
were as yet not, in the same sense as they became at
a later period, acts of public worship and marks distinguishing the Christian religious fellowship from the
Jewish. Baptism was originally a symbolic act of
purification and dedication,[1] and was already in use
in the Essene community and among the disciples
of John, who nevertheless remained "good Jews";
it therefore did not necessarily involve a breach with
Judaism, or the foundation of a separate community.
It was the same in the case of the Supper, which at
the first had, even less than Baptism, the character
of an act of worship; this is only acquired later in
the Pauline churches and through the Pauline
theology. Among the earliest Christians it consisted
at first simply of a meal partaken of in common, in
which the loving union of the brethren received
practical expression. Private religious assemblies of
this kind, with common meals, were already usual
among the Essenes and Pharisees; their relation to
public worship was similar to that of the prayer-
unions of the present day to the public services of
the Church. What, however, gave to the Christian
fellowship-meals their higher sacredness and special
religious significance, was the intimate union of the
brethren through the focussing of their thought upon
Jesus as Messiah. As they prayed and studied the
Scriptures and gave themselves to absorbing medita-
tion upon the life and death of Christ, recalling His

[1] Baptism, like the Lord's Supper, first acquired its specifically
Christian sacramental significance—as a means of mystical union
with Christ in His dying and rising again—from the Pauline
theology. Cp. Rom. vi. 2 ff.

promises with full assurance of faith, their hope
of His return in the near future rose to a pitch
of enthusiasm which enabled them to overcome the
world by deeds of faith and love, and to make the
Kingdom of God not only a hope but a present
reality.

As an outcome of their faith in Christ and as a
practical preparation for the new social order of the
Kingdom of Christ, the regular relief of the poor out
of the common funds was of great significance. A
formal and complete community of goods such as
the writer of Acts, idealising a little, represents,
was, no doubt, not actually established. Had it been,
the poor, for the care of whom it was necessary to
appoint deacons, would no longer have existed ; it
could no longer have been singled out as a praiseworthy act when an individual sold his land for the
benefit of the common funds ; and it would not have
been possible for any one hospitably to place a private
house at the disposal of the church for its meetings, as
is recorded of Mary, the mother of Mark, in Acts xii.
But even if we reduce the exaggerated legend of
community of goods among the first Christians to
its historical substratum—to the constant relief of
all poor persons by means of a common fund, and
especially by means of the meals partaken of in
common—this still remains a fact of remarkable
importance. Imaginative hopes were here transformed into practical acts, the dream of the apocalyptic Kingdom of the Messiah here became the
reality of a brotherhood of the children of God. It
was the grandest and at the same time the boldest
and the purest scheme for the regeneration of the

world which was here entered on by a narrow circle
of quiet and simple people, not in the spirit of self-
seeking and aggrandisement, but in that of serviceable and patient love, which found in Jesus, the friend
of the poor and heavy-laden, its pattern and the
pledge of final victory. Not in the dogmas, and not
in the legends, which now began gradually to arise,
but in these wonders of love, lay the mystic power
by means of which, from the first, Christianity overcame the world—in the first place, it is true, the
world of the poor and humble, of the simple and
weak, of the ill-used and oppressed, of the hungry
and the sad, of the helpless and the lost. To all
these the Brotherhood of Jesus opened a place of
refuge where they found, in the comforting and
helpful sympathy of the brethren, a foretaste of the
Kingdom of God, where God "shall wipe away all
tears from their eyes."

CHAPTER II

PERSONALITY

JUST as, in mountainous country, the true height of the loftiest peaks is not recognisable from the immediate neighbourhood, but only from a more distant standpoint, so in human history it is a common phenomenon that the full significance of the loftiest personalities is much less clearly recognised by those immediately about them than by those standing at a distance. Only for the latter does the picture of such personalities stand out in its characteristic completeness; while for those near at hand the comprehensive general impression is often obscured by the multitude of more limited impressions drawn from daily intercourse. This was precisely what happened in the case of the relation to Jesus of the original Apostles and of Paul. Paradoxical as it may seem that Paul, who never saw Jesus in the flesh or listened to His words, nevertheless grasped the innermost spirit of Jesus more purely and more deeply than the first disciples, yet it is by no means unintelligible. Precisely that which seemed to constitute the advantage of the latter, and in certain respects really was so, the fact,

3

namely, that they had enjoyed personal intercourse with Jesus, nevertheless involved the disadvantage that their view of Jesus was limited by the standard of His outward life, in which He showed Himself a devout and law-abiding Israelite. Of the essential originality of His character and of the side of His work which conflicted with Judaism, as it had historically developed, no complete understanding had ever dawned upon them; and, as a consequence, even the decisive fact of His death could not open their eyes to these things. Their desire was to get away from this offence of the cross as quickly as might be, to excuse it, to justify it; and for that very reason they did not come to the point of deliberately facing the full significance of the fact, the breach of principle with Judaism which it involved, and drawing the necessary inferences. As they themselves had gradually and without any decisive breach with their Jewish way of thought come to believe in Jesus as the Messiah, so it appeared to them that in the future the belief in Christ would be perfectly compatible with Judaism. The idea that they could come to be mutually exclusive opposites, alternatives of which one or the other must be chosen, had not entered their minds. If there had been no advance from this conservative attitude of the first disciples, it is clear that Christianity would never have torn itself loose from the fetters of Judaism, but would have remained a Jewish sect, and in the political upheavals of the ensuing period, which culminated in the overthrow of the Jewish State, Christianity would have been carried down with it in its fall.

It was therefore of the utmost importance for the
whole future of Christianity that its cause received
the accession of a man whose eyes were open, in
consequence of his character and training, in a way
in which those of the original disciples were not, to
the new elements in the belief in the crucified Christ
Jesus—to the universal, non-Judaic elements which
were present in the character and spirit of Jesus,
and which had found expression to some extent in
His life and teachings, but still more in His death.
It was Paul who saved the life-work of Jesus from
the danger of remaining in bondage to Jewish
traditionalism and thus coming to nought, by setting
free the belief in Christ from the religion of the
Law, and thereby making it, for the first time, an
independent religion, and a religion for all mankind.
For this achievement of permanent importance in
the history of the world, God had, as Paul himself
says (Gal. i. 15), set him apart from his mother's
womb, and called him by His grace. For, as in the
case of every historical hero, his inborn disposition
and the outward circumstances and experiences of
life combined in a marvellous manner to provide the
means conducive to the furtherance of his life's task.

Paul was one of those rare personalities in which
an extraordinary depth and tenderness of feeling is
united to keen understanding and energetic will.
Born of Jewish parents whose tendency towards a
strict Pharisaic observance of the law seems to have
been only heightened by the careless life by which
they were surrounded in a Gentile commercial city
like Tarsus, Paul had received through inheritance
and upbringing the best characteristics of the Semitic

race: the deep sense of dependence upon God and of obligation towards God. In every experience of life, great or small, joyful or sorrowful, he recognised the providence of God, the purposeful working of His gracious will, which moved him to thanksgiving and self-dedication. To have peace with God, or, in the language of his school, to be just before God, was at every period of his life his highest aim and highest good. But a passionate disposition stood in conflict with this tender, deeply earnest conscience, a choleric, irritable temperament, a nervous, easily excited sensibility. The grim picture which at a later time Paul draws of the strife between flesh and spirit in which the better will of the inner man is so often worsted by the overmastering impulse in the members, is certainly not entirely derived from general considerations, or from the experience of others; it is a confession of his own experiences, the experiences which the strict Pharisee Paul had undergone in his efforts to attain a legal righteousness by rigorous asceticism. These were the experiences which later wrung from him, even in the recollection, the cry of pain, " O wretched man that I am, who shall deliver me from this body of death?" (Rom. vii. 24). But the severity of the struggle, the painful sense of incapacity to reach the ideal goal of righteousness, did not weaken his zeal for the law, but rather raised it to a passion. That at which he himself had toiled so hard must stand to others also as the highest, the unassailable; and whoever assailed it was an enemy of God and must be rooted out. This zeal of the true Pharisee still remained with him in later life, the only difference being that the object of his zeal was then no longer the Law, but the truth of the Gospel, as he had apprehended it.[1] It was for the same reason, too, that he saw in the Jewish-Christian opponents of the Gospel downright enemies of Christ and of God, ascribed the worst motives to their opposition, and pronounced an inexorable anathema upon them (Gal. i. 8 ; Phil. iii. 2, 18 f.).

And yet this passionate zealot possessed also a tenderness of feeling, an intensity of sympathy, a selfless altruism, a capacity for loving self-devotion, such as are scarcely to be found elsewhere among men of action, and which seem indeed to be the special property of the noblest type of feminine

---

[1] Cp. the excellent characterisation of Paul in Orello Cone, *Paul : the Man, the Missionary, and the Teacher*, p. 28 : " His nature was of the eager, tempestuous sort in which intensity of conviction and resoluteness of purpose are leading characteristics. He could do nothing by halves. His aim, once clearly before him, became the dominant power of his life and pushed him to its realisation, without fear of consequences and without self-regard. As a Jew, he believed that the Christian sect was an enemy of his religion, an offence to God, and a menace to the institutions of his race, and he threw himself into the cause of an unsparing extermination of them. On the other hand, 'When it pleased God to reveal His Son in me,' he writes, 'immediately I conferred not with flesh and blood, neither went I up to Jerusalem to them who were Apostles before me.' This consciousness that he had a revelation, a divine commission, induced immediately a resolution to act independently of all human counsels, and to preach the gospel in his own way—a resolution to which he adhered with all the intensity and energy of his determined nature throughout his life. Opposition, persecution, the attempt to estrange his churches from him, could not prevail to turn him from his great purpose, the mission to the Gentiles, nor to shake his conviction that the Gentile Christians were entitled, without submission to Jewish ordinances, to an equal rank with the Jews in the coming Messianic Kingdom."

character. He himself compares his love for his
churches and his tender concern for the well-being of
each individual Christian with the tenderness of a
mother or a nurse. In his letters, from the severest
censures and threats he will turn again and strike the
most moving chords of the heart, and he woos the
trust and affection of his wavering converts with the
selfless humility of tender and forgiving love. The
man who wrote the incomparable hymn of love in
1 Cor. xiii. must have had a nature in which love
glowed still more warmly than zeal.[1]

But this glowing warmth of heart which made Paul
the greatest missionary of Christendom, was united
in him to a remarkable energy of mind. What he
felt, he made also an object of reflection, in order to
grasp it in his thoughts and exhibit it as truth to
himself and to the world. Thus it was that he created
for the young Christian community a doctrinal form,
a comprehensive view of the world, a "Theology."
No doubt his thinking was very far from being
scientific in the modern sense of the word. In this,
as in much else, he was a true son of his race; his
thinking remained throughout practical. He based
his reflection on the received authorities, he combined
the new revelation with that which was laid down in
the Holy Scriptures of his people. We shall see

[1] Cp. Norden, *Kunstprosa,* ii. 509 : "Those two hymns on the love
of God and the love of men (Rom. viii. 31 ff. ; 1 Cor. xiii.) gave back
to the Greek language what it had lost for centuries, the fervour
and enthusiasm of the initiate mystic inspired by union with God,
such as meets us again in equal perfection only in Plato and, finally,
in Cleanthes. How this speech of the heart must have struck home
to the hearts of men accustomed to listen to the foolish garrulence
of the Sophist."

later that Paul's proofs from Scripture are often very
forced and arbitrary, and had very little of generally
illuminative or demonstrative power; and indeed we
see that it was precisely the Jews, who were the
most familiar with the Old Testament Scriptures,
who were least convinced by Paul's argument.
Nevertheless it is certain that this practical, dogmatic
character of Paul's thought contributed greatly to
advance the cause of Christianity as a universal
religion. By its means Christianity was equipped
with a system of doctrine which on the one hand
offered to the Gentile world a comprehensive view
of life, in which that desire for theoretic truth which
always plays a part in religion could find satisfaction,
and which, on the other hand, had an advantage
over the systems of the Philosophic Schools in that
it was not a mere subjective scheme of thought, but
was based on the positive ground of objective and
long recognised authority — upon the venerable
records of ancient revelations of God, to which the
new revelation in Christ attached itself as the last
link in a divine world-plan which embraced mil-
lenniums of human history.

CHAPTER III

EDUCATION: GREEK INFLUENCE

PAUL, or, to give him his Jewish name,[1] Saul, was born of Jewish parents in the Greek city of Tarsus in Cilicia. The Jewish home and the Greek city gave him his Jewish-Greek education, which fitted him to be an Apostle of the Gospel in the Grecian world. He who could say that he had become a Greek to the Greeks and a Jew to the Jews in order to win all for the Gospel must have from the first known Greeks as well as Jews. And Tarsus was an excellent place to learn to know them, as regards not only their outward conduct, but their deepest thoughts and feelings. For Tarsus was not only a flourishing commercial city, but also an important seat of Greek Philosophy, especially of the Stoic School. Several famous teachers of that school came from Tarsus, among others the teacher of Augustus, Athenodorus, who had also been of some service to Cicero when

---

[1] The combination of a Greek with a Hebrew name was frequent among Hellenistic Jews, and it is probable that in the case of Paul-Saul it does not date only from the incident recorded in Acts xiii. 7 ff., but from his home in Tarsus, the twofold designation corresponding to the dual character of his interests and education.

writing the *De Officiis*,[1] and who is frequently mentioned by Seneca. This Athenodorus exercised, after his return from Rome to his home in Tarsus, a considerable influence in a political direction. He obtained from the Emperor a remission of taxes in the interests of his fellow-citizens, and for this was elevated by the grateful populace to the position of a hero, and celebrated in a yearly memorial festival.[2] Of such a celebrity of his own city the young Saul-Paul would be sure to hear, and would no doubt learn something of his life and teaching. Moreover, he would not need to visit the lecture-rooms of the Stoic teachers in order to become acquainted with the Stoic philosophy of life. This, in the practical popular form in which we know it from Seneca and Epictetus, was daily set forth in the streets and markets of the town by the popular orators, who called themselves Philosophers (Cynics), Soul-doctors, Messengers of Truth. The Stoic philosophy was at that time the religion of the thoughtful, of the seekers, of the progressive elements in Græco-Roman society. How could it remain unknown to a keen-minded Jewish boy or youth in Tarsus, however narrowly Jewish and strictly Pharisaic the spirit of his parents' house might be ? That it did not remain unknown to him is proved by the Epistles of the Apostle Paul, which contain such remarkable parallels with thoughts and phrases in the writings of Seneca, that it has been sometimes proposed to find in Paul a pupil of Seneca, and sometimes in Seneca a pupil of Paul.

[1] He supplied Cicero with a précis of the views of Posidonius on conflicting motives. See *Ad. Att.* xvi. 11 and 14.

[2] Susemihl, *Griechische Literaturgeschichte*, ii. 249 f.

Though the one is as impossible as the other, yet the fact that these parallels exist points to a common source. This we can find only in the Greek culture of the time, which was deeply imbued with Stoic conceptions, and by which, moreover, the Hellenistic Jews had not remained unmoved. That the dominant Stoic philosophy, if not as a scientific theory of the Schools, yet certainly as a popular ethico-religious view of life, belonged to those elements of education which nourished the youthful mind of the future Apostle of the Gentiles, can hardly be called in question by an unprejudiced student of history. As the best means of enabling the reader to form an opinion upon this point for himself, I have thought it useful to put together a short anthology of sayings from the writings of Seneca.

We begin with those in which the weariness of life, the desire to flee from the world, and the serious ascetic spirit of the time, of which Stoicism was not the sole but the most important representative, finds expression. " If thou wilt believe those who have looked deeply into Truth, then all life is torment (*supplicium*). Cast forth into this deep and unquiet ocean, we find nowhere any solid ground, we swing and toss and collide with one another, suffer ship-wreck, and are ever in alarm; to the shipmen on this stormy sea there beckons but one harbour of safety, namely, death " (*ad Polyb.*, ix. 6). " Nought is so deceitful and full of snares as human life. Truly no one would have accepted it, had it not been given him without his knowledge" (*ad Marciam*, xxii.). " Why weep for a particular sorrow, the whole of life is matter for weeping! What is man? A frail vessel lying at the mercy of every blow, a weak body, naked, maimed, needing the help of others, a butt for every scurvy trick of Fate! Of all the outward good that shows so fair around us, children, honour, wealth, a beautiful wife, and whatsoever else lies in the power of fickle Fortune, none is truly our own, it is only lent to us to dress the stage of life withal, but sooner or later the owner demands it back again! We enjoy only the usufruct of that which is lent us for a limited time, and must at all times be prepared to render it back without complaint. Therefore we should love our families, friends, and goods, only as a temporary possession. Make haste to enjoy the love of your children and to let them enjoy your love and to drain every drop of joy, for you have need of haste; death is at hand!" (*ad Marc.*, x. 11; *cf.* 1 Cor. vii. 29 ff.). " It was the complaint of our forefathers, and will be the complaint of those who come after us, that morals are corrupt, that evil reigns, that human life grows worse and worse, and all that is sacred is at the point to fall. But this (evil) remains ever the same, only that it tends now in this direction and now in that. In general, we must be prepared to hear the same judgment passed upon us, that we are bad, that we have been bad—alas, I must add--that bad we shall remain" (*de Benefic.*, i. 10; *cf.* Rom. iii. 9 ff.). " Why do we deceive ourselves? Evil is not without us, it has its seat within us, in our inward part! And therefore is it that we come so hardly to healing, because we know not that we are sick. Now indeed we seek a physician, but he had had an easier task if we had called him to our aid at the right time " (Ep. l. 4).

The source of evil Seneca sees in the body, which is for the God-related soul of man a confining prison; while its lusts give rise to a hard and constant struggle. The body is the soul's burden and punishment; under its pressure the soul feels herself weighed down and fettered, unless Philosophy comes to her aid and raises her from the earthly to the divine. " I am a higher being and born to higher things than to be a slave of my body, which I look on as nought else than a shackle laid upon my freedom. It is all of me that is capable of suffering—in so miserable a habitation dwells the free soul; never shall this flesh (*caro*) drive me to fear, nor to a hypocrisy unworthy of a good man, never will I lie for the sake of this wretched body. When I choose I can terminate my connection with it; but for the present, so long as we hold by one another, we shall never be comrades on equal terms, but the soul shall reserve all authority to itself. The contempt of the body is the soul's true freedom " (Ep. lxv. 21–23). " These bones and skin and whatever else belongs to our outward coverings, make a prison and a darkness round the soul; the soul is oppressed, blinded, infected, by it; held back from the true and spiritual, and ensnared in the false; its whole struggle is directed against this grievous flesh—not to let itself be dragged down by it; it strives to return whence it came, where everlasting peace awaits it, when after the confusion of the material it at length beholds the pure serene " (*ad Marc.*, xxiv. 4; *cf.* Gal. v. 17; Rom. vii. 14 ff.; Col. iii. 1). " There is something great and noble about the human spirit; it tolerates no limits save those which it has in common with God. It claims no mean fatherland; its father-

land is whatsoever the All contains.   Then too it lets
itself be bounded by no narrow time, but says: All
the years are mine, to great spirits no century is
closed.   When that day comes on which this (earthly)
mixture of human and divine is disentangled, then
will I leave this body behind in the place where I
found it, and will give myself back to the gods.
True, I am not without them even now, but I am still
held fast by the grievous constraint of the earth.   This
temporal life is but the prelude to that better and
longer life.   As we are prepared in our mother's
womb to come forth into this earthly life, so through
the period between childhood and age, we ripen for
a new birth.   A new beginning, a new condition,
awaits us.   Meanwhile we can bear heaven only at
a distance.   Gaze, therefore, unmoved on that
decisive hour; not for the soul is it the last, but only
for the body.   Regard the things about thee as the
furniture of an inn; as for thee, thou must travel
further.   Thou canst take no more with thee than
thou hast brought hither, nay, even of that a great
part is to be laid aside.   That day which thou dost
dread as thy last, is the birthday of that which abides
for ever (*aeterni natalis*).   Lay aside thy burden,
why dost thou hesitate?   Once thou didst weep as
thou didst enter into this life which was strange to
thee; now it is no more a new thing to thee to
separate from that of which thou hast been a part;
calmly, then, let the limbs thou needest no longer
sink in death, and lay aside the body thou hast long
inhabited.   The day will come which shall free thee
from the husk of the flesh, and deliver thee from the
companionship of the hateful body.   Soar aloft even

now, so far as thou canst; turn thy thoughts towards what is higher and nobler. One day the secrets of nature shall be disclosed to thee, the darkness will disappear and the clear light dawn everywhere" (Ep. cii. 21–27 ; *cf.* Rom. viii. 18–25 ; 2 Cor. iv. 16–v. 8).

To point the soul upon the way to this high goal of its heavenly vocation, and to heal it of the weakness and disease which attaches to the sensuous nature, that, the Stoic holds, is the task of Philosophy. Philosophy is not to occupy itself with useless accumulations of knowledge, or with empty logomachies, but to teach practical wisdom, to educate men in virtue and happiness. "Wouldst thou know what philosophy promises to mankind? Counsel! In face of the manifold needs and wants of men, there is no time to trifle (with words). Thy mission is to the unfortunate, thou hast promised to bring help to the shipwrecked, the prisoner, the sick, the needy, to men lying under sentence of death. From all sides men stretch forth their hands to thee, and beseech thee to save them from this sea of troubles, and to show the clear light of truth to those who wander aimlessly" (Ep. xlviii. 6–8). This philosophy effects chiefly by awaking men from the sleep of error, making them conscious of the true cause of their sufferings—their soul-sickness—and thereby calling forth the desire for amendment, the inner reformation. "'The first step towards a cure is to recognise one's sin'—an excellent saying of Epicurus, for he who knows not his faults desires no amendment; therefore examine thyself, be first thine accuser, then thy judge, finally thine advocate, sometimes chastise thyself!" (Ep. xxviii. 7). "It is otherwise

with the sicknesses of the soul than with those of
the body; the worse one is the less he notices it;
even as, in sleep, a light sleeper is often conscious that
he sleeps, but a heavy sleeper ceases even to dream,
and loses all consciousness of himself. Why does
none confess his faults? Because he is still deep in
them; only after one has awakened can he tell his
dreams, and to confess one's faults is a sign that one
is cured of them. Let us awake, then, that we may
strive against our errors! But only philosophy can
awake us; it, alone, can shake off our heavy sleep"
(Ep. liii. 7, 8; *cf.* Rom. xiii. 11; Eph. v. 14). But a
single resolution does not suffice to make us good,
a progressive and thorough revolution is needed, and a
constant and unwearying struggle against the passions.
" I notice that I am not only growing better, but
becoming changed (*transfigurari*), nevertheless I have
as yet no hope or confidence that there is nothing
more in me which needs alteration. How should I
not have much that still needs to be amended, or
mitigated, or removed? And the proof that my
mind is turned towards what is better, is precisely
this, that it recognises the faults of which it was
previously unconscious" (Ep. vi. 1; *cf.* Rom. xii. 2;
Phil. ii. 10–13). " I must inure my soul to hardness,
and wrench it free from the allurements of desire.
We, too, have a warfare to wage, and one, truly, in
which there is no pause nor relaxation of effort.
Above all, we have to fight against pleasure, which
has cast even strong spirits into chains. We aim at
freedom, this is the prize for which we strive; but
freedom means not to be in bondage to any object,
to any constraint, to anything contingent. Never

let thy spirit slacken its efforts. Carry on a relentless and never-ending war with the vices, for they
themselves are relentless and never-ending. Cast
away from thee whatever inclines thine heart towards
the flesh, and if there is no other way of plucking it
out, tear out thy heart itself along with it. Especially
expel the fleshly lusts, and hold them for thy worst
enemies: they embrace us only that they may
strangle us" (Ep. li. 5, 8, 13; *cf.* Matt. v. 29; Rom.
viii. 13; Col. iii. 5).

Next to inner freedom and purity comes the
demand for gentleness, for serviceableness, and
philanthropy, by which the Stoic Ethic, especially in
its later phases, was distinguished, and by means of
which it prepared the way for Christian morality.
The universal need of the period awoke the altruistic
feelings of mutual dependence and obligation.
Under the pressure of the universal political servitude, the national and social barriers gave way, and
out of this dead level of political equality rose the
moral respect for the dignity of the human personality
purely as such. Thus the proud and harsh self-
sufficiency of the ancient Stoics softened and
deepened to a mild humanity, in the consciousness
of our organic union in human society. From the
multitude of utterances of Seneca which might be
quoted in this connection, we choose out only a few.
" All that we ought to do and avoid, may be summed
up in the brief formula of human duty: we are all
members of one great body. Nature, by producing
us from the same material and to the same end, has
made us all members of one family. She has im-
planted in us mutual love, and instilled into us the

principles of justice and equity; in view of the order
she has established, it is worse to do than to suffer
ill: at her command helpful hands are stretched
forth. Let that verse be ever in our mouths and
hearts: 'I am a man, and nought that interests
human kind is foreign to me.' Human society is
like an arch which falls to ruin, if every stone does
not support the other " (Ep. xcv. 52 f.). " Human life
acquires stability by means of well-doing and concord;
not by fear but by love does it become a league of
mutual helpfulness " (*de Ira*, l. 5). " So long as we
live among men let us exercise humanity " (*de Ira*,
iii. 43, end). The Stoics applied this principle in
particular to the condemnation of slavery, that most
fatal characteristic of ancient civilisation, and were
here, also, the precursors of Christianity. " What
else is the human soul, I mean the right-doing great
and good soul, than a god dwelling as a guest in the
human body? This soul may come down into a
freedman or a slave, just as well as into a Roman
knight. What is the meaning of ' Roman knight,'
' freedman,' ' slave ' ? Mere names, arising out of
ambition or injustice! One can soar to heaven out
of any corner. Only raise thyself and make thyself
worthy to be a dwelling of God! " (Ep. xxxi. 9).
" Gladly have I heard from thee, that thou dost
associate familiarly with thy slaves; that accords with
thy discernment and thy culture. Are they slaves?
nay, they are men, housemates, lowly friends, yea our
fellow-slaves in regard to the dominion of fate over
them and us alike. Despise not a man on account
of his low estate, seeing that to-morrow thou mayest
pass into the same. Make it thy rule so to behave

4

towards those below thee, as thou wouldst wish those
above thee to behave to thee. As a man would act
foolishly who, in buying a horse, should examine
not the animal himself, but only its stable and
harness, so, and much more, foolishly does he act who
judges a man by his position or his clothing. Though
one is a slave yet he may be in spirit a free man.
And what harm does it do him to be a slave? Show
me anyone who is not a slave! One is a slave of
pleasure, another of avarice, a third of ambition, and
all are slaves of fear; no slavery is shameful save
that which is of our own choice! Therefore let not
the arrogant dissuade thee from being affable towards
thy servants, let these respect thee rather than fear
thee! Should not that suffice the master of a household which suffices the Deity, who desires to be
honoured and loved? Love cannot mix with fear!"
(Ep. xlvii.; *cf.* 1 Cor. vii. 22; Philem. 16; Eph. vi. 9).
Just as in face of the thought of the universal
and equal dignity of men, social divisions lost their
power to separate, so was it also with national
divisions; the Stoics were the first cosmopolitans.
"A man should live in the conviction, 'I was not born
for one little corner only; my fatherland is the
whole world'; for what thou seekest, namely, to live
aright, is possible everywhere" (Ep. xxviii. 4). "I
will look upon the world as my fatherland, and the
Gods as my rulers, who stand above me and about
me, governing my deeds and words. I desire to be
able to say that no man's freedom is curtailed by me,
and mine by no man" (*de Vita Beata*, xx. 4; Ep. cii.,
see above). "We are born under the rule of a King;
to obey God is freedom" (*de Vita Beata*, xv. 6).

Even from the passages quoted, it is clearly evident that the ethical philosophy of Seneca (as of the later Stoics in general) was based on a religious interpretation of the world. The early Stoic conception of a World-Spirit which was at once dynamic and material, was deepened in the direction of an ethical monotheism. Just as men had learned to prize goodness of will in human character more than mere force, just as in earthly rulers men had come to look on power as morally ennobled only by gentleness and benevolence, so it was natural that in the character of the Deity they should place the goodness and wisdom of its administrative providence above mere efficient force. Along with this ethicising of the idea of God the religious sentiment acquired a more inward character than it had had before; mere resignation to the necessity of fate became free obedience, trust, reverence, and love. What representations people might form to themselves of the character of God, whether they called the cause and ruler of the whole Fate or Providence or Nature or World, whether they thought of Him as incorporeal Intelligence or as all-penetrating Spirit (Breath), or as the power of Fate which holds all things together (*Nat. Quæst.*, ii. 45; *ad Helv.*, viii.), is of less moment. The main thing, for Seneca, is the pious belief in a Providence which guides all in our best interest, and the ratification of this belief by moral obedience to the Divine will. "Between the good man and God there subsists a friendship founded on virtue; nay, more than a friendship, a relationship and likeness, since indeed the good man, differing from God only in regard to time (as being non-eternal)

is his pupil, and imitator, and true offspring, whom
that exalted Father educates, like a true Father,
somewhat sternly. God cherishes a fatherly feeling
towards the good, and loves mankind; amid trouble,
pains, and evils, He bids them win strength. Without adversaries virtue weakens; its powers are known
to no one who has not put them to the test; therefore
God teaches those whom He loves to endure hardness, puts them to the proof, exercises them. As a
tree grows strong only by braving the blast, so it is
to the interest of the good to learn fearlessness and
calm by exposure to alarms. Therefore the wise
man will say: 'There is nothing to which I am
compelled, there is nothing which I suffer against
my will; I serve God not as servant, but am in
concord with Him, I follow Him from the heart,
not because I must'" (*de Provid.*, i.–v.; Ep. xcvi.).
"God heaps upon us a multitude of benefits without
hope of return—of which He has no need, while we
are powerless to give it; therefore beneficence itself
must be a thing desirable" (*de Benefic.*, iv. 10).
"Wouldst thou imitate the Gods, then give to the
unthankful; for the sun rises on the ungodly, and the
seas are open to pirates; the wind blows not only as
suits the good, and the rain is not turned aside from
falling on the fields of the godless" (*ibid.* 26, 28;
cf. Matt. v. 45). "What moves the Gods to well-
doing? Their nature. He who holds that they desire
to injure men, is wrong; that they cannot do; they can
do injustice as little as they can suffer it. The first
point in the service of the Gods is to believe in the
Gods, the next to recognise their majesty, and their
goodness, without which there is no majesty; the next,

to know that they are those who rule the world, guide the whole by their power, take the race of men under their protection, and sometimes concern themselves even about individuals. They neither give, nor have they, any evil, yet they chasten many and award penalties; at times they punish under the appearance of doing good. If thou wouldst make the Gods gracious unto thee, then be good; he has honoured them enough who has become like them!" (Ep. xcv. 48 f.). It is not needful to lift up the hands to heaven, or to make petition to the temple-servants to permit us to come close to the ear of the image of the God, as though he could better hear us there; God is nigh thee, God is with thee, God is in thee. Yes, I say again, a holy spirit dwells in us, to mark and observe our evil and our good; as we treat him, so he treats us. No man is good without God's aid; nor can any, unhelped by Him, rise superior to Fate. He alone it is who gives us great and high thoughts and purposes. In every one of the good dwells some god or other." "When thou seest a man undismayed in danger, unmoved by passion, happy amid adverse fortune, serene amid the storm, art thou not moved by reverence, wilt thou not say: 'That is something too great and high to be thought of as the same in kind with the poor body in which it dwells'? A divine force has here come down to earth, a heavenly power by which the soul, with its splendid powers of thought, raises itself above all lower things, and laughs to scorn all our fears and desires. As the rays of the sun touch the earth indeed, but have their true home in that place whence they come forth; so is it with the great and

holy Spirit which is sent down hither in order that
we may learn to know the Deity better; he has
intercourse with us, indeed, but retains his connection
with his origin; thence is his dependence, thither he
directs his gaze and his endeavour. He dwells with
man like a guest of higher rank. What is this
guest? He is the spirit who places dependence on
good that is not his own. That which is man's 'own'
is the soul and the perfect intelligence which dwells
therein; for man is essentially an intelligent being,
therefore his good is complete when he has fulfilled
his destiny" (Ep. xli.). "The gods are not proud or
envious; they let us approach them and they stretch
forth a hand to those who are mounting up to them.
Dost thou wonder that man goes to God? Why,
God comes to man, yea, He comes closer still, He
enters into men. No disposition is good apart from
God. Seeds of the divine are planted in human
bodies; if they are well tended, they germinate and
grow up into likeness with That from whence they
sprang" (Ep. lxxiii. 14). "Certainly, a man must so
live as before the eyes of all; so think as though there
was one who could see into our innermost hearts.
And so it is. For what use is it that anything
should remain secret from men? Nothing is hidden
from God, He is present in our hearts, He enters
into our inmost thoughts" (Ep. lxxxiii. 1). What use
is it to hide oneself and avoid the eyes and ears of
men? A good conscience challenges the verdict of
men; a bad conscience is full of fears and cares even
when alone. Oh unhappy man, if thou despisest this
witness!" (Ep. xliii. 4).

These sayings of Seneca last quoted (Ep. xli., xliii.,

lxxiii., lxxxiii.) are of especial interest, because the same question arises here as will meet us in connection with the Pauline doctrine of Salvation: whether the principle of the good is man's own spirit, his God-related intellect and conscience, or whether it is a supernatural power working upon man from without, a divine spiritual being sent from above, to help him. Zeller[1] understands all these sayings in the former sense only. He writes: "The statement that no one can be good without the aid of the Deity is always to be understood in Seneca in the sense of this (the Stoic) system. The divine aid for which he calls is nothing supernatural, but coincides with the use of our reason and its natural powers. This is obvious from the context of the passages in which he enunciates this thesis. The help of God consists, accordingly, in this—that in the spiritual endowment of mankind an emanation of the Deity as λόγος σπερματικός unites itself with a human body." However accurate this may be as a logical inference from the system, yet it is difficult to rid oneself of the impression that Seneca also conceives of a supernatural divine influence coming to the support of weak human nature, when he says that the Deity gives us his aid, comes down to us and into us, especially when he sees in the truly good man a great and holy spirit who is sent down as a messenger from the higher world in order that we may learn to know the divine better, and who, still

[1] *Philosophie der Griechen,* 2nd ed., iii. 1, 649 *sq.* Besides this classical work, we may refer, in connection with what is said above, to Baur's essay upon Paul and Seneca; Havet, *Le Christianisme et ses Origines,* ii. 249–294; Bruno Bauer, *Christus und die Cäsaren,* 20–60. [Add Lightfoot, *Philippians,* Dissertation II., St Paul and Seneca.—TRANSLATOR.]

maintaining his connection with his home, dwells in our world only as a stranger of nobler origin (Ep. xli.). Turns of thought such as this, although, doubtless, something is to be put down to Seneca's rhetorical style, nevertheless betray a certain vacillation between the philosophic rationalism of his school and the religious belief in revelation and salvation, such as was common in connection with the enthusiasm of the mystery - cults in the Orphic-Pythagorean circles of the time, and found a natural support in the widespread pessimistic sense of powerlessness and need of help. Moreover, points of contact with the philosophy of the Orphic mysteries are found elsewhere in Seneca's system of thought. His belief in immortality, his estimate of the earthly life as a mere prelude to the life beyond, his description of the day of death as the birthday of that part of us which is eternal, are not Stoic at all, but Platonic and Orphic. As the Orphics believed in divine saviours (θεοὶ σωτῆρες) and divinely inspired mediators of salvation who had been sent in the past, and continued to be sent in the present, to the help of mankind who stood in need of help, similarly Seneca points men who strive after ethical perfection to leaders and load-stars, with the picture of whom the struggling soul should fill itself completely. " We must," he writes, "seek out some good man and keep him constantly before our eyes, in order that we may so live and act as though we were in his sight. So Epicurus prescribed, giving us in this way a guardian and guide; and not without reason. Many sins are suppressed if a witness comes on the scene before the deed is done. Our heart must have someone to honour, someone

by whose example it may consecrate its inner life.
Happy is he who can find such an one to venerate
that he himself becomes moulded to the image which
abides in his memory! We need one by whose
example our morals may be formed : without a
standard, what is wrong will not be set right " (Ep. xi.).
" Clothe thyself with the spirit of some great man
and separate thyself from the opinions of the
multitude! Grasp the image of the fairest and most
exalted virtue, which is to be honoured not with
garlands, but by the expenditure of sweat and blood
(*i.e.* toilsome imitation)" (Ep. lxvii.; *cf.* Rom. xiii. 14 ;
Gal. iii. 27). " If we might cast a glance into the
soul of a good man, what a fair picture we should see
there, how impressive in its splendour, its grandeur
and its calm! There we should see in glowing
colours, righteousness, courage, prudence and wisdom
. . . . and over all, humanity, that rare excellence,
would pour forth its brilliancy . . . . everyone would
recognise him to be worthy of love and at the same
time worthy of honour. If anyone were to see this
picture, nobler and more splendid than is commonly
seen among men, would he not stand still as before a
divinity and pray in the stillness of his heart that this
vision might be granted to him continually. Then,
drawn by the attractive goodness of that vision, he
would fall on his knees to adore it, and after long
contemplation would break out with awe and amaze-
ment into the words of Virgil, ' Hail to thee, whosoever thou art : heal thou our grief.'[1] And it will help
and heal us, if we honour it, not with offerings of

[1] "Sis felix, nostrumque leves quaecunque laborem." Aen.
i. 330.

beasts or gold or silver, but of a pious and good heart.
There is none, I repeat, who would not be fired with
love, if it were granted us to see an ideal picture such
as that. Now, it is true, our eyes are blinded by
many things ; but if we would purify them and clear
our vision, then we should be able to see virtue
beneath the veil of the body, beneath the burden of
poverty, humility and ignominy : we should see her
beauty even under the most sordid vestments"
(Ep. cxv. 3 f.).

It is not to be wondered at that sayings of this
kind have made the impression upon many that
Seneca must have known Jesus Christ and have been
referring to Him when he spoke with such enthusiasm
of the inspiring power of the ideal of ethical perfection embodied in a person. But this is out of the
question. For the historical student, the special
importance of these sayings consists precisely in the
fact that they are not dependent on the Christian
Gospel, and are therefore of the more significance as
witnesses of a widespread ethico-religious mode of
thought and feeling in the Græco-Roman world of
that period, which, from its close affinity with the
Christian view had, among the heathen, prepared
the soil for the Gospel. There was here a morality
which led a man to look into his heart and freed him
from the outer world, with its allurements and its
terrors ; which purified his soul by demanding the
mastery of the passions, especially of sensuality ;
which taught him to find in this inner freedom and
purity the dignity of the human personality, and
called into being a respect for the individual as a
man ; which, finally, found in the rational God-

related nature of man a bond of union for all mankind without distinction of nation or rank; and from
this conviction derived the motive to a new virtue
which put the crown on all the rest—brotherly love
of men, "humanity" (the word *humanitas* was first
used by the Stoics in this sense). This morality
based itself upon a religious interpretation of the
world: in the latter, as in the former, the pagan
Naturalism was spiritualised and moralised; the gods
of the national polytheism lost their significance and
were conceived partly as symbols for the powers of
Nature, and partly as servant-gods, something in the
nature of the Biblical angels. These, however, did
not interfere with the sole administration of the one
supreme God, the author and ruler of the world. In
the character of this Supreme Ruler the naturalistic
and anthropopathic traits of mythological tradition
were eliminated; He was thought of as perfect
Intelligence and Goodness, His administration of
the world as a wise providence, caring for us with
a fatherly solicitude, and wisely ordering evil to our
best interests as a factor in our education. To this
world-ruling intelligence, man, as an intelligent
being, feels himself closely related; nay more, he
is conscious of the presence of God within him as
a holy spirit, a warning and watching conscience, a
motive power to good, to victory over the world.
Finally, this religious experience is also a guarantee
of the hope that the God-related soul, after its
separation from the earthly body, shall find in the
heavenly world of light the perfect freedom and
peace and repose for which here below it could only
strive. This hope of the hereafter was borrowed by

the Stoic rationalism in the period of the Empire, from the Platonic philosophy and the teaching associated with the Orphic mysteries, where it was likewise based upon enthusiastic experiences, though, it is true, rather of an ecstatic and orgiastic than of an ethical and idealistic character. The Orphic belief, too, in authoritative mediators of revelation and salvation, was rationalised to some extent by Seneca in his ethical Hero-worship. In general, therefore, we may describe that idealistic conception of the world, which meets us especially in the writings of Seneca and Epictetus, as a first attempt to bring the enthusiasm of the religious mystic into the service of the ideals of a rational ethic. Neither Stoicism nor the mystery-cults could give the world the religious satisfaction which it longed for; both had outgrown the official popular religion, and sought to provide a substitute for it, but both essayed the task with inadequate means. Stoicism had, it is true, a rational ethic, with a religious background, and there was not wanting to this ethic a certain enthusiasm, an idealistic impulse and sentiment; but this idealism was still much too abstract to give substance and form to a religion. It lacked the definite authority of a revelation as a basis for its teaching, and definite mystical acts whereby to express and intensify the belief of the religious community. In these two respects, it is true, the mystery-unions possessed an initial advantage over the philosophic schools. But their deliverer-gods and mediators of salvation were still too closely connected with the old pagan Naturalism, and consequently the enthusiasm produced by their mystic initiations partook too much of a wild, irrational, ecstatic orgiasm to satisfy and permanently hold the more finely touched spirits and the more rationally thinking minds. Their expiatory rites, moreover, since they were divorced from an ethical ideal, seemed rather to blunt, than to intensify and deepen, moral feeling. What neither the Stoic teachers nor the priests of the mystery-cults were able to effect—the overcoming of paganism by the foundation of a new universal and enduring religious organisation—Paul accomplished by means of the gospel of the historical Saviour Jesus Christ. This was a saviour who could take the place both of the saving gods of the mysteries and of the ideals of virtue of the Stoics, because in His life and death faith saw the moral ideal fulfilled and the divine salvation manifested, and thus possessed the source of an enthusiasm which united the strongest religious motive-force with the purest ethical content.

The mystery-cults too, which received such a strong impetus about the beginning of the empire, could be studied at that time scarcely anywhere better than in Tarsus, where Paul had lived as a youth, and again, later, for some time as a Christian. As we know from Plutarch's Life of Pompey (cap. xxiv.) Tarsus was, as early as 63 B.C., when Pompey was engaged in suppressing the Cilician pirates, a seat of the Mithras-cult, which there became known to the Romans for the first time, and worked its way westward from that point. As I shall have to go into more detail regarding the Mithras-cult in a later connection (vol. iii.), it may suffice to say here that it was from the beginning a mixed religion formed by combining Persian Mazdeism with

Babylonian theology. Subsequently, after its diffusion over Syria and Asia Minor, it received a further admixture from the cults of Sun-deities which prevailed in those regions, in particular in Phrygia and Lydia; it took over from the orgiastic religion of Attis or Sabazios and of Cybele, the Great Mother of the Gods, certain ritual usages such as the expiatory blood-baptism, the Taurobolium or Kriobolium.[1] In the bas-relief which we find on many monuments representing Mithras himself sacrificing a bull for the salvation of the world, he is always shown with the Phrygian cap, from which we may conclude that the cultus-myth thus represented and, consequently, the corresponding ritual, viz. the Taurobolium itself, is of Phrygian origin. From the proximity of Phrygia and Cilicia we may infer that in the cult of Mithras as established in Tarsus also, the Taurobolium, conceived as communicating an expiatory and lifegiving influence through the sacred blood of the sacrifice, formed a main feature of the ceremony of initiation. Besides this, their sacraments included a sacred meal at which the symbols of the life which Mithras had communicated to the faithful stood on the table in the form of consecrated bread and a cup (of water or wine), as may be recognised from many representations of the ceremony. At one side stand the initiated of various grades, in animal masks which

---

[1] The person who was to be initiated stood in a pit covered with boards in which holes had been pierced. Over this the sacrifice of the bull or ram was performed in such a way that the blood of the sacrifice, streaming down, poured over the man's whole body as an effectual means of expiation, purification, and new life.

represent the being of the God under various different attributes; thus they have "put on" their god in order to place themselves in the closest fellowship with him.   Involuntarily we remember the words of Paul, that all who are baptized into Christ have "put on" Christ, and that the consecrated cup and the bread that we break in the Lord's Supper are the "fellowship of the blood and body of Christ."   I do not of course mean to assert that Paul borrowed these thoughts and words direct from the mysteries of Mithras.   But the possibility cannot, I think, be denied that Paul the citizen of Tarsus had some slight knowledge of the heathen cults practised there, and that pictures and representations of this kind so impressed themselves upon his memory that, later, when they were called forth by natural association of ideas from the background of his consciousness, they became the prepared material for the combinations formed by the genius of the Apostle. This possibility will at least not be unconditionally rejected by anyone who, on the one hand, reflects that Paul cannot have drawn his doctrines of the mystical ceremonies of Baptism and the Lord's Supper from the tradition of the Christian community, because this tradition before his time knew nothing of these doctrines; or who remembers, on the other hand, that Paul himself appeals in 1 Cor. x. to the analogy of the pagan sacrificial meal.

CHAPTER IV

EDUCATION: JEWISH INFLUENCE

IT is time to turn from the possible Greek culture of Saul-Paul of Tarsus—which after all must remain problematical—to the Jewish side of his education, where we stand on surer ground. That he was a Pharisee and the son of a Pharisee, he himself testifies; that he was a pupil of the famous head of the Pharisaic school, Gamaliel, is asserted in Acts, and I see no valid reason for doubting the statement. Nay more, it has in its favour the well-established fact that Gamaliel had among his scholars many Hellenistic Jews, and was himself more favourably inclined than the other Palestinian teachers towards the Hellenistic tendency in Jewish theology. If Paul, therefore, sat as a pupil at the feet of Gamaliel it is all the easier to explain his familiarity with the Alexandrian Book of Wisdom, and with the allegorical method of interpreting Scripture which was more usual in Hellenistic than in Palestinian circles. But however that may be, whether Paul received his Jewish education only in his parents' house and in the synagogue at Tarsus, or whether he studied also in the school of Gamaliel in Jerusalem, it is in any

case certain that he was brought up in the strict
spirit of the Jewish faith, and in the form of theological tradition which was represented by the
Palestinian teachers of his time. That this religion
and theology was not identical with that of the
prophets and Psalms is so manifest a fact that no
serious religious historian can ignore it. It is impossible really to understand the Apostle Paul without
knowing the presuppositions of his Jewish faith as
determined by the theology of the Pharisaic school.
The best source for this is Weber's book, *Die Alt-
Synagogale Palästinensische Theologie*, which has not
been superseded even by Dalman's more recent
Worte Jesu. Besides these we may refer to Schürer's
well-known work *Neutestamentliche Zeitgeschichte*,[1] and
to Holtzmann's *Neutestamentliche Theologie* (i. 42–85).
I must limit myself here to the following sketch.[2]

The doctrine of God as it developed in post-exilic
Judaism and became fixed in the Pharisaic theology,
differs in two directions from that of the Old Testament prophets. It is, on the one side, more spiritual ;
anthropomorphisms are eliminated, the transcend-
ence above the world is more strictly carried through ;
but, on the other side, the religious relationship is
conceived in a narrower and more external fashion.
God's will is completely set forth in the book of the

---

[1] Eng. trans., *A History of the Jewish People in the Time of Jesus
Christ.*

[2] Of the development of the religion of Israel down to the time
when Pharisaism arose, I have given a comprehensive survey in
my *Religionsphilosophie auf geschichtlicher Grundlage*, third edition,
pp. 46–96. [The corresponding section in the English translation,
The Philosophy of Religion on the Basis of its History—made from
the second edition—is vol. iii. pp. 127–176.]

Law (the Torah), and as He has given the Law to
the Jewish People only, it is to them alone that He
has a positive relationship : there is not even the
expectation of a later extension of it to all nations,
as the prophets had held.   According to the Pharisaic
view the Jews are for ever the sole People of God,
while the heathen, as such, of whatever kind their
moral character may be, are enemies of God, and are
destined to eternal damnation.   In regard to Israel,
God's relationship is completely defined by the Law,
which He has given to that People for the very
purpose that they may by fulfilling it win for themselves merit and a claim to reward in this world and
the next.   In the requital of human action the Divine
will is as absolutely bound to the Law as the human
will.   Thus the Law is exalted as a higher power
above God, and became indeed the veritable idol of
Pharisaic Judaism ; indeed the Rabbis did not hesitate
to represent God Himself as studying the Torah !

The more God was conceived as removed into
an inaccessible elevation above the world, the more
pressing became the need to fill the gulf between
God and the world by interposing intermediate beings.
Divine attributes and activities, Wisdom, Word,
Spirit, Glory of God, were hypostatised into personal
beings who acted as representatives of God and
carried out His will, especially in connection with
the revelation to Israel.   In particular, the old conception of angels and demons (originally the friendly
and hostile spirits of the animistic religion which had
maintained itself in the popular belief alongside of
the belief in Jahwe) now received an extension and
application which were foreign to the prophetic

religion. Various ranks were distinguished among the angels, names were given to the most exalted of them, and definite functions in the administration of the world were assigned to them. Nations and individuals had guardian-spirits allotted to them (in which we may perhaps see an imitation of the Persian Fravashis) and even the different phenomena of Nature were placed under the direction of special angels, a proceeding which restored the heathen nature-gods, though under the limitations demanded by the monotheistic principle. The demons again (originally malevolent ghosts) were now set over against the heavenly "messengers of God" as "fallen angels" and were organised under a leader, Satan, who is now first conceived as the adversary of God. This was not originally his essential character; in the didactive poem of Job he still belongs to the heavenly retinue of God, and plays the part of a Crown-prosecutor who comes before God as the "accuser" of sinners, though even here, it must be admitted, not without an obvious satisfaction in raising suspicion and causing injury. But as early as the (post-exilic) Book of Chronicles Satan is represented as tempting David to sin (1 Chron. xxi. 1), whereas the earlier historian (2 Sam. xxiv. 1) represented the same action of David, the numbering of the people, as directly caused by God. It is evident, therefore, that the theological necessity of exonerating God from responsibility for the wickedness and evil which is in the world favoured the transformation of Satan from a servant of God into an adversary. Another contributory cause was, that, since the Maccabæan war of liberation, the opposition, in the mind of pious Jews, between the Kingdom of God and the Kingdoms of this world had reached that extreme tension of which we find the typical expression in the apocalypse of Daniel; consequently the Guardian-Spirits or Angel-Princes, which according to the earlier view (Deut. iv. 19) were placed by God as regents over the nations, came to be looked on more and more as rebel vassals hostile to God, who, under their head, Satan, are at war with the Kingdom of God — a similar conception is implied by the description of Satan as "the Prince of this World." The demons under his command fill the earth and the air and make themselves felt by men as scourges in sickness and misfortune of every kind. The fear of them brought to the surface again many of the hobgoblin-superstitions which the prophetic Jahwe-religion had forced out of sight, and the official Jewish theology did not, like the old healthy prophetism, ban this belief in all manner of spirits working upon men and taking possession of them, which had survived from the animistic nature-religion, but rather sanctioned it and found a place for it in its own system; just as the Stoic and Platonic philosophies had done with the Greek belief in gods and demons. If we consider, on the one hand, what a large space the belief in angels and demons occupied at that time in the Jewish consciousness, in spite of the monotheism of the Bible, and on the other, that for educated pagans the multiplicity of the mythological divinities had no longer any real significance (since the one-ness of the deity that rules the world was generally recognised either in a pantheistic or monotheistic sense, while the other gods were reduced to symbols of the powers of Nature or mere tools in the hand of the supreme world-ruler); it must be admitted that the distinction between the Jewish and the Greek beliefs in God was not so great but that an understanding between them, on the basis of a rational ethical monotheism, was perfectly possible. As a matter of fact, God-fearing Gentiles were accustomed to hold friendly intercourse with Hellenistic Jews on the basis of this belief, as on a common ground; and this was the basis upon which Paul founded his churches. It was not the belief in God, but the belief in the Law and the meticulous observance of the Law, which formed the insuperable barrier which divided strict Pharisaic Judaism from the Gentiles, and, consequently, also from Gentile Christians.

According to the Pharisaic theology, the world was created for the sake of the (Mosaic) Law, and therefore for the People of the Law, and Zion is its centre. Above the earth rise seven heavens, of which the highest is the seat of God. The under-world was now divided (in a fashion still unknown to the canonical Scriptures of the Old Testament) into a place of reward for the pious, Paradise, and a place of punishment for the ungodly, Gehenna (the counterpart in the other world of Gehinnom or the "valley of abomination"—so called from the sacrifice to Moloch which had been practised there—near Jerusalem). Man is not created in the immediate image of God, but of the angels. He remained only a short time in the Paradise of innocence, then fell, through the transgression of his First Parents, into a deep and ever-advancing corruption. This doctrine of the Fall and corruption, which is foreign to the canonical Old Testament, is current throughout the Pharisaic theology, and plays an important part in the Apocalypses of Esdras and Baruch; but to the further question as to the cause of the Fall, different answers are given.[1] Sometimes the original sin seems to have been the free act of Adam, whereby he brought judgment upon himself and his posterity; but another version runs thus : " One little grain of bad seed was sown from the beginning of the creation in Adam's heart, and what fruit of sin that has borne already and will yet bear until the harvest is finished ! " According to that, Adam's sin was not the first and free cause of evil, but only the first appearance of that which lay already in his nature, con-created with him, the evil impulse of sensual lust. Finally a legend which is very old (for it is alluded to in 2 Cor. xi. 3) derives the corruption of mankind from Eve's having been seduced by the devil in the form of a serpent, the nature of her whole posterity being thus physically infected with the demonic poison of sin and death.

However the case may stand in regard to this last-named cause of sin, there is at all events general agreement among the Jewish theologians of the period that the sin of our First Parents was fateful for the whole of mankind, nay, for the whole world : when Adam sinned the world was judged and sentence of death was passed upon his posterity (*cf.* Rom. v. 12). Moreover, the evil consequences extended also to the spirit-world, for some of the angels came down

---

[1] *Cf.* 2 Esdras iii. 21, iv. 30, vii. 11, 48 ; Apoc. Baruch xxiii. 4. See Weber, *altsyn. Theol.*, p. 211 ff.

from heaven and had intercourse with women, and as a punishment were imprisoned and given over to torture, while the giants whom they begot became evil demons, who tempt men to all evil and injure them in every way.[1]   In spite of this terrible corruption, to which the present world is given over until its future renewal in the Messianic age, man retains freedom to withstand the evil impulse and to avoid sin, or to make up for the sin he has committed by penitence and good works.   There were, according to Jewish theology, in spite of the corruption which originated from Adam, a few holy men; who were not indeed sinless, but were so rich in merit that their little sins were of no account in comparison.   The Jewish Patriarchs, Moses, famous teachers of the Law and notable martyrs, were counted of this number.

The righteousness of man rests upon a Divine judgment which pronounces him either just, *i.e.* guiltless, or guilty, and it may have reference either to a single command or to the general conduct of the man.   But the recognition of righteousness carries with it also the claim to reward.   Righteousness depends on a comparison of the fulfilments and transgressions of the law.   The account is kept in heaven both for Israel as a whole and for each individual, and is provisionally made up every day, while the final balance is struck at death.   There are, on this basis, three classes of men: the righteous, whose merits preponderate; sinners, whose demerit preponderates; an intermediate class in whose case the balance is even.   As perfectly righteous, are ranked in Jewish

[1] Apoc. Baruch lvi. 10; Enoch vi., x., xv., xviii., lxvii., lxix.

theology all whose merits are out of all proportion greater than their failings, and, in particular, the Patriarchs; absolute sinlessness is not an essential condition, since minor faults may be atoned for by penance in this world, so that only reward for merit is to be expected in the next. Conversely, great sinners receive the reward of whatever small merits they have acquired in the form of happiness in this life, so that in the world to come they have only eternal punishment to look forward to; hence the prosperity of the ungodly heathen. As good works deserve reward, so sins must be atoned for, expiated, by penances or services: for sin is a debt for which God exacts payment. God does not forgive without payment, according to the Pharisaic theology, any more than an earthly judge. The expiation is a "compensation" or "restitution" in so far as it sets right the relation to God which sin had disturbed; it is a "propitiation" in so far as it appeases God's wrath against the sinner and alters His relation towards him. Means of expiation which effect either delay of punishment or complete remission of punishment are (1) Penitence [Germ. "Busse," which includes, but is not limited to, the meaning "penance"], consisting less in an alteration of mind than in confession, fasting, and restitution; (2) Suffering and death, which, as the endurance of the temporal penalty for sin, mitigate the severity of the sentence in the other world; (3) Good works, among which study of the Law and the performance of the ritual observances (e.g. the Temple sacrifice) are of special importance, after them come fasting, almsgiving, and voluntary martyrdom; finally (4) the Day of

Atonement as a general expiation for the whole community. The efficacy of these meritorious acts and means of expiation is not, however, confined to the sole person of the doer, but is also communicable to others ; there are vicarious merits and penances of the righteous on behalf of sinners, there is a store of mercy, an accumulation of merit which belongs as a hereditable possession to individual families and to the whole people. Thus, above all, the merits of the holy Fathers of Israel constitute a national fund in which every true Israelite has a share in virtue of his birth. But even the merits of contemporary righteous men can be credited to their whole generation, and deliver them from the divine sentence of punishment, since their intercession is efficacious with God. Most powerful of all, however, in the atoning and saving influence which it exerts on behalf of the whole community, is the martyr-death suffered by the righteous for no sin of their own. Its saving power is esteemed equal to that of the Day of Atonement, since it effects, as that does, a general atonement for living and dead—as is implied indeed by the descriptions applied to it, "atoning sacrifice" and "ransom price." The well-known Isaian interpretation of the suffering of the righteous as a means of salvation and a ransom for the sinful multitude (Isa. liii.) is obviously influential in this Pharisaic doctrine of the vicarious suffering of the righteous for sinners ; but it must not be overlooked that the ethical communication of this saving influence implied by the prophet, was coarsened in Pharisaism into a purely juridical substitution, more like the discharge of debts by one for another which civil law recognises. Here as elsewhere there betrays itself the predominantly juristic spirit of this theology, which externalised religion into a legal relation between God and man. It is, moreover, to be remarked that in this doctrine of vicarious expiation, as well as in the previously-mentioned doctrine of intermediate beings and demons, the Judaism of that period was in the closest touch with those conceptions of the contemporary paganism which underlay, especially, the expiatory ritual of the mystery-cults. The conception took, no doubt, a somewhat different form in the one and the other; in the one it was a juridical act, the payment of a ransom on behalf of another; in the other it was a magic act, the removal of a corrupting infection through the sacred blood of a sacrifice, whether of animals (Taurobolium), or, in some cases, of men (self-mutilation of the priests of Cybele): but ultimately both come to the same thing —that the guilt of sin can be removed by outward, ethically indifferent means. But the fact that this unethical conception, which is as contrary to the spirit of the Hebrew prophets as it is to that of Greek philosophy, had then an equal vogue among both Jews and pagans, points, without doubt, to a soul-sickness of mankind at that time, to a morbidly intense consciousness of sin and feeling of apprehension, such as is constantly met with in times of extreme distress and social disorder (as, for example, in the last centuries of the Middle Ages). But as this irrational conception of the necessity and value of these bloody sacrifices for sin did, as a matter of fact, rule the sick world, it was almost inevitable that the new religion which came to bring salvation

should take account of the morbid delusions of men
and administer its healing medicine in forms which
appeared scarcely distinguishable from that of the
poison.

A certain counterpoise, however, to the deadening
unspirituality of legalism was offered by the Jewish
Messianic expectation, which may be not unjustly
described as the soul of the Jewish religion, inasmuch
as all the courage and enthusiasm which remained to
that unhappy people, under the double misery of the
Roman political, and the Pharisaic legal, tyranny, had
concentrated itself in Messianic hopes and dreams.
Of a Messianic system of doctrine in any strict sense
it is, however, impossible to speak, since there was
never any Jewish dogma regarding the Messiah, nor
any systematised and officially sanctioned doctrine of
the Messiah in the sense that there was later a Church
doctrine of Christ; but vague conceptions of very
various origin and content, which, indeed, partly contradicted each other, were current in different circles
without coming into conflict with one another. The
one fixed point which formed the centre of the
Messianic conception was that God would victoriously
and magnificently assert His kingship over His People,
and through them over other nations, by means
of miraculous deeds of power. But opinion wavered
even on the question whether this restoration of the
theocracy would be directly effected by God Himself,
or through the agency of the Messiah as the instrument and representative of God. According to the
apocalypse of Daniel, the theocracy realises itself in a
" kingdom of the saints "—that is, of pious Jews, without a Messianic king, for the form " like unto a son of

man " (Dan. vii. 13) seen by the seer in his vision, is only a symbol of the people of God, as the preceding appearances of beasts are symbols of the nations of the world. Similarly in the apocalyptic writing " The Assumption of Moses," there is no mention of the Messiah, but the final salvation comes when the Most-High Himself arises and comes forth to punish the heathen and bring to nought their idols ; then shall Israel be happy and mount up on eagles' wings and look down from the stars of heaven upon its enemies (x. 7–10). On the other hand, in the older part of the Apocalypse of Enoch, after God Himself has conquered the heathen and held judgment upon the Jews and the angels, the Messiah comes on the scene under the form of a white bull—*i.e.* as a pre-eminent member of the Jewish nation, whose victorious greatness He personally represents, while He is feared and supplicated to by all the heathen (cap. xc.). A much more prominent part is played by the Messianic king in the " Psalms of Solomon," which were composed by a Pharisee after the first Roman invasion under Pompey. In these He is the " Son of David " of the ancient prophets, chosen of God and girded with strength that He may smite unrighteous rulers, purify Jerusalem, and destroy the ungodly heathen with His rod of iron and with the word of His mouth, gather the tribes of Israel, judge the nations and bring them under His yoke. Under the rule of this righteous king there will be no injustice done, and He Himself is pure from sin because God has strengthened him by His holy spirit with wisdom and power (xvii. 20–40). On the other hand, in the later Apocalypses, the Similitudes of Enoch, 2 Esdras, and Baruch,

amid the growing pessimism and despair of the
present world, the Messianic conception took a
transcendent direction.   In the Similitudes of Enoch,
Daniel's vision of " one in the likeness of a son of man "
is referred to the Chosen One, or Messiah, in such a
way that an origin and dignity is ascribed to Him
which wavers between ideal predestination and real
pre-existence, but is in any case supernatural.   " The
name of the Son of Man was named by God before
the world was ; the Son of Man was chosen out and
hidden in God's presence before the world was created,
and will be eternally in His presence.   The wisdom
of the Lord of Spirits revealed Him to the saints, for
in His name were they delivered.   The Chosen One
stands before the Lord of Spirits, and His glory is for
ever and ever ; in Him dwells the spirit of wisdom
and the spirit of Him who giveth understanding, the
spirit of doctrine and might, and the spirit of those
who have fallen asleep in righteousness.   He will
judge that which is hidden ; when the earth and the
under-world give up their dead, then will He choose
the righteous and holy among them, for the day of
their deliverance has come " (xlviii., xlix.).[1]

[1] Against the hypothesis that this and other passages were interpolated by a Christian, Schürer remarks (Eng. trans., Div. ii. vol. iii.
p. 68), as it seems to me justly, " the view of the Messiah here set
forth is fully intelligible on purely Jewish premisses, and does not
need for its explanation the hypothesis of Christian influence ; in the
whole section there is nothing specifically Christian."   There seems
to be more doubt about the Jewish origin of the Messianic passage
in the Sybilline Oracles, v. 414 : " There came from the vault of
heaven a blessed man, who bore the sceptre given him by God, and
brought all things under his power, and restored to all the good,
the wealth which former men had taken away from them "

That this Son of Man, pre-existing in heaven, is to be derived from the symbolic figure of the son of man in the vision of Daniel, is self-evident and is confirmed by the Apocalypse of Ezra, where the seer sees something like a man brought up from the sea by a storm and flying with the clouds of heaven (xiii. 3), which he proceeds to explain as a reference to him "whom the Highest has long held in reserve, through whom He will deliver the creation, and who will create a new social order among the survivors" (viz. the Messiah). "When the foregoing signs occur, then shall my Son appear, whom thou sawest ascend as a man, and will go up to the summit of Mount Zion, rebuke the nations for their sins, and will annihilate them without effort by his mere word" (32 ff.). His rising out of the heart of the sea betokens that "none of the inhabitants of earth shall behold my Son or his companions (angels) before the hour of his day (the day of his revelation) has come" (51 ff.). Here too, therefore, the Messiah shall not come from beneath, but from above, from a heavenly pre-existence, in which God has long kept Him in reserve and hidden Him until His manifestation on the day of redemption. It is true that this higher origin is not quite in accordance with the further saying that the Messiah, with all that draw human breath, shall die after four hundred years, and then will come the Last Judgment and the eternal world (vii. 28 ff. ; cf. Apoc. Baruch xxx.). In this contradiction there is betrayed very markedly the

(Kautzsch, *Pseudepigr. d. A. Ts.*, p. 214). As the whole Fifth Book of these Oracles is a conglomerate of various origin, it is not possible to arrive at any certain conclusion in regard to these verses.

hesitation between the old prophetic outlook upon the present world and the apocalyptic other-worldliness of the Messianic idea of that period. The same inconsistency shows itself in the description of the Messianic Age: sometimes a solid earthly happiness of the pious Jew, with fabulous blessings of children and fruitfulness of Nature (Enoch x. 17 ; Baruch xxix. 4–8), the heathen conquered in battle, and destroyed, or subjugated and laid under tribute ; again all is more or less spiritualised ; the redeemed will become heavenly angels (Enoch li. 4) ; the gates of heaven will open before them, they will shine as the stars of heaven, rejoice like the angels, be members of the heavenly host, have peace and joy as children of the truth (Enoch civ. f.), the redeemed Jews will mount aloft upon eagles' wings to the stars of heaven, and thence look down with scorn upon their enemies (Assumption of Moses, x.) ; the countenance of the pious shall then shine as the sun, and they shall be like the stars, imperishable as they, and shall behold the face of God and receive from Him praise and reward (2 Esdras vii. 97).

The Messianic hope thus spiritualised and transferred to the other world can scarcely be distinguished from the Hellenistic hope of immortality as we find it in the Alexandrian Book of Wisdom and in Philo: " The souls of the righteous are in God's hand, no suffering can touch them, they are at peace. . . . The righteous live for ever, their recompense is of the Lord, and the Most-High careth for them " (Wisd. iii. 1 ; v. 15). This hope of blessedness in the other world for the soul when freed from the earthly body was borrowed by Alexandrian Judaism from the

Greek philosophy and Mysteries; it was foreign to genuine Palestinian Judaism. The hope of the latter was directed towards the earthly blessedness of the Theocratic nation; and when the Palestinian Jews began to postulate a share in the future Messianic happiness for the pious dead, they could only represent that to themselves in the form of a bodily resurrection: therefore the resurrection of the sleeping righteous forms an essential act in the apocalyptic drama. But how could the Alexandrian Jew feel any enthusiasm for the resurrection of a body which he regarded, quite in the manner of Plato and Seneca, as a mere perishable envelope and heavy burden of the soul! (Wisd. ix. 15). It is therefore intelligible that in Hellenistic Judaism the hope of immortality prevailed over the Messianic idea, and either forced this so completely into the background as we shall find it in the case of Philo and the Essenes, or modified it greatly in the direction of a spiritual hope concerned with the other world, such as we have found in the later apocalypses. It is also quite possible, though not clearly demonstrable, that the conception of a Messiah pre-existing in heaven before His manifestation upon earth, has a historical connection with the Platonic-Alexandrian philosophumenon of a heavenly ideal man, who was the prototype of the creation of man upon earth, a doctrine which passed from Alexandrianism into the Rabbinic theology. It is in any case certain that the Alexandrian-Jewish religious philosophy, which I reserve for fuller treatment in a later context (vol. iii.), was an extremely important link of connection between

Judaism and Greek thought; it afforded to Hellenistic Jews of the Dispersion the possibility of building a bridge from their ancestral Faith to the Greek culture by which they were surrounded.

Paul too was affected by the influence of the Hellenistic Jewish philosophic doctrine—it matters not whether he made its acquaintance in his Tarsus days or only in the school of Gamaliel at Jerusalem. He can hardly have known the writings of his contemporary Philo, but certainly knew the Book of the Wisdom of Solomon, written in the last century before Christ at Alexandria, as is proved by the numerous striking echoes of this book in the Pauline Epistles. I may refer in this connection to the careful study of E. Grafe on " The Relation of the Pauline Writings to Sapientia Salomonis," in which the dependence of Paul on Wisdom in several points [1] is demonstrated with a high degree of probability, and the conclusion is drawn that " the influence of Sapientia on Paul deserves to be called important . . . . he borrows from it a considerable number of phrases, conceptions and images, and makes use of them for the expression of thoughts and convictions which he had drawn from other quarters. In some not unimportant points, however, he shows himself really influenced by Sapientia, as for example in his doctrine of eschatology and in his condemnation of heathenism

[1] *Cf.* Rom. ix. 19 ff. with Sap. xii. 10 ff., 20 ; xv. 7 (predestination); then for condemnation of heathenism, Gal. iv. 8 ff. and Rom. i. 18 ff. with Sap. xiii. 1–10, xiv. 23–31 ; further, for eschatology, 2 Cor. v. 1–4 with Sap. ix. 15, iii. 1 ff., vi. 20 ; finally (less certain), anthropology, 1 Cor. ii. 8 ff. with Sap. ix. 17, vii. 27 f., Rom. v. 12, viii. 19 f. with Sap. i. 13 ff., ii. 24. There are besides many scattered parallels the convincingness of which is open to controversy.

and its idolatrous worship. In these departments of
doctrine, passages from Sapientia throw light upon
obscure and difficult arguments of the Apostle. And
Paul has yet another point in common with this
peculiar book ; just as Sapientia unites within itself
Judaic and Hellenistic elements, and in such a way
that a complete adjustment of the disparate elements
is not always arrived at, so too, in the breast of the
Christian Apostle, these two forces struggle with
one another." But from the Alexandrian - Jewish
theology Paul also learned the way to bind together
these two heterogeneous elements, and to overcome
their opposition—the allegorical method of interpreting Scripture. We shall see later how Philo developed
it into a fixed and regular method ; but he was not the
discoverer of it. It is found two centuries earlier in
the Jewish philosopher Aristobulus, who had used it in
order to read into the books of Moses the spiritual conception of God which he had found in the Greek philosophers, and to explain away the anthropomorphisms
of their naïve religious narratives. The same method
was employed by the Stoic philosophers in order to
father their religious conceptions upon Homer, and
to reconcile in some degree the popular mythological
beliefs with their own enlightened views. The
Alexandrian Jews were the more disposed to follow
this example because it enabled them to adopt the
imposing conceptions of Greek thought without
denying their ancestral Faith. By interpreting their
sacred Scriptures in such a way as to make the letter
only the symbol and outward envelope of a spiritual
sense which was often far removed from the literal,
they were able not only to maintain the agreement

of their sacred writings with those of the philosophers, but even to indicate with proud satisfaction that the ancient revelation of Moses was the source from which the much later philosophy of Greece had drawn its wisdom.

The same service which the allegorical method of interpretation had already rendered to the Stoic interpreters of Homer and to the Alexandrian-Jewish theologians, it rendered also to the Apostle Paul, and subsequently to all the Christian teachers—that of concealing from the consciousness of those who believed in authority the gulf which actually divided the old from the new, and of compelling, with gentle force, the venerated literature of the past to bear witness to a truth which in reality rendered it nugatory. That this everywhere took place quite *bona fide*, without any scruple as to the violence and arbitrariness of the procedure, gives us less cause for surprise if we reflect, in the first place, that we ourselves in our treatment of the Bible for purposes of practical edification and instruction consider ourselves justified in employing exactly the same procedure; and, secondly, that the feeling for historical reality in general, and for the original meaning of ancient historical documents in particular, was almost entirely lacking in that age, in spite of its otherwise high mental culture. This lack of the " feeling for reality " was the condition not only of its weakness in scientific knowledge, but also of the greatness of its creative power in art and religion.

CHAPTER V

Conversion and Call

WHETHER Paul was present in Jerusalem in the days when Jesus fulfilled His destiny there, and had seen Him in the flesh, we cannot tell—from 2 Cor. v. 16 no definite conclusion can be drawn either for or against a personal acquaintance of the apostle with Jesus, while 1 Cor. ix. 1 can only refer to a vision of the risen Lord. The first historical appearance of Paul is connected with the martyrdom of the Hellenist Stephen, who seems to have been the first to draw from the belief in Jesus as the Messiah far-reaching inferences as to the reform of the Jewish religion, to which the other disciples had not yet approached, for it was made a special charge against him that he had declared that Jesus would destroy the Temple and alter the Mosaic customs (Acts vi. 14). If, then, Paul the Pharisee, with his zeal for the Law, heard bold assertions of this kind maintained by those who confessed the faith in the crucified Messiah Jesus, and openly defended in the synagogues, it is intelligible that this aroused his bitter indignation against a sect whose belief in a crucified Messiah was in itself irrational, while in

view of the revolutionary consequences drawn by
Stephen it became nothing short of impious; and
made its extirpation appear to him as a conscientious
duty.   Accordingly at the death of Stephen he
played the part of the principal witness, at whose
feet the executioners laid down their clothes.   And
not content with making the one capital example,
he displayed such zeal in the continued persecution
of the Christian community that the Council at
Jerusalem gave him authority to hold penal jurisdiction in the Jewish colony at Damascus over the
Christians who had taken refuge there.   But the
persecutor was to enter Damascus as a convert.

The Book of Acts gives a threefold account of the
conversion of Paul, in chaps. ix., xxii., and xxvi.
The particulars of this threefold narrative can make
no claim to historical accuracy, if only because they
contradict each other in several points.   The words
which one account ascribes to Christ at His appearance
are represented in the other as spoken by Ananias
at Damascus ; in one the companions of Paul fall to
the ground along with him, in the other they remain
standing ; according to one they hear, indeed, a voice,
but see nothing ; according to another, they see,
indeed, a light, but hear nothing.   If we deduct these
subordinate features, which are to be credited to the
narrator, there remains as the essential kernel of the
story only this—that Paul on the way to Damascus
suddenly saw an appearance of light that shone down
from heaven, and heard a voice in which he believed
he recognised a personal communication from Jesus.
With this, Paul's own utterances in his letters are in
essential harmony, since they agree in indicating that

the decisive experience by which he was called to be
not only a believing disciple, but also the Apostle of
Christ to the heathen, consisted in the manifestation
of the Lord Jesus exalted to heaven and glorified
with heavenly splendour (δόξα). When, for example,
he asks in 1 Cor. ix. 1, "Have I not seen the Lord
Jesus?" it is evident from the context that this
"seeing" can only refer to the experience on which
Paul based his claim to apostolic rank, therefore to
his call at his conversion. Again, when in 1 Cor.
xv. 9, after the enumeration of the earlier appearances
of Christ to the other disciples, he continues, "Last
of all he appeared unto me also, as to one born out of
due time, for I am the last of the apostles, and am
not worthy to be called an apostle because I persecuted the church, but through the grace of God I
am what I am," it is clear that here too he refers his
call to the apostleship to an appearance of Christ
which he places in line with the other appearances of
the risen Christ as of essentially the same character.
Now though this makes it certain that Paul was
convinced of the objective character of the appearance of Christ which he witnessed, yet other passages
show just as clearly that he did not regard this seeing
as the perception by the senses of an earthly, material
body, but as the vision of a supersensuous being by
the inner eye of the spirit. He says in Gal. i. 16,
"It pleased God to reveal his Son *in me*, that I might
preach him among the heathen"; and in 2 Cor. iv. 6,
"God .... hath shined in our hearts to give the light
of the knowledge of the glory of God in the face of
Jesus Christ." It is quite in accordance with this that
in 1 Cor. xv. 45 ff. he describes Christ as the Heavenly

Man, whose likeness we shall one day bear at the resurrection, and whose body has nothing to do with flesh and blood, but is a " spiritual " or " heavenly " body such as pertains to heavenly beings.[1] A spiritual or heavenly body of this kind cannot, however, be an immediate object of sense-perception to the bodily eyes; what is seen by these is only an appearance of light to which the inner sense or the consciousness of the percipient gives the definite significance of an appearance of Christ. But that is as much as to say that this appearance belongs to the category of inner or visionary perception, and stands therefore in the closest relationship with the visions and revelations which are frequently mentioned elsewhere in the apostle's life..

Specially significant in this connection is 2 Cor. xii. 1 ff., where his subjective ecstatic state of consciousness in visions of the objectivity of which, in other respects, Paul entertained no doubt, is made quite clear by his adding that he does not know whether, when he was caught up into the third heaven, he was "in the body or out of the body." When, further, he speaks in the same connection of peculiar bodily suffering and exhaustion which was connected with these high visions, that points unmistakably to such conditions of nervous excitation as are usually connected with ecstatic states of consciousness and form in a measure the physical basis for them. We may therefore confidently draw the conclusion that the bodily and mental organisation of Paul had a general predisposition to experiences

[1] $\sigma\hat{\omega}\mu\alpha$ $\tau\hat{\eta}s$ $\delta\acute{o}\xi\eta s$, Phil. iii. 21 ; $\sigma\hat{\omega}\mu\alpha$ $\dot{\epsilon}\pi o\upsilon\rho\acute{a}\nu\iota o\nu$, $\pi\nu\epsilon\upsilon\mu\alpha\tau\iota\kappa\acute{o}\nu$, 1 Cor. xv. 40, 44, 48.

of that kind. There are some other instances which give us a glimpse into the psychological pre-conditions for the occurrence of "revelations." When, according to Acts xvi. 9 f., his resolve to extend his missionary activity into Europe was caused by a vision in the night, or when, according to Gal. ii. 1, his eventful journey to the Apostolic Council at Jerusalem was the result of a revelation, it is clearly evident that in such cases the "vision" or "revelation" was the form of consciousness which a mental struggle, issuing from doubt to clearness, from indecision and un-certainty to a definite resolution, was wont to assume in the case of Paul. These visionary experiences, therefore, did not occur spontaneously; they had their immediate causes in pre-existing conditions of mind, from which they may therefore to a certain extent be psychologically explained. The same is the case with the visionary experiences which led to Paul's conversion : historical criticism claims the right and the duty of investigating its psychological pre-conditions and the motives which gave rise to it. Moreover, this question cannot be avoided even by those who believe themselves bound to maintain the strictly miraculous character of the occurrence, for were there no psychological preparation or motive for this "miracle," it would be a purely magical act, in which the soul of Paul was subjected to a force acting from without—a thoroughly unevangelical conception which would stand in complete contra-diction with the Pauline definition of faith as an act of personal obedience to the truth which has been inwardly experienced.

The Book of Acts gives us a hint which helps

us to understand the situation which we have to presuppose, by attributing to the Jesus of the vision the words, "Saul, Saul, why persecutest thou me? It is hard for thee to kick against the goad!" It seems therefore that the persecutor of the Christians had felt a goad in his soul against which he had striven in vain. In what else can this have consisted than in the painful doubt as to the righteousness of his persecution of the Christians, and that must mean the doubt whether the truth was really on his side, or whether it was not, after all, on the side of the persecuted disciples of Christ? But how could the fanatic Pharisee come to entertain such a doubt? The occasion for its arising came, we may suppose, from his coming in contact with the persecuted Christians and from the conversations which he must inevitably have held with them. The mere sight of the joyful courage with which they confessed must have made a deep impression on Paul's sensitive spirit, and have forced upon him the question whether a faith that led men to face martyrdom with such heroism could be based on mere delusion or impious deceit. Then, too, on such occasions Paul could not avoid hearing the defence which they offered for their Christian faith, and becoming acquainted with the proofs of its truth which they advanced. If in these controversies he urged against them that a criminal, rejected by the rulers of Israel, could not possibly be Israel's Messiah, they would reply with the Scriptural saying, "The stone which the builders rejected is become the head of the corner." If he maintained that one hanged on a tree was, according to the Law, accursed, they would point

to the passage in Isaiah in which it is said of the
Servant of God that it was our punishment which
was laid upon Him in order that we might have peace.
That this way of regarding the death of Jesus as a
vicarious expiation would make an impression on
Paul the Pharisee is the more probable because it
was quite in harmony with the view prevalent in the
Pharisaic theology, according to which the undeserved
sufferings of righteous men in general served as an
atonement and expiation for the sins of their nation.
It is true Pharisaism had not applied this theory to
the Messiah, since the rôle of a sufferer was of course
incompatible with the political Messiahship which
formed the ideal of the Pharisees. But when once
the Christians had given a Messianic interpretation
to the passage in Isaiah it was not possible, from the
standpoint of the Pharisaic atonement-theory, to raise
any valid objection against it. On the contrary, this
idea offered to the Pharisee the solution of a difficulty
by which his faith was seriously oppressed. For
while the Pharisees expected at that time a speedy
coming of the Messiah to deliver His downtrodden
People, it was, at the same time, one of their fixed
principles that only a righteous People should see
the day of the Messiah. But where was this
righteous people who completely answered to the
divine will and had shown themselves worthy of the
coming of the Messiah? Could it be said that the
convulsive effort of the Pharisees to bring the people
to righteousness had had any success worth speaking
of? Did not they themselves ban with the bitterest
contempt "the multitude which knows nothing of
the law"? And must not a conscientious Pharisee,

such as Paul was, confess even of himself that he was
ever unable to attain the ideal of righteousness which
hovered before him ?   Was he not conscious that all
his zeal for righteousness did not avail to break down
the resistance of the sinful tendencies, but rather
increased and intensified them ?   That Paul as a
Pharisee had actually had experiences of that kind
and had felt them bitterly, we may conclude with
confidence from the picture which he draws at a
later period of the inner conflict in the natural man
(Rom. vii. 7 ff.).   All the more easily, then, might
the question force itself upon him and lay hold upon
his mind : Could it be that the righteousness of the
Messianic kingdom, since it is unattainable by us,
shall be established by the Messiah Himself?   Might
it be, not so much the condition of His coming, as
its purpose and result ?   Might it not be possible
that the innocent sufferings of so righteous a servant
of God as Jesus, according to the representations of
His followers, must have been, might be the means
ordained by God to supply the lacking righteousness
as a gift of God ?

The psychical conditions which rendered possible
the events which happened upon the Damascus road
can therefore be, so far, clearly recognised : a nervously
excitable organisation, predisposed from the first to
visionary conditions, a mind fearfully agitated and
torn by painful doubts since it had become uncertain
as to the righteousness of his fanatical activity, seeing
that the possibility of a Messiah who should suffer
vicariously and rise again from the dead could not
be denied.   If along with all this we remember the
necessity for a prompt decision entailed by his near-

ness to Damascus, the lonely stillness and the burning glow of the desert, we shall be justified in coming
to the conclusion that the occurrence of visionary
experiences under such conditions lies well within
the range of the analogy of other similar occurrences.
But as to what was the exact character of the perception which filled the consciousness of Paul in that
moment, in regard to the complex of sense-impres-
sions and conceptual images, we can have no certain
knowledge, since the report of Acts is secondary and
Paul himself nowhere gives a detailed account of it.
We can, however, form conjectures which have some
degree of probability. It is at any rate certain, to
begin with, that it was not a man of flesh and
blood that Paul saw; that is, in view of what has
been said above about Paul's conception of Christ's
spiritual, heavenly " body of glory," simply out of
the question. It would even be easier to suppose
that he saw a shining human form, in which his
conception of the risen Jesus was objectified, and
which by means of an inner stimulus acting on
the nerve of sight, had presented itself as the
perceptual image of something external. Such
seeing of inner conceptual images as external appearances not infrequently occurs in the conditions of
vision which are associated with ecstasy and halluci-
nation. But it is quite possible, and, indeed, more
probable, that what he saw was only an undefined
splendour which he took to be the appearance of
Christ's " body of glory " or of the glory of God in
the face of Christ (2 Cor. iv. 6). And, as it often
happens in psychical conditions of this kind that an
impression upon the auditory nerves is combined with

that upon the visual, Paul may well have heard at the same moment in which he saw the appearance of light, a voice which was in essence nothing else than the accusing voice of his own conscience, but which he involuntarily objectified as the voice of Christ calling to him from without and from above, " Saul, Saul, why persecutest thou me ?" Acts may therefore have described what happened at Paul's conversion quite correctly in representing him as seeing, not Jesus Himself but only a light, and hearing a voice in which he believed he recognised the voice of Jesus calling him. Here, too, we may recall again the events of Pentecost, when many at one time experienced something essentially similar : an appearance of light and a mighty noise from heaven in which they believed they recognised the presence of Christ. Finally, a further confirmation of the explanation here given is to be found in the many analogous cases which history—especially Oriental history—records. Wonderful appearances of light were often seen by the Rabbis when in a state of rapt devotion. In the life of Mahomet, too, visions and voices of heavenly beings played an important part. The desert is a specially favourable region for such things. " In Arabia it happens so often that men who have lost their way hear a voice answering when they call, that there is a special word for a voice of this kind, namely, ' Hatif,' while in Africa they call the phantom who appears to the rider the ' Ragol' or Companion.[1] If in the case of appearances of this kind there no one doubts the trustworthiness and accuracy of the

[1] Sprenger, *Mohammed*, i. 216 (cit. Hausrath, *Neutestamentliche Zeitgesch.*, ii. 451).

psychological explanation, historical criticism is justified in explaining in a similar way the similar appearances of the Biblical history. At the same time, Paul's experience, just like the similar experience of the first apostles, remains none the less a true revelation, in which their minds became possessed with the conviction of the truth of the Gospel, but here, as always, the truth presents itself to consciousness in forms determined by psychological conditions. Even in this explanation, therefore, Paul's saying retains its full significance, " God hath shined in our hearts to give the light of the knowledge of the glory of God in the face of Christ " (2 Cor. iv. 6).

On this ecstatic visionary or " enthusiastic " experience there ensued a complete revolution in the mind of the former Pharisee and legal zealot. It was to him as though he were a new creation ; crucified with Christ to the world and the world to him ; as though there lived no longer his Ego as it was before, but now only Christ in him (Gal. ii. 19 f., vi. 14 f. ; 2 Cor. v. 14 ff.). He had now, through an experience similar to that of the first disciples, acquired the conviction that the crucified Jesus had not remained under the power of death but had been raised again by God, exalted to heaven, and made Lord and Christ. But for Paul this experience was of much deeper significance than for the first disciples. For them the effect of the Easter vision was to restore and strengthen the faith in the Messiahship of Jesus which had been shaken by the Crucifixion, and to enable them to rise superior to the offence of the cross, but, as regards its content, their belief was not essentially altered—it did not prevent them after, any

more than before, from remaining good Jews, loyal to
the Mosaic law as the basis of the national Messianic
hope.   Paul, on the other hand, had persecuted the
disciples so fanatically for the very reason that he
saw with the utmost clearness the irreconcilable
opposition between the belief in a crucified Messiah
and the Jewish way of thought.   " Cursed is every
one that hangeth on a tree ! "—by this word of the
Law the belief in the crucified Jesus had seemed to
him inexorably condemned (Gal. iii. 13).   Now,
however, he had become convinced that this belief
was justified, since the Crucified had been shown by
the resurrection to be the Messiah and Son of God.
But if so, then the Law could no longer be in the
right in pronouncing a curse upon the Crucified.
Condemnation of the Crucified because of the Law,
was now reversed in the mind of Paul into condemnation of the Law because of the crucifixion of
the Messiah Jesus.   Thus the crucifixion of Jesus,
combined with His vindication by God in the
resurrection, became for Paul the basis of a new
religious system in which the Mosaic law was set
aside in virtue of a new and higher principle.   And
what was this new principle ?   What was, according
to the divine purpose, the object and significance of
the death and resurrection of Jesus the Messiah ?
How far had these events, set in motion by God,
disclosed a new way of salvation, independent of the
old way of the Law and accessible to all men without
distinction of race ?   These were the questions which
agitated the mind of Paul from the moment of his
conversion ; and out of his reflection upon them arose
what it is the custom to call the Pauline theology,

that is, the intellectual expression of his personal faith
in Christ; it can hardly be called a "doctrine," and
still less a dogmatic "system." It is a complex of
very various lines of thought, interconnected and
intersecting, complementary and contradictory. To
harmonise them into a systematic unity did not
enter into the mind of the apostle himself, who was
anything rather than a systematic thinker; therefore
we need not attempt to do so. Any attempt of the
kind can only have the effect of obliterating the
distinctive character of his thoughts and thereby
rendering unrecognisable their historical connection
and affinities; and to exhibit these is one of the first
duties of the religious historian. On the other hand,
we should never forget that the various trains of
thought of Paul the theologian, although it may not
be possible to combine them into a unity of system
and logic, had yet a unity of their own in the religious
personality of Paul the Christian and Apostle. It
was his own most intimate beliefs, based on experiences and feeling, that he moulded in various media
according to the needs and purposes of the moment
—now using the forensic categories of the Jewish
scholastic theology, now the poetic imagery of the
apocalyptic writings, now the animistic forms of
speech of universal popular metaphysics, now the
symbolism of the Mysteries, now the phrases of the
Hellenistic-Jewish religious philosophy, or of the
Stoic and Cynic popular philosophy. Paul was in
sympathy with all these elements in the culture of
his time, his way of conceiving and expressing
religious ideas was influenced by them all; yet with
all this, he remains the original Christian thinker

who with the freedom of true genius made use of all forms of presentation which the world and the time offered him as a vehicle—even so, inadequate—for the imperishable treasure of the truth of the Gospel as apprehended by faith (2 Cor. iv. 7). As a result, one who would describe the Pauline theology finds himself confronted with a twofold duty: on the one hand, he must neither overlook nor efface the variety of the trains of thought which are interwoven in it; on the other hand, he must not seek to isolate any one of them and to fix it down with logic-chopping exactitude, a method which results only in caricature, but must endeavour constantly to refer the diverse theories to their living unity, to the mighty spiritual personality of the apostle, to whose rich religious life and fine ethical sensibility they gave expression in so many diverse forms. As the Pauline theology will at a later point occupy us more in detail I will here merely cast forward a rapid glance over its principal thoughts, so far as seems necessary for the explanation of Paul's position as Apostle of the Gentiles, without attempting to follow out historically the way in which this theology arose in the mind of the apostle. That is, indeed, not possible, since we know only the finished product and not the steps by which it came into being.

To the question regarding the purpose of the crucifixion of Jesus the Messiah, the Pharisaic theory that the sufferings of the righteous served as a vicarious expiation for the sins of their fellows, offered a ready answer. Applying this theory to the special case of the crucifixion of Jesus, Paul saw in it the expiatory sacrifice prepared by God with a view to the

7

forgiveness or acquittal of those who believed in the Messiah. There had been somewhat similar teaching, no doubt, among the first believers, but they had understood the effect of the death of Christ in procuring the forgiveness of sin as consisting only in a supplementing of the inadequate attainments of the pious, without in any way calling in question the obligation to fulfilment of the whole Mosaic law. Paul, thinking back to the principle involved, drew inferences of much wider scope. According to his conviction the death of Christ Jesus signifies the reconciliation of the whole world, the abrogation of the law of Moses as a condition of salvation, and the opening up of a new way of salvation to all without distinction, Gentiles and Jews alike, through faith in Jesus as the mediator of salvation and Lord of the new People of God. This conviction of the central significance of the death of Christ as the means of a salvation destined for all, was closely connected, however, with Paul's higher view of the person of Christ Jesus. He was no doubt at one with the first disciples in holding Him to be a man naturally born and a Jew "made under the law"; but that, he held, had reference only to the outward, earthly manifestation, which formed only a short episode in the heavenly existence, before and after, of the Son of God. Identifying, as he did, the exalted and glorified Lord Christ who had appeared to him on the way to Damascus with the Son of Man of the Jewish apocalypses who should manifest Himself from heaven, having been hidden there by God since the foundation of the world—identifying Him perhaps also with the Ideal Man of Platonic-Alexandrian specu-

lation—Christ became to him a super-earthly being,
heavenly man, son and image of God, prototype,
final cause, and head, of mankind, mediator of
the creation of the world and of the ruling of Israel,
who finally in the fulness of time had been sent
to Earth by the Father to become the mediator
of salvation and the founder of a new humanity,
the Second Adam. This purpose of His divine mission
was fulfilled not only by His life and teaching, but
in still greater measure by His death. When the
sinless Head of Mankind as the representative of
sinners suffered in His flesh the death sentence which
had been passed upon sin, the curse of sin and of
death, which since Adam's Fall rested on the whole
race, was broken, and a new era for mankind was
inaugurated under the emblem of " Life and Righteousness." This effect of the sacrificial death of
Jesus is available for every one who believes on Him
as his Lord and Saviour: the believer is declared
righteous by God and adopted to sonship, he enters
into the relationship to God of a son to a father,
knows himself the object of the divine love, and as
the free son and heir who is no longer under the
chastening rod of the Law. But how can that be?
asked the adherents of the Law—will not all morality
and discipline be destroyed by such teaching, will not
sinful lust receive a charter of indemnity, and Christ
be in the end degraded into a minister of sin? By
no means, answered Paul; for the same faith in
Christ which frees us from the tyranny of the letter,
binds us by a new law which has the advantage
that it gives life, that is, that it gives power to will
and to perform—this is the " law of the spirit of

Christ." And here commences a new line of thought
which we may call the "pneumatic" or enthusiastic.
That the believers in the Messiah received the Spirit
was known before Paul; proof of it was seen in the
wonderful phenomena of enthusiasm which were
continually repeated in their assemblies, ecstasies,
speaking with tongues, prophesyings, thought-
reading, healings and other miracles; phenomena
which, in conformity with the "animism" of popular
metaphysics in all peoples and periods, were attributed to the influence and momentary indwelling
of a higher, supernatural spiritual being. Paul himself set out from these enthusiastic phenomena and
assumed the popular interpretation of them, but, on
the ground of his personal religious and ethical
experience, gave it a profound and peculiarly fruitful
modification. The "Pneuma" of the Christians is
not merely the cause of those wonderful momentary
phenomena, but is also, and primarily, the Divine
power which dwells in them continually, and trans-
forms their whole life into the likeness of Christ;
and causes, more especially, the recognition of divine
truth and the willing and doing of the good.
What led him to this conviction may be con-
jectured from passages like Gal. ii. 20, 2 Cor.
v. 14, etc.: it was the inspiring enthusiasm of
his faith in Christ, and his grateful love to Christ,
which swayed him so completely, raised him so far
above his former Ego, that he seemed to himself a
new creation, a continual miracle. Now, since this
miraculous transformation went back to the appearance of Christ at his conversion, he regarded this
transformation as the supernatural action of the

Spirit which then came forth from the heavenly Son of God, and entered into himself, and which, since it was identical with Christ's own being, established a mystical community of life between the believer and his heavenly Head. In this way he made the enthusiasm of the early Christians, which in its original form was closely related to the orgiasm of the Mysteries, into the principle of a religious ethic which brought the depth and strength of the enthusiasm into the service of the ethical ideal of a life realised in an ordered community. In this way, he solved most successfully a problem which haunted other religious thinkers of his time. Seneca, as we saw, made use of the mystical conception of an indwelling of God in man, in the interest of his ethical idealism, speaking of a holy spirit (*sacer spiritus*) who dwells in us to mark and watch over our evil and our good, and of a divine strength and heavenly power, by which the soul of the good man is moved, and which is sent down to us in order that we may learn to know the Divine more fully, but has its home in the heavenly world (Ep. xli. *sup.*, p. 53 ff.). So, too, in the Book of Wisdom it is the Divine Wisdom, passing from one generation to another in the souls of holy men, which makes them prophets and friends of God; while without the holy spirit sent down from on high, none can understand the counsel of God (Wisd. vii. 27 ; ix. 10, 17). Impossible as it may be to suppose any direct borrowing of the Pauline doctrine of the Pneuma from these analogous theories of his contemporaries, yet it is certainly worthy of notice that, even before Paul, similar thoughts and phrases are met with both in Gentile and Jewish circles, for this betrays the need common to the age, the need of giving to religious mysticism an ethical content, and of inspiring ethics with religious enthusiasm. This need found its deepest satisfaction, as the problem of the time found its solution, in that classical saying of Paul, in which he combines his doctrine of the Spirit with his doctrine of Christ, and both with his ethic : " The Lord is the Spirit, but where the Spirit of the Lord is, there is liberty." From this central point in his theology two ways diverge : one in the direction of his ethics, the other in that of his ecclesiastical and mystical teaching. Paul's ethic is an autonomous Idealism nearly related to that of the Stoics,[1] but on a more religious foundation. Its three main points are : freedom from the world, the overcoming of sensuousness, and universal brotherly love. The parallels in particulars are often very striking, especially in sayings referring to the conflict between the flesh and the spirit, and to the vanity of the earthly life in comparison with that which is to come, and to the weakness and sinfulness of men, against which, as against a foil, the ideal of the Christian (Stoic : wise man) shines out in the brighter relief, but whereas, on that presupposition of human weakness, the realisation of the ideal remained for the Stoic always problematical—whereby his motive power was enfeebled— Paul, on the other hand, looked upon the ideal of

---

[1] *Cf.* Zeller, *Stoics, Epicureans and Sceptics* (Eng. trans. by Reichel, 1870), p. 126. " Moral philosophers were already familiar with the notion that the Good and Law are identical ; it was reserved for the Stoics to insist on this point with peculiar zeal ; and it was on this point that Stoicism subsequently came in contact, partly with Roman jurisprudence, partly with the ethics of Jews and Christians."

the good as perfectly realised in Christ Jesus, and as progressively realised in the believing community, whose task is simply that of becoming in actual moral life and conduct what they already are in their religious consciousness—spiritual men, children of God, saints.   The community of believers is the body of Christ, the social organism, in which the spirit of Christ, the Heavenly Ideal Man, finds its universal (macrocosmical) manifestation, just as in Jesus it receives its individual (microcosmical) manifestation.   As the community is thus a mystic whole, membership in it can only be established and maintained by mystic actions: in Baptism the " old man " is put away and Christ is " put on," the Lord's Supper is a " communion of the body and blood of Christ," whereby the partakers entered into a mystical union with their Head, as the heathen did with their divinities at their sacrificial meals.   The affinity of these conceptions with those of the heathen Mystery-cults is obvious.   The association of heterogeneous trains of thought which is characteristic of this whole theology, shows itself with especial clearness in Paul's view of the history of religion and eschatological expectations.   Heathenism is for him sometimes the period allotted in the divine education of mankind to nonage and ignorance, sometimes an impious apostasy from the knowledge of God which merited the divine wrath.   The Jews are the people of the covenant, the object of the divine love for the fathers' sake, yet now rejected, hardened in disobedience, put in a lower position than the heathen, but nevertheless with the hope of being finally restored to .favour.   The Mosaic law is, on the one hand, holy

and spiritual, just and good; on the other, it is the
letter which "killeth," it produces only wrath, makes
transgression to abound, is only a tutor and guardian
appointed for a limited time, standing on the same
footing with the nature-divinities of the heathen.
[The reference is to such passages as Gal. iv. 3, where
some exegetes interpret στοιχεῖα τοῦ κόσμου in this
sense.] In the heathen world, too, there is a natural
moral law written in the heart, and a social order
which tends to good, and praiseworthy efforts directed
to high ends; nevertheless all men have sinned and
come short of the praise of God, and are justified
only by grace for Christ's sake. Believers in Christ,
as being justified and chosen, are assured of the
salvation foreordained for them by His gracious
counsel, have no accusers, no condemnation, to fear,
cannot be separated by any hostile power from the
love of God which is assured to them in Christ; yet
they, too, must appear before the judgment-seat of
God, or of Christ, to receive the reward of their deeds,
and the possibility of their rejection is not excluded.
Christians who have died remain asleep until the
second coming of Christ, when, awakened by the
last trump, they shall arise and meet Him in the air,
and thenceforward continue in His presence; on the
other hand, the apostle looks forward joyfully to his
"departure" in the conviction that he will immediately be at home with the Lord, will receive the
habitation prepared for him in heaven, and will never
be found naked (disembodied). At the final End,
when all enemies have been overcome, even Christ
will submit Himself to the Father in order that God
(alone) may be all in all; and yet Christ is made

Lord over living and dead, that all in heaven and in earth and below the earth may acknowledge Him as Lord.

Here is a rich field of activity for the systematic and harmonising framer of dogma ; the historian, however, lets these disparate assertions stand as they are, and explains them by the inter-play of various motives; now the religious interest preponderates, and now the ethical. Sometimes the continued influence of the Jewish groundwork of his beliefs is traceable, at others the distinctive note of Christian piety is emphatically sounded. That Paul himself felt no need, and made no attempt, to smooth down these unevennesses and harmonise these dissonances, need not surprise us in an apostle who expressly testifies of himself that his speech was not with persuasive words of (scholastic) wisdom but in the demonstration of the Spirit and of power, that his word was not of man, but of God, not learnt from human wisdom but from the Spirit which we have received from God (1 Cor. ii. 4, 12 f. ; 1 Thess. i. 5, 13). And, as a fact, his theology is not artistically composed but " inspired," not a result of cool re-flection, of scholastic dialectic and argumentation, but of that enthusiastic intuition which is less akin to scientific thinking than to the method of conceiving and producing which is proper to the artist. In religious, as in artistic, intuition, what has long moved and stirred the soul in its very depths, comes to immediate, unsought, involuntary expression, and for that very reason makes the impression of being a truth of experience, laying hold with irresistible power of the souls of the hearers : it was the intuitive character of Paul's doctrine that made his missionary preaching so marvellously successful. But the reverse of this practical strength is theoretic weakness. Intuition gives, so to speak, an instantaneous photograph of the soul-life, it brings out the state of consciousness and mood of mind at the moment with wonderful vividness and freshness, but it is for that very reason wholly subjective, one-sided, aphoristic, inconsistent; for the different elements of objective truth are photographed by intuition, not in their mutual relations, but each as at a given point of time it fills and dominates the soul to the exclusion of all else. The different sides of Christian truth, which in the living personality are bound together by the unity of the character in such a way that now one and now another comes into the foreground of consciousness, can only be presented in the utterances of the inspired prophet and apostle in a fragmentary form, and subject to many inconsistencies and obscurities.

CHAPTER VI

Paul and the first Apostles

Moreover, Paul contrasted the "spiritual" ("pneumatic") origin of his gospel not only with human wisdom, with his own thought and with the teaching of the Schools, but also with communication by tradition through the intermediary of an earthly teacher. Conscious of having been called to be an apostle directly by the will of God, or by God and Jesus Christ (1 Cor. i. 1; Gal. i. 1), he declares solemnly that he did not receive or learn the Gospel which he preached from any man, but by the revelation of Jesus Christ (Gal. i. 12). With the special purpose of demonstrating his independence of the original apostles he writes (*ibid.*, 15 ff.): "When it pleased God to reveal his Son in me, that I might preach him among the heathen, I conferred not with flesh and blood, neither went I up to Jerusalem to those who were apostles before me; but went away into Arabia, and returned again to Damascus. Then after three years I went up to Jerusalem to talk with Peter, and remained with him fourteen days, but of the other apostles saw I none, save James the Lord's brother." Strange as it may appear to us that the

newly-converted apostle of Christ had no desire to
obtain more detailed information regarding the life
and teaching of the Lord whom he was to preach from
the older apostles, the immediate pupils of Jesus, yet
the correctness of this self-witness cannot be doubted,
for it is confirmed by the content of his own preaching
as we ·know it from his letters. The sole historical
material upon which Paul built up his theology
consisted of the crucifixion of Jesus and the appearances of the risen Lord.   He himself spoke of his
teaching as the "word of the cross" (ὁ λόγος τοῦ
σταυροῦ) and desired to know nothing else than Jesus
Christ and Him crucified (1 Cor. i. 18, 22 ; ii. 2) ; on
the other hand, the earthly life of Christ remains
quite out of view, and sayings of Christ are only
four times referred to : 1 Cor. vii. 10, ix. 14, xi. 24 f. ;
1 Thess. iv. 15.   The saying of eschatological import
mentioned in the last passage is nowhere found in
the Gospels, and so far as concerns the words of the
institution of the Supper in 1 Cor. xi. 24 f. we have,
as will be shown later, very strong grounds for the
conjecture that Paul did not receive them by
historical tradition, because they contain a theory
of the Supper which was unknown to the primitive
community, and which must have been originated by
Paul himself.   Perhaps the apostle himself wished to
suggest that this was the case by the peculiar turn
of expression which he uses : " I have received from
the Lord " (ἀπὸ τοῦ κ. ver. 23) which seems to point to
a revelation or inspiration coming direct from Christ.
Strange as it may appear to us, it is certainly
characteristic of Paul to derive even representations
of historical matters such as the words of institution

reported in 1 Cor. xi. 23 ff., from a spiritual communication which for him was more authoritative
than any human tradition.   The weakness of his
sense of historical reality was proportionate to the
strength of his religious faith in the truth of the
intuitions which were given to him by the Spirit,
or (as we might say) which sprang from the
creative power of his religious genius.   In view
of this habit of thought, it becomes quite intelligible
that he should hold the immediate revelation of
Christ which he had received inwardly (Gal. i. 12) as
a completely sufficient source for his knowledge of
the Gospel—as a so absolutely divine authority, far
superior to that of men, that any teaching from the
older apostles might well seem to him superfluous,
and indeed rather disturbing than desirable.   At the
present day no doubt many will be inclined to ask
whether it would not have been better if Paul after
his conversion had conferred with flesh and blood, and
had got the older apostles to give him exact information concerning the life and teaching of Jesus when
on earth, and had made abundant use of it in his
apostolic teaching and frequently referred to it in his
letters.   We may share the last-named wish, and yet
may fairly confront such critics with the question :
Is it probable that Paul if he had formed his faith in
Christ in strict dependence on the historical tradition
of the original apostles, would have been so successful
in proclaiming that Lord who is the Spirit and whose
spirit signifies freedom from the whole system of
Jewish law ?   But how, without this " Christ after
the Spirit," could the Gospel of Jesus have freed
itself from Judaism and become a world-religion ?

Accordingly, the apostle Paul retains his epoch-making importance in the history of Christianity, not in spite of, but because of, the spiritual character and orgin of his gospel.

That this independence of Paul in regard to the original apostles was considered even in the early Church unaccountable or even incredible, may be concluded even from the fact that the writer of Acts represents him as being introduced at the very beginning through the agency of Bárnabas to the original apostles, and as having, to a certain extent under their oversight and sanction, come forward publicly in Jerusalem and disputed with the Hellenists (Acts ix. 26 ff.).   That obviously contradicts Paul's own statement that he did not immediately after his conversion go to Jerusalem, but into Arabia, and thence returned to Damascus, and that it was three years afterwards that he made his fourteen days' visit to Jerusalem and became acquainted with Peter and James — without as it appears being officially introduced to the apostles and without making a public appearance in Jerusalem (Gal. i. 16–20).   It must, of course, be admitted that this short notice of Paul's own itself leaves much in the dark.   What was his object in going to Arabia?[1] Where did he sojourn while there and how long did he remain?   Why did he go back again to Damascus?

[1] Did Paul perhaps write not Ἀραβία but Ἄραβα and mean thereby a town of Galilee which Josephus mentions (*Vita*, li.)? (So Fries in *Zeitschr. für N.-T. Wiss.*, 1901, Heft 2.)   There was also a place named Ἄραβα in Samaria according to Hieron., lxxxviii. 29.   A retirement of Paul to a Galilæan or Samaritan town would no doubt be less surprising than to Arabia, but in any case the matter remains obscure.

Did he begin even there his missionary preaching? Was it at the end of his first, or of his second, visit that the dangerous persecution took place, from which he was only able to make his escape by being lowered from the town-wall in a basket? What moved him after he had stayed away for three years to make his short visit to Jerusalem? Was it intentionally or by chance that he there made the acquaintance only of Peter and James? What was their attitude towards him? Was there even then a discussion of the two ways of regarding the Christian faith? How is it to be understood that during the next fourteen years the missionary activity of Paul in Syria and Cilicia aroused no misgivings among the churches of Judæa, but rather joy and thanksgiving? (Gal. i. 21 ff.) Had Paul perhaps not yet developed the implications of his gospel in regard to the freedom from the Law of the Gentile Christians? Are we to infer from Gal. v. 11 that there was a time when he still preached circumcision, *i.e.* a Judaising, legalistic Christianity? Or was he quite clear from the first as to his call to be the apostle of the Gentiles and as to the characteristic features of his non-legalistic gospel for Gentile Christians? To all these questions it is either difficult or impossible to give a certain answer. In regard to the last point, however, the preponderant probability is [1] that from the moment of his conversion Paul knew himself called to be the Apostle of the Gentiles (Gal. i. 16), and therefore was convinced from the very beginning that the Law was not binding upon Gentile Christians—for that was the necessary condition of any successful mission

[1] Cp. O. Cone, *Paul*, p. 78 ff.

among the Gentiles—and that he never concealed this conviction in his missionary activity in Syria and Cilicia. That is evident from Gal. ii. 2, where Paul mentions that at his second visit to Jerusalem he laid before the apostles his gospel which he preached among the heathen, that they might judge whether he was running, or had run, in vain; the question at issue therefore was the legitimacy of his distinctive way of preaching the Gospel to the Gentiles as he had employed it up to that time—therefore, certainly, in Syria and Cilicia—which he desired to make good as against the recent attacks of the legalist "false brethren." Why these attacks had only lately begun to be made, while for fourteen years previously Paul's mission to the Gentiles in Syria and Cilicia had been viewed by the churches in Judæa not only without misgiving but as a subject for thankfulness to God (Gal. i. 24), is a question which can only be answered conjecturally. The most probable explanation is that the churches of Judæa had only a vague knowledge of the state of things in the mixed congregations of the Pauline mission, and that they attributed no special import-ance to the Gentile Christian element in them so long as it was in a weak minority. This is the more comprehensible if, as was generally the case, these Gentile Christians had already been proselytes to Judaism : in that case they could be regarded even after their conversion to faith in Christ as guests and dependents [Ger. Beisassen, = "metics "] of the Jewish-Christian congregation, and not as in any way endangering the position of the latter.

It may be remarked in this connection that while

the native population of Syria and Cilicia was of
course Gentile, yet everywhere in the towns there
were Jewish colonies and that many " God-fearing "
Gentiles used to attend the synagogue-services as
guests, so to speak.   Now, that Paul in his missionary
journeys made a practice of turning first to these
synagogues of the Jewish Diaspora, where he would
also find a gathering of Gentile proselytes, and that
it was precisely among the latter that he had his
chief success, is not only repeatedly evidenced by
Acts (and, it is to be noted, in the " We-Sections,"
which are founded on the report of a travelling-
companion of Paul), but even without this evidence
it must have been held to be extremely probable
on general grounds, since it was, in the given circumstances, the only procedure calculated to effect his
purpose.   The most favourable soil for the missionary
preaching of Paul was neither pure Judaism, to
which a crucified Messiah was an offence, nor pure
heathenism, to which it was a folly — something
quite impossible to grasp, because all the presuppositions necessary to a comprehension of it were wanting
—the most favourable soil was found among the
Gentile associates or proselytes of the Jews, who by
taking part in the synagogue-services had acquired a
certain acquaintance with the Old Testament and
the Messianic hopes of Israel without becoming
biassed by the national and legalistic prejudices of
the Jews.   With these circles Paul was familiar from
his Tarsus days; he knew their earnest religious
temper, their longing for a morally pure religion,
their profound sympathy with the faith in God and
providence set forth in the Psalms and Prophets,

8

and also their antipathy against Jewish pride of race
and against the meticulous formalism of the Rabbinic
law-worship. How could these barriers be over-
thrown, how could the multitude of heathen who
longed for salvation be won over and saved for the
true God ? This question must often have occupied
the mind of the Jew of Tarsus ; now it was solved
for the apostle of Christ, in whom there is neither
Jew nor Greek, but a new creature. Therefore he
felt, immediately upon his conversion, an irresistible
impulse to bring the knowledge of the grace of God
in Christ, which was destined for all, to the heathen
as being the most needy and also the most receptive.
And now he must become to the Greeks a Greek,
not suffering Jewish legal scruples to fetter him ; and
he, moreover, better than another, could become a
Greek to the Greeks, since as a Hellenist he knew
their ways of thought and spoke their language.
Hence his inner certainty that he had been destined
and called by God Himself to be the apostle of the
Gentiles—a certainty that received practical confirmation from the notable success of his preaching
among the heathen.

But with the growth of his success, with the
increase in the number and importance of the Gentile
converts in the mixed churches, there arose among
the Christians of Judæa serious misgivings as to
the soundness of the principle which directed his
missionary efforts, against his preaching a Christianity
without the Jewish law, against the recognition of non-
Jews who believed in Christ as full members of the
community and Christian brethren. Some brethren
from Judæa, who had formerly been Pharisees and

were therefore especially zealous for the Law (Acts xv.
1, acc. Western Text[1]) thought they ought no longer
to concur in looking with complacency upon the pro-
ceedings of the apostle of the Gentiles, and came
themselves to Antioch in order to observe on the
spot the freer customs which were there coming into
vogue, and to put a stop to them.   The agitation set
on foot by these " false brethren who insinuated themselves surreptitiously," as Paul describes them in Gal.
ii. 4, caused no small stir in the mixed church at
Antioch, especially as these agitators appealed to the
authority of the mother-church.   If the legalist
party succeeded in enforcing their demand that the
believing Gentiles must submit, by circumcision, to
the Jewish law, and if it was confirmed that the
mother-church, with the apostles, really sided with
them in this demand, then any large measure of
success among the heathen was no longer to be
thought of, and the life-work of the apostle of the
heathen was brought to nought.   For if he had
submitted to the exactions of the legalists, the Jewish
law would have become an insuperable obstacle to
the conversion of the heathen to Christianity.   On
the other hand, if Paul had simply ignored the
demands of the Judaisers, without coming to an
understanding with the original apostles, and without
obtaining their sanction for a mission to the heathen
independent of the Law, he would have severed the
connecting links between the Gentile churches and
the mother-church ; and Gentile Christianity, thus

[1 The reference is to the reading of 8, 137 and the Later Syriac
marg. which, after ἀπὸ τῆς Ἰουδαίας, insert τῶν πεπιστευκότων ἀπὸ τῆς
αἱρέσεως τῶν Φαρισαίων.—TRANSLATOR.]

from the beginning isolated and reduced to a mere
sect, would hardly have been able to maintain its
existence permanently. The preservation or destruction of his life-work depended therefore on whether
he could succeed in winning from the original
Church and its leaders a recognition of the claim
of the Gentile Christians, as such, to a place in the
Christian brotherhood.

When matters were in this difficult position, it was,
as Paul himself narrates in Gal. ii. 1, an inner voice
or "revelation" which crystallised in his mind the
resolution to bring the crisis to an issue in the most
direct and, certainly, also in the boldest possible
fashion—by a personal discussion of the matter with
the mother-church and its leaders. Whether Paul
suggested this plan to the church at Antioch and
the latter thereupon dispatched him and Barnabas as
official deputies to Jerusalem, as is recounted in
Acts (xv.), must remain undecided. It is not
inherently impossible, but, on the other hand, it is in
accordance with the purpose of Acts to make Paul
appear as the instrument of the official authorities and
not as acting independently. When Paul had given
an account before the assembled church at Jerusalem
of his missionary activity and its success among the
Gentiles, the party of the zealous legalists, to which
the "false brethren" and agitators who had crept in
at Antioch, belonged, formulated the demand that
the converted Gentiles should be made Jews by
circumcision; and, moreover, that a beginning should
be made by circumcising Titus, the Gentile travelling-
companion of Paul. Paul does not directly tell us
what attitude the assembled church took up towards

this demand, but he gives us grounds for forming a conjecture. In the first place we have to note that he indicates as the immediate cause of the sharp contention over the circumcising of Titus the false brethren who had crept in at Antioch, and therefore obviously distinguishes these, as the extreme zealots, from the remainder of the community. This distinction must certainly not be overlooked, but on the other hand its significance must not be exaggerated. There is nothing to justify us in assuming that the Church as a whole was from the first completely on the side of Paul, and that the zealots formed merely an insignificant fraction. On the contrary, we cannot conceal from ourselves that on this traditional assumption it would be hard to understand how such sharp contentions as both accounts undeniably report could come to be at all. The most probable view of the case is therefore, certainly, that the Jerusalem church, when for the first time the definite question was put before it whether there should exist in the future a Christianity without the Mosaic law, at first took up no decided attitude towards it, but wavered irresolutely between opposite views and considerations. To their strict Jewish conservatism it was without doubt a very surprising idea that in the future they were to recognise as brethren in the Christian faith uncircumcised heathen, on whom they had hitherto looked down as sinners and unclean. It was also to be feared that if they thus fraternised with Gentiles, the good repute of the young Christian community would be seriously compromised in the eyes of their own countrymen, and that its character for righteousness might be damaged, a result which would naturally not be favourable to the success of the mission-work among Israel. Further, the question might well be raised whether Jesus the Messiah, who had certainly all His life long submitted to the Jewish law, would, when He returned in the near future to establish His kingdom, recognise as citizens of that kingdom Gentile believers who were unwilling to accept the law? Under the influence of considerations of this kind the sympathies of the community doubtless at first inclined towards the demands of the legal zealots. Nevertheless it was, on the other hand, difficult to escape from the powerful impression which the reports of Paul and Barnabas of the success hitherto of their mission to the Gentiles produced even upon their opponents. Even though the zealots were uncompromising and the multitude remained doubtful, the three leaders of the Church who were accounted " pillars "—James, Peter, and John—were sufficiently free from prejudice to recognise in the successes of the Pauline mission a pronouncement of God in its favour; they were therefore ready to grasp " the right hand of fellowship " which Paul and Barnabas held out to them, and made an agreement with them that thenceforward Paul should go to the Gentiles, Peter and the other original apostles, to the Jews. For the rest, "nothing was added " to Paul, *i.e.* no limiting conditions were laid upon him (such as are mentioned in Acts xv. 20, 28 f.), the single condition being that he should remember the poor (of Judæa), namely, by making a collection for them among the Gentile churches (Gal. ii. 6–10).

Thus Paul had attained his immediate object—the

recognition of the freedom of his Gentile converts from the Jewish law; to make demands of a more far-reaching kind, to contest the obligation of the law for Christians in general, including the Jewish Christians, would only have frustrated his immediate aim, and he had no reason for attempting it. The securing of an understanding on the question which was of the greatest practical importance, the authorisation of a Gentile Christianity which did not undertake to keep the law, was certainly an inestimable advantage to the progress of the Pauline mission-work; but it must be admitted that this understanding was only arrived at by evading the question of principle regarding the relation of the Christian Faith and the Christian Church to the Jewish law. The treaty of peace was only a compromise in which each retained his own opinion, the agreement being confined to the point that each party should leave the other unmolested in its own territory "in peace and quietness." Any solution dealing with the principle of the opposition between Gentile Christianity free from the law and Jewish Christianity zealous for the law was then, and for a long time to come, far to seek. For that reason the formal treaty of peace could not prevent the outbreak of ever-renewed contentions and dissensions, to which the Epistles of Paul, especially those to the Galatians and Corinthians, so clearly testify. But even Acts, which elsewhere deliberately passes over those matters which disturb its ideal picture of the Church of apostolic times, cannot avoid reporting (xxi. 21) that on Paul's last visit to Jerusalem the reproach was brought against him by the zealous legalists among the Jewish

Christians that he taught the Jews to repudiate the law of Moses. Even though it characterises this reproach through the mouth of James as a groundless calumny, it allows us to perceive clearly that the great majority of the members of the Jerusalem church were antagonistic to Paul, as appears from the fact that none of the Christians there seem to have come to the aid of the apostle when so sorely persecuted by Jewish fanaticism.

An earlier contest over the question of the law, which he had with Peter at Antioch, is described by Paul immediately after the negotiations at Jerusalem which have just been referred to (Gal. ii. 11 ff.). It must therefore, in any case, have happened after these, but whether soon after, or some time later, Paul gives no indication. The latter seems to me the more probable, and I conjecture that the course of events was somewhat as follows. While Paul and Barnabas were away in South Galatia on the so-called First Missionary Journey [1] Peter had come to Antioch to visit the church there; he wished to convince himself by first-hand observation of the success of the Pauline mission of which so much had been heard in the negotiations at Jerusalem. When he now saw in this mixed church in which, for the first time, the Gentile Christian element was strongly represented (Acts xi. 20 ff.), that under the liberating and elevating influence of prophetic enthusiasm—

[1] That this journey, described in Acts xiii. and xiv., happened, not before, but after, the Apostolic Council, follows neccessarily from the fact that Paul prior to Gal. ii. 1 speaks only of a mission in Syria and Cilicia, to which neither Cyprus nor South Galatia belonged. For the explanation of the anachronism in Acts, I refer the reader to the analysis in a later chapter.

which likewise seems there first to have acquired a
significant import[1]—the majority even of the Jewish
Christians had begun to cast off the narrow and
exclusive Jewish legality and to eat in company with
their Gentile fellow-members of the church at the
fraternal meals, he too in his impulsive fashion
allowed himself to be hurried into conforming to
these freer customs.

When, however, some who belonged to the party
of James, who was a strict observer of the law, came
from Jerusalem, he became so alarmed by the fear of
offending them that he withdrew himself again from
brotherly intercourse and fellowship at table with
the Gentile Christians.   His example and exhortation
so strongly impressed the other Jewish Christians
that they returned one after another to a strict
observance of the law; and in order not to make a
complete breach of intercourse with the Gentile
brethren they demanded of them that, in the interests
of the peace of the church, they should accommodate
themselves to the Jewish customs.   Thus the church
at Antioch was again thrown into dangerous confusion; under the pressure of Peter's authority the
retrograde movement towards Jewish illiberality was
attaining more and more threatening dimensions,
all that Paul had gained seemed to be once more
called in question.   This was the state of affairs
when Paul and Barnabas returned from their
missionary journey in South Galatia.   Confronted
unexpectedly by this new situation, they were obliged
to take sides at once; one party expected of them
that they would submit to the authority of Peter

[1] Acts xi. 27, 28, Cod. D., xiii. 1, xv. 32.

and follow the example of the other Jewish Christians ;
the other party, however, made " accusation " [1] against
Peter that he had been disloyal to himself since he
had at first himself eaten with the Gentile Christians
and thus sanctioned by his own conduct the freer
customs which he now wished to condemn as illegiti-
mate. How great was the danger at this critical
moment is shown most clearly by the fact that even
Barnabas, hitherto the friend and missionary companion of Paul, was so carried away by the general
pusillanimity and retrograde tendency that he
repudiated the opinions which he had hitherto held.
In such a case Paul could not keep silence; he had
a public encounter with Peter and rebuked him,
saying that his conduct was not in accordance with
the truth of the Gospel; how could he require the
(Christian) Gentiles to live as Jews after he himself
had formerly lived like a Gentile (associated himself
with the free, non-Jewish, manner of living) ?   Men
who, in the conviction that they were justified not by
the works of the law but by the faith of Christ,
regarded themselves as dead to the law, that is, as
once for all released from its compulsion, but only in
order to live in free obedience towards God, did not
thereby make themselves sinners. But men who,
after they had " destroyed " the law (viz. by their
partial emancipation from its ceremonies, or, it may
be, through their belief in a Messiah who had been
crucified and therefore lay under the curse of the law)

---

[1] Gal. ii. 11, ὅτι κατεγνωσμένος ἦν. This seems to imply that Paul
had heard from others the report of Peter's vacillating conduct;
therefore that he had not been an eyewitness from the beginning
of the progress of these events.

again establish the law, put themselves in the position of transgressors.   It was not therefore the Pauline Christian, who drew from his faith in Christ the logical inference that he was free from the law, but the illogical Jewish-Christian who alongside of his faith in Christ wished to hold fast to the law as a way of salvation, who " frustrated " the grace of God, as manifested in the death of Christ, " for if righteous- ness come by the law, then Christ is dead in vain " (Gal. ii. 21).

By thus rejecting in principle a Christianity of this kind, which desired to remain at the same time legal Judaism, Paul made a breach with Jewish-Christianity which was never healed, and which could not be healed, because the principles on either side were irreconcilable.   In comparison with this conflict of principle it is a question of quite subordinate im- portance how the personal relation between Paul, on the one hand, and the original apostles and the Jerusalem church upon the other, is to be conceived. That Paul worked hard and loyally at the gathering of a collection for the poor of the Judæan churches is well known ; and he never directly attacked the authority of the original apostles.   But the tone of asperity in which he speaks in Gal. ii. 6, 9 of those " who seemed to be somewhat," of the " pillars " of the Church whose past history " made no matter to him " since God accepteth no man's person, betrays certainly no very friendly feeling.   And in fact he had no grounds for feeling very friendly.   For at every step of his further missionary travels the Judaising agitators who crept into his churches and stirred up disaffection against him, made his life bitter to him. And when we consider that these agitators gained admission to the Pauline churches by the use of Peter's name and by means of letters of recommendation which they had undoubtedly brought with them from Jerusalem, it is difficult to suppose that the original apostles were in no way concerned in their agitation. Of the ill reception which Paul met with when he brought up the collection to Jerusalem, and of the at least coldly reserved attitude of the whole church there, mention has already been made. Finally it is to be remembered that a hundred years later the uncompromising Judaic Christianity represented by the Clementine Homilies had not forgotten the controversy at Antioch, but directed the bitterest reproaches against Paul on account of his conduct towards Peter on that occasion—in fact, caricatured him, with the traits of Simon Magus, as Antichrist. But the very intensity of this fanatical hatred is a testimony to the unique greatness of the apostle of the Gentiles—who could say of himself with justice, "I have laboured more than they all."

CHAPTER VII

THE LETTERS TO THE THESSALONIANS

THE foundation of the church at Thessalonica is described in Acts xvii. 1–9. It consisted essentially of Greeks, especially of Greek women, who had probably been previously connected with the synagogue, and who had been converted by Paul's preaching to faith in Christ. In comparison with the "great multitude" of these the few converted Jews need hardly be considered. This success of Paul's preaching among the Greeks aroused the jealousy of the Jews of Thessalonica to such an extent that they incited the populace to mob the house where the missionaries were lodging, and the latter were in consequence turned out of the city. Anxious about the condition of the young converts from whom he had been obliged to separate himself so hastily, Paul had sent back Timothy from Athens to Thessalonica. Timothy brought to him at Corinth a report of the church at Thessalonica, which, indeed, reassured and rejoiced him so far as concerned their firmness in the faith and their loyalty to himself in spite of the suspicions cast upon him by his opponents, but from which also he judged it advisable to combat, in a

letter, the dangers that threatened them. It was
of the first importance to confirm his converts in
their loyalty by repelling the suspicions cast upon
his motives, and by reminding them of their first
enthusiasm of faith, and also by pointing out to them
the universality of this enmity against Christianity
among the Jews, who were thereby only filling up
the measure of their guilt. But it was also important
to warn the Church against moral aberrations, due
in part to the influence of their former heathen
habits, but in part also to their new faith, the product
of their enthusiastic hope of the Second Coming of
Christ. Then, too, the occurrence of some deaths
among the members of the church had given rise to
anxieties and doubts, which needed to be calmed by
teaching, as to the "last things." In general, the
life of the young community, still swaying between
excessive enthusiasm and timid depression in a very
unstable fashion, needed to be reined in and guided
by rebuke and regulation. These are the ends aimed
at in the First Epistle to the Thessalonians, which
first treats (chaps. i.–iii.) of the personal relations of
the apostle to the church both at and after its foundation, and then (chaps. iv. and v.) deals with the ethical
and dogmatical points suggested by the situation, in
both cases without fixed order, and quite in the
unconstrained fashion of a letter called forth by the
occasion. The apostle testifies in the first place that
his thoughts constantly dwell with thankfulness and
joy on the Christian standing of the Thessalonians,
on their faithful activity in serviceable love and patient
hope. Yea, he had from the beginning been assured
of their election to be beloved children of God from

the fact that at the very first preaching of the Gospel among them, teachers and hearers alike had felt themselves laid hold of by the power of the Holy Spirit and by joyful confidence. The success of his preaching among them had been so remarkable that it was reported throughout Macedonia and Achaia how the Thessalonians had "turned from idols to serve the living and true God, and to wait for his Son from heaven, whom he raised from the dead, even Jesus which delivered us from the wrath to come." (It should be noticed that the apostle here gives a summary of that which obviously formed the subject of his first preaching in the heathen city and of the faith of the newly converted: Belief in the one true God and in the Second Coming of the risen Jesus, who guarantees to His people deliverance from the imminent catastrophe of the judgment of the world. How this deliverance was effected, what significance the death of Christ had therein, in relation especially to the old legal covenant, are questions of a secondary order which do not appear from this summary to have belonged to the elementary doctrines of the faith which Paul was accustomed to make the first subject of his preaching on heathen soil.)

After recalling the lofty experiences of his readers in the glorious beginning of their faith, the apostle goes on to remind them of his own conduct as the ambassador of the Gospel which was committed to him by God, and which he therefore taught in such a way as to please, not man, but God who trieth the heart. He calls God to witness that his motives in preaching the Gospel were not, as his adversaries calumniously alleged, of an impure and treacherous character, not the desire to gain favour by flattery, not coveteousness, nor vain ambition, but the impulse of a love as tender as it was deep, which was ready to offer not only the Gospel but his own life for the salvation of his beloved converts. He had spared neither toil nor suffering, but laboured day and night in order that he might make his service in the Gospel a (pecuniary) burden to no one. While he had himself conscientiously practised an upright and blameless walk, he had with fatherly insistence charged each one "to walk worthy of God who had called them to his kingdom." And they, on their part, had received his words in the same spirit in which he spoke them, not as the word of man, but as from God, whose power showed itself effectually working in the believers, especially in enabling them to endure the persecutions which the Thessalonians now experienced at the hands of their fellow-countrymen; just as earlier, the churches of Judæa had been subjected to them by the Jews. These latter now evinced their hatred of Christ and their spirit of enmity against God and men, by endeavouring to hinder the preaching of salvation to the Gentiles, and were thereby filling up the measure of their sins and calling down upon themselves the final judgment of reprobation.

This charge against the Jews of being the instigators of all the persecutions of Christians—even those carried out by the heathen in heathen districts—certainly suits the situation of the church at Thessalonica according to Acts xvii. 5 ff., while it is no longer suitable to the circumstances of a later time. But the "final consummation of the wrath of

God upon the Jews" is suspicious, since the most obvious way of interpreting it is as a reference to the conclusive judgment on the Jewish people which took place at the destruction of Jerusalem. Even if understood in a more general sense with reference to the exclusion of the Jews from the Messianic Kingdom, it would be difficult to reconcile with the hope which the apostle expresses in Rom. xi., of the final conversion of Israel. On these grounds the conjecture of several critics[1] that it is an addition by a later hand seems to me well founded.

In the following chapters (ii. 17 – iii. 13) the apostle expresses his fervent desire to see his converts—with whom he was, indeed, constantly present in spirit—face to face, a desire which had been intensified since Timothy had been with them, and had reported what a "good remembrance" they had of him and how they longed for his presence. It was, therefore, his constant prayer that it might be granted to him to see them again and to fill up what was lacking in their faith (by further instruction). Meanwhile, he could only pray that "the Lord would establish their hearts" that they might be found blameless, in a state of holiness before God, at the solemn appearing of the Lord Jesus.

This introduces the transition to the exhortation with which the second part of the letter begins, to advance in the Christian walk, seeking to please God, as they had learned to do from him (iv. 1 ff.).

---

[1] Spitta, *Offenbarung Johannis,* p. 501 ; Schmiedel, *Comment.,* p. 21. The latter holds verse 15 also to be spurious, since, in view of the fact that the persecution originated with the heathen, the attack on the Jews is without motive.

As our sanctification is God's will for us and the goal
of our Christian calling, the Thessalonians must cast
off the heathen vices of unchastity, and dishonesty
in business relations, since all such deeds fall under
God's condemnation ; and Christians should endeavour to do God's will the more conscientiously
because they have received from Him the Holy
Spirit, and therewith both the impulse towards, and
the capacity for, sanctification. From the inward
teaching of the Spirit also came brotherly love, which
they had indeed already exercised in a way that
deserved recognition, but which they should learn ever
better. Especially should they make it a point of
honour to gain their own living through quiet fulfilment of the duties of their calling, and thus to make
the Christian name honoured by the world (instead
of causing offence by pietistic idleness and dependence
on alms, as had doubtless occurred in the case of
many in consequence of a misinterpretation of the
brotherhood of Christians in a communistic sense, and
of excited, enthusiastic expectations of the appearing
of Christ).

The expectation of a speedy " Parousia," which
formed one pole of the early Christian consciousness
in the Pauline churches as well as elsewhere, had
given occasion, not only to moral aberrations of an
enthusiastic nature, but also to religious scruples and
difficulties. As some members of the community
had died, their fellow-Christians were troubled as to
whether, and, if so, how, these could share in the
blessings of the coming Kingdom of Christ ; and the
doubt thus raised extended itself over the whole
domain of the Christian hope of the future, for,

since these had died without seeing the realisation of their hopes, the same might happen to others, and even to all. On this point Paul reassures his readers, in the first place by giving a firm basis to the certainty of the resurrection of Christians in general as a necessary consequence of the belief in Christ's resurrection (iv. 14), and then, further, showing by referring to a saying of the Lord [1] that the living will not at the Return of Christ be preferred before the dead ; nay, rather, the latter will first at the approach of Christ rise again, and then they and those who were alive will together be carried away upon the clouds, to meet the coming Lord in the air. (For this a previous transformation of their present earthly body into a heavenly body is a necessary presupposition, here implicit, but made explicit in 1 Cor. xv. 51 ff.). The essential point in these representations, in which Oriental imagination has lent wings to the faith of the early Christians, is, moreover, so far as Paul's conviction is concerned, nothing else than the simple certainty that we shall be constantly in the presence of the Lord. And this hope remained, even when the Church's expectation of the Parousia became less vivid, the standing consolation of the Christians in the face of death and the grave. The Thessalonians seem also to have been concerned about the time of the Second Coming of Christ, and to have asked for information about it. The apostle,

[1] As a saying of Christ of this import is not found in the Gospels, it must remain uncertain whether Paul has here preserved a saying of Jesus recorded by a tradition which is unknown to us, or whether we are intended to think of an inner revelation of Christ given in prophetic intuition. (Paul's phrase is τοῦτο λέγομεν ἐν λόγῳ κυρίου, 1 Thess. iv. 15.)

however, holds this to be unnecessary, and leads the
interest of his hearers away from the useless questions
of a subtle curiosity to the practical consideration :
since we know that the Lord will come suddenly and
unexpectedly like a thief in the night, the important
thing for the Christian is to be ever ready for His
coming. They must show themselves children of
the light and of the day by watchfulness and sobriety,
putting on the armour of faith and love and the
helmet of a hope which is confident that we are not
destined by God to condemnation, but to the
obtaining of salvation through Jesus Christ, who has
suffered death for us in order that we might live
together with Him, whether we wake (living in the
body) or sleep (having died).

In conclusion, the apostle proceeds to give a further
series of rules of life for the well-ordering of the
Christian Church (v. 12 ff.). He exhorts them to show
respect and love towards all who by their voluntary
labours (for there is no reference to definite office),
whether in serving, or in guiding, or in teaching, have
deserved well of the community ; to be at peace
among themselves, to warn those who are unruly, to
comfort the discouraged, to support the weak, to be
long-suffering towards all, to overcome evil with
good. The habitual mood of the Christian should
be one of joy and thankfulness, resting upon constant
intercourse with God by prayer. The fire of the
Spirit is not to be quenched, his utterances in prophesying are not to be lightly esteemed, yet all prophetic
utterances are not to be accepted without testing, but,
with sober judgment, only the good is to be retained.
From evil of every kind they must hold aloof. If

this self-discipline of the church is maintained, the faithfulness of God who has called them gives ground to hope that He will complete in them the work of sanctification which He has begun, so that throughout, in body, soul, and spirit, they may be kept blameless until the appearing of the Lord Jesus Christ. The conclusion is formed by the apostle's request to his readers for their intercession on his behalf, and the exhortation to greet one another with the kiss of brotherly love, and to communicate the epistle to all the members of the church.

The genuineness of this epistle has been called in question by critics, but on insufficient grounds. Language and thought are throughout thoroughly Pauline. To lay stress on the absence in the Epistle to the Thessalonians of the arguments which we find in the Epistles to the Galatians and Romans on faith-righteousness and work-righteousness, law and gospel, is to lose sight of the fact that there was no occasion for explanations of this kind in a letter to a young Gentile Christian community, in which there was no Judaistic error to oppose. His readers would neither have understood, nor been interested in, the elaborate dialectic by which he proves his dogmas from Scripture, since their theological purview was limited to the elementary truths of the Christian faith (i. 9 f. ; v. 9 f.) and their interest was concentrated upon the hopes of the future ; as, indeed, was entirely natural in their circumstances. Besides, the thoughts which formed the religious centre of the Pauline theology are not wholly wanting in this epistle. There is mention of the wrath of God, whose judgment is coming upon the godless heathen world, which is held in the grip of the passionate impulse towards sin, as well as upon the Jewish world, which has filled up the measure of its sins in its enmity towards Christ. There is mention also of the election and calling of Christians to salvation through Jesus Christ and to sanctification of life. Their salvation is mediated by Christ's death and resurrection (iv. 14, v. 10), and is to be perfected at His second coming (i. 10). That Christ died on our behalf in order that we might share His higher life (v. 10) is a thoroughly Pauline conception, even though the explanation of this in detail, by means of the theory of atonement, is lacking; it is, indeed, very probable that Paul only went into this at length when he was writing for Jews and consequently made use of theological categories, and that when he was dealing with Gentile Christians he confined himself to the thought of universal application which formed the religious kernel of the matter, namely, that Christ had died for us in order that we might live with Him, in Him, and for Him (cf. 2 Cor. v. 15; Phil. iii. 10 f.; Rom. xiv. 7–9). "Justification," too, belongs to the categories of Jewish theology, which were out of place in teaching a purely Gentile church, and therefore it falls quite into the background in the Epistles to the Corinthians, without anyone's making that a ground of suspicion against these. On the other hand, the significance of faith as the effect of the grace of God which chooses men and calls them by the word is brought out even in the Epistle to the Thessalonians (i. 3, 8; ii. 13; iii. 5 f., 10). That the ethical duty of sanctification occupies the principal place is fully justified by the circumstances of this church, and, besides, it is based in genuine Pauline fashion upon the obligation to gratitude towards God who calls us and gives us His Holy Spirit (ii. 12 ; iv. 1, 8) ; moreover, it is not merely man's duty but is quite as much the effect of the divine influence upon man (v. 23 f.). "To sum up : the dogmatic system of the apostle is for obvious reasons not fully unfolded in this epistle but merely touched on incidentally, but this is done in thoroughly Pauline fashion." [1] Moreover, not only are the objections drawn from the general character of the epistle not convincing, but there are several positive considerations which tell decidedly against later composition. One is the charge brought against the Jews, of being the constant instigators of all persecutions of the Christians, which is as appropriate to Paul's situation at the time as it would be inappropriate to the situation subsequent to 64 A.D. Another, still more decisive, argument against later composition is to be found in the expectation expressed in iv. 15, 17, that Paul himself will be among those who will be alive at the second coming of Christ : this could not possibly have been written after the death of Paul. The anxieties, too, of the Thessalonians about their fellow-Christians who had died (iv. 13) would no longer be psychologically natural at a later period of church-life ; only the first deaths in a quite young community could call forth such questionings in a natural way. The weight of these arguments on the other side so greatly preponderates over that of the slight grounds for suspecting the genuineness of the First Epistle to the

[1] P. Schmidt, *Der erste Thessalonicherbrief.* Berlin, 1885.

Thessalonians that the genuineness of this epistle may be confidently maintained.

It is quite otherwise with the Second Epistle to the Thessalonians. Its contents consist for the most part of amplified repetitions of the first, in which may be recognised at the first glance not only dependence on the first epistle but also the heightened colouring which betrays the hand of the imitator. What is peculiar to the epistle is only its eschatology, and it is precisely in this point that it stands in strong contradiction to the views of the first epistle. According to the latter the Thessalonians know that the Parousia will come suddenly and unexpectedly, without any sign beforehand, like a thief in the night. According to 2 Thess. ii. 5, they are, on the contrary, reminded that Paul had previously told them that the Parousia would not take place until various premonitory signs had preceded it; namely, first, a general apostasy in consequence of an epidemic of falsehood and error (ii. 3, 11), then the appearance of the Adversary who shall raise himself up against all that is divine and holy, desecrate the Temple and give himself out to be God—a manifestation with Satanic powers, and at the same time the counterpart, in caricature, of the Parousia of Christ (ii. 4, 8 f.); finally the restraining power (τὸ κατέχον and ὁ κατέχων) must be removed which, until that time, prevented the manifestation of the rival of God (ii. 5). Only when this restraining power should be taken out of the way would the Adversary reveal himself, and then Christ would appear and would destroy him with the " spirit of his mouth " and execute retributory justice upon all heathen and unbelievers, especially upon the persecutors of the Church (ii. 8 ; i. 6, 8 f.). Of all this the Paul of the First Epistle to the Thessalonians knows nothing, and expressly refuses to have anything to do with apocalyptic calculations of this kind (1 Thess. v. 1 ff.). Against this it has been urged from the side of Apologetics that between the expectation of premonitory signs of the Parousia and the sudden occurrence of the latter there is no necessary contradiction ; even in the Gospels we find both side by side. That is, no doubt, true in a certain sense, in so far as the signs refer to events of the present which in their rapid passing give grounds for inferring the speedy coming of the end, as in the parable of the fig-tree putting forth leaves (Mark xiii. 28 ff.). But it is otherwise when in Matt. xxiv. 14 the completed evangelisation of the heathen is named as one of the signs. That unmistakably sets back the period, and is intended to weaken the expectation of the nearness of the Parousia. The description in 2 Thess. ii. is of this latter kind ; it implies unmistakably a historical development of considerable length, which is simply not reconcilable with the expectation which Paul expresses in First Thessalonians that he himself will be alive at the Parousia, but is rather intended to combat the expectation of a Parousia in the immediate future which Paul and his contemporaries had aroused in the church.

As regards the interpretation of this apocalypse, ii. 1–12, it is only possible to say that it rests upon an earlier Jewish basis which in course of time has been transformed and added to. Its origin is to be

sought in Dan. xi. 36 f., where it is said of the
Syrian King Antiochus Epiphanes that he would
exalt and magnify himself against every god and
speak insolently against the God of Gods. For this
prophecy the Jews found a second application as a
reference to the Roman Emperor Gaius Caligula,
who caused himself to be everywhere worshipped as
God, and cherished the plan of setting up his image
in the Temple and causing himself to be worshipped
there. The plan was not, indeed, carried out, but
the imagination of the Jews could never rid itself of
the thought of this threatened desecration of the
Temple, and expressed itself in apocalyptic utterances
such as we find in Mark xiii. 14 ff. and Rev. xiii.
With this may well be connected the new features
which are added in 2 Thess. ii. 4–6 f. to Dan. xi. 36 :
the Adversary will not only exalt himself against
God, but will seat himself in the Temple of God and
give himself out to be a God, and the " mystery of
iniquity " (godlessness) is already at work, and is only
restrained until he who now hinders it is taken out
of the way.   Since the " Adversary " is described as
Antichrist, whose " Parousia " in Satanic might,
encompassed by all manner of signs and wonders,
will have the effect of leading astray all those who
love not the truth, but whom the Lord Jesus, when
His Parousia takes place, will annihilate with the
spirit of His mouth ; the close affinity of these representations with those of Rev. xiii., xvii., xix., xx., can
hardly be overlooked, but whether a direct use of the
Johannine apocalypse by the author of Second Thessalonians, or the dependence of both on the common
material of apocalyptic tradition, is doubtful.   In any

case the distinctive features which in the Johannine apocalypse point to the legend of the return of Nero are completely wanting in 2 Thess. Moreover, the conflict between the opposing powers has here lost its original realistic features and been transferred to the spiritual region; the "mystery of iniquity" has its Satanic strength in the misleading power of error, to which those fall victims who have not laid hold unto the love of the good, and have not believed in the truth. This obviously refers to the same kind of offences, aberrations, and errors as are mentioned in Matt. xxiv. 10 ff. also, as signs of the Parousia. That points, however, to the second century, to a period when Christianity found its most dangerous enemies in its own heretics rather than in the Jews and heathen. That in this case the symbolic language of the apocalypse, once adopted, should be retained and merely have a new sense given to the words, is quite natural. The author of Second Thessalonians might quite well take over from an earlier tradition the representation of the Adversary who set himself in the Temple of God and gave himself out to be God (ii. 4), applied originally to the worshipping of the Emperor in the Temple at Jerusalem—even though there had long been no Temple at Jerusalem. In that case he explained it as referring to the spiritual temple of the Christian Church in which this new form of impiety—Satanic error—threatened to assume large dimensions. In the same way he retains, out of the common mythical material of the traditional apocalyptic, the "Restrainer." What he understood thereby, or whether he attached to it any distinct meaning whatever, it is impossible for us to discover.

All we can say is that evidently at that time something or other hindered the consummation of wickedness, and consequently deferred the Parousia. The
writer's special object was to combat the enthusiastic
expectation of a near Parousia which led to practical
excesses and to disorganisation of the life of the
Church; he represents in marked fashion the recoil
of early Christianity from the enthusiasm of the
first century to the opportunism of ecclesiatical
organisation in the second century. In the prosecu-
tion of this legitimate and timely purpose he must be
credited with adopting the somewhat heroic plan of dis-
placing the old Pauline letter, in which the enthusiastic
tendency seemed to find support, by means of a letter
which in general imitated it and was altered only in
reference to the expectation of the Parousia. For
that that is the natural inference from the very
curious relationship of the Second to the First
Epistle to the Thessalonians can scarcely be denied,
in spite of all Apologetic protests, by an unprejudiced
criticism. Only in this way is it possible to explain
the fact that the writer never in the whole epistle
makes a direct and positive reference to the earlier
one (which nevertheless had, according to the
traditional opinion, been written only a few months
before !), but appeals only to what he had said during
his visit to Thessalonica (ii. 5), which, however, is the
opposite of what the real Paul had written. Only
once does he refer to the first letter, and that in an
indirect fashion and with polemical intent. He
warns the Thessalonians in ii. 2 that they should not
let themselves be so easily shaken out of a sound
frame of mind or excited, whether by a spiritual

revelation, or by a word, or by a letter purporting to be written by us (*i.e.* Paul) to the effect that the Day of Christ is immediately at hand. But that is just what the genuine Pauline letter to the Thessalonians, in which Paul himself, along with the majority of the church, hopes to survive till the Parousia, did convey ; therefore the author of the second letter desires to discredit the first as only purporting to be written by Paul (this is the only possible meaning of ὡς δι’ ἡμῶν). To that end he has copied the leading thoughts of the genuine epistle (omitting the personal elements), but has substituted for its enthusiastic eschatology one more conformable to the requirements of ordinary church life. In order to give this new epistle the authority of a genuine apostolic communication he makes Paul, at the conclusion, iii. 17, write an autograph greeting as a sign (of genuineness) "as he is accustomed to do in every epistle." That, of course, never entered Paul's mind ; his autograph greetings were the natural expression of the cordial relationship of the apostle to his churches, not a precaution against possible forgeries, to which at the time when his literary activity had only begun there would have been no motive. Weizsäcker's remark, therefore (*Apostol. Zeitalter*, p. 260), precisely meets the case :. " It is just these words (iii. 17) that betray the writer ; not only because their purpose is so obvious, but also from the very fact of their suggesting this as the motive of Paul's adding a final clause in his own handwriting. The statement finds no confirmation elsewhere, not even in Gal. vi. 11. Paul adds in his own handwriting what his temperament makes him feel the need of saying in a specially

personal way; he desires, so to speak, to come before
the church in his own person. There is no trace of
the intention that these autograph conclusions should
be a sign and seal of genuineness. But the deliberate
design of a third party betrays itself elsewhere in the
epistle also; the warning against forged letters which
might mislead them into believing in the nearness of
the Parousia, is calculated, from the writer's point of
view, to enhance the significance of. this genuine
epistle. His exhortation to hold by his teaching,
whether received by word of mouth or by letter, his
command to punish, in particular, anyone who does
not obey his written words, must also be intended to
facilitate the acceptance of the present epistle."
Schmiedel in his commentary comes to the same
conclusion (*Handcom.*, II. i. p. 12 f.), and Holtzmann
sums up the result of his investigation as follows
(*Zeitschr. für N. T. Wissensch.*, 1901, 2 Heft, p. 107):
" The delay of the Parousia, which Paul expected
in the lifetime of the first generation, was the primary
and predominant motive for putting in the place of
the first epistle a revised edition, which was designed
to preserve the essential religious content of Paul's
letter, while omitting the personal and historical
elements, and which therefore makes the impression,
in comparison with the first epistle, sometimes of
lifeless imitation, sometimes of a solemnity adapted
to liturgical use (*cf.* the elaborated phraseology of
i. 3–12). It is a recasting of the first epistle
intended to make it suitable and acceptable to a
wider circle of readers, to whom the local circumstances of the first readers were no longer of
interest, and to a later generation which was no

longer content with a so narrowly bounded view of the future."

That this later epistle was not put, as the writer probably intended, in the place of the older one, but alongside of it, is quite in accordance with the customs of the early Church. It retained what had become traditional even when the circumstances and views of a younger generation had outgrown it, but placed beside it newer compositions more suited to the time (whether whole writings or single sayings) to correct the old and form a standard by which to interpret it. Thus we have the Fourth Gospel alongside of the three earlier ones, and these earlier gospels themselves include many later elements. As the advantages of this procedure in the interests of the regularity of the religious development of the Church's life are obvious, we ought not to take offence at the fact that later writings, or sayings, were introduced under the name of an ancient and revered authority. Only in this way could they attain their end, the edification of the generation then in existence on the foundation of the ancient and holy faith.

CHAPTER VIII

THE LETTERS TO THE CORINTHIANS

DURING Paul's stay of a year and a half in Corinth he had founded a church there which consisted almost exclusively of former heathen, and for the most part of people of the lowest classes. When he left Corinth for Ephesus he maintained relations with the Corinthian church. He probably wrote, soon after his departure, an epistle, now lost, in which he called upon the Corinthian Christians to break off fraternal intercourse with any who continued the practice of heathen immoralities (1 Cor. v. 9). Thereupon the Corinthian church sent the apostle a letter in which it seems to have described this demand as too rigorous and impracticable, pointing out that on the principle that we ought to have no intercourse with any immoral person (v. 10) it would be necessary to go out of the world altogether. Besides this, the letter also contained a series of questions upon points of conduct on which divergent opinions, stricter and laxer, prevailed in the Church. Was married life in any case worthy of a Christian, and in particular was it permissible for a Christian husband or wife to continue to live with one who was not a Christian? Was the eating of meats which had been offered to idols allowable for a Christian? What was the right opinion as to the value of "spiritual gifts," and in particular of "speaking with tongues"? How were they to organise the collection which Paul desired to have made? Might they not hope for the return of Apollos in the near future?[1] These questions, asked in the letter of the Corinthian church, formed one motive for the writing of a second letter by Paul—our "First Epistle to the Corinthians." But a further motive was supplied by the verbal reports which the apostle had received, partly from the messenger who brought this letter, partly from the servants of a Corinthian lady (Chloe) who had come to Ephesus. These reports were by no means of a nature to cause him satisfaction; they drew the picture of a congregation which was in a condition of religious confusion and dissension, and of moral disintegration and degeneration.

To the formation of religious factions an unintentional impulse had been given by the activity of Apollos, a Jewish Christian versed in the Alexandrian philosophy, who had come to Corinth after Paul's departure. His method of teaching differed from that of Paul, in the first place in being presented in a strikingly rhetorical form, and also by the use of Alexandrian speculation and allegorical interpretation of Scripture. It had so impressed many members of the church, not only by its eloquent presentation, but also through the suggestion of a deeper wisdom,

---

[1] *Cf.* 1 Cor. vii. 1, viii. 1, xii. 1, xvi. 1, 12, where the recurrent περὶ δέ indicates a reference to a point in the letter of the Corinthians.

through the charm of mystery in its idealistic speculations, that they saw in Apollos their true master,
the teacher of a higher Christianity. No doubt
Apollos himself did not propound any teachings
essentially at variance with Paul's; he only sought
to reinforce the Gospel which was common to both,
by means of the Alexandrian philosophy and methods
of exegesis. We find him later among the companions of Paul at Ephesus and on the best of terms
with him (1 Cor. xvi. 12). But, as always happens
in such cases, the adherents went much further than
their masters. They were not content with a mere
use of the forms of the Alexandrian philosophy, but
worked out, by means of it, a gnostic Christianity for
themselves, which doubtless differed in essential
points from the simple gospel of Paul. Of what
kind are we to suppose it to have been? Was it a
Christianity adapted to the world on the lines of
the secular heathen philosophy? But that would
by no means correspond to the character of the
Alexandrian religious philosophy, which was based
on the principles of the dualistic Platonic idealism,
and took throughout a spiritualistic, mystical, and
ascetical direction nearly akin to that of Essenism.
Of the errors to which such a philosophy might give
rise on Christian soil, we have a clear example in the
case of the false teachers at Colosse ; their spiritualism
led to an undervaluing of the historical saving work
of Christ, to mystical intercourse with the spirit-world,
and to an ascetic dread of all that was material as
something unclean and standing in close relation
with the world of evil spirits. When, therefore, we
find among the errors combated by Paul in writing

to the Corinthians (alongside of quite other and opposite errors) traits of precisely the same kind as those of the gnostic heresy at Colosse, the conjecture, in my opinion, naturally suggests itself that we should see in these traits the distinguishing marks of the Alexandrian-Gnostic Apollos-party. In this connection it is worthy of notice that Paul at the outset, in the first chapter, where he is opposing especially the Apollos-party, emphasises the unique saving virtue of the death of Christ upon the cross against their so-called philosophy which tended to depreciate it; no doubt, therefore, they substituted a spiritualistic theory of redemption for this unique historical redemptive work of Christ. Since they despised the material body, they naturally could not believe in its resurrection, any more than did Philo or the Essenes; we may therefore see in the deniers of the resurrection, against whom the polemic of 1 Cor. xv. is directed, the followers of Apollos. It was not Epicurean indifference but dualistic Spiritualism which formed the motive of this denial. But they seem also, like the Essenes (and also probably the Colossian ascetics—Col. ii. 21) to have held marriage in aversion, and to have forbidden the entering on, or continuance in, that state as unworthy of the Christian; so the protest of Paul against this rigorism in chapter vii. is doubtless addressed to the Apollos-party. The anxious avoidance of any partaking of meat offered to idols also looks like a characteristic of theirs, though in this they may well have made common cause with the party of Peter. We may regard all these traits, which suggest an Alexandrian-Gnostic Christianity, as a mark of the Corinthian

Apollos-party. It was not in principle opposed to
Paul, but emphasised in a one-sided fashion the
idealism and dualism which were not inherently
foreign to his mode of thought. On another side
their rigorous asceticism was in touch with the
legalistic standpoint of the Petrine-party. Thus the
Alexandrianism of the Apollos-party formed in this
early instance, as it continued to do throughout the
whole of early Christianity, the middle - term and
bond of connection between Paulinism and Judaism
—it is perhaps significant that in i. 12 the Apollos-
party is placed in the middle, between the parties of
Paul and Peter.

If the Apollos-party had so travestied the attitude of
Apollos that he no longer cared to identify himself
with them (his refusal to return to Corinth, xvi. 12,
proved that), the same thing had taken place in a
still more marked fashion in regard to the Pauline
party and to the apostle Paul. The two things hang
together. The ascetic exaggerations of the former
party naturally provoked the latter to push their
master's principles of liberty to an extreme on the
other side. Not that a loose morality had been first
introduced into the Corinthian church by the Pauline
doctrine of freedom from the law ; it had always been
the prevailing tone of Corinthian life. But it can
quite well be conceived that the Pauline doctrines of
the expiation of all sins by the death of Christ, of
justification by faith, of the abrogation of the law,
of the liberty of the spirit, of the brotherhood and
equality of all in Christ, had been misinterpreted by
many as giving licence to sin, and abused to the
deadening of conscience and the abandonment of

chastity and morality. That is so much in accordance with human nature in general and the nature of hot-blooded Greeks in particular, that we should have had cause to wonder if it had not happened. Indeed Paul again and again found reason, in Galatia, Antioch, Corinth, Rome, and Philippi, to warn his converts against such misunderstanding, and abuses of Christian liberty and the blessedness of faith. It is therefore entirely probable that the various moral evils and excesses of the Corinthian church ought to be set down, if not exclusively, at least mainly, to the Pauline party. When Paul said in regard to meats and drinks " all things are permitted unto me," his Corinthian followers could not see why the same principle should not be applied to justify sexual licence. Paul had therefore to make them understand the essential difference between the two, and, further, was obliged to exhort them to seek in marriage a defence against the temptations of their hot blood, though he made no concealment of the fact that he regarded the state of celibacy as essentially preferable, without, however, making it a precept as the ascetic Apollos-party did. Again, since Paul had said that the idol was nothing and meat offered to an idol was not different from ordinary meat, his Corinthian followers drew the inference that it was open to the Christian to enjoy himself without scruple at the banquets which accompanied the heathen sacrifices, without concerning himself about the offence thus caused to weaker brethren. Since Paul had said that in Christ master and servant, man and wife, were one, many a Christian slave thought himself justified in running away from his master, and many a Christian woman ventured to appear unveiled at the meetings of the church and to come forward as a speaker. Of the confused and unedifying babel made by those who felt moved to speak with tongues and prophesy, all parties may share the blame, and so, too, in regard to the grave disorders at the Lord's Supper, which developed into a banquet of the rich at which the poor were spectators. Here, therefore, social cleavages came in, in addition to the religious factions, as a further element of unsettlement in the disordered life of the community.

Into this church, in which advocates of liberty who exaggerated Paul's teaching, and ascetics who exaggerated the teaching of Apollos, were already contesting the field, there had come finally Jewish Christians from without, bringing letters of recommendation from foreign (? Palestinian) churches. They had set up in this arena of individual opinions and extravagances the external rule and standard of the Jewish law and of the tradition preserved by the original apostles, a banner of authority inscribed with the name of the chief apostle, Peter. No wonder that their teaching took root in a soil so well prepared for it. Amid the stormy sea of opinion (to vary the metaphor) the fixed law of Israel, to which, moreover, the original church of the apostles was firmly attached, might well appear to many, especially of the more serious and sober thinkers, as a haven of refuge. And this was the more likely to be the case since the tactics of these Jewish brethren and guests were cleverly adapted to the circumstances of a Gentile Christian community. They avoided bringing forward certain demands of the law, in reference to which it was

easy to see in advance that they would not have been
likely to find a ready acceptance with the Greeks;
e.g. the ordinance of circumcision, the keeping of the
Jewish festivals, the regulations in regard to food, but
sought in the first place only to gain admission for
the general principle of legal righteousness by exalting
the authority of the original apostles as the personal
representatives of this principle, and by depreciating
the authority of Paul.   Thus the question of principle
took the form of a personal question, a struggle of
opposing authorities.   It was not their own authority
that the Jewish teachers at Corinth opposed to that
of Paul—they would not have accomplished much by
that; they rested their cause on the authority of the
original apostles, above all on that of Peter as their
recognised and revered head.   That very fact made
the situation difficult for Paul, who was far from
desiring to undermine the respect in which Peter was
held, and it was rendered all the harder for him
because his opponents were by no means disposed to
show him the kind of consideration that he made a
point of displaying towards Peter.   On the contrary,
they prosecuted their campaign against Paul with all
the weapons of dishonest and spiteful abuse and
calumny.   That his gospel was obscure and mysterious,
so that no one could make out what its real meaning
was, that he preached not Christ but himself, and
falsified the word of God with his own imaginations—
these were the least of the charges they brought
against him.   He had, moreover, never himself seen
Christ Jesus, and it was therefore impossible that he
should know better than the original apostles what
Christ's teaching was; he was therefore not really a

true "minister" of Christ at all, for such an one must
be above all a minister of (legal) righteousness, as the
genuine Jewish apostles, and they themselves as the
helpers of these, actually were (2 Cor. xi. 13 ff.).
They were now bringing to the Corinthians for the
first time the genuine Gospel and the true Jesus and
Spirit of Christ, who were quite other than the Spirit
and the Jesus whom Paul had preached to them.
Therefore they were justified in claiming to be supported and maintained by the Corinthians. If Paul
had not done that, the very fact betrayed his consciousness that he was not justified in claiming the
rights of an apostle, as not being a true apostle and
minister of Christ. In other respects also his modest
and timid manner showed that Christ's spirit of
power, of which he boasted, did not really dwell in
him. In his letters he used impressive language,
but when it was a question of making it good in
person he was weak and foolish. Besides, he was
untrustworthy in character; his speech was now yea,
now nay; no one could rely on him. Even as regards
disinterestedness his conduct was by no means so
admirable as he pretended; for if he took no direct
support from the church at Corinth, he knew how to
indemnify himself by using the pretext of the collection for the Palestinian Christians in order to exploit
the church for his own advantage. Thus the great
question of principle between Jewish legalistic
Christianity and Pauline Christianity without the
law, took the hateful form of personal intrigue and
vulgar scandal-mongering. But, after all, it was only
a few of the Judaising fanatics who had come in from
without who had the hardihood to use such weapons

in their agitation against Paul. And their action was not at first conspicuous, for in the First Epistle to the Corinthians, while Paul does indeed already mention the party of Peter, he makes no further direct reference to them, but only alludes indirectly and incidentally to their personal attacks upon himself (iv. 1 ff., ix. 1 ff.). But in the interval between the first and the second epistle—probably on the occasion of a short visit of Paul to Corinth—matters suddenly took a turn for the worse, so that in the second letter, written immediately thereafter, Paul took up the battle which had been forced upon him with all the energy and passion of which he was capable. To that we must recur later. Here we have only to remark that Peter is not to be held responsible for the appearance of the " Peter-party " in Corinth, any more than Paul and Apollos for the aberrations of the " Paul-party " and " Apollos-party "; in every case the partisans were only a caricature of the leaders under whose names they fought.

Besides these three parties, each of which is easily understood in itself and in relation to the rest, and which are in their general outline typical of the tendencies which are found throughout the whole of ancient Christianity, it is very generally thought that in view of 1 Cor. i. 12 we are to understand that there was a fourth party which called itself specially the " Christ-party." But as, with the exception of this problematical passage, Paul nowhere else makes mention in either epistle of this supposed fourth party, there was here a free field for the most various hypotheses of exegetical scholars. However ingenious these may be, I cannot conceal that none of them seem to me to have much probability, for the reason, if for no other, that no clearly definable character by which it might be differentiated from the others can be discovered for this fourth party. In whatever way the attempt was made to characterise the Christ-party, its characteristics so nearly coincided with those of the Apollos-party or (and this more frequently of late) of the Peter-party, that it was difficult to understand how so slight a *nuance*, a mere difference in the degree to which the tendency was carried, could have become the basis of the formation of a special party, and how it was that this difference could be indicated by the peculiar appellation of " Christ-people." If the intention was to express a specially close relationship to the historical Jesus, that was possessed by Peter, the chief of the apostles, in a degree which could be surpassed by no one, not even by James the brother of Jesus, since he had never been His disciple.[1] Again, if the founders of the Christ-party had appealed to the fact that they

[1] Had the Christ-party been associated with the stricter tendency of James, why did they not simply name themselves after him as the less strict Judaisers named themselves after Peter? Besides, how can anyone tell whether these two tendencies subsisted in Jerusalem after Peter had at Antioch deferred to, and associated himself with, the spirit of James? And even supposing — what is not capable of proof — that there was in Jerusalem a milder tendency identified with Peter and a stricter identified with James, can it be supposed possible that this, in any case subordinate, difference would have been at once so strongly emphasised in the Judaising propaganda among Gentile Christians that it would have given rise to a division of the Judaisers into different parties? This would have shown a degree of stupidity which we cannot well credit to the astute Judaising agitators. So that this hypothesis, not less than the others, makes the impression of being artificial and wanting in probability.

themselves had personally seen and heard Jesus, had
been, in fact, His disciples in the wider sense (as distinguished from the twelve), that would not have
given nearly so strong a point of support for their
opposition to Paul, as did the appeal to the famous
name of the chief apostle, Peter. This, the very
fact that no sufficient explanation can be found of
this fourth party and its distinctive name, and that
there is no apparent room for it alongside of the
three natural parties of Paul, Apollos, and Peter,
suffices to make the existence of this fourth party
doubtful for us. And this doubt is strengthened
into a decided denial when we observe more closely
how Paul himself speaks of these Corinthian parties.
The decisive passage is 1 Cor. iii. 21 ff., where the
attack upon these factions which Paul has carried
on up to this point is concluded with the words,
" Therefore let no man glory in men, for all things
are yours; whether Paul or Apollos, or Cephas, or
the world, or life, or death, or things present, or
things to come ; all are yours ; and ye are Christ's ;
and Christ is God's." This is the passage in which he
most markedly censures the factions ; the fourth party
which (according to the usual acceptation) was for
him the most dangerous, is passed over in silence ;
and further, he has used, in combating the other
three parties which were less unfavourable to him, a
turn of expression which could only have the effect
of favouring the Christ - party, which was (by
hypothesis) the most unfavourable to him. They
would not feel themselves at all affected by the
warning against over-estimating the authority of the
various teachers, but might rather say that what

Paul here demanded of all the Corinthians, namely, to belong to Christ only, was precisely what they did, and therefore the other parties must simply come over to their position. An attack upon the factions which would have the effect of strengthening the position of the worst of them does not look like Paul's wisdom. The inference is that he knew nothing about a Christ-party, and that no such thing really existed. The polemic against the parties in 1 Cor. i. 13 leads to the same conclusion : " Is Christ divided ? Was Paul crucified for you ? or were ye baptized in the name of Paul ? " *i.e.* do you suppose that the one Christ can be divided into a Paul-Christ, an Apollos-Christ, and a Peter-Christ ? or is the ground of salvation which you acknowledged at baptism no longer the one Christ but the particular teachers whom you are thus putting in the place of the crucified Saviour ? This argument, too, is appropriate only to the three parties who by professing allegiance to particular teachers tear asunder, as it were, the one Christ, but it is absolutely inapplicable to a " Christ-party " which would not have felt itself touched by this argument at all. Therefore the conclusion is inevitable that in the foregoing verse, too, the words " But I am Christ's " do not refer to the designation of a fourth party, however strongly the literal meaning of the words seems to favour this misunderstanding. Paul would not be likely to think of this misunderstanding, precisely because there was no need to guard against it in the case of readers who knew nothing of a Christ-party. This negative result must be taken as determined by the arguments from fact and exegesis which have been advanced, whatever be the positive interpretation of the words "but I of Christ." According to the interpretation put upon them by the early Church, they contain the confession of those who were of the same mind as the apostle in desiring to keep themselves outside of party divisions, those of no party, the neutrals who, for the very reason that they did not themselves form another party, would not feel themselves affected by the polemic against factiousness. More ingenious is the interpretation proposed by Räbiger,[1] that "but I of Christ" expresses the common affirmation of the three parties which have been previously indicated by their special professions : each advanced for itself a superior, if not an exclusive, claim to belong to Christ, precisely on the ground that they interpreted and confessed the faith of Christ in the sense of Paul or Apollos or Peter ; thus to the three separate confessions there is added in the fourth clause the claim which was common to them all, and for that very reason became in turn a subject of contention. The simplest interpretation is certainly to take the words "but I am of Christ" as Paul's own confession, which he desired to contrast with the other party mottoes as the only true one—in which case, of course, these last words are not dependent on "each one of you saith," and should be divided from what precedes by a colon.

After a brief introduction, in which the apostle declares his thankfulness and rejoicing over the vigorous life of the church at Corinth, so rich in

---

[1] In his critical studies on the Corinthian Epistles (second edition, 1886). Even though his interpretation of i. 12 is problematical, he is doubtless right in denying the existence of a Christ-party.

knowledge and other spiritual gifts, he proceeds at once (i. 10) to speak of its grave defect, the factious spirit. He first reminds his own party that he has given them no pretext for an over-valuing of his own person; they were not baptized in his name, nor had he, except in a very few cases, himself adminis- tered baptism, since his office was to preach the Gospel. This Gospel he had expressly refrained from preaching in the forms of secular rhetoric (as the Apollos-party boasted that Apollos did), lest he should obscure the divine wisdom and might that lay in the word of the cross. It was precisely that which in the eyes of the world appeared the weakness and foolish- ness of the Gospel which constituted the divine power and wisdom, by means of which God willed to save them that believe. Therefore God had expressly chosen the foolish things, the weak things, and the base things, of the world to confound the wise and the honoured. In His presence the boasting of the flesh was nought, the only ground for glorying was Christ, "who of God is made unto us wisdom and righteousness and sanctification and redemption." Accordingly, he, the apostle, had despised all the arts of eloquence which human wisdom teaches, in order that his influence might be only "in demonstration of the Spirit and of power." He would indeed "speak wisdom among them that are perfect" (those who were advanced in knowledge), a wisdom of God which is to the natural man an unintelligible mystery but is revealed unto us by the Spirit which comes forth from God, and which teaches us to think the thoughts of God Himself. A man filled with the Spirit was capable of exercising an independent judgment in all (religious) matters, and did not need to submit himself to the judgment of any other (therefore not to that of the heads of the parties and their adherents). But the Corinthians had not yet, it must be admitted, reached this spiritual standpoint, but were still, in religion, babes, involved in fleshly weakness and only capable of receiving the spiritual nourishment of children, as their carnal dissensions clearly showed. To quarrel over Paul and Apollos was to forget that it was the highest office of both to be fellow-labourers with God in the building up of the church, one of them having laid the foundation and the other built thereon; Christ remained the one unmoved foundation; as to the stability and worth of the materials which the different builders had erected upon this foundation the judgment—"the day of Christ"—would declare it. Only let each one see that he did not, under the semblance of philosophic teaching, disturb the church, the temple of God, by faction. Therefore the church must not think of itself as belonging to any human teacher, since in reality all these teachers, as indeed all human circumstances and advantages, belonged of right to the church, as it, in turn, belonged to God. The only requisite in a servant of Christ was that he should be found a true steward of the mysteries of God. He who could give himself, as Paul could, this testimony, needed not to fear any human judgment, but could confidently leave the decision in the hands of the coming Lord. As each had received his special gift from God, none had reason for vain self-exaltation over others.

The Corinthians might learn this humble and unselfish frame of mind from both their teachers, Paul and Apollos. It was indeed a fine thing that they, in the consciousness of their wisdom, strength, and greatness, felt themselves exalted so high above their foolish and despised apostles who were mishandled by all the world (as to be able to sit in judgment upon them). Yet it was not his purpose to shame them, but to remind them that although they had various instructors (among them even schoolmasters in the law) yet they had him alone for their spiritual father, and therefore ought to be imitators of him (rather than lofty-minded judges). When he came again he would see what substance there was behind the proud words of the puffed-up partisans, and whether he should come to them with the rod or in the spirit of meekness.

Thus far the reproof of the Corinthian factions. Paul handles this delicate point with great skill and fineness of feeling. Although he takes the high stand-point of the Gospel, and from this point of view holds before his readers the ideal of a united Church of Christ, he most skilfully avoids giving the appearance of any partiality on his side towards his own adherents, and yet combines with his defence of his own apostolic activity a criticism of the supposed advantages, which were in fact weaknesses, of the Apollos-party. For to this refers the whole argument about the false wisdom of the world, which only served to empty the Gospel of its power. In contradistinction to this, Paul sets the true wisdom, derived from the Spirit of God and thinking the thoughts of God, but which of course assumes that its hearers are filled with the Spirit, and are mature in the Christian life ; and the very factious-ness of the Corinthians showed that they were not fit to receive it. To the Peter-party there is, up to this point in the argument, no direct reference; it is named only twice in all, and there is perhaps an indirect allusion to its dictatorial and proudly censorious attitude in iv. 3, 8, 15, 18 ff.

The threat, in iv. 21, to come with the rod, forms the transition to the earnest rebuke and admonition about the offence which had occurred in the church, the illicit intercourse of one of its members with his stepmother. He was to be delivered over, Paul solemnly declared, to Satan for the destruction of the flesh, in order that his spirit might be saved in the day of judgment. What is meant by this is not mere exclusion from the church, but something in the nature of a punitive miracle brought about by means of imprecation or handing over to the Satanic power. In general, members of the church were to break off all intercourse with notorious sinners, and to dismiss them from their midst. Again, going to law before the heathen courts about questions of property was not seemly for Christians, who should one day judge even the angels, and should therefore now much rather suffer wrong than do wrong. The heathen vices of unchastity and rapacity exclude those who practise them from the kingdom of God. If they formerly lived in these, yet they are now, through the name of Christ and the Spirit of God, washed and sanctified and justified, and must therefore not fall back into the old heathen life. To think that unchastity could be excused by the Christian principle of freedom was a gross error, since the body of the Christian was a member of Christ and a temple of the Holy Spirit, and therefore must be consecrated to God.

11

On this follows appropriately the discussion of the questions regarding marriage (chap. vii.). On the question raised by the Corinthians the apostle gives his decision in the following sense : Celibacy is in itself the better state, since the unmarried person is not so likely as the married to be entangled by the cares of the passing world, but is able to direct his cares exclusively to the things of the Lord, that he may be holy both in body and soul (26-34). But this advice was not to be interpreted as a binding injunction ; it was indeed much better that those who did not possess the gift of continence should marry (verses 9 and 35 ff.). So also those who were in the married state should not withdraw themselves from each other permanently, that they might not be led into temptation (2-5). Divorce was, according to the teaching of Jesus, not permissible. Even a mixed marriage must not be dissolved, so long as the non-Christian partner desired to maintain it. On the other hand, if the heathen partner wished to dissolve the marriage, the Christian partner was thereby released from his or her obligations (10-16). In general, the principle held for this as for other relations of life—for example, slavery— that the Christian calling altered nothing in the earthly position and vocation. Just because the Christian was freed by his redemption in Christ inwardly in his religious consciousness from all slavery to man, he could the better adapt himself with pious mind to the worldly relationship in which he was placed (17-24).

In chaps. viii. and x. Paul answers the questions which had been addressed to him about meat offered to idols, and in doing so takes the middle course

between opposite opinions. First he blames those
who inconsiderately assert their enlightenment to
the offence of their neighbours. Then he concedes
to the more liberal thinkers that they are actually in
the right, inasmuch as the heathen gods have no
longer any religious significance for the Christian,
who acknowledges only one God the Father and
one Lord Jesus Christ (viii. 4-6). Therefore, the
Christian need have no scruples in using the meat
offered for sale in the market or set before him at a
feast given by a heathen host, as to whether it came
from an idol sacrifice. Here the principle applied :
The earth and whatsoever is in it is the Lord's, and
may therefore be thankfully enjoyed (x. 25-30).
But this liberty in "things indifferent" must be
limited by consideration for the weak brother, who
might find an offence therein and thus be morally
injured. Just because eating or not eating is morally
indifferent, no one must by inconsiderate insistence
on his own liberty give offence to the weak brother
(viii. 7-13 ; x. 23 f., 28 f.). Moreover, the Christian
should be restrained from actually partaking in idol-
festivals by the thought that the offering made
thereat was made, not to gods indeed, but to demons,
and that to partake in them would place them in a
relation to the demons similar to that in which the
enjoyment of the Lord's Supper placed them towards
the Lord—for the partakers of the Lord's table to
be also partakers at the table of demons was to
tempt God (x. 14-22). Such a tempting of God
had had calamitous results for the Israelites in the
wilderness, therefore the Christians must take
warning by their example (x. 1-13). In fine, the

eating of meat which came from the idol sacrifice is permitted, so far as it does not cause offence to the weaker brother; but partaking in a sacrificial feast which had the character of worship is for the partakers of the Lord's Supper wholly inadmissible, and fraught with danger.

Between chaps. viii. and x., which are connected by unity of subject, there is inserted in chap. ix. a discussion of the apostolic rights of Paul. The immediate occasion for the digression was the admonition that the Corinthian Christians should not, for the sake of this question of meats, cause offence to one another, but should rather deny themselves the exercise of their Christian liberty for the sake of the peace and edification of the church. The apostle then refers to himself as exemplifying this principle, pointing out that he himself had hitherto made, and intended in the future to make, no use of the undoubted right which he as an apostle possessed of receiving support from the church, because he gloried in preaching the Gospel freely and in denying himself what was his personal right for the sake of the cause (ix. 15–18). Similarly, it was his custom in all other respects to subordinate his personal freedom to the purpose of his apostolic office, adapting himself to all, living among Jews in conformity with the law and among Gentiles as free from the law—though inwardly constrained by the law of Christ—that by thus becoming all things to all men he might by all means win some for the Gospel and thus make certain that he himself should share in its blessing (19–23). He practised, like a competitor in the Isthmian games, strict self-discipline, that he might not, while preaching to others, himself become a castaway (24–27). Although this discussion does not stand out of connection with the preceding and following treatment of the questions about things which are indifferent and as to what is permissible regarding the eating of meats offered to idols, it is impossible not to recognise that it has other points of connection outside the immediate context. Paul defends his right as an apostle with such energy, not merely in order to emphasise the voluntary nature of his renunciation of this right as an example of the Christian use of liberty, but also because his apostolic right in this respect had in some quarters been denied, and his non-use of it had been interpreted as a practical acknowledgment that he did not possess it. From what quarter this denial came is made clear by the comparison with the other apostles, and especially with Cephas. It was the Peter-party who endeavoured to depreciate Paul's free preaching of the Gospel in the eyes of the Corinthians by denying his right to be maintained by the Church, and this they could only do by means of an attack on his claim to apostolic rank and equal authority with the original apostles. To this end they urged, among other things, that he had not known Christ personally, and therefore could not be an apostle in the same sense as Christ's personal disciples, or possess the rights of an apostle. Against this hostile judgment (verse 3) Paul offers his " apologia," first by reminding them (verse 1) that he too had seen our Lord Jesus (and therefore had received a direct call from Him, no less than the earlier apostles), and secondly (verse 2) by appealing to the consciousness of his converts : " If I be not an apostle to others (to the Judaisers and founders of the Peter-party who had come to them from without), yet surely I am so to you (my own converts), for the seal of my apostleship are ye in the Lord " (*i.e.* the fact of your existence as a Christian Church). We shall meet with this thought again in the second epistle, where it is further developed : here he has only touched on it, desiring to hasten on to the point on which question had arisen—his right as an apostle to be maintained by the Church, and his renunciation of that right. It seems as if in this first epistle Paul still desired to avoid any direct polemic against the Peter-party, and only where the occasion demanded it entered upon it almost against his will, dropping it again immediately and passing on to the main subject.

In chaps. xi.–xiv. he discusses a series of points connected with the meetings for worship, some of them suggested by questions which had been addressed to him, some by reports received through other channels. In the first place, he censures the practice which was growing up of the women appearing at the meetings of the church with unveiled heads ; he finds therein an injury to the modesty and sobriety which are prescribed for women by the very order of the creation ; and another reason for veiling their heads was that they might not offend the eyes of the angels (or place temptation before them ?). In any case, for the women to be veiled was the custom in the churches of God (xi. 3–16).

A matter deserving of severer censure was their conduct at the Lord's Supper, each seeking to secure

his own meal first, so that one was drunken and
another hungry. That was to despise the Church of
God, and by taking the Lord's Supper in an unworthy
way, to sin against the body and blood of Christ. He
who ate and drank as though the bread and wine of
the Lord's Supper was only common food, without
reflecting on its sacred significance and its reference
to the body of the crucified Christ whose death was
symbolically celebrated in this meal—he who so acted
ate and drank judgment to himself, and with this are
connected the numerous cases of sickness and death
which had occurred among them (xi. 17–32). (We
shall recur later to this interpretation of the Supper.)

In xii. 1 Paul begins his reply to the question
which had been addressed to him regarding those
who possessed spiritual gifts (that is, those who spoke
with tongues or prophesied) by pointing to the fact
that the possession of the Spirit is the universal mark
of distinction of Christians in contrast to the heathen.
Whereas the latter are driven by a blind impulse to
have recourse to dumb idols (and thus come to no
clear consciousness and confession of their unspiritual
faith), in Christians, on the contrary, the Holy Spirit
(which is the principle of the Divine thought and
knowledge, and, consequently, of a thought and
knowledge like the Divine, 2, 10 ff.) inspires the
confession of a faith which is clearly conscious of its
object: "Jesus is Lord." This confession is therefore an unfailing token of the possession of the Spirit,
and it is proportionately unthinkable that the contrary
declaration rejecting Jesus could proceed from the
same Spirit. But although it is the same Spirit that
·dwells in all Christians, yet the spiritual gifts in

which he manifests himself in individuals are different, corresponding to the various services or offices in the church for which the gifts of the Spirit are intended to qualify them. The necessity and appropriateness of this variety of the functions and organs in the unity of the Church is explained by the illustration of a body with its various members. Before entering on the discussion of the point to which the question refers, the apostle prefaces it with the splendid hymn of love ; which is greater than speaking with tongues and prophecy, greater than all knowledge of mysteries, greater than faith and hope ; for when our partial knowledge and partial prophesying shall pass, and our childish speaking and thinking be put away, there will remain the triad of virtues, Faith, Hope, Love, and the greatest of these is Love. Then, in chap. xiv., the value of the speaking with tongues is put on a lower level than that of prophesying. The former is an ecstatic speech of men who feel themselves inspired, and wholly absorbed in God, but is unaccompanied by clear consciousness, and therefore serves only to the edification of the speaker himself, not to that of others, who are unable to understand the inarticulate forth-pouring of feeling, unless, indeed, someone interprets the ecstatic monologue in intelligible language, much in the same way as the wordless language of music can be translated into definite thoughts by one who understands it and is able to clothe his impression of the feelings which are expressed therein in articulate language. For this reason speaking with tongues, while it is of value for the private edification of individuals, has no direct value for the Church, and is only useful when the interpretation is given with it. On the other hand, the gift of prophecy contributes directly to the edification of the Church, since it reveals the thoughts of men's hearts (and also the counsels of the Divine will for man's salvation), or, out of a deeper knowledge (of the meaning of Scripture and of the acts of God in history) communicates instruction and direction by means of which the consciences of the hearers are impressed and their hearts powerfully moved to acknowledge the presence of God in the church (xiv. 6, 23 ff.). For this reason the Corinthians should especially strive after the gift of prophecy, while not rejecting the speaking with tongues. Moreover, all is to be done decently and in order, and women are not to come forward as speakers in the services of the church.[1] Thus the general

---

[1] This prohibition (verse 34 f.) of women's speaking in the assemblies for worship stands in striking contradiction to xi. 5, where, while it is forbidden that women should appear unveiled when preaching or prophesying, it is implied that their speaking in public is permissible. The contradiction cannot in my opinion be removed either by means of the distinction between public and private worship, of which there is no hint, nor by means of the distinction between "spiritual" and ordinary speech, since the prohibition in xiv. 34 f. is expressed in quite general terms and makes no exception in favour of "spiritual" speech. There seems therefore to be no way out of the difficulty except to suppose that verses 34 f., perhaps also 33 b. and 36, are a later addition, probably from the hand of an ecclesiastically-minded admirer of Paul in the second century, perhaps the same who wrote the similar prohibition in 1 Tim. ii. 11 ff. In favour of this is the surprising appeal to the law in verse 34, which would come strangely from Paul ; also the fact that in some MSS. verses 34 f. are placed after verse 40, and may therefore very likely have crept into the text from a marginal gloss ; cf. the Commentaries of Holsten and Schmiedel.

tendency of the apostle's teaching is to give the predominant place in the meeting for worship to the
word which impresses and edifies, and to deprecate
the over-estimation of enthusiasm, which so easily
leads to a morally unprofitable excess of feeling.
This effort to ethicise the religious enthusiasm while
freely acknowledging its religious significance, is
characteristic of Paul, and testifies not only to the
keen religious insight but also to the skill of the great
apostle and missionary in educating his converts.

In chap. xv. he turns to the treatment of the
question raised by the Corinthians regarding the
resurrection. That those who doubted the resurrection entirely denied any continuance of life after
death, is wholly improbable, especially as the belief in
immortality was widely prevalent among thoughtful
heathen, and was certainly a cardinal point in the
system of the Alexandrian Platonists, while it is not
easy to suppose that pure Sceptics or Epicureans
would at that time have strayed into the Christian
Church. The denial of a bodily resurrection must
therefore have had its grounds in the dualistic repug-
nance to the body as material, the protest being
directed against the traditional Jewish, grossly
material conception of the resurrection. But for
Paul, of course, the denial of the resurrection involved
the denial of immortality, because according to the
Hebrew psychology personal life was thought of as
closely connected with the body. It is on this
assumption that his proof of the fact of the resurrection is based (xv. 1–34); but further on, when he
treats of the manner in which it takes place, he so
largely spiritualises the Jewish conception, that even

Apollos, with his Alexandrian ideas, could well have accepted Paul's version of it. Thus, here also, as in the controversial questions previously treated, he mediates between the opposing opinions from the standpoint of the higher Christian knowledge. First he reminds the Corinthians of that which he had delivered to them as one of the earliest lessons in the Gospel, the death of Christ for our sins and His rising again on the third day, the latter supported in part by Scriptural proofs (verse 4) and in part by the tradition of the original Christian community regarding the appearances of Christ (5-7), and, lastly, in part by his own vision of Christ in which the mercy of God had revealed itself to him also, last of all the apostles, and made him from a persecutor into its most effectual instrument (8-10). This teaching he held in common with the other apostles. But anyone who denied the resurrection in general denied also the resurrection of Christ, and with that the whole Christian faith stood or fell (12-19). On the other hand, the truth of Christ's resurrection ensured that of the Christians, since it was the beginning, which was to be continued and perfected by a general resurrection of Christians, just as the death of Adam had its necessary consequence in the death of all men. Moreover, the vocation of Christ, according to the Scriptures, to rule until all enemies were placed under His feet, would not be fulfilled until the last enemy, Death, was put away (namely, by the resurrection of the dead). Not until then could Christ lay aside His office of ruler, and God be all in all (20-28). But the great practical importance of the hope of the resurrection for the Christian life Paul proves by the argument that only on this assumption would there be any meaning in the custom which was prevalent among them of receiving baptism on behalf of those who had died, in order to ensure them a share in the Messianic kingdom. Moreover, the whole warfare of the Christian against a hostile world would be meaningless without that hope; the heathen saying would be justified: " Let us eat and drink, for to-morrow we die." Therefore the Corinthians should guard against being misled by such false teaching (29–34). But as regards the question as to how the resurrection would take place, the apostle recalls the analogy of the grain of corn to which God gives a new body differing according to its kind, and then he refers to the differing flesh of animals, and the heavenly bodies which differ from one another in glory. Similarly the resurrection-body will be essentially different from the earthly: just as the latter is after the image of the earthly man Adam, so the former will be after the image of the heavenly man Christ, and therefore a heavenly and spiritual body. The earthly body of flesh and blood is corruptible, and therefore cannot share in the incorruptible life of the kingdom of God. Therefore not only those who have fallen asleep in the meantime will arise at Christ's second coming with a new and imperishable body; we who are alive will be transformed, receiving an imperishable and immortal body. That will be the crowning victory which God will grant to us through Christ. In the consciousness that the success of our work is thus ensured, we should be untiring and advance steadily in the work of the Lord (35–58).

The conclusion of the epistle (chap. xvi.) gives directions for the collection, promises a visit of some length, informs them of Apollos' decision against returning to Corinth in the near future, exhorts them to give a friendly welcome to Timotheus, to accord due authority to Stephanas in recognition of his services to the church, to stand fast in the faith, and to live in love and concord. Then Paul adds the greeting with his own hand, giving the solemn watchword, " The Lord is at hand," and finally assures the members of the church of his love to them in Christ.

Despite all the evidence which this epistle contains of Paul's apostolic wisdom and love, it did not succeed in producing the desired effect in Corinth. So far from the factious spirit now subsiding, it took a turn which from his point of view was far worse. The Peter-party, who in the first epistle are quite in the background, seem immediately thereafter to have won so much ground, that there was reason to fear the estrangement of the whole church from its founder. With this turn of affairs there stands in the closest connection *a short visit* which Paul must have paid to the Corinthian church between the writing of the first and second (canonical) epistles. For whereas the first epistle bears no trace of Paul's having been more than once in Corinth, several passages of the second epistle point unmistakably to his having been there twice previously.[1] Moreover, it appears from many indications that the apostle, in the immediately preceding—therefore the second—visit to Corinth, had had a painful experience,

[1] 2 Cor. xii. 14, xiii. 1, τρίτον τοῦτο ἔρχρχομαι πρὸς ὑμᾶς. xiii. 2, ὡς παρὼν τὸ δεύτερον.

had, indeed, received a personal affront at the hands
of his opponents. For only in view of some such
occurrence can we understand the desire which he
expresses not again to come to them in distressing
circumstances ; not when he came a second time, to
undergo a "humiliation" among them (ii. 1, xii. 21).
And there is expressly mentioned in ii. 5 ff. a personal
insult to the apostle which was at the same time an
insult to the majority in the church : " If any have
caused pain, he has not pained me (alone), but you all,
or at least a part of you, not to say too much. . . .
To whom ye forgive anything, I forgive also ; just as
I, on my part, when I have forgiven anything, have
done so for your sakes, as in the presence of Christ."
To the same circumstances we must refer also vii. 12 :
" If I have written to you it was not for the sake of
the offender or the offended, but rather in order that
your zeal for us may be openly manifested in your
midst before God." That is, in order to evoke a
declaration of the loyal adherence of the majority of
the church to the person of the apostle, and therewith a formal disavowal of the mortification to which
he had been exposed at the hands of his opponents.
He means that it was not for the sake of avenging
himself upon the offenders, or of having satisfaction
made to himself as the aggrieved party,[1] that he had

[1] This explanation of τοῦ ἀδικηθέντος is the most appropriate to the
tenor of the whole passage, and also in view of the parallel in ii. 5.
On the other hand, to refer it to the incestuous person in 1 Cor. v. 1
is a complete misunderstanding which needs no refutation, since
there is not a word to favour it, but everything against it, and it
implies a complete failure to understand the whole situation of the
second epistle, which is entirely different from that to which the
first epistle applies.

written his previous letter; he wrote for the sake of the church itself, to rouse them from their temporary failure in duty and loyalty towards their founder and teacher, from whom they had for a moment allowed themselves to be estranged by the machinations and calumnies of his opponents. The same passage, moreover, vii. 8–12, shows us, further, that Paul immediately after the short visit which had been broken off with so harsh a discord, wrote, under the vivid impression of his painful experience, a severe letter, which in turn caused such pain to the Corinthian Christians that the tender-hearted apostle almost repented that he had spoken so sharply, while the report which Titus brought of the salutary effect of this letter gave him the more satisfaction because he had previously been anxious and troubled about the consequences (vii. 6–9). Of this same letter he says in ii. 4 that he had written out of much affliction and anguish of heart, with many tears, not in order to grieve them but to make them feel the jealous keenness of his love—since the warmest love is always the most jealous. That the epistle here alluded to is not our First Corinthians is self-evident, for the latter is neither written in great affliction and anguish of heart, nor could there be any ground for anxiety as to the reception of this calmly didactic letter. The only question is, Has that epistle, which must have been written between First Corinthians and Second Corinthians, been lost, or is it still extant?

Although this question cannot be answered with unhesitating confidence, it seems to me a very happy and probable conjecture that the letter in question has been preserved in the last four chapters of the

Second Epistle to the Corinthians.[1]   That these four
chapters, 2 Cor. x.–xiii., cannot have been written as
a continuation of the foregoing chapters i.–ix., admits,
in my opinion at least, of no doubt.   Not only is
there a difference in the prevailing tone in the two
parts—which might be explained by a change of
mood during the writing—but an exactly contrary
tone which cannot be explained even by supposing
that Paul had in view in the first part the majority
of the church, which was friendly to him, and in the
second the party of his opponents.   On an unprejudiced examination it is difficult to rid oneself of the
impression that in the second part the whole situation
both of the writer and the recipients of the letter
is a different, and, moreover, an earlier one.   Whereas
in chaps. i.–ix. the apostle has already made his
peace again with the Corinthian church and addresses
it with kindly gentleness, excusing, consoling, and
cheering it, in the last four chapters, on the contrary,
he is fiercely at feud with it and is obliged to defend
his rights as an apostle, and even his personal honour,
against its doubts.   So far from there being any
mention of forgiveness for his adversaries, not to
speak of intercession with the church on their behalf
(as in ii. 6–11), they are described in the most
vehement language as false apostles, as servants of
Satan.   And whereas according to vii. 11 the

[1] This hypothesis, which had previously been suggested by
Semler, Weber, and Weisse, was taken up again by Hausrath (*Der
Vier-Kapitelbrief*, 1870).   It is a pity that a somewhat perverse
method of presenting it has obscured the essential correctness of
the hypothesis.   It has been most thoroughly and instructively
defended against all possible objection by Schmiedel in the introduction to his commentary on the Epistles to the Corinthians.

church had again turned to the apostle with penitent zeal, there is no suggestion of this to be found in chaps. x.–xiii., but on the contrary everything tends to show that the whole church stood at the time under the influence of Paul's enemies. Otherwise the anxiety of the apostle in xi. 3, and his bitterly sarcastic references to the good-natured Corinthians who allowed themselves to be fleeced and plundered by deceitful swindlers (11, 18 ff.), would be hardly intelligible. This contradiction is certainly too remarkable to be explained by a mere subjective change of mood on the part of the writer, whereas it is easily explained on the hypothesis that chaps. x.–xiii. were written earlier than chaps. i.–ix. Apart from this, ii. 4 and vii. 8 ff., as we have pointed out above, imply a sharp letter of fault-finding and threatenings, written shortly before, and as we have a writing of this character actually before us in the fragment 2 Cor. x.–xiii., it is a very natural conjecture that the letter referred to in ii. 4 and vii. 8 is identical with that of which a fragment has been preserved to us in these four chapters. This conjecture is confirmed when we observe that in x. 1 Paul introduces himself in a fashion which is quite unnatural in the middle of a letter, and only becomes intelligible on the supposition that the writer here takes up the word on his own account after someone else had previously —or at any rate he in the name of someone else— had an explanation with the Corinthians. Who this other was we do not indeed know, but it is a natural conjecture that it may have been Timothy, who, according to 1 Cor. xvi. 10, had been in Corinth in the interval between the two epistles, and therefore

12

may well have been there at the time of Paul's second visit ; and in that case would certainly have suffered the same ill-treatment as the apostle. It is also quite possible that Timothy had been the *immediate* object of the hostile action, in which case the objective way in which "the injured one" is spoken of in vii. 12 would be even easier to explain than if we understood Paul himself thereby ; and as in any case the master would feel himself attacked through the disciple, Paul might feel himself the aggrieved party not less in one case than in the other, as occurs in ii. 5. That then, after hurrying away from Corinth, both teachers unburdened their hearts by letter of their complaints against the church which had suffered itself to be turned against them, is easy to suppose, and also that, in the letter, first Timothy had his say, and then Paul took up the word with the emphatic "I, Paul, speaking in my own person, exhort you." It would also be easily intelligible that the church should especially prize the portion of the letter of which Paul was the author, and, since it had not an independent commencement, add it to Paul's previous letter. These are of course mere conjectures which are far removed from certainty, but which are at any rate those best adapted to clear up in a more or less satisfactory fashion the obscurities of the second epistle, and especially of the relation of the second part to the first.

We have now, therefore, following the historical order, to examine first the "Four-Chapters" epistle, 2 Cor. x.-xiii., the polemic of which gives us a clear picture of the position of affairs as the apostle

found them at the time of his second visit. He
begins by admonishing the Corinthians not to give
him cause to show them when present in person the
boldness (trenchancy) in regard to which some (the
hostile partisans) asserted that he only dared to give
expression to it in his letters, while in his personal
bearing he showed the want of confidence of one who
was conscious of the unsoundness of his cause. On
the contrary, he knew himself to be, amid all the
weakness of his outward appearance, a soldier of God,
and possessed of weapons which were not carnal,
but through God were mighty to the overthrowing
of all strongholds which human sophism endeavoured
to set up against the true God, and to the bringing
into captivity of every thought under the obedience
of Christ; and he was ready to avenge all disobedience (upon those who had seduced them) so soon as
the church should have returned to full obedience
(which therefore was not the case up to this time).

After this vigorous exordium the apostle begins
(x. 7) his self-justification as against the Judaising
adversaries who were endeavouring to discredit him
in the eyes of his converts. In these opponents we
recognise the Peter-party of the first epistle, which
is not specially mentioned here only because in the
actual state of affairs it was regarded as the sole
hostile party. If these people boasted of outward
advantages, and arrogated to themselves the honour
of being Christ's ministers as their exclusive privilege,
he could claim that honour with much more reason.
No doubt he could not rival them in the effrontery
with which they praised themselves and thrust themselves into another's field of work; for not he that

praises himself is approved, but he whom the Lord
commends by the practical success of his work. At
the same time the Corinthians might well pardon
him now a little foolishness of boasting, for he in-
dulged in it only in the godly jealousy on behalf of
the Church which he was bringing, as a pure bride,
to Christ, and whose innocence he was now forced
to see endangered, like that of Eve through the
wiles of the serpent, since they were so ready to
allow another Jesus to be preached to them, and
another Spirit and another Gospel, not such as they
had received from him (namely, that Judaising
Christianity with its legalistic Spirit and Jewish
Messiah which the Judaisers were at this very time
endeavouring to force upon the Galatians also,
Gal. i. 7 f.). And yet he was, he held, not a whit
behind these "arch-apostles."[1] Even if he was
feeble of speech, yet he was not so in knowledge ;
that, he had demonstrated among them in everything.
Or was he, perhaps, supposed to have committed an
offence in abasing himself that they might be exalted,
inasmuch as he preached the Gospel to them freely
and preferred to be a charge upon other churches,
in order not to be burdensome to them ? But this
boast he will let no man take from him, in Achaia at
least. People who wish to find an excuse for their
own selfish claims shall not be able to refer to him.
Such men are false apostles, deceitful workers,

---

[1] By those who are ironically called ὑπερλίαν ἀπόστολοι are not
meant the Jerusalem apostles, but the same insinuating Judaisers
to whom the whole context refers. That they stood in more or
less close connection with the Jerusalem circles cannot be confidently asserted, though it is natural to suppose so.

ministers of Satan, who are only masquerading as apostles of Christ and ministers of righteousness. And wherein, then, consisted these advantages of which they boasted, and with which they were able to impose upon the clever Corinthians so that they allowed them to bring them into bondage, to plunder them, to smite them in the face? Apart from this insolent boldness, for which he, Paul, must certainly confess himself too weak, he would venture in other matters to measure himself with them. Hebrew, Israelite, of the seed of Abraham, minister of Christ —all these he also was, and he could—if he might for a moment speak as a fool—make good still higher claims for himself. Therewith the apostle recounts the sufferings which he had undergone from the beginning of his Christian course, and to which he was still daily exposed. In this weakness he glories. But if it was a question of giving his grounds for glorying he would recall his visions and revelations of the Lord; how fourteen years before he had been caught up into the third heaven—whether in the body or out of the body he could not tell—-and had heard in Paradise words which it was not lawful for man to utter. Yet there had been given him also to humble him a "stake in the flesh," an infirmity in which he felt the buffetings of the demonic powers, and his prayer for deliverance from this plague had been met with the divine answer: "My grace is sufficient for thee, for my strength is made perfect in weakness." Therefore will he rather glory in his infirmities, that the power of Christ may descend upon him. Finally he would remind them, since they themselves had compelled him to this boasting, that the signs

of an apostle, wonders and mighty deeds, had been
performed by him in their midst.

After giving this proof that he is in nothing
behind these "arch-apostles" whom the Corinthians
so much admired, he puts to them the question:
Wherein had they been at a disadvantage compared
with other churches, except in that he had not been
burdensome to them? This wrong he begs them to
forgive him; it will be the same at his next visit, for
he seeks not theirs, but them. Instead of demanding
a sacrifice from them, he would rather sacrifice himself on their behalf. Did he, because he loved them
with so exceeding a love, deserve to be less loved by
them? Had he ever given them any grounds for
the suspicion that he had caught them with guile,
had exploited them by those whom he sent to them?
Had not Titus behaved in the same spirit as himself?
These things he said, not for the sake of justifying
himself, but of edifying them, for he feared lest when
he came again they would have little joy in one
another, but that God was preparing a new humiliation for him—grief for the many sinners who had not
repented. But the next time he came to them, as he
had said on his last visit, and now repeated, he would
not spare them. They should, as they had desired it,
experience the power of "Christ speaking in him."
He begged them also to prove themselves, whether
Christ was in them. Not that he desired to demon-
strate his power to their hurt; he would rather he
himself appeared weak, and they strong; his one
concern was that they should be perfect. Therefore
he wrote these things now in order that he might not
be obliged when present in person to make a harsh

use of the power which was intended for edification and not for destruction. The contentious letter closes with a heartfelt aspiration after peace.

Soon after Paul had sent this epistle to the Corinthians by the hand of Titus, a fierce persecution by the incensed populace of Ephesus, in which he stood in utmost danger of his life, brought his activity there to an end (2 Cor. i. 8.; *cf.* Acts xix. 23–xx. 1). He then betook himself to Troas in the hope that he might there meet Titus on his return from Corinth ; and not finding him there, travelled on into Macedonia to meet him (ii. 12 ff.). Here, at length, he met Titus, and the news which the latter brought him of the effect of his epistle on the Corinthian church gave the anxious apostle the consoling certainty that he had won back again the church which had been half lost to him. His irate letter had moved them deeply, and brought them to reflection and repentance. The church which had been led astray now turned to him again and sought to atone for its injustice to him by vigorously taking the part of the injured apostle, so far as the majority of the church was concerned, and visiting their strong displeasure upon the instigators of the unhappy discord (vii. 8–12, ii. 6 f.). Thereupon Paul wrote from Macedonia another letter to the Corinthians to express his joy at their conversion, and to remove completely the last traces of annoyance or misunderstanding, in order that he might, in his contemplated third visit to them, be able to rejoice unreservedly in his complete reconciliation with his church. This, the third of our epistles (2 Cor. i.–ix.), is, like the second (2 Cor. x.–xiii.), mainly occupied with Paul's self-defence and his account of his apostolic activity, but the mood and tone are entirely different. Conciliatory gentleness and cheerful confidence take the place of violent polemic and bitter irony. The calm mood allows the self-justification to rise above the purely personal to more general and positive points of view, and to give expression to thoughts of the deepest nature.

The apostle begins by thanking God who comforts him in all tribulation, in order that he may be able to comfort his converts in their sufferings for Christ's sake. God had even now delivered him from sore distress and peril of death in Ephesus, and his hope was in God that He would still deliver him in answer to the intercession of the Corinthians on his behalf. On this he might reckon· with the more confidence, since his conscience testified that he had walked by the grace of God in genuine sincerity, not in fleshly wisdom, in relation to the world generally, and more especially towards the Corinthians. His letters were without ulterior meaning; there was nothing in them except what they understood from them, and would indeed understand even better in the future— as they had, in part at least, understood and recognised in the past—that he was their boast even as they were his. The reproach of ambiguity was undeserved even as regarded his plans of travel ; [1] his word to them had never been yea and nay at the same time, any more than Jesus Christ Himself was yea and nay, in whom was given the fulfilling yea to all the promises

---

[1] .The alterations of plans here implied can hardly be completely cleared up, since we cannot tell what Paul had planned and promised in this respect at the time of his second visit to Corinth.

of God. Moreover, they might be assured that it was only from his desire to spare them that he had not come sooner ; he did not want to lord it over their faith, but to be the helper and partaker of their joy ; therefore he desired to let the clouds of dejection pass away before making another visit. To the same end, in order to clear up the dissensions by letter first, he had written his last epistle to them amid great affliction and anguish of heart, with many tears, not to grieve them, but that they might know the exceeding love which he had towards them. Now that this end was attained, since the majority in the church had inflicted a rebuke upon the instigator of the injury which had been done to them and him alike, he begged them now to pardon this person, as he himself had pardoned him for their sake, so that Satan might not bring trouble upon them. The thought of the satisfactory effect of the letter written amid so much affliction, leads the apostle, at the close of this first, wholly personal, section, to give thanks to God who always caused him to triumph, and everywhere made manifest the savour of the knowledge of Christ through him—to some for salvation, to others for destruction. In this success lay the practical proof that he did not, as some did, preach the Gospel from greed of gain, but with pure motive, ever conscious of his mission from God and responsibility towards God (ii. 17).

When about to pass, in iii. 1 ff., to a defence of his conduct of his apostolic office which moves on the higher plane of the principles of the Gospel, he guards himself first against the reproach which had been brought against him, especially on the ground of his

last letter, that he was constantly commending himself.
He turns the reproach by an allusion to the letters of
commendation by means of which his Judaising
adversaries had gained admission for themselves in
Corinth. Such letters of commendation he had
no need of, since the Corinthian church was itself a
living letter of commendation given to him by God
(iii. 1–3). He did not ascribe to himself any sufficiency
in his own strength; his only sufficiency was given
him by God for the service of the new covenant, the
essence of which was not the " letter which killeth "
but " the Spirit which giveth life," not condemnation
but righteousness, not bondage but freedom, as much
more glorious than the old covenant as the splendour
which streams from the face of Christ, the image of
God, upon His people, is more glorious than the
transient splendour upon the face of Moses (at the
giving of the law). Therefore the servant of the
new covenant can act with frank open-heartedness ;
he needs no veil like Moses, he knows no bashful
timidity, he disdains to act covertly as though
ashamed, he scorns all craftiness and deceitful hand-
ling of the word of God ; and seeks only by manifestation of the truth to commend himself to every man's
conscience in the sight of God. Since he preaches
not himself but Christ Jesus the Lord, the knowledge
of whom God had caused to arise in his heart like the
radiant light, he knows that his gospel is not veiled
for any except the lost, whose mind has been blinded
by the spirit of this world and made insensible to the
glorious splendour of Christ the image of God
(iii. 4–iv. 6).

It was true, he bore this exceeding power of God

in a weak earthen vessel. The splendour of the evangelical office had as its reverse afflictions and persecutions of every kind, amid which, however, he had never lost heart, for he saw therein only the dying of Jesus, which he, in imitating the sufferings of Jesus, bore in his body, and therefore they were at the same time the pledges that the living power of Jesus would manifest itself in him, as well as in the church for whose sake he bore all this. His present affliction, by which his outer man was being worn out, was the means of a daily inward renewal, and won for him a far more exceeding and eternal weight of glory, which is in store for those who look not at the things which are seen but upon the things which are not seen. If our earthly tabernacle is dissolved, we have a building of God, eternal in the heavens, a habitation which we now, under the oppression of our bodily existence, desire with painful eagerness to enter into for ever. Yet since God has given us "the earnest of the Spirit," we are even now always confident, as we walk in faith, not by sight, gladly though we would exchange our home in the body for our home with the Lord. Whether here below, or above, the main thing is to be well-pleasing to Christ, before whose judgment-seat we must all appear in order to receive the reward of the things done in the body (iv. 7–v. 10).

It is precisely this conscientious striving to please the Lord which is, Paul goes on to assure the Corinthians, the sole motive of his activity in his apostolic office, of his efforts to win men. He can appeal to God and to their own consciences to testify to his sincerity. They must give him this witness

in face of those whose reputation was founded on outward appearance and not on inner reality. Whether
he appeared beside himself or over-astute (both reproaches were brought against him by his opponents),
he looked ever to God and their cause. For he felt
himself constrained by the love of Christ, since, surely,
the lives of all belong to Him who died for all. Therefore from henceforth we must estimate no one—not
even Christ—according to his outward manifestation;
whoever is in Christ is a new creature, for whom
old things are passed away and new have come into
being. But that is the work of God, who has through
Christ reconciled the world unto Himself, making the
sinless the bearer of the guilt of sin for us, that we in
Him might become possessors of the righteousness of
God. And it is God who causes this reconciliation
to be offered to the world through the ambassadors of
Christ, who in His name beseech men to be reconciled with God (v. 11–21).

After portraying in the foregoing chapters (iii.–v.)
the office of a missionary of the gospel in the splendour
of the faith which he proclaimed, the hope which was
his goal, and the love by which he was sustained, he
comes at last to speak of his own conduct in his
office, and shows how he had endeavoured to prove
himself in every situation a blameless minister of
God, not turned aside either by honour or dishonour,
through good or ill report, " as deceivers, and yet
true; as unknown, and yet well known; as dying, and
behold we live; as chastened, and not killed; as sorrowful, yet always rejoicing; as poor, yet making many
rich; as having nothing, and yet possessing all things."
And as his heart has thus been opened to the

Corinthians, he begs them that they in their turn will open their closed hearts to him.[1] He had desired only the good of all of them, had drawn them into his heart to live and die with them; he was full of confidence and glorying on their behalf, full of comfort and joy. He could no longer regret that he had grieved them by his last letter (chaps. x.–xiii.), since this grief had wrought a wholesome repentance and a turning to good, and thereby the aim of this letter had been fulfilled. Titus also shared this confidence and rejoicing (vi. 1–vii. 16).

In the last section (chaps. viii. and ix.) he goes on to speak of the arrangements for the collection, admonishing them—pointing to the good example set by the Macedonians, and to the pattern of Christ Himself, who for our sakes exchanged His heavenly riches for earthly poverty—to give with liberality, each according to his means. He desires also to take with him when he goes to deliver the gift, a deputation chosen from the church, as a security against malicious calumnies regarding his honesty in the application of the money. As a consequence of this rich gift he hopes that many will with him thank and praise God for this proof of obedience to the gospel and the loyal and loving fellowship of the Corinthians with all Christians; and so concludes with an expression of thankfulness to God for His unspeakable

[1] The section vi. 14–vii. 1 is out of place here, as it evidently breaks the connection between vi. 13 and vii. 2, which manifestly belong together. If the intervening verses were written by Paul they must have belonged to a previous epistle; it is possible that they originally followed 1 Cor. vi., but it is also possible that we have in them a fragment of the lost Epistle to the Corinthians which was the first of the series.

gift (ix. 13).   The formal conclusion of the epistle
has either fallen out, owing to the addition of the
" Four-Chapters Epistle " (see above), or alternatively
—and this is probable—is to be sought in xiii. 11 ff.,
since the words there, " Rejoice, be perfect, be of good
comfort, be of one mind, be peaceable, and the God
of love and of peace be with you," seem much more
appropriate to the final letter of reconciliation than
to the previous letter of condemnation.

The last Epistle to the Corinthians has, no doubt,
like the second, the self-justification of the apostle as
its main topic, and it is not wanting in occasional
thrusts at his opponents (*cf.* i. 12 ; ii. 17 ; iii. 1, 15 ;
iv. 2 f. ; v. 12, 16 ; vi. 8 f. ; vii. 2 ; viii. 20), but the
defence rises above the purely personal attitude of
the previous letter to questions of principle, and
thereby takes its place alongside of the epistles to
the Galatians and Romans, to which it also stands
near in point of time, as of equal rank.   Controversy,
on the other hand, takes quite a subordinate place,
in incidental allusions, as is natural, since the apostle
now knows the majority of the church to be on
his side; it is only like the last rumbling echo of
a storm which is passing away, after discharging its
tremendous thunder-claps (x.–xiii.).   That this letter
effected a complete reconciliation may be inferred as
probable, since the Epistle to the Romans, written
shortly afterwards from Corinth, manifests a calm and
peaceful mood on the part of the apostle.

CHAPTER IX

THE LETTER TO THE GALATIANS

THE answer to the question as to when the churches to which this letter is addressed were founded, depends on where we have to seek them, whether in the district of Galatia upon the Halys, inhabited by a Celtic population, or in the Roman province of Galatia, which, in addition to that district, included the districts of Pisidia, Phrygia, and Lycaonia. The following reasons seem decisively in favour of the latter : (1) Paul elsewhere in his designation of places uniformly employs the official Roman names of provinces, not the ethnic names. It is in the former, not in the latter, sense that he speaks of Syria, Cilicia, Asia, Macedonia, and Achaia ; it is therefore extremely improbable that he made an exception in the case of Galatia only, and understood thereby only the little strip of territory with Celtic inhabitants on the Halys, instead of the very much more extensive Province.[1] (2) It is improbable that Paul could have

---

[1] It is true that Schürer, in the *Jahrb. f. prot. Theol.*, 1892, endeavoured to establish the proof that no one ever understood by Galatia, at least in the period which has here to be considered, anything but Galatia proper in the narrower sense ; but Theodor

founded in the region of Galatia several flourishing churches, since the use of the Celtic language, which was still prevalent there, would have placed serious difficulties in the way of his missionary activity ; and why should the apostle have turned at all to the non-Greek-speaking heathen of Asia Minor, so long as there remained everywhere so many Greek-speaking heathen to be converted ?   And would he have spoken in an epistle to Celtic readers of Jews and Greeks? (iii. 28).   Would it not have been more correct to say " barbarians " instead of Greeks ?   (3) It is improbable that no trace should remain in tradition of the foundation of the Galatian churches which attained

Zahn (*Einleitung in d. N.T.*, i. 123 ff.) has convincingly proved that the establishment of the Roman provinces, while it did not banish the old ethnic names, did give rise to the use of a new terminology. Romans like Pliny the Elder, Tacitus, and the geographer Ptolemy, understood by Galatia the whole province.   Paul could address his readers, even if they were not of Galatic, *i.e.* of Celtic, race, as " Galatians " in view of their belonging to the Roman province, just as at the present day the Frankish inhabitants of Würzburg are called Bavarians, although they have not been united with the Bavarian national territories very much longer than the Lycaonians had at that time been united with the Galatic tribes in the province of Galatia.   The more various was the composition of a circle of Christians in regard to nationality, the more natural was it in addressing them to choose a designation unconnected with nationality and drawn from the political district in which they lived.   This view has been supported by Hausrath, Weizsäcker, and Renan, and lately by the English scholar Ramsay (*St Paul the Traveller and Roman Citizen*, 1892), who also understands in Acts xvi. 6 and xviii. 23, by τὴν Φρυγίαν καὶ Γαλατικὴν χώραν or τὴν Γαλατικὴν χώραν καὶ Φρυγίαν, not Galatia in the narrower sense, but the Phrygian country so far as it belongs to the Roman province of Galatia.   This is contested by Zahn, who, however, remarks with justice that the linguistic usage of Luke is in no case decisive for that of Paul.

such importance, as would be the case if we had to think of churches in the Celtic region. The foundation of these could thus only have taken place on the journey through this region which is mentioned in Acts xvi. 6, but so far from there being any mention here of the foundation of churches, it is directly excluded by the statement that Paul was forbidden by the Holy Spirit to preach the word in Asia.[1]

If, on the other hand, we understand by the Galatian churches those in the Roman province of Galatia, to

---

[1] It has no doubt been remarked in opposition to this that Acts is in general fragmentary, giving, e.g., no account of the foundation of the Roman church, and it might have a special reason for drawing a veil over the founding of the Galatian churches on account of the unsatisfactory state of affairs which obtained there. But the case of the church at Rome, which was not founded by Paul, is quite different. In the case of the Galatian churches there would, according to the traditional view, be a deliberate concealment of their having been founded; and that is surely very improbable. A hypothesis has, it is true, been proposed which seems to offer a way of escape from this difficulty, namely that Paul did not intend any permanent missionary activity in the Galatic region, but was obliged by the accident of his falling ill to make a short stay there, of which the foundation of these churches was the fruit. Against this theory, however, it may be pointed out (1) that the statement in Acts xvi. 6, "at all in Asia," is too definitely worded to leave room for the supposition of a missionary work which, however accidentally caused, must at all events have been of some duration ; and (2) that the supposition of an illness being the cause of a missionary work is too strange and improbable to make that interpretation of iv. 13 satisfactory. Instead of δι' ἀσθένειαν τῆς σαρκὸς εὐηγγελισάμην ὑμῖν τὸ πρότερον, we ought perhaps to read δι ἀσθενείας, or even if the text stands it should doubtless be translated "amid weakness of the flesh." Besides this, it is to be noticed that the τὸ πρότερον = "the former time," does not necessarily refer to the first visit to Galatia, on which the church was founded. In any case this very obscure reference furnishes no argument against the South Galatian theory, which rests on the grounds given above.

13

which belonged Phrygians, Pisidians, and Lycaonians, the above-mentioned difficulty is completely solved by the fact that their foundation falls in the first missionary journey of Paul, which is narrated in Acts xiii. and xiv., and, moreover, on the basis of a first-hand description, as is indicated by the exact record of the route of travel. The cities through which, according to this narrative, Paul and Barnabas travelled —Antioch, Iconium, Lystra, and Derbe—were therefore the seats of the Galatian churches. The Galatian churches were thus founded on Paul's first missionary journey, soon after the Apostolic Council. That the council preceded this journey is rendered extremely probable by Gal. i. 20–ii. 1, according to which Paul, previous to the Apostolic Council, had not gone beyond Syria and Cilicia, for which reason, too, the apostolic decree is only addressed to the Gentile Christians of these countries and not to the Galatians also (*cf.* what is said below on Acts xi. 30, xv. 1). Paul subsequently visited the Galatian churches on two occasions (Acts xvi. 1–6, xviii. 23). The customary assumption that the Epistle to the Galatians was written soon after the visit in Acts xvi. is extremely improbable, and derives no support from Gal. i. 6, since there is no indication that the words "so soon" imply a short interval since the last visit.[1]

[1] See Steck, *Galaterbrief*, p. 42. "It is absurd to understand it as describing a mere interval of weeks or months. Even if the Galatians had not turned to another gospel until twenty years after their conversion, that would still be in Paul's estimation much too soon." A change of religious attitude such as that in the Galatian churches, which expressed itself in the "keeping of days, months, seasons, and years" (v. 10), necessarily implies a longer period than a few weeks or months.

Moreover, the persecution of Paul by Jewish opponents mentioned in v. 11 is not appropriate to this early period, is not indeed appropriate to a situation earlier than which obtained at the time of the Second Epistle to the Corinthians. The same period is indicated by the affirmation in ii. 10 that he had been active about the collection for the poor of Judæa, for it implies an action which had been completed, and this we find to be the case in the Second Epistle to the Corinthians, but not earlier. If we take into consideration also the remarkable affinity in vocabulary, purpose, and thought[1] of the Epistle to the Galatians, Second Corinthians, and Romans, the hypothesis that Galatians was composed between the other two becomes extremely probable. The complaints of the apostle in 2 Cor. vii. 5 and xi. 28 f., about "fightings without and fears within," which the "care of all the churches" caused him, since their weakness and the attacks to which they were exposed caused him to suffer with them, are explained most easily by supposing that just at this time anxiety about the seduction of the Galatians was added to that about the errors at Corinth. The latest news about this ill turn of affairs, and therewith the immediate occasion of the writing of the letter, may have come to the apostle from Gaius of Derbe, who appears in Acts xx. 4 as one of the companions of Paul on his journey from Corinth to Jerusalem, and therefore probably joined Paul some time before, bringing the collection of the Galatian churches.

---

[1] Pointed out by Clemen in his *Chronologie der Paulin. Briefe*, p. 281 ff. The above view is shared by Bleek, Lightfoot, and Brückner; Jülicher, too, is inclined to this hypothesis.

The opponents of Paul in the Galatian churches were Judaising agitators of the same type as at Corinth. They troubled the churches by endeavouring to turn them away from the gospel which Paul had brought to them, to another gospel, namely, to that of the Judaising Christianity which held fast to the recognition of the Mosaic law alongside of the Christian faith. The tactics of these agitators, too, were everywhere the same. The main point was to oust Paul, with whose personal authority the gospel of liberty was at the first inseparably bound up, from his position of influence with his own churches. They endeavoured, therefore, to persuade them that Paul had no independent apostolic authority, since he had not received either his call to apostleship or his knowledge of the Gospel directly from Jesus Himself. He knew nothing of Jesus' preaching concerning the kingdom except from the tradition preserved by the immediate disciples of Jesus; therefore he had no independent authority to teach as an apostle, but was the subordinate and envoy of the true apostles, and was bound to abide by their authoritative opinion. Accordingly, his gospel ought to be judged by the view prevailing in the mother-church, and as, according to this, the obligations of the Mosaic law upon the Christian congregations remained inviolate, the contrary teaching of Paul was proved to be a false gospel. If he had been able heretofore to preserve an appearance of harmony with the original apostles, that was to be explained by the dishonesty with which he framed his speech to be acceptable in all quarters; among the Jews he behaved as a Jew, but among the Gentiles he repudiated Judaism in order to curry favour with them.

Moreover, his aims were as insincere as his double-tongued dealings; he only pretended to seek their welfare, in reality he sought only honour for himself, the vainglory of an apostolic dignity which he had arrogated to himself. How could he, then, be their true friend when he wished only to allow them to become semi-Christians, and prevented them from obtaining, by incorporation with the People of Promise, a full share in the blessings of the Messianic kingdom? For it was clear that only those could have a part in the promises given to the seed of Abraham who belonged to the commonwealth of Israel, whether by birth or by voluntary incorporation with it by means of circumcision. All the promises of salvation were conditional on circumcision and the fulfilment of the law of Moses, for it was written, "He that doeth it shall live." How, then, could teaching be true which declared, in contradiction to the Holy Scriptures, that the doing of the law was unnecessary and was set aside by faith? To what end, then, had God given the law unto the Fathers by Moses, if not to the end that it should be fulfilled, and by being fulfilled make the people of God worthy of the blessing of Abraham? And why had the Messiah Jesus appeared, if not in order to lead His people to the fulfilment of the law, and thereby to prepare them to receive the blessings of the promised kingdom? Only in following the law did the special dignity of the people of God consist; apart from the law they stood on the same level as the heathen whose life was ruled by the unbridled impulses of the flesh. The Pauline doctrine of emancipation from the law was not only untrue from the point of view of religion, because in contradic-

tion with the revelation of God given to the Fathers,
but also morally destructive; it gave the flesh a
charter of liberty to fulfil its lusts. Therefore, if the
Galatians desired to share in the Messianic salvation,
they had no choice save to be, at the least, circumcised, and to keep the Jewish feasts, even if they need
not in other matters follow the customs prescribed by
the law quite strictly.

Somewhat to this effect ran the arguments by
which the agitators sought to win the Galatians for
their Jewish Christianity. And they produced in this
way so powerful an impression that Paul speaks of
his converts as being " bewitched." What made the
power of this witchcraft we can conjecture. In the
first place, it is not to be denied that, admitting the
assumption of the divine origin of the law, the Jewish
manner of thought was simpler and clearer to the
minds of ordinary men than the elaborate dialectic by
which Paul reached his anti-Judaising results. A
further point was the appeal of his opponents to the
views of the original apostles, who had had the
advantage, as compared with Paul, of being immediate
disciples of Christ. That these men would be able
to give better information as to the teaching of
Christ than Paul could, who had never known Him
personally, was, again, to the ordinary man, a more
convincing argument than Paul's appeal to the
revelation given by a spiritual and heavenly Christ.
Finally, the ceremonial of Judaism appealed much
more strongly to the natural instincts of the Galatians,
who had just been converted from heathenism, than
the spiritual service of mere faith, and for their moral
conduct, too, a firm rein such as the law offered might

still appear advantageous, since love, the inner spiritual motive on which Paul laid all emphasis, was not for everyone. When, moreover, the astute agitators told people that if they allowed themselves to be circumcised, and kept the Jewish feasts, they need not be strict in their observance of the other burdensome ordinances of the law, but might observe them or not as they pleased (v. 3), it was very natural that many should think an experiment in this direction could do no harm. Thus they had already gone the length of keeping days and months and festivals and years (iv. 10), and therewith had fallen back into a worship of the elements of the world similar to their former heathen cultus. They had not actually undergone circumcision, but this step had been seriously considered. It was true the authority of Paul was still respected in the church, and they had at his second or third visit again felt the powerful influence of his personality and testified their zeal towards him (iv. 18). But he had on the last visit strongly opposed the Judaising efforts and tendencies and relentlessly urged the truth[1] upon all, and this had produced an irritation which the agitators turned to account and increased by representing that Paul had become their enemy (iv. 16, 12), and had abandoned

---

[1] This ἀληθεύειν (iv. 16), which points to the anti-Judaising polemic, is not likely to have taken place at the second visit to Galatia (Acts xvi. 1 ff.) at a time when the Judaising agitation was still in its less dangerous beginnings, and was confined to Antioch in Syria; we should refer it rather to the third visit to the Galatians when Paul was returning from Antioch to Ephesus (Acts xviii. 23 and xix. 1). According to the noteworthy reading of Cod. D. Paul was at that time prevented by the "Spirit" from the carrying out of his purpose to journey to Jerusalem (see below on Acts

them, and that they had therefore the more reason
to join their new friends the Judaisers. The news of
this turn of affairs, which Paul had probably received
during his last journey to Corinth, or on his last visit
there (57 or 58 A.D.), gave the occasion for the
writing of his Letter to the Galatians, that splendid
monument of his lofty religious genius. We may
divide it into three parts, of which the first (chaps. i.
and ii.) meets the personal attacks of his adversaries
by a narrative of his Christian course; the second
(chaps. iii. and iv.) proves the truth of his doctrine from
Scripture and experience, the third (chaps. v. and vi.)
exhorts them to use the true freedom, which is not of
the flesh but of the Spirit.

At the very beginning, in his opening address,
Paul emphasises the independence of his apostolic
dignity, given him, not by man, but by Jesus Christ.
Then he proceeds, without further digression, to
express his painful surprise at the fickleness of the
Galatians in giving heed to men who professed to
offer them another gospel, whereas they were only
distorting the one true Gospel. They should take
it as an axiom that whosoever preached to them
another gospel should be accursed. This was his
answer to the assertion of his opponents that he was

---

xix. 1). · As such indications of the Spirit had usually a basis in real
circumstances, the conjecture is natural that Paul received news in
the course of this journey through Syria of the violence and extent
of the Judaising agitation, of which the centre was Jerusalem. It
appears, therefore, that this marks the beginning of the systematic
campaign of the Judaising agitators against the Gentile congregations founded by Paul, the success of which we observe in the
disorders which manifested themselves in Galatia and Corinth at
about the same time.

a hypocritical person who adapted his speech to please everybody, and bowed to every authority. But that his gospel was not of man nor of human origin, but had been given to him by revelation from Christ, was proved by the facts of his life-history. Once a strict Jew and zealous for the law, he had been called by the grace of God, who had revealed His Son in him, in order to proclaim the Gospel among the heathen. Thereupon he had not, in the first place, sought counsel from men; in particular, not from the older apostles, but rather, instead of going to Jerusalem, he had gone into Arabia and thence returned again to Damascus. Not till three years later had he made a fourteen-days' visit to Peter, and had at that time also seen James, but no other member of the church. During the following fourteen years of his missionary activity in Syria and Cilicia he had remained personally unknown to the churches of Judæa, and therefore in no relation of dependence upon them. Subsequently at his second visit to Jerusalem, when discussions arose concerning his preaching of the gospel to the heathen, he had not for a moment yielded to the claims on behalf of the law which were advanced by the false brethren; while on the part of the men of highest standing (whose past experience made no matter to him, since God accepteth no man's person) there was no attempt to question his independence, but an admission of the right of himself and Barnabas, in view of the blessing upon their mission to which its success bore witness, to continue the same line of independent missionary activity. Thus they had parted on that occasion in brotherly concord. Later, it is true, a conflict had arisen in Antioch with Peter, but through the fault of the latter, because he had repudiated on the arrival of emissaries from Jerusalem the freedom which he had begun to practise; and had led astray others with him, including Barnabas, into this hypocrisy, whereupon he, Paul, had earnestly urged upon him before the whole church the inconsistency and unchristian character of this conduct.

Having thus repelled the attack made by his opponents on the independence of his apostolic authority, he goes on (iii. 1 ff.) to establish positively the truth of his gospel. He first reminds the Galatians of their own Christian experience, that it was not legal observances and ceremonies, but simply faith in the crucified Christ, vividly portrayed before their eyes, by means of which they had received the Spirit and experienced the divine wonder-working power. How could they now be so void of understanding as to endeavour to complete in the flesh, that is, in the legal sphere, what they had begun in the Spirit? The paramount importance of faith is confirmed in many points by the history of Abraham (verses 6–18). It is said of him that his faith was reckoned to him for righteousness; therefore believers are the true sons of Abraham and heirs of the promises. Moreover, he was told "in thee shall all the Gentiles be blessed." Therefore it is implied from the outset that God will justify the heathen by faith. Further, the promises were given to him and to "his seed"; this single seed is Christ, with whom believers are united and are therefore partakers of His blessing. Finally, the promise was given to him as long as 430 years before the law; therefore, as a valid legal agreement cannot be annulled by subsequent conditions, the Divine promises could not afterwards be invalidated by having the condition of the law appended to them. Such a condition would contradict the essence of the promise, since the promise rests upon faith, but the law on works. In the one case the word is : The just shall live by faith ; in the other : Cursed is everyone who doeth not all that is written in the law—and that, Paul tacitly assumes, no one can do. Thus everyone who rests his confidence in the works of the law is under a curse. From this curse of the law, Christ has redeemed us by His accursed death — for such, according to the law, was the death on the cross — in order that instead of the curse of the law the blessing of Abraham might be given to the Gentiles, and so we might receive the promised Spirit through faith instead of through works of the law.

But if the law can contribute nothing to the fulfilment of the promise, of what possible use is it ? So the Judaisers had demanded. To this Paul replies (iii. 19–iv. 7), it was added because of transgressions, and, indeed, not directly by God, who was the sole giver of the promise, but by the administration of angels and through human mediation, this very fact betraying its subordinate position.[1]

---

[1] The words of iii. 19b and 20, ἐν χειρὶ μεσίτου· ὁ δὲ μεσίτης ἑνὸς οὐκ ἔστιν, ὁ δὲ θεὸς εἷς ἐστιν, refer back to Levit. xxvi. 46, LXX., where it is said of the law that the Lord gave it ἀνὰ μέσον αὐτοῦ καὶ ἀνὰ μέσον τῶν υἱῶν Ἰσραήλ ἐν χειρὶ Μωυσῆ. A mediator has nothing to do with a single person, but has his place when a matter lies between (ἀνὰ μέσον) two parties, where a covenant-relation is to be established between two or more contracting parties. That was not the case with the promise to which God on His own part gave binding force ;

But the law is not on that account opposed to the promise; on the contrary, it serves the ends of the latter in that, like the ruler of a prison or a house of discipline, it held mankind in the bonds of sin until Christ came. With His appearance its pædagogic function is at an end, and faith takes its place, making us free sons of God and all one in Christ, so that there remains therefore now no spiritual prerogative to the sons of Abraham after the flesh; all who belong to Christ, the true seed of Abraham, are the rightful heirs to the promise. When under the restraints of the law, we were in the position of an heir who is still in his nonage; we did not possess the full right of sonship and heirship, but were still under bondage to the elements of the world.[1]

But now, when God has sent His Son into the world to redeem us from the law, and has sent the Spirit of His Son into our hearts to awaken our childlike trust, we are no more servants, but sons, and so heirs by the Divine adoption. Therefore it is inconceivable that those who have once known God as their Father

---

but it did apply to the giving of the law, as the concluding of a treaty between God's plenipotentiaries, the angels, on the one hand, and the people of Israel, on the other. Thus, in this point also, the inferiority of the law is manifested in comparison with the promise, which cannot therefore be annulled by it.

[1] By στοιχεῖα τοῦ κόσμου are meant the powers of nature which all antiquity thought of as living and semi-divine beings; and on them not only the heathen, but also in a certain sense the Jewish, cultus (cp. the Feast of the New Moon) was dependent. How widespread this conception was among the Jews we see from the Book of Jubilees, where in chap. ii. there are mentioned the spirits of Fire, Wind, Clouds, Storm, and of special years and days, and also in Enoch, where in chap. lxxxiv. the angels of the stars appear as the " Rulers of the Seasons."

should desire to have recourse again to the service of the beggarly world-elements by continuing to keep Jewish moon-feasts, as they had formerly kept heathen moon-feasts.   To do that would be to exchange one form of bondage to the world for another, and they would have gained in truth nothing; Paul's work among them would have been in vain.

This brings the apostle back again to the point from which this exhortation started.   He appeals once again (iv. 12–20) to the Galatians' own experience, reminds them of their blessed enthusiasm and self-devotion on his behalf, when he, a sick and suffering man, preached the Gospel to them the former time. If their feelings were now different the blame did not lie on him, as though he were their enemy because he told them the truth, but to the fact they had listened to the persuasive tongues of false and selfish zealots, instead of continuing constant in their former zeal for good, not only in his presence, but in his absence. He concludes with the moving appeal: "My little children, of whom I travail in birth again until Christ be formed in you, would that I might be present with you again and use every tone of appeal to you, for I am in despair about you."

This properly forms the transition to the third, hortatory, section (v. 1 ff.), but before entering on this, he inserts an addendum to the Scriptural argument (iv. 21–31).   According to the allegorical exegesis of his time, he sees in the bond-maid Hagar, whose name resembles in sound the Arabic name (Hahar) of Mount Sinai, a symbol of the earthly Jerusalem which, along with her children, is now in bondage (political and religious); in Sarai, on the other hand, a symbol of the heavenly Jerusalem above, which is the mother of the free. As once Ishmael the son of the bondwoman persecuted Isaac the son of the freewoman, so now again the children of the earthly Jerusalem, *i.e.* the Jews, persecute the children of the heavenly Jerusalem, the kingdom of Christ, *i.e.* the Christians. But now, too, the word spoken to Abraham applies; the handmaid and her son shall be cast out, for the son of the bond-woman shall not inherit with the son of the free-woman. That is, Christians alone shall be the rightful heirs of Abraham; the natural sons of Abraham, *i.e.* the unbelieving Jews, shall be dis-inherited.

After thus arguing that Christ has freed us from bondage, and given us liberty, he adds in the last section the exhortation to abide in this liberty and to see that it is a true liberty (v. 1 ff.). To fall back into the servitude of bondage to the law would be to fall away from Christ and from grace, for in Christ neither circumcision is anything, nor uncircumcision, but faith which worketh by love. Those who are seeking to persuade them to keep the law are tempters, on whom God's judgment shall fall. They cannot appeal to his (Paul's) example, for if he still preached circumcision he would no longer be persecuted, the offence of the cross would have ceased (inasmuch as that lay for the Jewish consciousness in the antinomian implications of the Pauline theory and practice). The recollections of the virulent persecution which these Judaising fanatics directed against him wrings from the apostle the bitter jest, he would that these enthusiasts for circumcision would cut themselves off and have done with it.

But of course this freedom to which Christ has called them must be understood, in conformity with their calling, as a freedom from bondage to the sinful flesh as well as from the vain elements of the world. Liberation from the law must not give free rein to the caprices of sensuous impulse, but inspire to the service of love, in which the permanent ethical content of the whole law comes to fulfilment (v. 13 ff.). The apostle then sketches in broad outlines the works of the flesh, in which the sensuous and selfish impulses of human nature find expression, in contrast with the fruits of the Spirit, in which the new life awakened by Christ unfolds itself into the Christian virtues. As, in the case of those who belong to Christ, this new life in the Spirit is already present, it is a natural demand that in their conduct they should make use of and verify it. Vain and selfish factiousness was not in accordance with it, but modest self-restraint, the brotherly sharing of each in the burden of the rest, and, especially, harmonious co-operation with their teachers in all good. Since God does not suffer Himself to be mocked, let each be mindful of his responsibility for his actions, for the harvest will be according to the sowing. Therefore we should be unwearied in well-doing towards all, especially towards the household of faith.

In conclusion, the apostle recapitulates once more (vi. 11–18), in rapid vigorous strokes, the main thoughts of the epistle. Whereas in the case of Judaising agitators their chief concern is not the law,

about the fulfilment of which they are not themselves
too sedulous, but the glory to be gained for themselves by a successful propaganda, he on the contrary
can testify of himself that he desires to glory in
nothing else than in the cross of Christ, by means of
which the world is crucified to him, and he to the
world. Those who walk according to this rule are
a new creation and the true Israel of God, raised
above pre-Christian oppositions of a national and
religious character. Therefore henceforth let them
spare him such useless trouble, for he bears the scars
of a soldier of Jesus on his body.

The genuineness of the Epistle to the Galatians
has lately been called in question again by Loman,
van Manen, and Steck, following in the track of
Bruno Bauer, partly on the ground that it betrays in
some particulars dependence upon Corinthians and
Romans, partly on the ground that its strong anti-
Judaism must be later than the milder standpoint of
the other so-called Pauline epistles, and of the whole
body of the representative neutral literature of early
Christianity ; in particular, than that of the Acts of
the Apostles. The first argument rests in general
upon exaggeration, and perverse interpretation of the
actual relationship between Galatians and Second
Corinthians and Romans, which is easily explained
from their having been written about the same time ;
in details, too, there are some curious misunderstandings, as when, for example, in Gal. v. 21, " as
I said before " is interpreted as a reference to 1 Cor.
vi. 9 f. instead of to his teaching previously given
to the Galatians by word of mouth. Or when the
mediation of angels at the giving of the law, spoken

of in Gal. iii. 19, is explained as due to Gnostic
influence, whereas it is certainly found in Jewish
theology too (*cf.* Josephus, *Ant.* xv. 5, 3).   As regards
the second point, which is properly the main argument of these critics, it rests on an *a priori* theory of
development which cannot be maintained in the face
of the facts of history.   New ideas are usually at
their first appearance in the mind of the pioneers of
thought, not more faintly, but more strongly outlined
than in the case of their successors, who put the new
idea into practice, a process which is not accomplished
without compromises.   Holtzmann rightly remarks:
" What arrangement of Luther's writings would we
arrive at, if the order were decided by a standard of
regular development, whereas it was really determined
by the incalculable impulses and reactions of the
inner life! The breach of Luther with Zwingli
ought not to precede the tentatives of Melancthon,
Bucer, etc.,[1] if the history of the Reformation is to
follow the lines laid down by reason."   The spurious-
ness of Galatians would have as its consequence that
of all the Epistles of Paul hitherto accepted.   It
would, moreover, be impossible to explain the Pauline
elements in the writings of Luke, in the First Epistle
of Peter and the First Epistle of Clement, in the
Epistle to the Hebrews, etc., if the epistles of Paul
did not precede them.   Further, a Janus-headed
theology like the Pauline, which overthrows the Jewish
religion by the methods of proof drawn from the
Jewish schools, is perfectly intelligible in the case of
the historic Paul, who was converted from a pupil of
the Pharisees to an apostle of Christ; it would be

[1] Viz., their efforts to promote closer relations with the Zwinglians.

14

wholly unintelligible in a "Pauline Christian" of the second century. Finally, the realistic features of the life of the young church, the strife of parties, the phenomena of enthusiasm, the still quite undeveloped beginnings of church organisation which meet us in the Pauline epistles, are evidently taken directly from actual experience in a way which makes it impossible to explain them as a fiction of the second century.

CHAPTER X

THE LETTER TO THE ROMANS

THE Christian church at Rome was at the time when Paul addressed it[1] a mixed community of preponderatingly Gentile character. That is evident, in the first place, from Paul's own words, since at the beginning, and again at the end, he reckons his hearers as among the Gentile peoples[2] which formed his special field of labour as the apostle to the Gentiles. Since he had had committed to him the office of apostle to the Gentiles, since he felt himself under obligation to them, whether Greek or barbarian, wise or unwise (namely, to the service of the Gospel

[1] According to the commonly accepted chronology, in the year 58 A.D. In regard to the different chronology proposed by Harnack, I may refer to the criticism of Schürer (*Zeitschr. für wiss. Theol.*, 1898, Heft 1) and of Th. Zahn (*Einleitung z. N.T.*, ii. 626 ff.), also of Ramsay and Bacon (*Expositor*, March 1897 and February 1898), who are all united in rejecting it.

[2] To assume that by ἔθνη are meant the nations in general, including the Jews, is a wholly unwarrantable expedient which is contrary to Paul's regular linguistic usage, and which completely breaks down in view of the context of the passages in question, in which they are further defined—*i.e.* "Greeks and barbarians, wise and unwise," and the Jews therefore certainly cannot be understood as included among them.

211

among them), he had often desired to come to the
Romans also in order to obtain some fruit among
them, as among other Gentiles (i. 5 f., 13 f.).   This
is his justification for his epistle, in which he had
written to them somewhat more boldly (than would
otherwise have been admissible in dealing with a
church to which he was still personally unknown) in
order that he might perform the functions of a priest
of Christ (εἰς τὸ εἶναι με λειτουργὸν Χριστοῦ Ἰησοῦ, xv. 16)
towards the Gentiles, making them an offering
well-pleasing to God and consecrated by the Holy
Spirit (xv. 15 f.).   As he thus repeatedly bases his
relationship to the Roman church on his call to be
the apostle of the Gentiles, he must—the conclusion
is   inevitable — have   regarded   this   church   as
essentially Gentile Christian.   Besides, in xi. 13
he directly addresses his readers as Gentiles, and in
xi. 17 compares them with shoots of a wild olive,
which, through faith, have been grafted into the
noble olive tree of Israel; in xi. 28 ff. as former
unbelievers who have now attained the mercy of
God, while the Jews for their sakes had now as
enemies (as unloved) been shut up to disobedience.
That in all these passages the apostle had in view
only a small Gentile Christian party within a mainly
Jewish Christian church is hardly to be supposed.
How came it, in that case, that in that whole section
where he deals with the relations of Jews and
Gentiles to the Christian church, he never once
addresses the Jewish Christian church but always
the Gentile Christian minority ?   And would it not
be very peculiar that the apostle should write at
such length about the Gentiles being preferred

before Israel to a church mainly consisting of Jews, and should offer them consolation against the apparent rejection of Israel, for which their own condition gave no occasion? It is certainly much more natural to suppose that the Gentile Christians who are warned in xi. 20 ff. not to be high-minded because of their privileges, had the actual advantage, *i.e.* were in the majority, and that the Jewish Christians, who needed consolation on the score of their present rejection, were also really in a less favourable position, *i.e.* were in a minority in the Roman church.

We are led to the same conclusion by what is said in xiv. 1–xv. 9 about the two parties in the Roman church. Paul designates them as "the strong" who had no scruples about eating and drinking and keeping days, because they regarded these things as indifferent, and "the weak" who believed themselves obliged by conscientious motives to renounce the use of flesh and wine and to keep particular days holy. Now, it must no doubt be admitted that these contrasted parties of "strong" and "weak" are not to be identified without more ado with Gentile and Jewish Christians, since the observances about which the weak had scruples go beyond the Mosaic law and are connected with an ascetic tendency, which among the Jews was represented by the Essenes, but was also largely practised among the Gentiles at that time, as a consequence of a dualistic-spiritualistic system of thought. Thus the "weak" may have included ascetically-inclined Gentile Christians as well as Jewish Christians. On the other hand, since it is mentioned in regard to

the "strong" (xiv. 2) that they were convinced that
they might eat anything, it is clear that these, at any
rate, cannot have been Jewish Christians, who would
have felt bound by the Mosaic prohibition of unclean
meats. We should doubtless rather see in this
"strong" party in the Roman church, who boasted
of their freedom from scruple, the counterpart of
those Corinthian Christians who held the principle
"all things are lawful to me," and these were at the
opposite pole from the legal-minded Jewish Christians.
This impression is confirmed by the fact that Paul
exhorts those who were "strong" to receive their
weak brethren with loving forbearance, remembering
that Christ also had in undeserved and unexpected
mercy received them who were once heathen (xv. 7 f.).
As it was in the nature of things that such an
exhortation to forbearance should be addressed to
the majority rather than the minority, it follows that
at least the majority of the Roman church consisted
of Gentile Christians.

While these arguments concur in pointing to the
conclusion that Paul regarded the Roman church as
predominantly and essentially Gentile-Christian, yet
this must not be exaggerated by regarding it as a
purely Gentile Christian church. Without assuming
a Jewish minority, it would not be possible to explain
the Epistle to the Romans. The demonstration in
chap. ii., for example, that the Jews were not less
sinful and in need of redemption than the Gentiles,
would be purposeless for a purely Gentile-Christian
church, and in ii. 17 ff., indeed, the Jew is directly
addressed ; and this, moreover, can hardly be taken
as a mere rhetorical form, any more than the address

to the Gentiles in chap. xi., especially as in iii. 1–9 the address passes into a formal dialogue in which the objections which Paul had to expect on the part of his readers are brought forward and answered by argument. How superfluous for Gentile Christians would have been the question whether God was the God of the Jews only, and not also of the Gentiles! (iii. 29). And what would have been the object of the detailed explanation that through the doctrine of faith-righteousness, the law—that is, the Old Testament revelation—is not made void, but established? (iii. 31). The whole of the following argument from the history of Abraham can only have significance for the Jewish Christian as the means of showing him the harmony between the Gospel and the historically revealed faith. In vii. 1–6, too, the apostle seeks to remove, from the standpoint of the law itself, the offence caused to the Jewish Christians by his abrogation of the law, and the fact that he is here arguing on the basis of the legal consciousness is indicated by the words " I speak to them that know (the) law." It is true these words would not in themselves prove much, since a certain knowledge of law in the wider sense, or, for that matter, of the Old Testament, might of course be assumed even in the case of Gentile Christians, but the subsequent argument drawn from the law of marriage presupposes readers who had hitherto felt themselves so closely bound by the law, and, moreover, by the actual external law, and therefore the law of Moses, that the dissolution of the bond seemed to them like an act of disloyalty, of impiety. This could only be the case with Jewish Christians; the Gentile, even if he had

been a devout proselyte, could hardly have felt himself to be in so close a relation — comparable with
marriage—to the Jewish law. Similarly the following
discussion regarding the law, its holiness in essence
and its pernicious influence in fact, could only count
on being understood by those who knew the actual
law, not only by reading it, but by their own experience, by living under it, *i.e.* by Jewish Christians. In
chaps. ix.–xi., too, the apostle has them specifically
in view ; for a purely Gentile Christian church the
explanation of the deposition of the Jews from their
place of privilege, and of their imperishable hopes,
would have had little interest, and would in any case
have taken a different form and tone. When, however, towards the close, it is not the Jewish claim to
national privileges that is rebuked, but the Gentile
Christian self-exaltation in comparison with the
apparently rejected Israel, while the final restoration
of the latter is consolingly foreshadowed, it is possible
to draw a definite conclusion as to the position of the
Jewish Christians in the Roman church at that time.

Obviously they did not form the ruling majority,
holding an assured position and endeavouring to make
good their national privileges and to force their legal
customs and regulations upon the whole church, but
were an unprogressive minority which felt itself
numerically swamped by the rising tide of Gentile
Christianity, morally without influence, and in every
respect forced into a defensive position.[1] Of an

[1] How this had come about we cannot tell with certainty, but
it is natural to conjecture that the church had grown out of the
synagogue and its proselytes, and then, when the Jews were expelled
under Claudius, had lost the majority of its Jewish members, where-

aggressive Jewish agitation such as we find in
Galatians and Corinthians, the Epistle to the Romans
shows no trace. Had there been any such movement
the whole tone of the epistle would have been
different, as a comparison with Galatians shows. If
Paul had had to fear the influence in the Roman
church of fanatic Judaisers he would certainly not
have so persistently emphasised, as he does in the
Epistle to the Romans, the inviolable rights of the
People of the Promise, and the destination of salvation to the Jews first (i. 16, iii. 2, ix. 4 f., xi. 1,
18, 24, 29 ; xv. 8), which would have been playing
into the hands of the Jewish agitators whom it was
his object to oppose. Equally unintelligible, on this
assumption, would be the mild view of the Jewish
scruples of conscience on the question of days and
meats, which contrasts so strikingly with the stern
condemnation of the same practices in the Epistle
to the Galatians. In the latter, formal usages of
that kind are censured as a falling away from
Christian freedom into bondage to the miserable
elements of the world, and thus the Jewish law is
placed on the same footing as the sensuous cultus of

upon the Gentile membership increased the more rapidly because
it had no need to trouble about the Jewish customs of an incon-
siderable minority. In this connection it should not be forgotten
that the Jews in Rome were far from being loved, and that therefore even those Romans who found the God and Christ of the
Gospel a welcome provision for their religious need, would not on
that account have any great liking for the ceremonial law and the
aggressive theocratic nationalism of the Jews. Taking into account
all the circumstances of the time, the condition of the Roman congregation as evidenced by the Epistle to the Romans becomes quite
intelligible. A similar view of the origin of the Roman church is
given by Jülicher, *Einleitung*, second edition, p. 89 (= Eng. Tr., 113 f.).

the nature-religion. In the Epistle to the Romans, on the other hand, these practices are commended to Christian forbearance as "things indifferent," and the law, moreover, is recognised as holy, just, and good, and every appearance of depreciating it is carefully avoided. Such wide differences in his whole attitude towards the Jewish and Jewish-Christian conscious-ness cannot be explained merely by the fact that Paul had stood in a personal relation to the Galatians and not to the Romans, but imply an entirely different situation as regards the readers. The simplest explanation of it is to be found, in my opinion, in the supposition that Paul had not to fear in Rome, as he had in Galatia, a danger threatening the Gentile Christians from the side of the Judaising agitators, but rather had to win for his gospel the Jewish Christian minority which felt itself oppressed and aggrieved, and to reconcile them with the Gentile Christian majority which was pressing victoriously forward. The Roman Gentile - Christians who gloried with such self-satisfaction in their "strength," and looked down with scorn upon the scruples of their weak fellow-Christians, and indeed already rejoiced in the rejection of the hated Jewish nation, do not appear as if they, like the easily-influenced Galatians, had been in any danger of falling into the net of Jewish agitators. Even such polemics as some have found in the Epistle to the Romans against the attacks of opponents of this kind are undoubtedly very different from the anti-Judaising polemic of Galatians and Second Corinthians. There, it was a question of attacks by these fanatical agitators upon the apostolic rights and apostolic activity of

Paul—attacks of which the personal bitterness incited him to passionate and vigorous retort. In Romans, on the other hand, it is a question of natural and justifiable scruples of an honest Jewish-Christian conscience in regard to a Christianity which seemed to do away with the law of God and make void the promises of Israel, scruples which are therefore dealt with and appeased in a quiet practical fashion and with careful circumspection and consideration for the Jewish conscience.

It is in this connection a question of subordinate interest whether Paul had definite information of the existence of scruples of this kind among the Jewish-Christian members of the Roman church. It is quite possible that he had, just as he seems to have had of the difference of ethical opinion in the church ; but the assumption is hardly necessary, for those scruples were so certain to be felt that Paul must have met with them wherever he came in contact with Jewish Christianity, and especially in Corinth among the Peter-party. Even if Paul previously, during the heat of the party warfare, had been able to see nothing but injustice and malignity on the side of the Judaising opposition in Galatia and Corinth, yet it may well be supposed that now, when the fury of the fight had calmed down, he would not refuse to recognise the relative justification and personal sincerity of his opponents, and could therefore consider their scruples calmly and be content to meet them by the positive presentation of the truth of his own gospel. If he learned at this time that there was some tension in the Roman church between the Gentile-Christian majority and the

Jewish-Christian minority, he needed no detailed information as to the dogmatic opinions of the latter; the analogy supplied by his previous experience sufficed to make it seem his duty, by addressing an epistle to that church, to reconcile the Jewish Christians there to the contents and consequences of his Gentile-Christian gospel. This he endeavoured to do by removing their scruples regarding his doctrines of faith-righteousness and freedom from the law, and by explaining the paradoxical fact of the victorious advance and preponderating strength of Gentile Christianity as a dispensation of the Divine providence which was not in opposition to the Divine promises to Israel. Accordingly the object of this letter was not so much to oppose the Jewish Christians at Rome as to reconcile them with the Gentile Christians who were then in a majority, by means of a quiet, positive, and peacefully delivered defence of the Pauline gospel, of its contents as well as its consequences.

But this does not exhaust the purpose of the Epistle to the Romans. It is written to a preponderatingly Gentile-Christian church whose faith Paul could recognise as right in its main features and in sympathy with his own, as he unmistakably does in i. 12, vi. 17, xv. 14, using expressions which exclude the idea of a Judaising tendency in the majority of the church, and this confirms the result arrived at above regarding its Gentile Christian character. But it does not follow that in this church everything was necessarily all that could be wished. The cause of friction between the two parts of the church lay not merely in the legal and national exclusiveness of the Jewish minority; it lay not less in the disposition of the Gentile majority to carry on their old customs of life unchecked by Christian morality and to treat their Jewish fellow-Christians in an unloving and scornful fashion. They were not deficient indeed in goodwill and in knowledge of all kinds (xv. 14), but they were still wanting in full understanding of the moral demands of the Gospel of Christ Jesus, and of the spiritual power which inspires earnest self-discipline and a worthy conduct of life. Their heathen superficiality and levity in their way of apprehending the Gospel was just as fatal to a healthy church-life in general, and to the peaceful intercourse of the two parts of the community in particular, as the Jewish narrowness and obstinate cleaving to the tradition of the Fathers. To produce a harmonious and orderly church-life, it would not suffice to convince the Jewish Christians of the truth of the Pauline gospel and the legitimacy of Gentile Christianity; it was equally needful to guide the Gentile Christians into a deeper understanding of the moral essence of the Gospel, and to impress upon their minds the duty of humble and forbearing love. This is what Paul means when he says at the outset that he had long desired to visit the Roman Christians that he might impart unto them some spiritual gift to confirm them,[1] and again

[1] It is to be noticed that the "confirming" of a church implies the rightness in principle of its faith combined with a want of clearness and strength in the recognition and carrying out of the consequences of that faith. In the case of an essentially Jewish church Paul could not have assumed this, and therefore could not have spoken of "confirming" it; and as little could he have spoken of being cheered by his intercourse with it (i. 12). His experience with the Galatians and the Corinthians at the time

at the close, when he says that he had desired in his letter to give them some matters to ponder over, in order that he might as a true priest of Christ prepare them to be a consecrated offering acceptable to God (i. 11, xv. 15 f.). It was not therefore a question in regard to the majority in the church of first restraining them from going astray in their faith, nor of warning them against the danger of this going astray, but rather of giving to their as yet unstable Christian life the necessary stability and moral consecration.

A complete understanding of the Epistle to the Romans can, therefore, only be gained by keeping in view the two distinct parts in this Roman church, to which correspond this double purpose of the epistle. Paul desires not merely to convince the Jewish-Christian party of the truth of the Gospel which frees from the law, and of the legitimacy of Gentile Christianity as in accordance with God's providential ordinance, he also desires to remove those failings of the Gentile-Christian majority at which the Jews were justly offended, by deepening their moral earnestness. This double task Paul accomplished most successfully in the Epistle to the Romans, by combining these two aims in the most intimate fashion. He takes up his position at a point of view which is raised above these oppositions, and

when they were under the influence of the Judaisers was certainly not adapted to give him cause to hope for pleasant and cheering impressions from a Judaising church at Rome. If Paul really hoped for this (and we have no right to take his words as a mere formula of politeness) he must have known that he would find in the church at Rome a majority who were at heart not Judaistically inclined.

gives an objective exposition of the main truths of
the Gospel drawn from its own essence, showing that
it is the power of God unto salvation to every one
that believeth, to the Jews first and also to the
Gentiles, and that it must manifest itself as a sanctifying power in the life of every Christian, whether he
be Gentile or Jew.   But in this essentially objective
development of the main thoughts of the Gospel
Paul never loses sight of the needs of the Roman
church; in fact, he seems to keep one eye on the
Jewish-Christian and one eye on the Gentile-
Christian portion of his readers.   It is, of course,
in the nature of things that in the dogmatic
arguments upon faith-righteousness the adaptation
to the Jewish Christians, and in the ethical exhortations the adaptation to the Gentile Christians,
predominates.   The two aims are most closely interwoven in the middle sections, chaps. vi.–viii. and
ix.–xi.

The Epistle to the Romans has a more definite
structure than any of the other Pauline epistles.
At the first glance the eye is caught by the points of
division at ix. 1 and xii. 1, which make it into three
main sections — chapters i. – viii., ix. – xi., xii. – xv.
The first of these explains the content of the Gospel
of Christ as the power of God unto salvation to every
one that believeth: the second deals with the
paradoxical but divinely ordained result of the preaching of the Gospel, namely, that the salvation which
was intended for the Jew first and then afterwards
for the Gentile, has historically realised itself in the
reverse order—for the Gentile before the Jew; finally,
the third section shows how the divine power of the

Gospel must exhibit itself also as a sanctifying power in the moral life of the church, in its blamelessness towards those who are without and harmony among its own members.

Chap. i. 1–17: Introduction to the Epistle. Paul as the apostle of Christ greets the Roman church, and bases upon his commission to the Gentiles his right to enter into relations with the Gentile Christian church at Rome, which though personally unknown to him, belongs to the sphere of his mission. He assures the Roman Christians of the lively sympathy with which he had always thought of them, and desired to make personal acquaintance with them. Only external hindrances have hitherto prevented him from coming to Rome and there prosecuting the mission to the Gentiles to which he had been called. This resolution he still held to, for he was not ashamed (even in the face of the cultured metropolis of the world) of the Gospel of Christ, " for it is a power of God unto salvation to every one that believeth, to the Jew first, but also to the Greek. For therein is revealed God's righteousness from faith for faith ; as it is written, the just shall live by faith." In these words the apostle sets forth the theme with the development of which the first division, i. 18–viii. 31, is to be occupied.

And first, in the first division of this section (i. 18– iii. 30), he shows that the new principle of salvation by means of the righteousness which God gives on the ground of faith is needful for all because of the universality of human sin, and, through the mercy of God in Christ, has become effectual for all. But if the Gospel revealed a righteousness promised by

God in mercy to the believer, the question arises for the Jewish consciousness, What need is there of such righteousness; why cannot a man's works gain righteousness for him? This the apostle answers by proving that all men, Gentiles and Jews alike, stand as sinners under the wrath of God. First he speaks of the revelation of the wrath of God against all ungodliness and unrighteousness of men who hold down the truth in unrighteousness, by which he means the judgment of God which is actually being visited upon the heathen. For the heathen had the truth given them in their consciousness of God, based on the revelation of God in creation. But by their impiety they had lost this truth and put idols in the place of the incorruptible God. This was their guilt, for which God punished those who had first abandoned Him by allowing them to sink into such moral abandonment as to violate by unnatural vices the dignity of human nature, destroy the whole moral order of society, and reach such a pitch of degradation and moral insensibility, that, although they knew such conduct to be worthy of death, they gave it their (æsthetic) approval (i. 19–32).

But the Jew, too, though he, no doubt, did not by any means approve this sinful heathen life, but strongly condemned it, condemns himself at the same time, inasmuch as he, although he condemns it, does the same. The better knowledge, to which that condemnation of others testifies, of the Divine righteousness, which will reward every man according to his work, cannot help the man whose own works are equally deserving of punishment, but on the contrary, such an one will be the first object of the

15

righteous judgment of God (ii. 1–10). This judgment is visited quite impartially on all; there is no
advantage either in the possession or non-possession
of the law, for each will be judged according to his
own law—the heathen by the natural law written in
the heart, the law of conscience, the Jew by the
external law of Moses, upon which he bases his boast
of being a teacher of the blind heathen, whereas he
really, by transgressing it, causes God to be blas-
phemed among the heathen. Circumcision does not
give the Jew any advantage, any more than does the
possession of the law, since it is not the outward
circumcision but the spiritual circumcision of the
heart which is of value in God's sight (ii. 11–29).

But has the Jew, then, no advantage whatever?
This objection (iii. 1) Paul himself raises, knowing
that it would arise in the mind of his Jewish-
Christian reader, in order to dispel at once so gross a
misunderstanding of the principles which he had just
set forth. Certainly, he admits, the Jew had a great
advantage in every respect, especially because the
oracles (promises) of God were committed to him,
and they can never lose their value, since it rests
upon the faithfulness of God, which cannot be
annulled even by the unfaithfulness of men. This
remark Paul makes to console the Jewish Christians
and to correct those Gentile Christians who thought
they saw in the unbelief of the Jews the sign of their
rejection (*cf.* xi. 19 ff.). And this side-glance at the
Gentile reader gives him occasion also to remove
another misunderstanding which the assertion of the
unconditioned character of God's mercy and faithfulness gave rise to in the minds of many, who saw in

it a denial of the righteousness of God as judge and a charter of liberty to sin. This misunderstanding we need not suppose to have been merely a pretended inference maliciously drawn by hostile Jewish Christians, but to have been seriously drawn and actually put in practice by some of the Gentile Christians. Here, however, Paul only touches incidentally on this misunderstanding and deals with it quite briefly, since he intended later (vi. 1 ff.) to go into it more fully, so that verses 5–8 may be regarded as a parenthetic digression from the present theme. To this he returns in verse 9, where the question asked in verse 1 is taken up again, in order to add to the previously given answer the reverse side of the matter. The Jews are not in every respect at an advantage—not, namely, in respect of moral worth, but lie under the same general indictment which the Scripture brings against all without distinction. And this conclusion, which results from this whole description from i. 18 on, of the sin and misery of mankind, is summed up in the final verdict: " By the works of the law shall no flesh be justified, for by the law comes (only) the knowledge of sin " (iii. 20).

From this dark background there shines forth the more brilliantly the new revelation of a righteousness of God, which, though witnessed to by the law and the prophets, has nothing to do with the law, since it is received through faith in Christ or as a free gift of the divine grace. But this gift of grace is made possible by the redemption which God has accomplished in Christ Jesus, setting Him forth as a bloody sacrifice of atonement in order thereby to manifest His righteousness in such a way that He should at

once be just and the Justifier of him that believeth in
Jesus.   All Jewish boasting of works is excluded by
this new rule of faith, for now the only valid principle
is that a man becomes righteous by faith, not through
works of the law.   Just as surely as there is one God
for Jews and Gentiles, so surely will this one God
justify both in one and the same way, namely, by
·faith (iii. 30).

The content of his gospel, the revelation of a
righteousness of God for every believer, Jew and
Gentile alike, is thus set forth in its necessity and its
reality.   Now, however, the question arises in which
the principal difficulty of this teaching for the Jewish
conscience finds expression—the question whether
this new message of faith is not in contradiction with
the revelation of God in the law—*i.e.* in the Old
Testament in general ?   By no means, answers Paul ;
rather, it confirms that revelation (iii. 31).   And this
brings him to the next section, which gives a threefold confirmation of the gospel of faith-righteousness
—from the sacred history, in the example of Abraham ;
from Christian experience, in the witness of the Spirit
in the heart ; finally, from the cosmical antithesis of
Adam and Christ (chaps. iv. and v.).   It is the same
threefold argument which we have met before in
a somewhat different order in Gal. iii. 1 – iv. 7.
Abraham's faith was, according to the Scriptures,
reckoned to him for righteousness, and this reckoning
was, as a matter of grace, quite a different thing from
the reckoning of the payment of one who has done
work, for that is a matter of debt, not of grace ; but so
little is that reckoning of righteousness for the sake
of faith bound to good works, that on the contrary

it consists, according to the words of David, in the forgiveness of transgressions and the non-attribution of sin.   And inasmuch as this reckoning of righteousness to Abraham took place while he was in uncircumcision, it is typical of the faith-righteousness of all, including Gentile believers.   And the promise to Abraham and to his seed is not conditioned by the law either, otherwise it would have been no longer a matter of grace, and could not be secured to faith ; for the law, which brings upon sinful man the divine wrath, would annul the certainty of the promise.   If the promise is to stand fast, it can only be a gift of grace to which only the condition of faith is attached ; as such it is applicable to all Abraham's children, the followers of his faith without the law as well as the posterity of his blood with the law.   For this universal significance of Abraham's fatherhood Paul finds support in the scriptural saying that God has made him the father of many (heathen) nations. Lastly, he finds in the character of Abraham's faith in God—as the God who brings to life that which is dead (namely, the generative power of Abraham and Sarah) and calls into being that which is not—a type of the Christian faith in God as having raised from the dead "Jesus who was delivered up for (the expiation of) our sins and was raised again for our justification " (iv. 25).

To this argument from the history of salvation Paul adds, in v. 1–11, that argument from his readers' own experience which in Galatians he placed first (iii. 1 ff.).. That they have really been justified by faith shows itself in the peace which they possess in relation to God, in their free access to His mercy (in the intercourse of prayer) and in the joyful hope of (the manifestation of) His glory, a hope which enables us to maintain a joyful confidence even amid sufferings, because it rests upon the sense of the love of God (to us) which the Holy Spirit produces in our hearts. Since God has given the most amazing proof of His love, in that He let Christ die to make an atonement for us while we were still sinners and enemies of God, we may now, as reconciled and redeemed, cherish the more confident hope that we shall be delivered from the judgment (inasmuch as the life of Christ in heavenly splendour is the pledge of our partaking in the same in eternal life). Then the subject of our glorying is (no longer our own works but) God, whose love is assured to us through our Lord Christ.

Finally, the apostle closes the line of argument which he has pursued up to this point with a boldly-conceived philosophy of history, which finds its poles in Adam and Christ (v. 12–21). That the Gospel of Christ, in revealing a righteousness of God by faith, is a power of God unto salvation to all who believe, is confirmed by the formal analogy with the sin of Adam which passed upon all men. Through Adam's transgression sin came into the world as a tyrant to whose power all succumbed, and at the same time death acquired tyrannic power over all in virtue of a divine decree which, on account of the sin of one, has subjected all to the fate of sin and death. To this sin and misery, which by the sentence of God is entailed upon all Adam's children, and which had its cause in the one Adam, corresponds, upon the other side, God's verdict of acquittal, which gives righteousness and life to all who believe in Christ, and which has its cause in the righteous act of the one Christ.   Thus in both cases the act of the one Founder and Head has become for all who are His the cause of a condition which is determined by divine decree, and which individuals enter upon without reference to their personal merit or demerit; on the one side misery (the reign of sin and death), on the other salvation (righteousness and life).   Now, upon this assumption, what significance attaches to the law of Moses?   This question the apostle imagines to be raised by his Jewish-Christian readers, and answers it by an assertion which must have seemed to them highly paradoxical.   " The law entered that offence might abound, but where sin abounded grace did much more abound; that as sin has reigned unto death, even so might grace reign through righteousness unto eternal life by Jesus Christ our Lord " (v. 20, 21).

That might certainly occasion grave difficulties to the Jewish Christian, for this definition of the purpose of the law seemed to cut away the ground from beneath his whole moral system.   The apostle could not, therefore, well refuse the task which presented itself to him, of meeting the moral objections brought by the Jewish Christians against his gospel, and of showing that, so far from destroying, it first rendered possible the accomplishment of the moral content of the law.   This task he performs in the third section, chaps. vi.–viii.   Moreover, he had not merely to deal with theoretic objections from the Jewish side.   The question, " Shall we continue in sin that grace may abound?" (vi. 1, 15) had to be treated the more seriously, inasmuch as it was not merely an artificial inference drawn by his Jewish opponents; the question had actually been answered in the affirmative, both theoretically and practically, by many Gentile Christians. We ought not, because this now seems to us an absurd misunderstanding of the Pauline doctrine of salvation, to assume its impossibility in the case of the Gentile Christians of Paul's time; the Epistles to the Corinthians undoubtedly show us that there were Christians who understood the principle of freedom in a libertine sense. Accordingly, the subsequent exposition of the moral significance of the doctrine of grace is directed as much to the Gentile Christian majority as to the Jewish-Christian minority in the Roman church.

The apostle, therefore, now endeavours to show his readers that continuance in sin, so far from being the right inference from the Gospel doctrine of grace, is in complete contradiction with all that constituted a Christian, namely, with the mystical union with Christ which is effected in baptism, wherein we have become partakers in His death and life in such a way that we have become dead to sin and have entered upon a new condition of life—which can and must only be a life in Christ and for God. For the very reason that we are no longer under the law but under grace, the power of sin, which was intensified by the law, is broken, and we are enabled not only to cease from following the sinful impulse, but to dedicate our life to the service of God and of righteousness. But the possibility of doing this involves the obligation to do it. The will is always ruled by some power or other:

it is either under the tyranny of sin or in the service
of God. By being released from the former tyranny,
the Christian comes under the new obligation, and his
one concern is to be constant and earnest in this new
service, remembering that sin gives his servant death
for his wages ; but God, eternal life (vi. 1–23). The
central thought of this exposition is that the reign of
sin is not only not strengthened, but is rather, on the
other hand, abolished by the abolition of the law
(vi. 14). But is this latter really abolished for
Christians, and can it ever be abolished when one
who is under the law is bound for life to it, as the
wife to the husband ? This new difficulty of the
Jewish conscience necessitates a new explanation,
which is given in vii. 1–6, on the basis of the analogy
of the marriage bond. Just as the binding power of
the marriage law expires with the death of one of the
parties to the marriage, so the obligation of the law
in general is destroyed for those who in the power of
the death of Christ (which they have made their own
by baptism) have died to the law ; they can therefore
without disloyalty enter into the marriage bond with
the risen Christ in order that they may become
fruitful unto God. That they had not been under
the law, because the sinful passions intensified by the
law had been operative in their members to bring
forth fruit unto death. Only the Christian who has
died to the tyranny of the law is able to serve God
in the new way of the spirit instead of that of the old
(unfruitful) letter (vii. 6).

But the close connection assumed here (as in vi. 14)
between the law and sin raises for the Jewish
conscience a new and serious difficulty. Is, then,

asks the Jewish Christian, the law sin? Was the commandment given to produce death? These, from the Jewish point of view, scandalous assertions, Paul decidedly rejects. He admits that the law is in itself holy, the commandment holy, just, and good, and given to be a way of life; nevertheless, he demonstrates, it results in death to man, for the reason that man, as carnal, is in opposition to the spiritual essence of the law and is sold under sin, the impulse to which is stimulated, intensified, and brought to its full development by the law. The law is therefore not itself evil, but it is certainly the means whereby the evil which dwells in us, namely, in our flesh, is roused to activity, and its power to overcome our weak will and determine our action is made manifest. It is true, a willing of the good and hating of evil, in sympathy with the law of God, found place in our inner man, but this law (impulse) of the mind which forms our better ego, is so powerless that it is unable to conquer in the unequal strife with the law (impulse) of sin in our members, but instead is held captive. There man finds himself in a miserable condition of inner division between the law of God, towards which the good impulse of reason urges him, and the law of sin to which the flesh is in bondage. "So then I, for myself (apart from the power of the Spirit of Christ which works in me) serve with my mind, indeed, the law of God, but with the flesh the law of sin " (vii. 25), a confession which is by no means to be referred to the past of the apostle before his conversion, but pictures a present and continuous condition, but, of course, only as regards the "natural man," which continues to exist even in Christians

alongside of the supernatural " pneuma," and is here
portrayed by Paul with the same one-sided abstraction
with which he elsewhere portrays the new spiritual
life of Christians.   Only from a combination of the
one-sided pictures—the dark picture in chap. vii. and
the bright picture in chap. viii.—can we gather Paul's
complete view of the actual concrete Christian life
(*cf.* Gal. v. 17).

From the power of sin and death, to whose reign
man has been subjected since Adam by the sentence
of God (hence " law " of sin and death), the Christian
is set free by the higher power of the Spirit which he
possesses through his living union with Christ.   Not
merely the removal of the guilt of sin, but also the
overcoming of the power of sin—which was never
possible for the law because of the resistance of the
flesh, has been effected by God Himself, in that He
caused His Son to appear in the likeness of sinful
flesh, and in His death for us to fulfil the divine
sentence, in order that the moral demands of the
law might be fulfilled in us, by our walking not after
the flesh but after the Spirit.   This walking after
the Spirit is made possible for the Christian, and is
therefore morally demanded by his possession of the
Spirit of God and of Christ, whose mind is as fully
set upon life and peace with God, as the mind of
the flesh is set upon death and enmity against God.
In this same Spirit, which is the inspiring power of
true righteousness, the Christian possesses at the same
time the pledge and guarantee of the reanimation
of his mortal body through the quickening power of
God.   But it is a condition of this future possession
of life that the Christian must allow himself to

be directed by the holy impulses of the Spirit, and that the impulses and habits of sensuality must be fought with and slain. For only those who are led by the Spirit of God are the sons of God. Where he rules there is no longer slavish fear, but a childlike trust, which is confident of the fatherly love of God and the inheritance of the glory of Christ. Not all the suffering which we have now to bear can shake this confidence, for our fellowship with the sufferings of Christ is precisely the pre-condition of our being partakers in the future of His glory. Moreover, in our sufferings and hopes we are not alone in the world; the whole creation is in like condition, still groaning in its subjection to vanity and longing for its future emancipation. Similarly we Christians, although in possession of the earnest of the Spirit, must wait with patience for the full redemption which embraces the body also, and in which our dignity as sons will first be fully realised. Meanwhile the Spirit which " helpeth our infirmities " and represents us before God in inter-cession, guarantees to us the certain fulfilment of our hope. In the certainty that God is for us we are also certain that He helps all who love Him in the way which contributes to their highest good, to the fulfilment, namely, of the eternal divine purpose which has destined us to be conformed to the image of the first-born Son of God. Since God has given us the highest proof of His love in the delivering up for us of His Son, who ever represents us before God, we may be certain that no temporal nor earthly power shall be able to separate us from the love of God, of which we have the pledge in Christ (viii. 39).

In this hymn of the certainty of salvation exalted above the world and time, the apostle has given an impressive description of the power of the living Spirit of Christ which triumphs over sin and death, and this puts the crown upon his whole argument for the truth of the Gospel which produces such a lofty confidence. He has thus answered or excluded the objections of the Jewish Christians as well as the misunderstandings or misinterpretations of the Gentile Christians in regard to his gospel.

But Jewish Christianity found an offence not only in the content of the Pauline preaching, but also, not less, in the practical results of it, in the wholesale conversion of the heathen, whereby the original Jewish element in the church was being placed more and more at a disadvantage. If to be thus thrust back into the condition of a minority was disconcerting and humiliating enough for Jewish Christians in general, there was added as a special grievance for the Jewish-Christian minority of the Roman church the proud and unbrotherly conduct of the Gentile majority, who had seen in the small degree of missionary success among Israel, in comparison with that among the Gentiles, a proof of the divine decree of rejection against the hateful and hated Jewish people.[1] This state of things set the apostle a difficult task—on the one hand, to explain the actual numerical inferiority of the Jews as compared with

---

[1] In Tacitus, *Hist.*, v. 5, "odium hostile adversus omnes" is ascribed to the Jews, and this was certainly the prevailing opinion among the Romans, and the Roman Christians probably formed no exception to the rule. This condition of things should be kept in mind in reading Rom. ix.–xi.

the Gentiles in the kingdom of Christ as a dispensation of the divine will for man's salvation, which, however painful to Jewish feeling, was to be humbly recognised ; on the other hand, to defend the certainty of the promises to the Jews and to guard against the self-exaltation of the Gentile Christians. This task is discharged in chaps. ix.–xi.

Paul begins, in ix. 1, with an asseveration of his deep sorrow for the unbelief of his people—the People of the Covenant, so highly privileged above all others — and this is certainly not merely a " captatio benevolentiæ " for Jewish-Christian readers, but a genuine expression of his own pain as a lover of his nation. Immediately, however, he consoles himself as well as his readers with the assurance that God's word of promise has not on that account come to nought. The present dispensation of Providence does not stand in contradiction with the saving purpose of God as manifested in former revelations, since this will of God has always been accomplished in the form of an unconditional free choice, corresponding to the unconditional power of the Creator over the creature. As God had hitherto borne patiently with the vessels of wrath, in order, by a choice of vessels of mercy from their midst, to manifest His own special glory, so He had now followed the same principle by calling us Christians, not only from among the Jews but also from among the Gentiles, and making out of that which was not a people (the Gentiles), a new People of God ; while on the other hand He has saved of Israel only a remnant as the seed-corn of the future (ix. 1–29).

If by this argument the Jewish claim to preeminence at the kingdom of Christ was rejected and shown to be unjustified from the very premises of the Jewish doctrine of election, yet this deterministic explanation of the facts of the unconditioned divine decree was rather adapted to silence doubt than to give a satisfactory solution of it.   The apostle therefore next takes up the standpoint of the historical and moral method of explanation.   Israel, he points out, has stumbled, because in its self-willed and exclusive adherence to the law it was unwilling to receive righteousness in the way ordained of God. They had zeal towards God but without insight into the divine purpose, according to which the righteousness of God was to take the place of their own inner righteousness, since Christ was destined to be the end of the law and the mediator of righteousness for every believer.   By this righteousness which results from faith the problem which under the law was insoluble—how human effort could ever succeed in bringing about the coming of Messiah whether from Heaven or Hades—receives a practical solution.   He needs no longer to be toilsomely sought for, He is already there, namely, in the word of the evangelical preaching.   One need therefore only believe in Him with the heart, and confess Him with the mouth, to be already in possession of righteousness and salvation.   And this way of salvation is open to all ; there is no distinction between Jews and Greeks, as was foretold long ago by the prophetic word, " Whosoever shall call upon the name of the Lord shall be saved " (in which quotation Paul turns the Old Testament reference to God into a reference to Christ).   But in order to realise this universal saving purpose of God which is revealed by the prophet, there is needed also a universal missionary preaching addressed to all nations, and therefore the Gentile mission of Paul is not in contradiction with the promises of the prophets, but, on the contrary, is the means assigned by God for their fulfilment (ix. 30 – x. 15). Now, precisely this universal mission brings to the Jews of the Diaspora the preaching of Christ;[1] if they do not accept Him they have not the excuse of want of knowledge; it is a repetition of the old experience of which Moses and Isaiah had to complain—that God is found of those who have not sought Him, while His people proudly shut their hearts against the earnest wooing of God. As long ago, in the time of Elijah, only a remnant remained true to God in the general falling away of the people, so now again, only a small remnant of Israel was being taken up into the kingdom of Christ, and that, not on the ground of its works, but by the election of grace. The great mass of Israel, however, has not attained what it aimed at, but has become hardened, and thus only the threatenings of the prophets have been fulfilled in it, so that the non-success of the mission to the Jews, not less than the success of the mission to the Gentiles, is in full accordance with the counsel of God as testified to in the holy Scriptures (x. 16–xi. 10).

Does it seem, then, as if God had cast off His people?

[1] In this passage (x. 18–21) we have an unmistakable proof that Paul always on his missionary journeys addressed himself to the Jews of the Diaspora also, and constantly strove to win them to the faith, but always with the result which he here expresses in the two quotations (19 ff.). By this the corresponding representation in the Acts of the Apostles is undoubtedly confirmed.

Far otherwise, answers Paul. The fall of Israel was, no doubt, ordained by God, but it is not God's ultimate purpose ; it is only a means which, when its immediate end is attained, will cease to be. It is, namely, a means by which the riches of salvation are made available for the Gentiles. These have been grafted, in the place of the branch, Israel, which has been broken off, upon the root of the noble olive tree (the Old Testament covenant people), but—and here the apostle sounds a note of warning to the Roman Gentile Christians—they must guard against unloving self-exaltation and remember that they did not bear the root but the root them (*i.e.* that salvation comes from the Jews, to whom the Gentile Christians, therefore, should show themselves grateful ; *cf.* xv. 7 ff.), and remember also that God, who did not spare the natural branches, would not spare them, but might very well reject them if they were lofty-minded. Since, then, Israel's fall from God was only intended as a means to the salvation of the Gentiles, this mediate condition should only continue until the end was attained and the "fulness of the heathen " was brought in. The precedence of the heathen will then stir up Israel to rivalry, and thus will, on its part, contribute to the end of the salvation of all Israel, and in this way God's promise to the people of His choice, that in spite of all they are still for the Fathers' sake the object of the Divine love, will yet be fully realised. God has, therefore, indeed shut up all unto disobedience, but only in order to have mercy upon all. However unsearchable His judgments and unfathomable His ways appear to us, it will at last be seen that it was the very depth of

16

the riches of His mercy and of His wisdom which
was incomprehensible to our limited understanding.
"For of him, and through him, and unto him,
are all things, and to him be the glory for ever"
(xi. 11–36). Thus Paul raises the Roman church
above its inner divisions, leading it up to a point of
view from which the extensive prospect took in the
various destinies of the nations in history as merely
contributory means to the one end of the all-wise
love of God—a philosophy of history, which issues in
a most impressive theodicy.

Then, when the objections in principle against his
gospel and the results of his mission have been dealt
with from various points of view, he has still to bring
home to them the moral ideal of a Christian Church
and to show them that the divine power of the
Gospel must manifest itself as a sanctifying power in
all the various moral relations of life, xii. 1–xv. 13.
In,doing this he draws from what has been previously
established the general principle of Christian morality :
the mercy of God which has been shown to us is the
motive which should lead Christians to dedicate their
whole personality, even to the very body, as a holy
sacrifice to God ; they should shape their life into a
constant spiritual service, not allowing themselves
any longer to be ruled by the influences of the sinful
worldly life, but being transformed by the renewing
of their mind in order that they might be able to
judge what the will of God demanded in every case,
what was good and seemly and perfect in every moral
relationship (xii. 1 f.).

He then gives, in the first place (xii. 3 – xiii. 14),
general exhortations regarding the conduct which is

obligatory on Christians in their intercourse with one
another and with the world.   They should be diligent
in showing modesty, loyalty, hearty brotherly love,
cheerfulness in working and suffering, activity in well-
doing, hospitality, generosity, sympathy, harmony, and
once more, modesty (an exhortation mainly directed to
the Gentile Christians).   In their intercourse with the
outside world the first principle should be, not to
allow themselves to become infected with the evil that
ruled therein, but rather to bear themselves towards
all men decorously, and, so far as possible, peace-
ably, to leave vengeance to God, and to overcome
evil with good (xii. 3–21).   With this was closely
connected right conduct in regard to the power
whose duty it was to overcome evil and protect
good, the civil government, in which the Christian
should recognise a divine ordinance serving the ends
of good, and of which they should honour the
authority, not only from compulsion and fear of
punishment, but also from respect for its moral rights,
and should give free obedience to its demands
(xiii. 1–7).   That this exhortation is addressed especially
to the Jewish Christians, who in Palestine at least
(whether also in Rome is very doubtful) denied the
right of the Gentile government as inconsistent with
theocracy, is possible, but is by no means necessarily
the case ; the exhortation is couched in so general a
form that it is suitable to any Christian church.   And
there was need enough for it in the case of a Gentile-
Christian majority inclined to libertinism.   To the
obligation of civic obedience there attaches itself
naturally the universal legal obligation on which
rests the organisation of all social relationships—the

general principle of *suum cuique*, which, however, should find its Christian extension and deepening in the universal love for one's neighbour as a free fulfilling of the law. An exhortation, enforced by a reference to the nearness of the Parousia, to lay aside the evil customs of heathenism and to walk worthily, as befits the newly-risen day of the Christian religion, and especially to earnest self-discipline in restraining sensuous impulses, brings this section to a close, on the same note of moral principle with which it opened (xiii. 8–14).

The next section (xiv. 1–xv. 13) is chiefly occupied with an exhortation to mutual forbearance in view of the different parties in the church. Especially are the more liberal-minded, as being "the strong," exhorted not to give offence to their weaker brethren, who are still limited to the legal and ascetic standpoint, but in the use of their justifiable Christian freedom to allow themselves to be guided by the restraints of a considerate love. As motives to this patient bearing with the weaker brethren are assigned the general example of Christ, and more especially the condescending mercy with which Christ had redeemed them, the heathen, although He belonged by race and by promise to the Jews. For this reason the Gentile Christians have the more reason for gratitude. The hope of the prophets will be fulfilled in the united strain of praise rising to God from Jew and Gentile (therefore, neither have the Jewish Christians a right to look with disfavour on the Gentiles, nor the latter to exalt themselves above the former). The main body of the epistle closes with an aspiration for the growth of the church in joy, peace, and hope.

The conclusion (xv. 14–33) consists of personal explanations as to the justification and the purpose of this letter, as to the intention of the apostle to visit Rome soon and to travel on to Spain, as to his immediate journey to Jerusalem to convey the gifts of the Gentile churches, and as to his anxiety regarding the reception which awaited him there.

In this chapter, the genuineness of which has been called in question, but without sufficient grounds, only verses 19–24, with the closing words which belong to them in verse 28, give rise to serious critical difficulties.   The assertion that Paul had so fully preached the Gospel from Jerusalem and its neighbourhood right to Illyria, that there remained in those regions nothing more for him to do (19 and 23) is very surprising, for neither had he (according to Gal. i. 18–24; Acts ix. 28, it is true, gives a different account) begun his missionary activity in and near Jerusalem, nor did he ever go into Illyria, nor could he, after merely establishing a few churches in Asia and Greece, regard his missionary activity there as so thoroughly completed that he must now turn his glances towards the farthest west (Spain). Further, the resolution expressed in verses 20–24 to visit Rome only in passing on his way through to Spain, and not to work there for any length of time because he did not wish to work in another's territory, is obviously a contradiction with i. 13–15, where Paul connects his purpose of proclaiming the Gospel at Rome also with his duty as apostle of the Gentiles, and never implies by a single syllable that he regards the Roman church as "foreign territory," which he would only venture to touch upon as a passing guest.

Of the proposed journey to Spain there is no mention elsewhere, either in the Pauline or deutero-Pauline Epistles, or in Acts, nor is there any discoverable reason why Paul should have purposed a lengthened activity in the western outskirts of the empire, instead of at its centre. It would be much more intelligible that at a later period, when the name of Peter had begun to outshine the name of Paul at Rome, someone might have had an interest in representing the Roman church as foreign territory for Paul, to which he had only ventured to make a passing visit. I hold it therefore to be very probable that verses 19–24 and 28 have been either bodily interpolated or very much modified by a Roman bishop of the second century, who wished by this correction to limit Paul's relations with Rome and thereby to give scope to the Roman Peter-legend which was growing up in his time.[1] Of chap. xvi. only verses 21–24 seem to have originally belonged to the epistle, and to have formed its genuine conclusion. The long list of greetings in xvi. 3–16 would be very surprising in a letter to a church to which Paul was personally a stranger. The married couple who stand first, Prisca and Aquila, were, according to Acts xviii. 18 and 26, 1 Cor. xvi. 19, resident in Ephesus, and had there gathered round them a Christian "house-church"; that this couple should in the short time since 1 Cor. xvi. not only have migrated from Ephesus to Rome, but have there again become the centre of a church, is improbable. We may suppose,

[1] In confining the critical doubt to this section I follow Lipsius (*Handkomm.*, ii. 2, p. 86 f.); in the explanation of the interpolation I agree with Baur (*Paulus*, second edition, p. 397 ff.).

then, that all the greetings in verses 3–16 are not addressed to Rome but to Ephesus, the occasion being probably a letter of recommendation for the bearer, the Deaconess Phœbe, who no doubt travelled from Cenchræa, the port of Corinth, to Ephesus (verse 1 f.).   Verses 17–20 may also be explained as a portion of this short letter to Ephesus ; their sharp polemic, similar to that of Philippians, is directed against Judaising disturbers of the peace who cause divisions in the church and endeavour to deceive the simple with fair speeches, but amid these assaults the church had preserved its obedience to the faith (verse 19).   This polemic differs so entirely from the prevailing tone of the Epistle to the Romans that it cannot in any case have belonged to it.   It is possible that it belonged to the short letter of Paul to the Ephesians,[1] but it is probable that it has been added to the Epistle to the Romans by a later hand, in order to put into the mouth of the apostle a condemnation of the Gnostic heretics who were troubling the Roman church in the second century. Finally, the doxology, 25–27, is doubtless in thought and style deutero-Pauline, and it is wanting in some MSS.   How and whence it came here we do not know.   That the close of the Epistle to the Romans fell into disorder and confusion at an early date is shown by the several-times repeated closing formula (xv. 33, xvi. 20, 24).

[1] *Cf.* Jülicher, *Einleitung,* second edition, p. 86 f. (= Eng. trans., p. 110 f.).

CHAPTER XI

THE LETTER TO THE PHILIPPIANS

In the Epistle to the Philippians, the apostle, imprisoned at Rome, holds friendly converse with the church at Philippi—the earliest of his European churches—with which he stood in especially intimate relations. It had recently given him a new evidence of sympathy by sending him, through Epaphroditus, a sum of money for his support. Epaphroditus had fallen seriously ill in Rome, and desired to return to his own country. Paul then gave him this letter to take with him, in which, as was natural in the conditions under which it was composed, personal feelings, anxieties, and hopes largely preponderate over the doctrinal element, though this is not, indeed, quite unrepresented even here. It does not, moreover, follow a definite order of subjects, but passes quite freely from one theme to another, as is natural in a friendly letter, especially if, as was probably the case, it was not written continuously.

Paul begins with the assertion of his thankful joy over the happy condition of the church at Philippi, and then pictures his own present condition, which was not to be regretted, since the cause of the Gospel in Rome was making progress in spite of, nay, even because of, his imprisonment, not only in consequence of his own constant intercourse with the soldiers of the imperial guard, under whose ward he was, but also indirectly, because, in consequence of his imprisonment (and his trial, which had made the religious grounds of his arrest a subject of public interest), the majority of the Roman church had gained courage to preach the word of God in a way that had proved fruitful.   It was true this preaching of Christ had not been done universally with benevolent and pure intentions, but even, in the case of some individuals, from jealousy and contentious-ness and from personal ill-will to himself, the imprisoned apostle, with the intention of thereby making his condition worse ; but whatever the intention, he rejoiced, and would ever rejoice, that Christ was preached.   For he was firmly convinced that he would never be put to shame, but that openly before all men, as ever, so now, Christ should be glorified in his body, whether by his life or by his death.   For to him to live was Christ (*i.e.* a complete devotion to the service of Christ) and to die was gain.   Which of the two he should rather wish for himself he cannot tell ; so far as his personal feeling goes he would rather depart and be with Christ (a feeling which the apostle had expressed several years earlier amid sore affliction from without, 2 Cor. v. 28).   But for the sake of his churches, to which his service was so important with a view to their growth in grace, he desires and hopes to be able to continue his earthly ministry a little longer.

Then he exhorts the Philippians to make their

church life worthy of the gospel and not to allow
themselves to be intimidated by the sufferings
which for Christ's sake they were counted worthy
to bear with a view to their salvation (the "adversaries" are Jewish and heathen enemies of the church).
Above all, to be in hearty accord, free from
party-spirit and vainglory, living in the lowly and
selfless spirit of which Christ had given them
an example, in that "though he was in the form
of God he did not look upon equality with God
as a spoil to be grasped at, but emptied himself
and took upon him the form of a servant, and was
found in fashion as a man, humbling himself and
becoming obedient unto death, even the death of the
cross: wherefore also God highly exalted him and
gave him a name that is above every name, that at
the name of Jesus every knee, in heaven and earth
and under the earth, should bow, and every tongue
confess him as Lord." Therefore it behoves the
Philippians to apply all the power which God works
in them to ensure their salvation, showing themselves
blameless children of God in a perverse generation,
amid which they shine as stars in the world, giving
the apostle cause to glory that he has not laboured
in vain and can rejoice in and with them, even though
he should have to offer his life for their faith (i. 27–
ii. 18). Then follow some personal matters regarding
Timothy, whom he intends to send soon to the
Philippians that he may learn through him how they
fare. They know his capacity and how he has stood
by the apostle in his missionary work as a son by a
father; he had no one else (among those immediately
surrounding him) who was so much of the same mind

as himself, especially in regard to his care for his churches ; others sought their own, not the things that were Jesus Christ's (a judgment in connection with which we must take into account the melancholy mood of the apostle in his imprisonment and loneliness).   He was sending back, to reassure them, Epaphroditus also, who after his recovery from a severe illness longed to see them again.   Such men as these, who imperilled their lives for the sake of the Gospel, were to be held in honour (ii. 19–30).

Not in direct connection with the immediately preceding passage, but in conformity with the solicitude for the continuance and confirmation of the harmonious life of the church at Philippi which occupied the apostle's mind, and to which he has already alluded in i. 27, he begins the third chapter with a repetition of the warning of the danger which threatens their peaceful and joyous Christian life from the side of Jewish disturbers of the peace.   For in view of the context it is only as a reference to this that verse 2 can be understood : [1]   " Beware of dogs, beware of evil workers, beware of the concision.   For we are the true circumcision, who serve God in the spirit and glory in Christ Jesus, and have no confidence in the

---

[1] The characterisation of these men agrees so closely with that given in 2 Cor. xi. 13–23 and Gal. v. 10 f., vi. 12 f., that it must refer to the same, namely, to Jewish agitators who were endeavouring to tamper with the church at Philippi.   So far, indeed, these efforts had been without success, so that Paul could lavish praise upon the church while he held it necessary to give warning of the danger which threatened it on the part of these agitators.   These fanatical Jewish agitators have, however, nothing to do with the Jewish Christians of Rome, who were of quite another type. Therefore iii. 2 and 18 are not inconsistent with i. 18.

flesh." Though truly, if it were a question of out-ward advantages of this kind, he could make the same boast as these people — circumcision, Pharisaic zeal for the law, blameless righteousness (understood, of course, from the standpoint of the Pharisaic standard of strict legality, and therefore without reference to Paul's Christian conception of righteousness). But all these advantages, however valuable in Jewish eyes, he had counted but loss for Christ's sake, yea he counted them as dross, in order to win Christ in their stead ; and instead of his own righteousness, to obtain the righteousness of God through faith, that he might know Christ, and the power of His resurrection, and the fellowship of His suffering, being conformed to His death, in the hope of attaining the resurrection of the Lord. Not as though he had already reached the highest aim, but he could at least testify of himself that he had forgotten those things that lay behind (behind his call to be a Christian), and was striving unhindered towards the one goal, the prize of his heavenly calling in Christ. And this was the spirit which he recommended to all who desired to be perfect. However they might differ in other matters, let them only advance, upon the good way which they had begun, to Christian perfection. In doing so they might look to him and to those like him as examples, but not to those of whom he had warned them before, and now warned them again, as enemies of the cross of Christ, whose end was destruction, whose god was their belly, and whose glory was in their shame, since all their thoughts and imaginations were directed to what is earthly. We Christians, on the other hand, have our citizenship in heaven, whence also we expect our Saviour, who shall change our vile body and fashion it like His glorious body.   Therefore (since they have such hopes) he exhorts the Philippians, who were his joy and crown, to stand fast in the Lord (iii. 2–iv. 1).

Then follows an exhortation to concord addressed to two women in the congregation, the occasion of which is not known to us (our ignorance does not, however, justify us in making the two women into an allegory for two parties in the church—an eccentric idea in view of the simple natural tone of the whole epistle).   Then follows—again directed to the whole church—an exhortation to Christian joyfulness and to trustful prayer and to the exercise of all Christian virtue and seemly conduct.   An expression of thanks for the gift of the Philippians, and of the wish that God might visibly reward their offering, forms the close of the epistle.

The genuineness of this epistle has been attacked by the Tübingen school, and with especial keenness by Holsten,[1] but the arguments are not strong enough to stand against the general impression of genuineness which the epistle makes.   The language, in spite of many unusual expressions (but every Pauline epistle has its quota of these) is, in general, recognisable as genuinely Pauline.   As regards content, the points to which exception is taken are generally the following :—(1) The mention of bishops and deacons in i. 1 is said to point to post-apostolic conditions.   It is true this combination is not else-where found in St Paul, and on that ground the conjecture that these words at least are an inter-

---

[1] *Jahrb. f. prot. Theol.*, 1875 and 1876, where also earlier discussions of the question are collected.

polation by a later hand has something in its
favour. Paul mentions, however, those who preside
(προϊστάμενοι) in Thess. v. 12 and Rom. xii. 8, and a
deaconess in Rom. xvi. 1; so the possibility that,
in official actions such as the present to Paul, the
church at Philippi was even then represented by
bishops and deacons cannot be entirely excluded.
(2) The curious fashion in which the preaching of
Christ by Paul's opponents is spoken of in i. 15 does
not correspond to his uncompromising rigour elsewhere; e.g., Gal. i. 8 f. But does not Paul in the
Epistle to the Romans also deal with the Jewish
Christians at Rome much more gently than with the
Judaising agitators of Galatia? If we remember
that they were only a small minority (τινές), and that
the reproach brought against them is personal ill-
will to Paul, not actual false doctrine, we can quite
understand the gentleness of his judgment. And
it becomes perfectly comprehensible if we might
suppose (following Weizsäcker's noteworthy suggestion) that among those who with ill intentions
contributed to the extension of the Gospel there
were included not only hostile Christians but Jews
and heathen, who by their disputes about the Christian
cause involuntarily spread the knowledge of it. If
we take into consideration also that the apostle as a
prisoner at Rome was confronted with new and
strange circumstances which lay outside his own
control, we shall find the tone of mingled gentleness
and resignation in i. 15 ff. so exactly in harmony
with the situation that we can hardly suppose it to
be a later invention. (3) It is asserted that the
passage ii. 6 ff. is not in accordance with Pauline

Christology as set forth elsewhere, inasmuch as the pre-existing Christ is represented, not, as elsewhere, as the Heavenly Man, but as a God-like being, and the earthly Christ is represented not as real man but only as a being resembling man (docetically). This is so far true that the whole of the expressions in ii. 6 f. are unusual and seem to demand an interpretation which differs from the rest of the Pauline Christology; with reference to this I consider the suggestion lately put forward (Brückner, Schmiedel) that verse 6 f. was interpolated by a " deutero-Pauline " well worthy of notice.[1] (4) The judgment on Paul's past life as a Jew expressed in iii. 6 that he was "as touching the righteousness of the law, blameless," is un-Pauline, because it implies that the Mosaic law is only considered as a ceremonial law, contrary to Rom. vii. 12, 14. But in Galatians also Paul put the law on the same footing as the "beggarly elements of the world," and in Gal. i. 14 he estimates his legal righteousness in the same way as in Phil. iii. 6; Rom. ii. 6 ff., also, shows that where the doctrine of justification did not come into view he can recognise a relative moral judgment. (5) The doctrine of salvation in iii. 9 is un-Pauline, because it confuses the objective faith-righteousness with the subjective righteousness of life resting on union with Christ, making the latter a condition of salvation, and salvation therefore uncertain (εἴπως, verse 11). But a similar combination of inward and attributed righteousness is found elsewhere not infrequently in Paul (cf. 2 Cor. v. 14–21; Rom. vi. 4 ff., viii. 2 ff.),

---

[1] This will be referred to in greater detail below in connection with the Pauline Christology.

and the ethical condition of the final attainment of salvation is as definitely asserted in many passages (*cf.* Rom. viii. 17, 13; Gal. vi. 7 ff.; 1 Cor. ix. 23–27 *et al.*) as the unconditionedness of the certainty of salvation, from the religious point of view, undoubtedly is in others. This, like many other antinomies, merely shows that Paul was not the systematic thinker that he has often been supposed to have been. Finally (6 and 7), if objection be taken to the way in which Paul in iii. 15 ff. and iv. 9 holds himself up as an example of virtue, and to the elaborate manner of his thanksgiving for the gift of the Philippians in iv. 10–18, and these are held to be unworthy of the apostle, that is too much a matter of taste (others have taken exactly the opposite view) to quarrel about or build anything upon. While none of these grounds of doubt is convincing, they are confronted with a strong argument in favour of the genuineness of the epistle in the difficulty of inventing the individual traits and trains of feeling which are so unmistakably appropriate to the position of the imprisoned apostle, and especially the improbability that a later writer would, after the apostle's death, have attributed to him such a confident hope of a favourable issue of his trial and an early visit to the Philippians.

To that must be added finally the evidence of Polycarp, who in his Epistle to the Philippians expressly mentions one or more letters of Paul addressed to the church.[1] That our epistle had one

---

[1] *Polyc. ad Phil.* iii. 2: (Paul) καὶ ἀπὼν ὑμῖν ἔγραψεν ἐπιστολάς. According to Zahn, *Einleitung*, i. 378, the plural refers to the letters of Paul to the Macedonians, including Thessalonians.

or more predecessors has been inferred also from
iii. 1, since the remark that it did not weary him to
write the same thing to them cannot refer to what
had been already written in this letter, and must
therefore refer to earlier correspondence. Others
have divided our epistle itself into two separate
parts, first combined at a later date; a hypothesis
which finds a certain support in the abrupt transition
from iii. 1 to 2, but makes shipwreck on the difficulty
that in that case each of the two epistles had lost
one essential part: the first, in particular, lacking an
expression of thanks for the gift from the Philippians,
which must nevertheless according to ii. 25 have
already taken place. Moreover, the numerous
sudden transitions are quite intelligible in the case
of an occasional letter which is so little doctrinal and
so predominantly personal.

17

CHAPTER XII

The Letters to Philemon and the Colossians

THESE epistles are closely connected, both as regards the situation of the writer and the place of residence of the persons addressed. The church of the Phrygian city of Colosse was not founded by Paul, but probably by Epaphras, whom Paul speaks of as his beloved fellow-servant and a faithful minister of Christ (i. 7). He had come from Colosse, where his home was (iv. 12), to visit the imprisoned apostle in Rome, and had brought him cheering news of the loving sympathy of his church for Paul, and the orderly and steadfast character of its faith (i. 7, ii. 5), but at the same time reported the anxieties and struggles (iv. 12) which had been caused him, in all probability, by the appearance in the church of false teachers. To oppose the danger which threatened from this direction, and to confirm the Colossian church in the true faith, was the object of the epistle which Paul despatched by Tychicus to the Colossians (iv. 7). Along with him he also sent thither Onesimus (iv. 9), the slave of Philemon, whom he had converted, and to whom he gave a short letter to his master, in which he exhorted him for his

(Paul's) sake to receive Onesimus, who had become dear unto him, no longer as slave but as a Christian brother, and to set down his debt, if any, to him, Paul, who thereby undertook, by his own signature, to pay it. For the rest, he hopes soon to be restored to his friends, and desires even now to bespeak Philemon's hospitality on his prospective visit.

The Epistle to the Colossians begins with a thankful acknowledgment of the vigorous faith of this church, which was as yet personally unknown to Paul, but had sent him a message of love through Epaphras (i. 3–8). To this he adds an aspiration for their further growth in knowledge of God's will, and in all spiritual wisdom and understanding, and in fruitfulness in all good works, that they might walk worthy of the Lord and show gratitude towards the Father, who had delivered them from the dominion of darkness and translated them into the kingdom of the Son of His love, in whom we have redemption, even the forgiveness of sins (i. 9–14). That statement leads to a Christological excursus (i. 15–23) regarding the transcendent dignity of Christ as the image of the invisible God and the first-born of every creature, the mediator and the final cause of the universe, of the visible as well as of the invisible world, who also has become the Head of the Church and the first-born from the dead, because it pleased God to cause all fulness to dwell in Him, and to reconcile by Him, that is, by His death on the cross, all things in earth and heaven. Thus the Colossians, who were once enemies of God (heathen), have been reconciled through Christ's death in order that they may be presented holy and blameless before God,

provided that they stand fast in the faith and hope of
the Gospel. In the service of this Gospel, which is
destined for all the world, the apostle rejoices even
in his sufferings, which, as the "filling up of that
which is behind" of the sufferings of Christ, are pro-
fitable to the Church (i. 24). As he constantly,
through teaching and admonition, sought to make
every one perfect in Christ, so all his eager anxiety
on behalf of the churches of Colosse and Laodicea,
which were personally unknown to him, was directed
to the same end that they might come to a full
knowledge of the divine mystery in Christ, in whom
are hidden all the treasures of wisdom and knowledge
(i. 25–ii. 3). Then follows in ii. 4–23 the exhortation
to guard against being led astray by philosophy and
human ordinances, which were appropriate to the
world-powers, but not to Christ. It was by Him
alone, in whom dwelt the whole fulness of the Godhead bodily, that the Colossians were come to full
salvation; in Him they had the true circumcision,
not made with hands, namely, the laying aside of
the flesh, inasmuch as they had been buried with
Christ in baptism and raised again by faith; God
had made them, who were once dead in sins, alive
with Christ, forgiving them their sins after He had
blotted out the indictment in the form of ordinances
which was against us (the letter which condemns), set
it aside and nailed it to the cross, stripped the hostile
spiritual powers, made a mockery of them and led
them in triumph, through Christ. They should
therefore let no man judge them in matters of eating
and drinking or the keeping holy of days which were
only the shadow of things to come, whereas Christ

was the substance ; they must not allow themselves
to be robbed of their prize by any man who delighted
in false humility and worshipping of angels, boasting
mightily of his visions, puffed up by his fleshly mind,
not holding the Head from whom the whole body
(the Church) receives its divinely-given increase.
Having died with Christ to the elements of the
world they should no longer concern themselves with
ordinances of abstinence from this and that, which
was only the seeming wisdom of a capricious piety
whose maltreatment of the body had really the effect
of ministering to the satisfaction of the flesh (*i.e.* of
carnal vanity). Rather, they ought (in iii. 1 ff. begin
the positive exhortations), as those who have been
raised with Christ, to give their minds to the things
of the world above, in which their life is hid with
Christ in God, until His appearance at the Parousia.
They should, therefore, mortify their members which
are on earth and lay aside heathen vices, seeing that
they have put off the old man and put on the new
which is renewed in knowledge after the image of its
Creator, where there is no distinction in the unity of
Christ. Therefore, as the chosen saints and beloved
of God, they should put on all the Christian virtues,
above all, love, as the bond of perfectness. The peace
of Christ and gratitude towards God should rule in
their hearts and in their meetings for worship, and all
their words and actions should be in the name of
Christ and to the praise of God. Not less should
their home life, in the relationships of husband and
wife, parents and children, masters and servants, be
consecrated by the Christian spirit. This picture of
the virtues closes with exhortations to constant prayer,

including intercession for the success of Paul's missionary work, to watchfulness, to prudent conduct towards those without, to redeeming the time, to gracious speech seasoned with salt, and that they should be ready at any time to defend their faith. Finally (iv. 7 ff.) follow personal explanations about the sending of Tychicus and Onesimus, and greetings from the missionary helpers who were then gathered about the imprisoned apostle—Aristarchus, Marcus, Jesus Justus, Epaphras, Luke, and Demas. Greetings are sent also to the church at Laodicea, and especially to the church in the house of Nymphas, and the Laodiceans and Colossians are directed to exchange their epistles. Archippus, who belongs to the household of Philemon, is reminded to take heed to the due fulfilment of his Christian office. An autograph greeting and the request to " remember his bonds " bring this interesting letter to a close.

One can hardly fail to observe that these personal references are in exact agreement with those of the Epistle to Philemon. There, too, greetings are sent from the same helpers of the apostle, except that Jesus Justus is wanting in the latter, probably because unknown to Philemon. In Philemon Epaphras stands first, and is described as a fellow-prisoner, while in the Colossian epistle it is Aristarchus who occupies this position. Archippus, who in Col. iv. 17 is exhorted to zeal in his office, receives in Philem. 2 the distinguishing addition " our fellow-soldier "; he seems, like " the sister " Appia, to have belonged to the family of Philemon. It cannot indeed be denied that the historical and personal allusions of these two letters, while completely independent internally, supplement each other without the smallest contradiction between them emerging in any single point.[1] Now, as no valid grounds of objection have been raised against Philemon (even the difficulty of verses 5 and 6 admits of an exegetical solution), its relation to Colossians forms a strong argument in favour of the genuineness of the latter, or, at least, of an underlying original. Both point to the same situation of Paul, and in all probability to his imprisonment at Rome, not at Cæsarea, for it was only in the former, not in the latter, where he was confined in the palace of the governor, that he enjoyed sufficient freedom to have intercourse with his helpers and to convert a runaway slave. It is, too, less probable that Onesimus would have fled to Cæsarea and there have met Paul than that he sought harbourage in Rome, which was the rendezvous of all such people, and there made acquaintance with Paul, perhaps through the intermediary of a soldier of the Prætorian guard. The remark, too, in Col. iv. 11 that *only* the Jewish Christians who have just been named have been fellow-workers with the apostle unto the kingdom of God deserves notice, inasmuch as it points to a hostile attitude on the part of other Jewish Christians, such as would be inferred in the Roman entourage of Paul from Phil. i. 15 ff. also. Finally, the hope which Paul expresses in Philem. 22 of being set at liberty and of seeing his Colossian friends again, does not favour the imprisonment at Cæsarea, during which Paul's eyes were fixed on Rome, but suggests the situation at the time of the Roman imprisonment, in which Paul wrote to the Philippians also of his

[1] Zahn, *Einleitung*, i. 350.

hopes of being liberated and soon visiting them
(i. 25, ii. 24). Whether the Epistles to Philemon
and to the Colossians were written rather earlier or
later than that to the Philippians must remain an
open question.

If, in spite of all this, the genuineness of the epistle
has always seemed suspicious to critics and has been
denied by many investigators, there must be weighty
grounds for that. As a matter of fact its contents
as well as its language are, when compared with
other Pauline epistles, so peculiar that it is no
wonder they have given rise to serious difficulties
regarding its genuineness. Above all, the false
teachers whom Paul here combats are of a different
character from those with whom he had to do elsewhere. They certainly cannot have been mere
Judaisers; their position as regards eating and
drinking, keeping of feast-days, new moons and
Sabbaths (ii. 16) goes beyond the Pharisaic legalism
in that, for example, while the Mosaic law forbids
certain meats it does not make any reference to
drinks; with the worship of angels, too, Pharisaism
has nothing in common; and the Judaistic legalism
could hardly be described as a religion of caprice
resting on philosophy and vain deceit. It is more
natural to think of ascetics of an Essene tendency, of
a similar kind to the weak party at Rome (Rom. xiv.).
But then what is said further about worship of angels
and boasting of pretended visions (ii. 17) does not
harmonise with that supposition, for even if the
Essenes were taken up about the names of angels,
it is not recorded that they actually worshipped them,
and a philosophy which speculated about the world-

elements such as is ascribed to the false teachers in
ii. 8, was equally foreign to them.[1] A dualistic
gnosticism has therefore been suggested, but this
again cannot have been exactly similar to any
gnostic system known to us, because in this case the
worship of angels, the boasting of visions, and the
legalistic cultus (ii. 16) would be inappropriate, and
because, moreover, the combating of such a system
would, on the analogy of the later anti-gnostic
polemic, have taken a different form. Since it is thus
difficult to bring the false teachers at Colosse under
any definite historical category, there would seem to
remain only two possibilities open. Either, in one
epistle two kinds of false doctrines are combined
which were in reality different, an earlier Judaising
error such as Paul encountered elsewhere, and a
later gnostic heresy which someone who worked
over the epistle at a later date desired to oppose;[2]
or, the false teaching really consisted of a mixture of
various religions and speculations analogous to the
manifold forms of religious syncretism found in
the Asiatic mystery-doctrines and mystery-worship.
That there was a Jewish gnosticism in Paul's time is
not to be denied, as we shall see in a later chapter,
but this did not take elsewhere a legalistic, but an
antinomian form, such as we see in the Nicolaitanes
who are attacked in the Apocalypse, and the
Simonians, who were closely connected with them.

[1] According to Philo, *Quod Omnis Probus Liber* (Mangey, 458),
they despised theoretic philosophy and left physics (*i.e.* natural
philosophy) to those who dwell above the clouds, as transcending
human understanding.

[2] So Holtzmann and Weizsäcker, *Ap. Zeitalter*, second edition,
p. 544.

As these latter appear in the Church Fathers as the first gnostic heretics who penetrated into the Christian churches, it seems, on that ground also, at least very problematical whether we can suppose a Jewish-Christian gnosis like that of the Colossians to have been in existence in Paul's time.

The argument brought against this false teaching is of a Christological and soteriological character which certainly rests on a Pauline basis, while it doubtless also, both in thought and language, goes rather beyond the teaching of the previous epistles. The main points which appear suspicious to criticism are the following : (1) Christ appears here (i. 15 f.), no longer as the Heavenly Man, but as a metaphysical world - principle of the most universal character, not merely the mediator, but also the final cause, of the creation and the upholder of the universe (*cf.* Heb. i. 2 f. ; on the other hand, Rom. xi. 36) ; He is the first-born not only from the dead, and among many brethren (1 Cor. xv. 20 ; Rom. viii. 29), but also of all creation ; not simply the animating spirit (1 Cor. xv. 45), but the bearer of the whole fulness of the Godhead (i. 19, ii. 9)—a saying which, like some of the foregoing, has its nearest analogy in Philo's doctrine of the Divine logos. (2) The work of Christ, too, takes on cosmical proportions ; He is the reconciler not only of the whole world of mankind (as in 2 Cor. v. 19), but also of the whole spiritual world (i. 20), to which He is nevertheless not bound by that solidarity into which the Pauline Christ entered with sinful man in His incarnation and death. Peculiar also are the expressions in ii. 14 f. : the bond embodied in ordinances has been blotted out through Christ's

death, and nailed to the cross (*i.e.* the curse of the
law has been annulled, Gal. iii. 13), and the princi-
palities and powers are thereby despoiled (stripped of
their arms), made a mock of, and led in triumph—a
wholly gnostic expression, which carries with it a
suggestion of the myth of the harrying of hell—for
the victory over the hostile spiritual powers, which,
moreover, Paul did not elsewhere directly connect
with the death of Christ, but expected to result from
the future Lordship of Christ (1 Cor. xv. 24 ff.).
(3) Surprising also is the statement that Paul supple-
ments by his sufferings what was lacking in the
afflictions of Christ (i. 24); according to this the
sufferings of pious Christians appear to be, not a
mere imitation and continuation of the sufferings of
Christ (2 Cor. i. 5, iv. 10 f.), but also to possess a
saving power analogous to these and capable of
supplementing them — a thought which does not
occur elsewhere in Paul's writings, but which has its
parallels in the literature of the second century.[1]
(4) Peculiar, too, is the description of baptism as a
"circumcision of Christ not made with hands" (*cf.*
Phil. iii. 3; Rom. ii. 29). (5) The Christian consecration appears as a setting of the mind on things
above, not on things of the earth, and a mortifying of
those members which are on the earth (iii. 2–5)—
a cosmical antithesis instead of the anthropological
antithesis which is usual with Paul, between flesh
and spirit (Rom. viii. 12; Gal. v. 16, 24; *cf.* also
Phil. iii. 14, 19 f.). (6) The ceremonial system is

[1] *Cf.*, *e.g.*, Ign. ad Eph. viii. 1 and xviii. 1, περίψημα ὑμῶν
ἁγνίζομαι ὑπὲρ ὑμῶν. xxi. 1 : ἀντίψυχον ὑμῶν ἐγώ. Similarly Polycarp,
ii. 3.

described as a shadow of things to come, whereas the substance, the actual good, is in Christ (ii. 17)—a conception of the relation of the old and the new covenant which is elsewhere foreign to Paul's thought, but is characteristic of the Epistle to the Hebrews. (7) Christ is described as the Head of the body, namely, the Church (i. 18, 24, ii. 19), a new turn of the representation in 1 Cor. xii. 27, where the Church is also spoken of as the body of Christ, but in such a way that Christ is thought of as the animating Spirit of this body, not as the Head. The conception in 1 Cor. xi. 3 is different; Christ is the Head of every man as the mediator of creation, not of salvation. (8) Christ is called " the mystery of God " (i. 26 f., ii. 2), and is the object of a deeper knowledge, the value of which is emphasised by various expressions, all pointing to a way of regarding things which has its affinities in the gnostic mysticism.

The question naturally presents itself whether all these peculiarities of the Colossian epistle, which differentiate it so markedly in its lexical and doctrinal features from the earlier epistles in the direction of the church gnosis of the second century (*cf.* the Ignatian and Johannine theology), can be explained on the assumption of the genuineness of the whole canonical epistle ? Most writers answer this question in the affirmative, pointing out that even within the earlier epistles many differences and developments are found, and that in the present instance Paul was led by having to oppose the Colossian errors to enter on this line of thought and expression—" the new opponent compels him to adopt the new formulæ " (Jülicher, *Einleitung*, p. 106). That this is possible

I will not, indeed, deny, but I cannot hold it to be probable. The differences are so considerable that they are more easily explained as coming from the mind of some follower of Paul who was in close contact of time and place with gnosticism. This writer need not on that account necessarily have composed the whole of the Epistle to the Colossians, for he may have adapted and extended an original Pauline letter with a view to the needs of his contemporaries. Of such an adaptation another variant, whether from the same or from another hand, was the Epistle to the Ephesians, which is doubtless deutero-Pauline, and is so nearly related to Colossians that it gives additional weight to the argument of adaptation in the case of the later. Just as the Second Epistle to the Thessalonians is a later redaction of the first, recast to suit a different period, and as Romans certainly, and Philippians probably, contain later elements, and as 2 Timothy is probably worked up from older genuine fragments, so also, I believe, in the canonical Epistle to the Colossians we should see a church-gnostic adaptation of a Pauline original intended to oppose gnostic heresy ; but the reconstruction of the original does not appear to me possible.

CHAPTER XIII

The Natural Man

In his anthropology Paul is a dichotomist: man, he holds, consists of two parts—of the outer and the inner man, body and soul, or flesh and spirit. The outer man is called "body" in reference to its form as an organism, "flesh" in reference to its material substance: the two conceptions are, it is true, not identical, inasmuch as there are heavenly or spiritual bodies which do not consist of earthly material, or flesh, but of a supernatural light-substance, and are therefore not, like earthly bodies, subject to corruption—a distinction which has its importance, as we shall see, for Paul's eschatology. But since in the case of man on earth the body exists only as organised matter, or flesh, the distinction of the two conceptions is not here maintained. In point of fact, form and material coincide; therefore the terms "body" and "flesh" are for the most part used interchangeably. Paul speaks of "the flesh of sin" and of "the body of sin"; of the "body of death" and of "mortal flesh"; of "crucifying the flesh and its lusts" and of "mortifying the deeds of the body"; of the "purity of the body" and of "defilement of the flesh."[1]   Just as body and flesh are thus merely two names for the outer man, so are "soul and spirit" for the inner; the "spirit" of the natural man (which is to be distinguished from the supernatural or divine Spirit which is given to the Christian) is not something really different from the soul, but designates the inner man as the ego or subject of consciousness (1 Cor. ii. 11) in contradistinction to his outward manifestation or body; for example, in the formulæ "holy in body and spirit," "defilement of flesh and spirit," "absent in the body but present in spirit" (1 Cor. v. 3, vii. 34; 2 Cor. vii. 1).   But soul is also used for the whole man, "every soul" for "every man" (Rom. xiii. 1), Adam was made a "living soul" (1 Cor. xv. 45); but in this concept stress is laid, not so much on the distinction of the inner from the outer man (as in the case of spirit), but rather on their connection, for the soul is the principle which animates the body and makes the living man; as the life which dwells in the material body, it is not contrasted with the latter but thought of as constituting in combination with it a united whole, so that the formulæ "every soul" and "every flesh," the "soulish man" and the "fleshly man," are used as interchangeable terms for the natural man in general, in contrast with the spiritual man (1 Cor. xv. 45 f.; ii. 14 with iii. 1 and 3).   We must not conclude,

[1] *Cf.* Rom. viii. 3 and vi. 6; vii. 24 and 2 Cor. iv. 11; Gal. v. 24 and Rom. viii. 13; 1 Cor. vii. 34 and 2 Cor. vii. 1.   The critical objection to the last passage ($\kappa\alpha\theta\alpha\rho\iota\sigma\omega\mu\epsilon\nu$ $\dot{\epsilon}\alpha\nu\tauο\dot{\upsilon}\varsigma$ $\dot{\alpha}\pi\dot{o}$ $\pi\alpha\nu\tau\dot{o}\varsigma$ $\mu\omicron\lambda\upsilon\sigma\mu\omicron\hat{\upsilon}$ $\sigma\alpha\rho\kappa\dot{o}\varsigma$ $\kappa\alpha\dot{\iota}$ $\pi\nu\epsilon\dot{\upsilon}\mu\alpha\tau\omicron\varsigma$) is removed when we observe that it is a mistake to assume that Paul makes a strict distinction between the $\sigma\dot{\alpha}\rho\xi$ and the $\sigma\hat{\omega}\mu\alpha$ and its members in reference to the seat of sin.   See Orello Cone, *Paul*, p. 228.

however, from this intimate connection of body and
soul that Paul thought of the latter as a purely
animal principle with the exclusion of spiritual
functions; rather, he uses "soul" as well as spirit
for the subject of personal states of consciousness,
especially feelings, in which the whole undivided man
is concerned.[1]   It must therefore be maintained that
soul and spirit are not different parts, but only
different names for the one human being,[2] between
which we can only distinguish to the extent that in
the former it is rather the unity of the outer and
inner man, in the latter rather their contrast, which
comes into view.[3]

While body, or flesh, and soul, or spirit, designate
the two parts of man, outward and inward, mind,
heart, and conscience are the factors by which the
life of the inner man is carried on.   Mind (νοῦς) is
the power of theoretical and practical judgment; in
1 Cor. xiv. 14 it is used of the reflective consciousness in general in contradistinction to immediate
unreflective feeling.   According to Rom. vii. 15–22
the mind of the inner man is the subject of the
ethical will which is in sympathy with the law of
God.   There is a law of the mind, that is, an ethical

[1] Cf. Rom. ii. 9; 2 Cor. i. 23; Phil. i. 27; Col. iii. 23.

[2] Even 1 Thess. v. 23 is not inconsistent with this, since here
the apparent trichotomy πνεῦμα, ψυχή and σῶμα is only a rhetorical
emphasising of the completeness of the man, just as in Phil. i. 17
ἐνὶ πνεύματι, μιᾷ ψυχῇ, and in Luke i. 46 ἡ ψυχή μου, τὸ πνεῦμα μου,
are placed in rhetorical parallelism without any reference to
different subjects being intended.

[3] Cf. Simon, Psychologie des Ap. Paulus, p. 37 : "Man's inner
being is called ψυχή as dwelling in the σάρξ and closely united with
it; the name πνεῦμα is applied to it in so far as, in spite of that, it
still shows freedom and independence of the σάρξ."

impulse of the mind, which stands in contrast with
the law (impulse) of sin in the members. Similarly,
the mind is the religious sense by which the being of
God is recognised from the works of creation (Rom.
i. 20). Inasmuch as the mind thus possesses a
moral and religious tendency towards the divine, it
would be possible to speak of a certain relationship
of the mind to God. But according to Paul the
natural mind of man is not in itself an effective
power of knowing and willing the good; he makes
it only a mere form which can take up into itself a
content of a contrary nature, and which, in the case
of the natural man, is determined by the flesh in a
direction contrary to God. Therefore, he speaks of
a "mind of the flesh" (Col. ii. 18), of a "reprobate
mind" (Rom. i. 28), the thoughts of which are
blinded by the world-spirit (2 Cor. iv. 4), and his
judgment on the soulish (natural) man who does not
yet possess the mind of Christ is that he is incapable
of discerning the things of the spirit (1 Cor. ii. 14).
Hence the natural mind needs, in the first place,
renewal through the divine Spirit which finds in it
a receptive point of connection (Rom. xii. 2). The
heart (καρδία) is also, it is true, in harmony with the
Hebrew usage of לב, the theoretical and practical
capacity of apprehension and evil, but especially the
seat of feeling; in the heart the love of God is
poured out, joy and fear are experienced, faith is
formed (Rom. v. 5, x. 9 f.; 2 Cor. ii. 4). Like the
mind, the heart can be darkened, impenitent (Rom.
ii. 5, i. 21). On the other hand, he speaks of the
work of the law as written on the hearts of the
heathen (Rom. ii. 14), which means the same thing

18

as the law of the mind (vii. 23), namely, the ethical sense as a natural endowment of man.[1] Connected with this is the conscience (συνείδησις), a term which Paul adopted from the late Greek linguistic usage, but in its original wider sense, in which it included the theoretic consciousness of the truth of a statement (Rom. ix. 1) or the religious consciousness of the significance of an object.[2] As a rule, however, "conscience" is the ethical sense of the worth or worthlessness of one's own existence and action (Rom. ii. 15; 2 Cor. i. 12; 1 Cor. iv. 4), sometimes also of the worth of others (2 Cor. iv. 2); finally, it is the personal judgment on right or wrong, duty (Rom. xiii. 5), and things permissible (1 Cor. viii. 7–12), which is involved by religious conviction. The weak conscience in the last-mentioned case is the capacity for ethical judgment in so far as it is limited by religious prejudices, and does not yet possess the power of forming an objectively right judgment in regard to things indifferent. Since Paul ascribes to the natural man mind and conscience as a capacity for ethico-religious knowledge (Rom. ii. 7), it might be thought that we must draw the inference that the Christian Spirit is the development

---

[1] *Cf.* Norden, *Antike Kunstprosa,* ii. 497, note. "This phrase (Rom. ii. 14) is cast in a thoroughly Greek mould; the identity of the ἄγραφοι νόμοι and the φύσις had been keenly debated since the time of the ancient Sophists; but it is well known to classical scholars that through the intermediary of the Stoics this idea passed into the popular consciousness, so its use does not imply that it had been taken from books."

[2] In 1 Cor. viii. 7, συνείδησις τοῦ εἰδώλου = a religious conviction of the existence of the false god and of its connection with the flesh of the sacrifice.

and actualisation through historical experiences of
that God-given endowment of our natural spirit.
That is not, however, Paul's view of the case; for
him, it is no uninterrupted inner development of
the mind of the "psychic" man into the pneuma of
the Christian; the latter comes from without,
through the mystic act of baptism, into the man, as
another, purely supernatural, spirit which sometimes
stands in contrast with the man's own spirit (Rom.
viii. 16), sometimes represents him (verse 26), sometimes, again, appears as so closely united with him
(1 Cor. vi. 17) that there results, so to speak, a new
divine-human spirit, which in spite of its supernatural
origin is apprehended by the Christian as his own
ego, his new nature. We shall have to deal with
this later in a more detailed fashion; here it was
important to establish at the outset, that in Paul's
view there is an essential contrast between the spirit
which is identical with the personal soul of every
man and the supernatural Spirit, which is identical
with the person of Christ the Son of God, inasmuch
as the latter does not develop out of the former, but
comes to him from without and enters into him—
a strict supernaturalism which is as thoroughly
accordant with ancient methods of thought as it is
foreign to our modern psychological and evolutionary
views; but it is impossible, unless it be taken into
account, to understand the Pauline theology.

Paul, therefore, has a twofold conception of spirit :
the natural spirit, which belongs to the "psychic
man," is without power of knowing the true or
doing the good, can be stained with sin and fall into
corruption (1 Cor. v. 5; 2 Cor. vii. 1); and the

supernatural, which is essentially an eternal divine life, holiness and glory, and therefore a power able to animate, sanctify, and glorify a man to whom it is given. Similarly Paul has also a twofold conception of "flesh," the natural and the moral. According to its original meaning it is the visible, sensible material of the earthly world, which, as such, is also perishable (2 Cor. iv. 18). It is in this physical, ethically indifferent, sense that the word is always used where things, circumstances, or actions of a bodily kind are described as " carnal " or "after the flesh," as in 1 Cor. ix. 11, carnal goods ; in Rom. i. 3 and ix. 5, ancestry according to the flesh ; in Gal. iv. 13, weakness of the flesh (sickness); in 1 Cor. v. 5 destruction of the flesh (death). So also the formulæ " life in the flesh," " walk in the flesh," are often (Gal. ii. 20 ; Phil. i. 22 f. ; 2 Cor. x. 3) used in the natural sense of " bodily life " without any ethical implication. Now, inasmuch as it is the materiality of the earthly being which distinguishes the earthly creature from the Creator and from the heavenly spiritual beings, the " flesh " was already in the Old Testament associated with the conception of weakness and transiency in contrast with the divine strength (cf. Is. xxxi. 3 ; Jer. xvii. 5), and as this natural weakness of the fleshly creature expresses itself in the case of man in his moral relationships also, flesh appears even in the Old Testament as the explanation and excuse of ethical defects without being itself on that account evil or the seat of evil (Ps. lxxviii. 39, ciii. 14 ; Gen. vi. 3 ; Job iv. 17, xxv. 5 et freq.). In precisely this sense Paul sometimes speaks of flesh and blood, meaning weak man (Gal. i. 16), and describes the

Corinthians on account of their party spirit as
" carnal," who walk as men (1 Cor. iii. 3), *i.e.* in whom
common human weakness prevented a ripe Christian
life. But Paul goes a long step beyond the conception of the merely unspiritual weak flesh, and thinks
of the flesh as the seat of an active God-opposing
principle and consequently so hostile to the Spirit that
to be " of the flesh " or " in the flesh " is equivalent to
being " sold under sin," *i.e.* tyrannised over by sin.
In order to understand Paul's peculiar ethical conception of the " flesh " as the antithesis of the (Divine)
Spirit, we must first take note of his conception
of sin.

We have to distinguish in Paul's writings between
sin (ἁμαρτία) in the singular and sins or transgressions
(παραβάσεις, παραπτώματα). While the latter are
individual actions contrary to the law, which incur
personal guilt, the former is a general principle
underlying and giving rise to all sinful acts. Paul
understands thereby, however, not, as we might
think, a permanent tendency of the will, evil inclination, bias, or the like, but, with the usual personifying
tendency of antiquity, he makes the sinful principle
an independent entity, an active subject to which all
manner of predicates can be attached. Sin has come
into the world and exercised kingly rule, is a tyrant
to which the carnal man has been sold as a slave,
gives its servants death for their wages, but was
itself condemned to death in Christ's flesh ; before
the law it was dead (powerless, dormant), but in
consequence of the law it was vivified, causes all
manner of lusts, and through the commandment
deceives and slays men, makes evil actual in man in

spite of his better will, and thus holds the ego a
prisoner under its law (compulsive power) (Rom.
v. 12, 21; vi. 16, 23; viii. 3; vii. 7 ff., 20 ff.). That
may well appear to us at the present day as a mere
rhetorical form of speech, but for Paul it was
certainly much more than that; he really saw in
sin a demonic spiritual being, which takes possession
of men, sets up its throne in the material flesh of
his body, excites the lusts, kindles the passions,
enslaves the will, and delivers body and soul over
to death. Possessed by this demonic power, infected
with its deadly poison, the fleshly body becomes
" flesh of sin " and " body of death," the desires are no
longer the mere, morally indifferent, expression of
its life, but are sinful desires, because contrary to
God, its endeavours tend towards death, and are
involuntary rebellion against God's law, so that it
was quite impossible for those lying under its ban
to please God (Rom. viii. 6; Gal. v. 17). The last-
mentioned passage is especially significant in that it
makes the ego of the man the direct object of the
strife of hostile powers—the lusting of the flesh and
of the spirit—so that it never does its own will, but
always that to which it is driven from the one side
or the other (similarly Rom. vi. 16 ff.). According
as the one or the other power preponderates there
result works of the flesh, i.e. vices of a sensuous,
selfish, or even irreligious character, or fruits of the
spirit, i.e. Christian virtues (Gal. v. 19–23). Among
the works of the flesh sensuous sins take the first
place, since the sinful principle has its base of
operations in the flesh, and therefore expresses itself
most immediately in the form of the lusts of the

flesh ; but these are not the only works of the flesh, for the sinful principle forces the whole ego to submit to its sway and corrupts even its mind by occupying it with fleshly interests (Col. ii. 18; Rom. i. 28). Therefore all the explanations of the Pauline "flesh" which find favour at the present day in the sense of a sensuous direction of the will, "the love of worldly pleasure," or, more generally, the "natural condition" of man as he is, must be described as arbitrary modernisations of the idea. Holtzmann remarks excellently : " When a writer gives us so clearly to understand that he means by flesh just real flesh, that when he wishes to explain it further he speaks, on occasion, of 'beating the body' and of 'the law of sin in the members,' it is certainly not he who is to blame, but the fixed determination of his theological interpreters to misunderstand him, if they fail to recognise the one single sense and meaning which his words will bear, and have wrested from them an interpretation which seems to be alterable at will, which is inconsistent with itself, and is extremely difficult to define." It is no doubt true that the flesh is not identical with sin, but is the seat and organ of the demonic sinful principle ; but as such it becomes fused with the power by which it is possessed into such an indistinguishable unity that its own imaginations and interests become wholly sinful and tend to death. The case is thus exactly analogous with that which we touched on above ; the union of the natural spirit with the divine spirit by means of which the former becomes wholly life and righteousness (Rom. viii. 6–10). This Pauline view of the inherence of sin in the flesh is wholly misrepresented when freewill is inserted between the two in such a way that it is only through the voluntary surrender of man to the desires of the flesh that these become sinful and sin acquires power over him. That is a sound modern conception, but it is not Pauline, for Paul does not say, Because I have freely surrendered myself to the dominion of sin, therefore I have become carnal, but exactly the converse: I am carnal (σάρκινος), sold under sin (Rom. vii. 14), that is, because I physically consist of flesh I have become enslaved to the sinful power which dwells in this material substance. In fact, sin is for Paul so terrible a power, so immeasurably stronger than the natural will, that he cannot think of it as the result of the freedom of man but as the cause of his enslavement; and as he is accustomed to think of general principles, not as abstract conceptions, but, after the realistic fashion of antiquity, as concrete entities, it is wholly natural that sin should appear to him as a demonic spiritual being which dwells in the material body and holds man under its tyrannic sway until he is freed from its domination, and in this case too not by his own freewill, but by the overmastering power of a higher divine spiritual being (Rom. vii. 23–viii. 2).

However strange this "animistic" conception may seem at first sight to our modern way of thinking, it must not be overlooked that this obsolete form conceals actual experiences which were founded on the nature of our race and are the same in all periods. And these facts of experience, as for example, that unconscious desire becomes, under provocation of the

law, conscious sin, and that when a man becomes
conscious of legal prohibitions he feels himself divided
between his actual and his ideal will, a painful sensa-
tion which nevertheless carries with it the hope and the
possibility of salvation—these permanent facts Paul
has set forth with unsurpassed penetration and depth
in Rom. vii. 7–25. " I had not known sin but for
the law, for I had not known lust except the law had
said : thou shalt not lust [covet]. But sin, taking
occasion by the commandment, wrought in me all
manner of lust. For I was alive without the law once :
but when the commandment came, sin revived, and I
died. And the commandment, which was ordained
to life, I found to be a means of death. For sin,
taking occasion by the commandment, deceived me,
and by it slew me. Is, then, that which is good
become death to me ? Nay, it was sin, that it
might manifest itself as sin by working death in
me by that which was good ; that so, by means
of the commandment, it might display all its sinfulness." According to this, sin, as the actual
power of desire in man, is present, before he is
himself conscious of it, but, so far, it is "dead,"
i.e. latent, dormant, not yet recognised as sin and
therefore without conscious guilt ; that is the condition of childish innocence, of simply living the
life of nature under the unresisted rule of impulse.
Then comes the prohibition of the law and rouses the
potency of sin so that it comes to life, and, with the
consciousness that they absolutely ought not to be,
the hitherto innocent desires become contrary to
the law, morally condemned, and therefore formal
guilt and sin. It is then all over with the peaceful

unconscious life of childish innocence; man knows himself now as a sinner who lies under sentence of the law and is worthy of death — " but I died." Thenceforth he recognises his natural desires directed towards pleasure as a " deceit " ; inasmuch as, instead of the hoped-for satisfaction, it has rather death for its consequence. But though the evil effects of sinful desire are recognised, it is so far from being possible to suppress it by the law, that the provocation of the commandment rather incites it to greater energy and fuller development. Thus the law serves not only to bring sin to subjective consciousness as such, but to impel it to an actually increased manifestation in a multitude of transgressions (Rom. v. 20). But the more the destructive power of sin is brought to development and to consciousness, the more apparent becomes the division between it and the inner man whose intelligent will is in harmony with the law of the good, while nevertheless the actual deeds of the outer man remain under the sway of the sinful power. Thus, man finds in himself a painful disharmony between his inner ideal will and his actual deed as ruled by sin. These deeds now seem to him like the action of a hostile power opposed to his own will, by which he feels himself dominated against his will, which he repudiates and abhors, but without being able to free himself from it (verses 17, 20). This sense of bondage, of an irreconcilable self-contradiction, an incurable cleavage, breaks out in the cry of pain: " Unhappy man that I am ! who will deliver me from this body of death ? " (verse 24). But this question, with the cry of painful yearning for deliverance, itself implies the possibility and promise of deliverance, for it proves that the inner man is liberated from sin and feels himself identified with the law of God (verses 22–25). In this fact of the inner " crisis " which Paul represents as the outcome of the moral process under the discipline of the law, modern evolutionary thinking would see not only the consciousness but the actual beginning, the fertile seed, from which the transition from bondage to freedom has proceeded by gradual development and continues to develop; that, however, was by no means Paul's meaning, and on his presuppositions could not be so, not only because he himself felt the transition to be a catastrophe, the cause of which presented itself to his consciousness as a power which came upon him from without, but also (and this has been too little regarded) on account of the theoretic form of his religious consciousness in general. The primitive animism which personifies the state of consciousness as a spiritual being and places it outside the ego and in opposition to it, necessarily involves a thorough-going supernaturalism for which there is no regular inner development of the personal life, but only actions of the different spiritual beings, whose action man passively experiences. Thereby is to be explained the peculiar inconsistency that in Paul's teaching on sin and grace we find, on the one hand, deep ethical and religious truth and marvellously accurate description of facts of experience which constantly recur, while on the other hand we feel ourselves alienated by the theological garb in which they are clothed, and the more so the more closely we fix our attention on the immediate literal sense of the phrases. This literal study has its place, but is so

far from sufficing for the real understanding of the
religious interpretation of the apostle's meaning, that
on the contrary, the seemingly scientific process of
defining his theological conceptions in isolation and
abstraction from real experience gives rise to the most
perverse caricatures, which are much further removed
from the right interpretation than the earlier less
exact exegesis.

With this way of thinking is connected also the
difficulty in which the question of the origin
of sin and death is involved for Paul. Starting
from the above - mentioned passage in Rom. vii.
7 ff., it is possible to get the impression that
in this description of the appearance of sin in
the individual Paul had in mind the Biblical
account of the fall of man in Paradise,[1] and
therefore thought of our individual experience in
becoming sinful as an analogue of the Fall. From
that one might draw the inference that the sinful
power in the flesh, which must be assumed as a
pre-condition of the awaking of the moral consciousness, was present in our first parents from the outset
and did not originate from the Fall, but only made
its first appearance at the Fall. And this view
seems to be confirmed by 1 Cor. xv. 45 f., where the
first Adam, as living soul, is contrasted with the
last Adam, as quickening spirit, and the general
principle is asserted that, not the spiritual, but the
psychic, was first; and since life and righteousness
are the properties of the spiritual, but not of the
psychical-carnal man, the conclusion seems indicated

---

[1] Cf. Rom. vii. 11, " Sin deceived me and slew me," with 2 Cor.
xi. 3, " the serpent deceived Eve."

that the original condition of man is not to be thought of as freedom from sin and death, but that this was first effected by Christ; especially as there is no direct and express declaration that in consequence of the Fall corruption so affects the nature of the human race, that flesh then first became sinful. On the other 'hand, Paul says in Rom. v. 12–18, "that through one man sin came into the world and death by sin, and so death passed upon all, for that all have sinned;" through the disobedience of the one, many (the whole posterity of Adam) have become sinners and have fallen under the tyranny of death, so that in Adam (in consequence of their racial origin from him) all die (1 Cor. xv. 22). According to this, sin and death were not in the world from the beginning, but only entered after the historical Fall of Adam, inasmuch as this called forth a divine sentence of punishment ($\kappa\rho\iota\mu\alpha$ and $\kappa\alpha\tau\dot\alpha\kappa\rho\iota\mu\alpha$) in virtue of which all men are subjected to the power of sin as well as of death; the latter as a logical consequence of the former, but both in consequence of the original sin of Adam.[1] Here,

[1] "And so death passed upon all in consonance with the fact that ($\dot\epsilon\phi'$ $\ddot\omega$) all sinned." The following verses (13 f.) assert that sin was present before the law, but since it was not, as in Adam's case, the transgression of a positive command, it is not condemned (by God) as personal guilt and deserving of death. If, in spite of that, death even then reigned over all, the decisive reason for this cannot be in the actual sins of individuals but in the original sin of Adam, for whose sake the tyranny of sin and death was inflicted by a divine decree upon the whole race, in virtue of its solidarity, as its common fate. In verses 12–14 there is therefore clearly asserted both the causal connection of the universality of death with the universality of sin, and also the connection of both with the sin of Adam, the consequences of which were by a divine

therefore, the universal lordship of sin and death over mankind is not based upon the fleshly nature of man, but upon the historical fact of the free sinful act of Adam, and the divine sentence of punishment which that called forth. The question now arises, Have we here two views which run parallel, but cannot be united, as to the origin of sin and death ? Or did Paul perhaps think of them in combination, perhaps in the form that in consequence of the Fall, and in virtue of the divine sentence, the demonic powers of sin and death have taken possession of the human body, first in the case of our first parents and then of all their posterity, and have produced the evil effects which now form the nature of the flesh of sin and " body of death." The possibility of the second view can scarcely be contested, especially as it is found in Jewish theology also ; not, it is true, exclusively, but alongside of the other view of the originality of the evil impulse in man.[1] In favour of the probability of the second view the passages may be cited in which the Jewish theologoumenon of a corruption of nature both

sentence entailed upon all, involving the subjugation of all flesh under the demonic power of sin and death ; *cf.* viii. 20, vii. 14.

[1] *Cf.* Weber, *Altsynagogale Paläst. Theol.*, p. 211 f. According to the Apocalypse of Baruch, xxiii. 4, liv. 15, lvi. 6 ff., Adam's fall brought death and general physical and moral corruption upon the whole of mankind, yet at the same time each individual is the cause of his own miserable state. Similarly according to 2 Esdras, vii. 10, 118, Adam's fall became the cause of general corruption to all his posterity, yet nevertheless each bears, according to vii. 105, 128, his own guilt. According to iii. 21 and iv. 27 there was from the first in Adam as in all men a seed of evil, a bad heart, a germ of sin. There is thus here, throughout, the same unassimilated combination of common guilt due to the solidarity of the

human and non-human, caused by a historical
catastrophe, seems to be implied. In 2 Cor. xi. 2 f.
Paul represents himself as the friend of the bridegroom who has betrothed the church as a bride to
Christ the bridegroom, and is now anxious that she
should not allow herself to be deceived by another
as the serpent deceived Eve. It cannot be denied
that in view of the context this deceiving of Eve
can hardly be understood otherwise than as sexual
seduction by the serpent, thought of as an incarnation
of Satan, through which Eve lost her virginal purity,
as the church stood in danger of doing by the
seductions of the false teachers.[1] Now, while the
Biblical narrative indeed knows nothing of a sexual
seduction of Eve by Satan, this myth certainly plays
a prominent part in Jewish legend, which derived
therefrom a demonic infection and corruption of
human nature. That Paul could believe a Jewish
legend even where it departed from the Biblical
account is proved by many analogies.[2] Further,
Paul says in Rom. viii. 20, " The creation is subjected
to transiency, not willingly, but for the sake of him
who has subjected it, in the hope that the creation
itself also will be freed from the bondage of decay,

race, and individual guilt – of historical causation and natural
inherence of evil—as we find in the case of Paul, who therefore in
this closely follows the lines of Jewish theology.

[1] Everling, *Die Paulinische Angelologie und Dämonologie*, pp. 51–55.
Kabisch, *Eschatologie des Paulus*, p. 155 ff.

[2] *Cf.* Gal. iii. 19, the giving of the law through the mediation
of angels; iv. 29, Ishmael persecuted Isaac; 1 Cor. x. 4, the rock
that gave water in the desert was the Christ; 2 Cor. iii. 13, Moses
hid his face with a veil that the Israelites might not mark the
gradual disappearance of the glory.

and admitted to the glorious liberty of the children
of God.   For we know that the whole creation
groaneth and travaileth until now."   The "creation"
can, in view of the context, only betoken the world
of nature exclusive of man ; and of this it is asserted
that it has been subjected to the bondage of corruption, not for its own fault, but for the sake of him
who has subjected it; that can only refer to the
historical catastrophe of the fall, whether we understand by "him who has subjected it" the primal
man or his tempter, as in Wisd. ii. 23 death "came
into the world only through the envy of the devil."
According to this, corruption does not belong
originally, as might be inferred from 1 Cor. xv. 46,
to the essential character of the created world, but
has been imposed upon it (by the punitive sentence
of God, as may be understood from Rom. v. 16) on
the ground of human guilt, which, in turn, is the
result of Satanic temptation.[1]   For that very reason,
because this condition of corruption does not originally
belong to its essence, but has been imposed upon it
by another's guilt, there runs through all creation,
according to the apostle's profound view, an unconscious hope and yearning for liberation from this
condition of bondage.   Man's cry of pain, "Who
shall deliver me from this body of death?" finds an
echo throughout the whole world, because sin and
death did not originally belong to God's creation,
but found their way into it as hostile demonic
powers and subjected it—man and nature alike—to
bondage, but yet in such a way that there remained
to it a hope of final liberation when death, the

[1] Cf. Kabisch, *Paulin. Eschatologie,* p. 256 f.

last enemy, shall be vanquished, and all shall have become new.[1]

If the question is asked what are the sources or the affinities of Pauline anthropology in general, it must be said that it is neither Hellenistic philosophy nor Pharisaic theology, but a Christian modification of the popular anthropology which was common to the whole of antiquity, and which we usually call Animism, according to which the soul or spirit is a generally invisible yet not wholly immaterial being, but which stands in so loose a relationship to the body as its containing vessel that it can at times pass out of it (*cf.* 2 Cor. xii. 2), just as other spiritual beings can temporarily or permanently enter into it and dwell in it. The view of sin, especially, as a demonic power, a spiritual being which dwells in the material body, which rouses the passions, enslaves· the will, and causes death, corresponds exactly to the fundamental animistic view according to which all abnormal excitations of the soul life, whether in a good, or, more especially, in a bad sense, are referred to the over-

[1] On the assumption, which Paul adopted from contemporary thought, that evil is an actual entity in man, its existence cannot well be otherwise reconciled with the origin of man as a created being than by supposing a corruption of human nature taking place in Time and caused from without. The matter is, of course, otherwise conceived in our present-day evolutionary view, according to which evil is not an actual entity, but the disharmony, the as yet defective organisation, of the impulses which belong to our nature, but of which the harmonious ordering cannot be original, because, for a moral being, it must be the task of intelligent activity, of education and culture. The teleological idealism remains in this case the same as in Paul's view, but without the dark background of demonic depravation, that metaphysical reflection of ancient Pessimism.

19

mastering influence (the domination) of spiritual
beings who take possession of man.   This view of the
popular animism in regard to particular passionate
excitations is extended by Paul to a permanent
possession of the flesh by a demonic spiritual being
which has taken possession once for all of the human
race, and therein he did not stand by any means
alone, but only shared the views which, under the
influence of the prevailing pessimistic mood of his
time, had grown up in many circles.   The Pharisaic
teaching about the Jezer hara or evil impulse, which
as a hostile spirit, or Satan, dwelt in man's body
from birth and at an early age raised itself into an
effectual power,[1] stands quite on the same footing,
and in the Greek world also there are a multitude of
parallels in the Orphic theology and in the Platonic,
Stoic, Neo-Pythagorean, and especially the Philonian,
philosophies.[2]   But the Pauline anthropology is not
to be explained as derived from these parallels; it is
merely that it has the same roots as they in the
primitive fundamental conceptions of animism, which
at that period, owing to the prevailing mood of
pessimism and religious enthusiasm, had in many
cases been sharpened into a more or less logical
dualism.   But it is the more necessary for that
reason to notice the specific distinction between the
anthropology of Paul and that of his contemporaries,
Jewish as well as Greek.   While according to the
Platonic, Stoic, and Philonian philosophies, the spirit
which belongs to the nature of man, or, according to

[1] Weber, *Altsynagogale Paläst. Theol.*, 204 ff.
[2] See above, p. 43 f. ; of Jewish Hellenism we shall have more
to say at a later point.

others, the spiritual part of his soul, is from the first divine, immortal, unstained, and is the victorious power which overcomes sensuality, Paul, on the other hand, ascribes these characteristics, not to the natural spirit of man, but to the supernatural spirit which through Christ enters into the man from without, in contrast with which the natural spirit, while it has, no doubt, in its intelligence a certain divine endowment, has no real divine power, but is morally indifferent and exposed to corruption. In this respect it may be said that the dualism between the divine and the human being is more radical and pessimistic in Paul than in the contemporary Hellenistic philosophy. But, to counterbalance that, he holds out the prospect of a more complete overcoming of the dualism which now prevails: he expects not only, like the aforesaid Greek thinkers, a deliverance from the body, but a deliverance of the body itself through the life-giving Spirit of God at the resurrection. Pharisaic theology taught, it is true, something similar; but while its doctrine represents the whole body as restored in its earthly materiality, Paul does not think of a resurrection of the flesh but only of the body, the form of the organism, and in a different, heavenly substance. Paul, therefore, teaches, in agreement with the Pharisees, deliverance of the body, but not deliverance of the flesh; in agreement with the Greeks, he teaches liberation from the flesh, from earthly sensuality, not, however, in a disembodied, purely spiritual state, but in a new body appropriate to the circumstances of the heavenly life; therefore not a one-sided deliverance of the spiritual part of man with the permanent abandonment of the bodily, but a

deliverance of the whole man, body, soul, and spirit
(1 Thess. v. 23), effected, however, by the slaying of
the flesh as the present seat of the powers which
oppose God. On the basis of a most pessimistic
judgment of the actual world as ruled by demonic
powers and lying under sentence of the divine wrath,
Paul's hopeful faith rises to the ideal of a new
creation in which the glorious freedom of the children
of God shall receive a victorious manifestation, and
the groaning and yearning of Nature be thereby
satisfied and stilled ; and God, in short, be all in all.
And this bold idealism thenceforth remained the
faith of Christians, the faith which has overcome the
world and continues to overcome it.   The distinction
is only that we to-day, on the ground of what we
have learned from history, expect the realisation of
that ideal of a new world in which nature and spirit
are purified into harmonious organs of the divine will,
to be attained by the historical development of the
Christian spirit and by the ethical effort of the
Christian community, whereas ancient Christianity
expected it to result from a supernatural catastrophe.

CHAPTER XIV

HEATHENISM AND JUDAISM

WE have seen that Paul regarded the condition of the natural man as a universal subjugation to the bondage of sin and death, a fate brought upon the race by the sin of the first man, imposed by a divine sentence, and carried out by the oppression of demonic powers. If, again, we cast a glance at his description of the religious condition of the heathen and the Jews, we meet the same thought once more, but with this difference, that, in the one case, the enslavement of man under the God-ordained domination of spiritual powers is prominent; in the other, the freely-incurred guilt of man which calls down God's judgment.

To the Galatians, who had been converted from heathenism to Christianity, and who stood in danger of being led astray by Jewish legalism, Paul says in Gal. iv. 8 ff.: "Then, when ye knew not God, ye served them that are by nature no gods. But now that ye have known God, or rather been known of him, how can ye turn again to the weak and miserable powers of the elements, desiring to be again in bondage to them? Ye observe days and months and times and years: I am concerned for you, lest I have bestowed upon you labour in vain." According to this, Paul regards heathenism as the worship of beings who are not indeed, as the heathen think, really gods, but yet are not mere fictions, but the powers presiding over the world-elements, conceived as personal spirits.[1] These, as compared with the one God, are indeed weak and miserable, but to their domination mankind in its childhood, whether heathen or Jewish, has, according to the purpose of God, been subjected in the same way as a son who is not of age may be placed by the testamentary disposition of his father under the oversight of guardians and stewards (verse 2 f.). How far Paul maintained the subjection of the Jews as well as the heathen to the domination of the powers of the elements, and therefore considers the legalistic leanings of the Galatians as a turning back to the service of these weak powers, we shall see later. It is noticeable, however, that Paul does not here treat heathenism as a guilty falling away from the true God, but as a condition of childish immaturity (nonage) in which man, in ignorance of the true God, served the nature-powers, and that, moreover, in virtue of a divine ordinance which placed them, up to a certain appointed time, in this condition of

[1] On this interpretation of the στοιχεῖα τοῦ κόσμου, exegetes of the present day are pretty well agreed. *Cf.* Everling, *Paul. Angelologie,* p. 70 ff. It is of less importance whether we think of them as the spirits presiding over the heavenly bodies (Lipsius) or as including also those of earthly Nature, the different elements in which were thought of by the Jews as ruled by angels (Weber, *ut sup.* p. 167), and by the heathen as ruled by demons. The latter is more probable in view of 1 Cor. viii. 5, εἰσὶν λεγόμενοι θεοί, εἴτε ἐν οὐρανῷ, εἴτε ἐπὶ γῆς.

bondage. Not dissimilar is Paul's judgment as expressed in 1 Corinthians. When in xii. 2 he tells his readers that in their former heathen condition they were driven by a blind impulse to have recourse to the dumb idols, that is just the way in which the heathen consciousness is characterised in the above-mentioned passage of Galatians—as a condition of sensuous limitation, of bondage and ignorance, and as contrasted with the spiritual freedom and enlightenment of the Christian who has been enabled by the holy Spirit to confess Jesus Christ as Lord. This condition was no doubt regrettable, because in it man betook himself, in search of help, to the unspiritual dumb powers (" was subjected to the miserable and weak world-elements "), but, as being a condition of blind involuntary impulse, it was not a deliberately guilty denial of God. What is said in 1 Cor. viii. 4 f., x. 20, too, about the heathen gods agrees with Gal. iv. 8. Judged from the standpoint of the true consciousness of God, these supposed gods of the heathen are not what they are held to be ; they do not possess divinity, because there is only one God, the Creator of the world. But the heathen gods are not on that account wholly destitute of reality : there are, without doubt, "gods many and lords many in heaven and earth," namely, those very powers of the elements, whether of a sidereal or tellurian nature, which ruled over the elements, and which, it is true, possessed no deity in the true sense, for they are not creators but themselves created beings and instruments of the sole Divine Creator, but yet, as administrative powers of nature, they possess a certain authority, as is implied in their being made by God

guardians and overseers of mankind in its nonage.
That, further, these living creatures in heaven and
earth to which the heathen Nature-worship was
offered are described in x. 20 as demons, corresponds
to the views and linguistic usage of Hellenism, for in
this the Jewish judgment of Polytheism agreed with
that of the Greek philosophers. The term demon
did not yet, indeed, include the sense of devilish
beings hostile to God, but signifies only superhuman
and sub-divine spirits and intermediate beings which
can even stand in the service of God as instruments
of His administration of the world, as is doubtless
assumed also in Deut. iv. 19 and x. 17, in regard to
the heathen gods. But for Israel, which was pledged
to the exclusive service of the one true God, these
heathen divinities were false gods, who led them
astray—demons, therefore, in the bad sense, or devils
(so, *e.g.*, Deut. xxxii. 17, LXX.). Similarly it is easily
understood that for a Christian who knows the one
sole God and Father all intercourse with the heathen
divinities—*e.g.* in the sacrificial worship—is defiling
and corrupting, as being a falling back from the true
worship of God into the false worship of impure
World-Powers. All this, however, does not go essentially beyond the standpoint from which heathenism
is judged in Gal. iv.

But in Rom. i. 20 ff. matters stand quite differently.
Here Paul seeks to show that the heathen are
without excuse, since at the beginning they had the
true knowledge of God, but suppressed it in unrighteousness ; and because they refuse to render to God
the honour and gratitude which was His due, their
thoughts became vain, their hearts became darkened

and unintelligent. Thinking themselves to be wise, they became so foolish that, instead of the glory of the incorruptible God, they made images of men and beasts as objects of worship. As a punishment for this denial and dishonouring of God, He gave them up to the most degraded vices and self-abuse. According to this, heathenism is a deliberately guilty falling away from a God once known, and a consequent deeper and deeper fall into the lowest moral and religious error and abandonment. In this there is therefore implied an original true knowledge of God, founded upon the original natural revelation. The being of God, although itself invisible, has, since the creation, in view of His eternal power and majesty, clearly manifested itself to the perceptive intelligence of the mind, which accordingly is capable, by thoughtful consideration of the world, of understanding from that which is created the creative might and glory of God. And since this revelation of God in nature is ever the same, there remains ever the possibility of a natural knowledge of God as at the beginning. If it is, as a matter of fact, not found among the heathen, but, instead of it, the worst possible perversion of the God-consciousness in the worship of demons, this is, Paul here concludes, the consequence of their deliberate impiety, of their unwillingness to render to God due honour and gratitude. This practical impiety led in the first place to a darkening of the theoretic knowledge of God; the thoughts clave to the vain, the corrupt, the creaturely, instead of raising themselves to the Creator; the heart lost its capacity to receive the impression of the divine from the revelation in the world, and the deceptiveness of its seeming wisdom, which made the world itself into a false god, completely destroyed the possibility of knowing God in His wisdom (*cf.* 1 Cor. i. 21). The result of this process of religious degradation was the most complete perversion, the worship of images of men and beasts, of corruptible creatures in the place of the Creator. But according to the law of the moral order, that sin punishes itself by increase of sin, this religious depravity led ultimately to the loosing of all the passions, to lusts which are contrary to nature, to the destruction of all the bonds of society, to the unrestrained practice of all that is bad in spite of the knowledge of its ill-desert.

That the Græco-Roman world of that day gave material enough for this gloomy picture, no one can deny. Yet it is not to be overlooked that this severe judgment of heathenism as a process of theoretical and practical depravation brought about by deliberate guilt, stands in striking contrast to the milder view of the Galatian epistle, according to which heathenism represents a childishly immature and unenfranchised form of consciousness, which has been ordained by the Divine providence. This is not the place to inquire whether, and how far, both views might have a relative truth, the reconciliation of which might be conceived in some way or other ; but in any case, in the unreconciled fashion in which they here stand side by side they belong to different systems of philosophy, one of which has for its centre the Hellenistic thought of a providentially guided advance from the sensuous to the spiritual, while the other revolves round the Pharisaic thought of a free-willed fall, the guilt of which brings down judgment upon itself and can only be made good by expiation. It is, moreover, to be remarked that a similar inconsistency runs through the judgment of the heathen world in the Book of Wisdom, chaps. xiv. and xv., the arguments of which must have been in the apostle's mind when writing Rom. i. Only, the Alexandrian author of the Book of Wisdom distinguishes more definitely than Paul between the grossness of heathen idolatry and the higher efforts of the heathen philosophers, to whom but little blame is attached ; since they, after all, desired to seek and find God (*cf.* Acts xvii. 27), even if in doing so they went astray. But, on the other hand, the author of Wisdom immediately adds that these also are inexcusable. When they were able to learn so much and to search through the whole world, why had they not found the Lord of all this creation ? (xiv. 9). But really he had given the answer to this reproach at the beginning when he said that all men are by nature vain (foolish) and incapacitated by ignorance of God, and *are not able* from visible goods to recognise Him who essentially is (God) (verse 1). And this view, not the other, agrees with this assertion in ix. 16 f. of the incapacity of the human understanding, from its own resources, and without the gift of divine wisdom and of the holy Spirit, to recognise heavenly things. It is clear that the author of the Book of Wisdom wavers uncertainly between this Hellenistic explanation and the Jewish condemnation of heathenism, and thus offers a parallel to the inconsistency which we find in Paul between the judgment of heathenism in Gal. iv. and Rom. i.

Stern as is the condemnation of the heathen world

in Rom. i., Paul goes by no means so far as to deny, with Augustine, all good without exception to heathenism and to make its virtues only "splendid vices." On the contrary, Paul is sufficiently un-prejudiced to recognise the occurrence even among the heathen of ethically good and noble conduct, and to find therein evidence of the existence of an inner law in the heart, to which is added the con-current testimony of conscience, of the thoughts which mutually accuse or defend one another (Rom. ii. 14 f.). Paul, therefore, knows not merely the positive law of the Jews, but also a natural law written in every man's heart which manifests itself as the motive force and norm of reason (Rom. vii. 25) and as a judging voice of conscience. Further, Paul recog-nises the possibility and actuality of morally worthy conduct in the heathen corresponding to this law. " Where any Gentiles, who do not possess the (Jewish) law, do by nature [1] that which the law enjoins, then they who do not possess the law are a law unto them-selves." In this phrase, " When any Gentiles do that which the law demands," it is impossible, even on linguistic grounds, that a mere unreal and impossible hypothesis is intended, for Paul evidently assumes the

---

[1] φύσει τὰ τοῦ νόμου ποιῶσι refers to conduct which in its content answers to the demands of the positive (Mosaic) law—in its moral aspect, of course—but yet has not this law, but the natural law of the conscience, as its motive. Stoic ethics was accustomed to distinguish between φύσις and θέσις, natural and positive law. Moreover, that this φύσει ποιεῖν cannot refer to Christian conduct from the inner impulse of the Holy Spirit, which is, of course, not of nature, but grace, is obvious. The interpretation of this passage as referring to Christians is a misunderstanding which springs from the harmonistic effort to reconcile Paul's disparate lines of thought.

fact of such conduct really occurring in many cases.
It is just that assumption which enables him to apply
the principle of the divine retribution according to
human action and effort to the heathen as well as to
the Jews, as in the significant passage Rom. ii. 6–10 :
" God will render to every man according to his
works ; to those who by patient continuance in well-
doing strive after glory and honour and immortality,
eternal life ; but to the factious who do not obey
the truth, but obey unrighteousness, indignation and
wrath : yea, tribulation and anguish upon every soul
of man that doeth evil, of the Jew first and also of
the Greek : but glory and honour and peace to every
man that worketh good, to the Jew first and also to
the Greek." This passage has given much trouble
to exegetes, because it seems to contradict the
Pauline dogma of the righteousness and blessedness
which come from faith alone. Many have therefore
wished to apply the passage to Christians only, but
this expedient obviously comes to grief, in view of
the express emphasising of the unconditional inner
universality of the principle of retribution as applying
to every soul of man, Jew and Greek alike. Nor can
it be maintained with any greater success that Paul
here argues from the standpoint of the Jewish consciousness, while reserving his own personal opinion
in regard to such a " doing of good works " and
striving after noble ends and aims as an abstract
hypothesis without real truth. For there is no hint
that he is thus reserving his opinion ; any unprejudiced
reader must understand the words in their natural
sense, as implying the existence of men whose
actions and endeavours are worthy of praise and

reward among the heathen as well as among the Jews, and this is confirmed in the sequel, where he speaks of heathen who do by nature that which is according to the law. There is nothing for it, then, but to admit that Paul here recognises the possibility and actuality of a natural virtue, of noble endeavour and excellent conduct, which may look forward to reward according to the divine administration, among non-Christians also. How he reconciled that with his dogmatic teaching in regard to universal sinfulness, of the carnal man being sold under sin, of his incapacity to do good, of his complete failure to deserve God's praise, of his justification and liberation only through faith in Christ, is hard to say. For us, there might be a reconciliation between the recognition of natural goodness and the absolute value of Christian goodness in the thought of the relative character of the moral judgment according to the various stages of development, but this way out of the difficulty must not be assumed in the case of Paul, whose archaic supernaturalism excluded the modern idea of development and relativity. Probably he was unconscious of the contradiction between his humane judgment in Rom. ii. 6 ff. and his dogmatic theory, and gave no thought whatever to their reconciliation.

That the Jews have much advantage over the heathen in many respects, Paul, the Pharisee turned apostle, never questioned. Among these advantages he names in Rom. iii. 2, in the first place, the possession of the oracles of God, which, from the context, must mean primarily the promises of God to the fathers. The enumeration, which is not carried further at this point, is taken up again in ix. 4. In order to show how highly he esteems his people and how deeply he is pained by their disbelief in Christ, he recounts here all its glorious claims; to it belong the position of sonship in which God has placed Israel as His peculiar people above all others, and has thereby chosen them as the especial object of His fatherly care; for them there shone the glory of God in which He clothed His revealed presence amidst His people, to them belong the covenants which He made and confirmed to the fathers, the giving of the law through Moses, the Temple-service, the promises of future salvation; above all, the Patriarchs, those servants and friends of God, who are the pride and the confidence of Israel, because their righteousness gives the whole nation the *character indelebilis* of holiness (Rom. xi. 16). And in regard to this dignity of Israel, even its present hostile attitude to the revelation of God in the Gospel can alter nothing; their unfaithfulness cannot do away with the faithfulness of God. God, having once chosen the fathers of Israel and called them to be the bearers of His promises of mercy, cannot now repent, and accordingly the disobedient Jewish people is, and remains, the object of the saving love of God for the sake of the beloved fathers (Rom. xi. 28 f., iii. 3). Next to this inheritance from the fathers, the highest boast of Israel is the possession of the law which makes the Jew a leader of the blind, an instructor of the ignorant, a light amid the darkness of the rest of the world, and capable of obtaining righteousness for himself and therewith making good his claim upon life and salvation (ii. 17 ff., x. 2).

This is, however, the point on which Paul the

Christian rejects the opinion of the Pharisees as an error. Once he, too, had had all his pride in the advantages of the Jews, but what he then counted gain he has, since his conversion, counted loss, that he might win the exceeding glorious knowledge of Christ (Phil. iii. 8 f.). It is true Paul still holds fast to the fundamental conviction of his ancestral religion that the law is the infallible and indivisible expression of the revealed will of God, the clear outline of religious knowledge and truth, and in so far holy, just, and good, of a divine and spiritual character (Rom. ii. 20, vii. 12, 14). He recognises the written law as a divine authority and argues from it, and in doing so, follows Jewish usage in identifying the term law (Torah) with the book of the law (the Pentateuch), and occasionally extends it to Scripture in general (*cf.* Rom. iii. 19, 31; Gal. iv. 21). He does not dispute that the commandment was given with a view to life—"whoso does the law shall have life" (Rom. vii. 10, ii. 13; Gal. iii. 12). But of course this is only true in the abstract, apart from the relation of the historical law to man as in reality a fleshly, sinful being. On the other hand, when his judgment refers to this definite actual historical relationship, that abstract judgment is converted into its exact opposite and runs: the command, given to bring life, results in death; in itself holy, just, and good, it does not produce goodness or righteousness in man but only increases sin, gives the sinful lust occasion and incitement to activity, intensifies the energy of the sinful passions, holds man prisoner under the bondage of sin, so that to be under the law signifies the same

as to be under the dominion of sin (Rom. vi. 14,
vii. 5–13, iii. 20 ; Gal. iii. 21–24). These effects of
the law Paul discovered in actual experience, his
own as well as that of his nation in general. He
himself, in spite of the most zealous striving to fulfil
the law, had never succeeded in attaining a satisfying
consciousness of true righteousness, an inner victory
over sinful desires, and he recognised in the zeal of
the Jewish nation for legal righteousness the main
hindrance to its obtaining the true righteousness
of Christ. Being convinced of the impossibility of
legal righteousness, in the first place, as a fact of
experience, he sought now to give it a basis in
theological reflection, both indirectly by a doctrinal
inference from the significance of the death of Christ,
and directly from the nature of the law and the
nature of man.

"If there had been a law given which could have
given life, verily righteousness would have been by
the law." "If righteousness came by the law then
Christ is dead in vain" (Gal. iii. 21, ii. 21). But this
last would be unthinkable ; the death of Jesus the
Messiah must have served a divine end, and this can
only, according to the apostle's conviction, have
consisted in its being a means for the provision of
a righteousness which is to be given by grace to the
believer, not deserved as reward by a man's own
actions. But as grace and reward for work are
mutually exclusive (Rom. xi. 6, iv. 4 ff.), it follows that
righteousness is not the wages earned by the doing
of the law, but comes as a gift of grace from the
death of Christ, so that Christ is the end of the law
for every one that believeth (Rom. x. 4). This

20

result of doctrinal reflection on the death of Christ
finds confirmation also in the nature of the law and
of man.   In this proof Paul follows a twofold
method, arguing now from the character of the law,
and now from the condition of man.   According to
Galatians and Second Corinthians the law cannot
give life, because it is not a quickening spirit but a
deadening "letter," an objective precept standing
outside the will, directing and demanding as a cate-
gorical imperative, but conferring no power to fulfil
the law, since it is not able, like the Spirit, to inspire
the heart and fill it with the inner motive of love of
good.   Therefore the law is only a gaoler who holds
men in bondage, in the servitude of the eternal
ordinance, and under the sense of fear of the threatenings of punishment.   To the covenant of the letter
corresponds the spirit of bondage, which is oppressed
with fear, and for that very reason never attains to a
free and joyful performance of the good; on the
contrary, the literal and definite prohibition provokes
self-assertion, and instead of overcoming sin rather
incites and increases it.   And as the law of the letter
in general remains foreign and external to the heart
of man, so in its ritual portion, too, it refers to externals
which fall under the category of the sensuous and the
weak, of the flesh and of the world.   Therefore Paul
describes the falling back of the Galatians from
Christian freedom to legal bondage as a falling away
from the spirit to the flesh, and as a return to the
service of the miserable and weak powers of the
elements (Gal. iii. 3, iv. 3, 9), and therefore places
the legal ritual of Judaism on exactly the same
footing as the heathen nature-worship.   But this judg-

ment, though it reflects more on the ceremonial side
of the Jewish law than on its moral content, offended
the Jewish conscience so much that Paul in Romans,
where he is seeking to conciliate the Jewish Christians, gives the matter a new turn calculated to cause
them less difficulty. He now emphasises the fact that
the law is holy, just, and good, inasmuch as it has for
its content moral good, and for its origin a revelation
of God (Rom. vii. 12). If, nevertheless, it has as its
consequences not righteousness and life but sin and
death, the cause of that lies not in itself but in the
fleshly nature of man (vii. 14, viii. 3); but that
means, however, not that individual men from inconceivable wickedness are unwilling to fulfil it, but
that they are one and all, just because they are flesh,
and therefore sold under sin, unable to fulfil it. The
flesh which, whatever may be said, is as a matter of
experience ruled by an impulse hostile to God, cannot
obey the law of God (viii. 7), and the law, which is not
as a matter of fact a life-giving power but can only
oppose to the sinful impulse the lifeless commandment, can make no alteration in the fleshly nature of
man; that is possible only to the spirit of sonship
which overcomes the selfish impulse by the positive
and living power of love. This view is certainly in
form milder and less calculated to cause offence than
the other, in so far as it avoids the appearance of
attributing to the high and holy Divine revelation of
the Old Testament an injurious effect, which would
contradict its divine origin; but practically it comes
essentially to very much the same thing, whether one
says that the fault lies in the incapacity of the fleshly
man to fulfil the law, or in the incapacity of the law

of the letter to overcome the opposition of the flesh
and to make man obedient instead of rebellious. In
the one case, as in the other, the deficiency is not
merely accidental, caused by subjective ill-desert, but
is based on an inner necessity in the nature of the
case, in the essential character of the legal religion,
since it consists precisely in this external relationship
of the Divine and human will, of Master and servant,
in which it is naturally impossible ever fully to overcome either defiance or fear in the heart of man and
therefore ever to attain true goodness or true blessedness. This argument therefore issues in the conclusion
that the law is so far from being able to produce
righteousness that it is through it, rather, that man
first becomes really a sinner. For not only does it
set unconscious desire in the light of the ethical
consciousness, whereby it first becomes conscious sin
and is imputed as such (Rom. iv. 15, vii. 7), but it also,
by its prohibition, excites the sinful impulse of the flesh
to energetic activity, and thus multiplies transgression
(v. 20). Therefore Paul calls the law the "strength
of sin" and a "letter which kills," because it provokes
the wrath of God and condemns the sinner to death
(1 Cor. xv. 56 ; 2 Cor. iii. 6 ; Rom. iv. 15). Therefore to be "under the law" is for Paul equivalent to
being under the domination of sin and of the flesh
(Gal. iii. 22 ; Rom. vi. 14, vii. 5). Man under the law
is in disharmony with himself and with God, and feels
himself un-free and un-blessed (Rom. vii. 14, 24 f.,
viii. 15). That was the experience which Paul had
himself gone through, and the deep misery of it had
only fully come home to him when he had looked
back upon it from the standpoint of his Christian

consciousness of salvation. In the light of faith in
Christ, life under the law appeared only a hopeless
darkness.

We cannot blame the opponents of Paul because
this pessimistic view, in which the Pharisaic deifica-
tion of the law was transformed into its diametrical
opposite, appeared to them not only historically
unjustifiable—and it forms indeed a striking contrast
to the view of the law held by the saints of the Old
Testament—but also as morally obnoxious. The
only practical result which they could expect from
this depreciation of the law was the dissolution of
all moral discipline and order, and many occurrences
among Gentile converts seemed to confirm this
fear. Was there, then, no escape from this dilemma
between Jewish legalism and complete antinomianism? For our present-day thought there would be
a simple one in the conception of the Jewish law
as an imperfect preparatory stage of revelation of
which the essence is fulfilled in the higher Christian
morality not less really that its outward form is
abolished. And the application of this thought
was, as a matter of fact, made by deutero-Pauline
theology in order to obtain a view of the "new law"
which avoided at once the Pauline antinomianism
and Jewish legalism. But Paul himself could not
take this way. He was too much the Pharisee to
be able to distinguish in this critical fashion between
the transitory and the permanent, between the form
and the content of the law; the law was for him an
indivisible whole of divine revelation which must
be either the sole means of salvation or not a means
of salvation at all. The solution of the problem

which is offered in Gal. iii. and Rom. iv. is, therefore, that while the law is not inconsistent with the promises of God, it contributes only indirectly to their fulfilment.

His starting-point is that the promise of the inheritance, which was the foundation of the covenant of God with His people, was a promise of grace. This, its original character, the law, which was added 430 years later, could not annul. It would, however, be annulled if the aim of the law had been to make the obtaining of the inheritance conditional on obedience to the law, for then the inheritance of the promised blessing would have become the reward of human effort, and no more a gift of grace. The later addition of a conditional clause of this kind would have annulled the covenant of God as a covenant of mercy, which it was originally intended to be. If the voiding of a contract by subsequent condition is not permissible even in human affairs, how much less in the case of a covenant of God ratified so solemnly and with express reference to Christ! Accordingly, the later addition of the law to the promise can only have had the aim of making the obtaining of the inheritance as a gift of grace from God more certain by showing that every other way of obtaining this end, *e.g.* through a man's own work, was actually impossible. This came about through the fact that the law held men (the Jews) in the bondage of sin, constantly brought their sin, servitude, and unhappiness to their consciousness, and thus hindered them from enjoying the rights of sonship and the inheritance until the time of " coming of age " appointed by the Father.

"The Scripture" (*i.e.* God, according to the Scripture) has concluded all under sin, in order that the promise (the promised inheritance) might be fulfilled to those who believe, as a consequence of faith in Jesus Christ. Before faith came we were held in durance under the ward of the law with a view to the faith which should be revealed. Thus the law was our "paidagogos" up to the coming of Christ, in order that we might be justified by faith. But now that faith is come we are no longer under a paidagogos (Gal. iii. 22–25). In this paidagogic office of the law we are not to think directly of a positively educative preparation for redemption, but in the first place of tutelage under a guardian power which made it impossible to obtain salvation in any other way than that way of faith in Christ which God has provided. But indirectly this negative service includes the positive advantage that the law, by making men feel their powerlessness and want of freedom, awakens the desire for salvation and the receptiveness for it. Finally, Paul seeks (Gal. iii. 19 f.) also to show the subordination of the law to the promise by the manner in which the law was given, inasmuch as (according to Jewish legend, *cf.* Acts vii. 53; Josephus, *Antiq.* xv. 5, 3) the law was not, like the promise, given directly by God Himself but by the mediation of angels, and by Moses, again, acting as mediator between them and the people. God alone would not have needed a mediator, but in this case a mediator was needed, because the covenant of the law was not made immediately with God Himself, but with His representatives and envoys, the angels. Closely connected with this representation

that the angels were the agents of God in the conclusion of the covenant of the law, stands that
other, that in the pre-Christian period of mankind
as determined by the law, men were under the
tutelage of the poor and weak spirits of the elements,
inasmuch as these had a predominant influence upon
Jewish as upon heathen cultus (Gal. iv. 2–9; *cf. sup.*,
pp. 294, 306). These systems of spirits and angels
signify for Paul what we to-day should call the
"principles" of the religious consciousness of pre-
Christian mankind. These principles were, according
to the providentially ordered course of development
of mankind, needful and right at their proper time,
but were nevertheless not a direct and permanently
true revelation of God in the religious consciousness.
This conception clothed itself for Paul in the
mythical representation of demi-gods who, as representatives of God, gave laws and held mankind, while
in its minority, in tutelage, under their guardianship,
until the coming of the liberating faith of sonship.

We may admire this boldness of genius by means
of which Paul by his philosophy of history cuts the
knot of the question about the law with the sword,
but it must not be overlooked that this teaching was
far too individual a conception ever to find acceptance
in the church. That the law served directly only to
promote an increase of sin and misery is the morbid
judgment of the Pharisee who has had his own
experience of the law and the legal religion, and now
looks back from the peace which he has found under
the grace of the Gospel upon his former unhappy
condition, which seems the more gloomy to him in

contrast with the newly-risen light. Psychologically
this is quite intelligible, but from the purely historical
point of view this estimate of the law is certainly at
least one-sided. The historical aim of the giving of
the law was certainly not the increase of sin, but
the education of Israel, as a holy people of God,
to righteousness, in the relative sense of the Old
Testament stage of religion. And in this light the
law appeared to the good among Israel as a valuable
means of salvation and the highest gift of grace, as
the cause of their pious joy and refreshing, as so many
psalms testify. Since the Christian Church appropriated the Old Testament as a venerable record of
revelation and as a means of edification, it naturally
adopted the favourable view of the law held by the
pious authors of the psalms, and, as a necessary
consequence, could not accept the pessimistic theory
of Paul. But that was impossible on practical
grounds also. For antinomianism is, indeed, free
from danger when it is united with so high and
pure a religious inspiration as filled the hearts of
Paul and his rare spiritual congeners, but for far
the greater majority in an ecclesiastical community
antinomianism involved the gravest moral dangers.
The ancient Church had sufficient experience of that,
and the Lutheran Church knows something of it too.
Their regard for the practical conditions of the moral
life of the church was an urgent reason for replacing
the Pauline theory of the law by a more serviceable
one. Morally, too, it must not be forgotten that the
Pauline theory of the law stands in a relationship
to his doctrine of redemption of which the inherent
logical difficulty can be explained, indeed, by Paul's

individual experience, but could not possibly count on
being generally understood in the church. Since the
doctrine of redemption has for its starting-point a
ransoming of men from the curse of the law through
the atoning death of Christ, the absolute claim of
the law to the satisfaction of its demands and the
fulfilment of its threats is thereby assumed, an
assumption which is entirely based on the Pharisaic
doctrine of the law. But how does that agree with
Paul's new view that the law was only intended to
hold men fast in the prison of sin until the coming
of their deliverance through faith in the Son of God ?
How could the law, whose function was of so humble
a character and of only temporary duration, make
any claim at all to atoning satisfaction for transgressions which, after all, it had itself called forth,
and had been intended to call forth ? Either, one
might be inclined to think, the Pharisaic doctrine of
the law is valid, or the Pauline doctrine, but to
attempt to maintain both together, as is done in the
Pauline doctrine of the law on the one side and of
redemption on the other, is simply a contradiction,
which might remain concealed from Paul himself, in
whose breast the two souls of the Pharisee and the
apostle constantly struggled together, but which it
could hardly be supposed that the thought of the
church could assimilate. To make clear to ourselves
the state of the matter, to set clearly before us these
various practical and theoretical difficulties and
offences of Paulinism, is needful, because, unless this
is done, it is impossible to arrive at a right understanding and a just estimate of the post-apostolic
development of the theology of the Church.

CHAPTER XV

REDEMPTION THROUGH JESUS CHRIST

THE redemption from the power of sin and death which the law was unable to effect, since it was too weak to overcome the flesh, God, according to the Pauline teaching, accomplished by sending His Son, who was a heavenly Spirit, in a human and fleshly form. Through His death and resurrection sin and death were overcome, and a new life in the spirit of sonship to God was opened up to man. Paul, since the occurrence of his conversion through the vision of Christ, felt himself a new creature in whom the old man, the flesh, had passed away and a supernatural life had been produced by the heavenly power of the Divine Spirit; and he had seen in Christ the cause and the prototype of this transformation. He is the Lord, who in His essential being is a quickening Spirit, in His origin heavenly, who has appeared upon earth in the flesh, in order, through the surrender of the flesh to death, to wipe out the debt of sin, to annul the curse of the law, to break the power of death, and to bring the spirit of righteousness and life to victorious sovereignty. To express it psychologically we might say: What Paul had experienced

315

in himself through his faith in Christ—namely, that through the surrender of the natural ego the true life is won, the life of sonship to God, of peace, joy, freedom, love, inspiration,—it was this principle of the religion of Jesus which he saw embodied in the Person of Jesus Christ, and revealed in His death as man's exemplar. But this ethico-religious principle clothed itself for Paul—on the assumptions of that animistic popular metaphysic which had led to the hypostatising in Jewish theology of the Divine Wisdom as a personal mediator—in the representation of a personal spiritual being who descended from heaven and took human form in order, as the man Christ Jesus, to become, through His death and resurrection, the founder of a new Humanity. This conception was already a departure in some measure from the historical foundation, and prepared the way for the gnosticising doctrine of Christ of the later Church dogmatic; but, for Paul, this hypostatising of the Spirit of Christ was only the temporal form in which the truth of his Christian faith, of which his experience had convinced him, presented itself to his consciousness, and a way of expressing the universal value, going beyond anything that was individual, national, or temporal, of this truth. The religion of Jesus could only be made the universal means of salvation for the world at the price of setting the supra-temporal principle in abstraction from the individual person of the historical Jesus, personifying this abstraction as the Spirit of Christ, and transferring it to heaven. This psychological genesis of the Pauline representation of Christ explains how it was that the emphasis of the religious interest fell neither

on the earthly life of Christ nor the pre-mundane
existence of the Spirit of Christ, but on the post-
mundane life of the risen Christ Jesus as the "Son of
God in power," the "Lord who is the Spirit." On the
earthly life of Christ apart from His birth and death,
Paul seems scarcely to have reflected, and even to
the pre-temporal existence of the Christ-Spirit there
are found in the older letters only rare incidental
references, which nevertheless are sufficient to indicate that Paul, from the very beginning, attributed to
this metaphysical spiritual Being a peculiar position
as mediator between God and man and the People of
Israel.

We take as our starting-point Rom. i. 3 f., where
Paul attaches himself most closely to the view of
the primitive community, which thought of Christ's
elevation to theocratic sonship to God, *i.e.* to
Messianic dignity, as closely bound up with His
resurrection. While, however, according to the
belief of the primitive community, the sonship to
God only designated a position of theocratic dignity
in exactly the same way as the sonship to David,
Paul distinguished between the Davidic Sonship
and the Divine Sonship in such a way that they
describe two characteristics of the one Person of
Christ which spring from different origins. By His
human birth of the race of David (a statement which
implies His natural generation by a human father)
Christ became the Son of David according to the
flesh; but in this, the earthly form of His manifestation, He is still only the Christ according to the
flesh in the sense of the Jewish Messiah; His Divine
Sonship is not fully realised. That only came to

pass when He was "appointed Son of God in power according to the spirit of holiness from the resurrection onwards." Therefore, the Davidic Sonship, founded upon His birth according to the flesh, was followed, though only at the resurrection, by His appointment by God to the real and effectual Divine Sonship. The possibility of this lay in the fact that Jesus was the Spirit of Holiness; that means, not begotten as to His body by the Holy Spirit, nor having received the Holy Spirit as an endowment at baptism, but that His personal being, His inner man, consisted originally of a holy Spirit. "This practically gives the material ground of His Divine Sonship in the super-theocratic metaphysical sense, His descent from heaven" (Holtzmann). The latter is, it is true, not directly mentioned in our passage, but it is certainly implied, because a holy and spiritual being does not, like a fleshly psychic man, originate from the earth, but from heaven. For, according to 1 Cor. xv. 47, the first man was of the earth and therefore earthly, "the Second Man is the Lord from heaven," and (verse 45) "the first man, Adam, became a living soul, the last Adam a quickening spirit." According to this passage also Christ first became[1] by His resurrection a Spiritual Being, who, as the effectual

[1] Practically it is of subordinate importance whether in the second member of the phrase in verse 45, the ἐγένετο which is to be understood is interpreted strictly on the analogy of the first as "was created," or, as is equally possible, simply in the sense "became." In the former case the reference would be to the origin of the Spirit of Christ at creation, its influence, however (in the main point, namely, as life-giving power), being supposed to remain dormant up to the resurrection of Christ. The other interpretation has the advantage of simplicity.

principle of "quickening," that is, of the raising
again of Christians from the dead, is the pledge of
their future possession of a spiritual or heavenly
body; but the possibility of His *becoming* so in his
resurrection had its cause in what He *had been* from
the beginning; He could become the Second Man
or Founder of a new spiritual humanity destined to
heavenly and everlasting life only because He was,
in contrast with the first psychic and earthly
humanity, in His being Spirit, and in His origin,
from heaven. In these two passages, therefore
(Rom. i. 4 and 1 Cor. xv. 45 ff.), the emphasis undoubtedly falls on what Christ has become through
His resurrection, but the potentiality of this becoming lies in His pre-mundane being, in the assumption
of a metaphysical background of pre-existence.

This is directly expressed in the passages which
speak of the sending of the Son of God in the form
of fleshly man, or of His birth from a woman (Gal.
iv. 4; Rom. viii. 3), since He who is thus "sent"
must have had existence in another form; further,
there are the passages where the Incarnation is
described as an ethical act on the part of Christ
(2 Cor. viii. 9; Phil. ii. 5); finally, those where a
mediatorial activity is asserted of the pre-existent
Christ (1 Cor. x. 4, viii. 6, and xi. 3). These last
passages show clearly in how close relationship the
Pauline doctrine of Christ stands to Alexandrian-
Jewish speculation regarding divine intermediaries.
As, according to Wisd. x. 17, the cloud which
accompanied the Israelites in the wilderness was a
manifestation of the Divine Wisdom, and according
to Philo (I. 213 M.) the rock which poured out water

in the desert was a manifestation of the Divine Logos, so Paul, in 1 Cor. x. 4, says that the spiritual rock which followed the Israelites, and out of which they drank, was Christ. This is not, any more than the representation in Wisdom or Philo, a mere figure, but is to be understood as a reference to the actual form in which the Spirit of Christ manifested itself—a mythical representation which finds its explanation in the animistic popular metaphysic of the Semites—compare the stone at Bethel which was a house of God. As, further, it is said in Proverbs (viii. 22) that the wisdom which was prepared by God in the beginning of His creation, stood by His side as a master-worker at the making of the world; and as in Wisd., wisdom, in Philo, the Logos, acts as mediator of the divine causality in the creation of the world and of man, so Paul seems to ascribe a similar activity to the pre-existent Christ (1 Cor. viii. 6): "We have one God the Father by whom all things are (made) and we for him, and one Lord Jesus Christ through whom are all things (doubtless here too created) and we through him." And when it is said in 1 Cor. xi. 3 that Christ is the head of every man, as the man is the head of the woman, and God of Christ, the term head must, in view of the context, designate a relationship in which the subordinate has in the superior its origin, pattern, and end. According to this, Christ takes an intermediate position between God and man, as the latter between Christ and woman. In short: Christ is the mediator to man of dependence upon God and likeness to God; as the image of God (2 Cor. iv. 4, 6) He is also the creative pattern of man. To this conception an analogue is found in the Philonian theory of the original Heavenly Man, the perfect pattern of the imperfect earthly man (*De Op. Mund.* 32, M.).

The entrance of the pre-existent Spirit of Christ into our earthly human form of existence is touched on by Paul in only a small number of passages, but from these it is possible to form a fairly clear conception in regard to it. The cause of His appearing on earth lay in His mission from God (Gal. iv. 4; Rom. viii. 3), and in Christ's selfless love to men, who gave up what was His own that He might make us rich. This point of view is brought up in 2 Cor. viii. 9, Phil. ii. 5 ff., to reinforce the exhortation to a similar attitude of Christians towards one another. According to the former passage, "Christ, though he was rich, yet for your sakes became poor, that ye through his poverty might be made rich." The "wealth" which He, for our benefit, gave up when He entered into the "poverty" of His earthly life consisted in His heavenly glory, which He as the image and forth-shining of God had possessed in His pre-existence. Whether the sense of even Phil. ii. 6 f. can be fitted into the frame of 2 Cor. viii. 9 and Rom. viii. 3, is a question which is variously answered. In common with the majority, I formerly answered it in the affirmative, but I must admit that the justice of my former interpretation has become very doubtful to me, because I cannot conceal from myself that the whole of the expressions in Phil. ii. 6 f. are peculiar, and seem to involve conceptions which are divergent from the remainder of the Pauline Christology, and nearly related to Gnostic speculations.

21

When it is said of the pre-existent Christ that though He was in the form of God He counted not His equality with God as a spoil, but emptied Himself and took upon Him the form of a servant and appeared in the likeness of man, and outwardly was found in fashion as a man, a view of Christ seems to underlie these . assertions according to which, before His appearance on earth, He was a superhuman and God-like being, and even after His appearance not a real man but only having the form of man-like existence (Docetism). This difference of principle would be hard to set aside, however the details of the obscure passage Phil. ii. 6 f. are interpreted. It is very difficult to say whether the "being equal with God" refers to the same condition as the "being in the form of God," or is a higher good, distinguished from it, which might conceivably be the object of "robbery" or violent seizure; in any case the being equal with God is so closely related to the being in the form of God that it is only on the basis of the possession of the latter that the former can be regarded as the possible object of (or incentive to) the "robbery." By this an antithetic relation of the phrase in verse 6 to Adam, who was certainly not in the form of God, is excluded, and there remains scarcely any other possible interpretation than a reference to the myth in the Ophite and Valentinian Gnosis of the Sophia which desired to unite itself on equal terms with the primal Deity of the Father, or of the subordinate demiurge Jaldabaoth, who attempted to misuse his god-like power of lordship in order to put himself in the place of the highest God. The conception that Christ, who pre-existed in the form of God, could have thought, even as a possibility, of an act of violent self-deification, is, in fact, so strange that it hardly admits of explanation except as an implied contrast to an analogous myth of the Gnostics. That this interpretation of Baur's (*Paulus*, ii. 51 ff.) was vehemently resisted, is intelligible, since his opponents conceived themselves obliged to accept along with it the inference which he drew as to the late authorship of the Epistle to the Philippians. But that is not necessary. What is to hinder us from supposing that verse 6 f. is a later interpolation into a genuine Pauline epistle such as we find in Romans, and still more in Colossians? The two verses allow themselves to be taken out of the context without the slightest difficulty, so that verse 8, "he humbled himself," is attached immediately to the relative in verse 6. With this excision, too, the difficulty is solved which, on the assumption of a pre-existence in equality with God, is caused by the statement in verse 9 that God exalted Christ as a reward for His obedience, inasmuch as after His earthly life He would only have received back precisely what He had possessed before, and no real "exaltation" would have taken place. On all these grounds the hypothesis advanced by Schmiedel and Brückner, that Phil. ii. 6 f. is a later interpolation, seems to have much probability.

As regards the way in which Paul thought of the Christ Jesus who had appeared in the flesh we find in Rom. viii. 3 an indication which is, it must be admitted, somewhat problematical: God sent His Son in the likeness of sinful flesh, that is to say, in

a body resembling the usual human body, which
consists of sinful flesh. The term likeness seems
intended to indicate that the human corporeity of
Christ when on earth did not belong to Him as being
the mode of manifestation originally natural to Him
and corresponding to His essential character, but that
He had adopted it in the place of His own peculiar
heavenly mode of manifestation, for the purpose of
His entry into earthly humanity, like a foreign
garment, for the sake of making Himself like in form
to earthly men, much as a traveller in foreign lands
provides himself with clothing made in the fashion
of the garb worn there.   Whether according to Paul
the body of the incarnate Christ, which was formed
in the image of the sinful flesh of other men, itself
consisted of " sinful flesh," or of a flesh which was so
far distinguished from ours as to have no relation to
sin, is still a matter of contention among exegetes.
The former is incontestably the natural inference
from the Pauline anthropology, according to which,
as we saw above, the flesh of Adam's race has been
so infected with the poison of sin that flesh and sin
are for Paul inseparable conceptions. How could
the flesh of Christ form an exception to this common
condition of the race ?   That could only be supposed
if it had not originated in the natural way of the
race; but of a supernatural birth of Jesus Paul has
nowhere said anything; rather, he represents Him
as born, according to the flesh, of David's seed
(Rom. i. 3), which implies His derivation from an
earthly father.   And when it is further said in
Rom. viii. 3 that God, when He had sent His Son
in the likeness of sinful flesh and, for sin, condemned

sin in the flesh, and carried out the sentence of death upon it, this seems to imply that sin as an objective demonic power was really present in the flesh of Christ, and that this, therefore, was in fact a sinful flesh of the same kind as that of all men. Against this, appeal is made to 2 Cor. v. 21, " Him who knew no sin God made sin (the atoning bearer of the guilt of our sin) for us." But what is here asserted is only that Christ had no guilt of His own through personal commission of sin. That Christ was thus absolutely free from sin is necessarily the case, since the spirit of holiness constituted His very being; but this absence of subjective sin (transgression and guilt) does not exclude the presence of objective sin as a potential power in the flesh of Christ, in Paul's view, any more than in that of the Jewish theology, which, in spite of the universal sinfulness of the race, taught the sinlessness of the Patriarchs, who overcame the universal natural impulse to sin by their individual strength (Weber, *ut sup.* p. 224).

The purpose of the mission of Christ in the flesh is found by Paul, not in His earthly life, but in His death; to this, together with His resurrection, the whole saving work of Christ was for him exclusively attached. The death of Christ was, in Paul's view, of redemptive efficacy, because, as the expiation for the sin of the world, appointed by God and carried out by Christ in obedience and love, it did away with the religious misery of the consciousness of guilt and the moral bondage of legal obligation, and produced the blessedness and freedom of sonship to God. This, the fundamental view of Paul of the work of redemption, is set forth according to the point of view prevailing at the moment with very various shades of expression, in which there may be noticed a certain progress from the vaguer phrases of the earlier to the more definite and developed doctrinal statements of the later epistles.

According to 1 Thess. v. 10 Christ died in order that we might have life; according to Gal. i. 4 He surrendered Himself (to death) for our sins that He might deliver us from this present evil world (in which death holds sway). His surrender of Himself to the death which God willed, as a deed of obedience and love (Rom. v. 18 f.; Gal. ii. 20), was the costly "price" by which we have been "redeemed," that is, freed from the jurisdiction of death and dedicated to God as a peculiar possession (1 Cor. vi. 20, vii. 23). Since we thus "judge" His death as being substitutionary for the death of all, and delivering for all the life which was forfeit to death, the love of Christ which was thus displayed becomes for Christians a morally binding motive which compels them to live henceforth not to themselves but to Him who died and rose again (2 Cor. v. 14 f.). But in this offering of love Christ revealed also the love of God Himself from whom this whole plan of salvation originated, since it was God who through Christ reconciled the world unto Himself, and did so in that He "made him who knew no sin to be sin for us, that we might be made the righteousness of God in him." The thought of the apostle is quite clear: God has made the sinless Christ in our stead[1] the bearer of

---

[1] ὑπέρ means, of course, primarily "for the sake of," but can also bear the nearly related meaning "instead," as proved by verse 20; 1 Cor. xv. 29; Philem. 13. In the passage cited above this meaning is demanded by the context.

the guilt and the punishment of sin, by causing Him
who had not deserved death to die as our substitute,
in order that we, in virtue of our connection with
Him, might be counted guiltless, or righteous,
although we really are as far from being so as
Christ was from being really a sinner. There thus
takes place *idealiter*, in the judgment of God and
in our faith, an exchange of rôles between Christ
and the world of sinners: He takes their guilt
which deserves death and wipes it out by His
substitutionary death; in return they receive from
Him righteousness, that is, freedom from guilt,
and become, instead of objects of the wrath of
God, objects of His love, as Christ is. It is
precisely this transformation of the relations of God
to the sinful world which constitutes its reconciliation with God; it therefore does not consist,
according to Paul, in man's giving up his hostile
attitude towards God, but in God's giving up the
hostile attitude which men's sin compelled Him to
assume towards them, removing its cause by the
atonement for human guilt which He has Himself
appointed in the death of Christ, in order that His
forgiving grace might have effect, "not imputing
to them their trespasses" (2 Cor. v. 19). It is true
Paul does not say that God has been reconciled,
because He is the author of the reconciliation; but
this is nevertheless a transformation effected from
the side of God, of His relation to the world from
one of wrath to one of mercy—an objective fact
which has been brought about without the aid of
the sinful world by Christ alone, and the effects of
it are offered to the world as God's gift and received

by faith (Rom. v. 11).   Since, then, reconciliation is
made possible by an atonement which in a sense
effects a compromise between righteousness and love
in God, it can be looked upon as a proof of the one
as well as of the other.   According to Rom. iii. 25
God set forth Christ as a means of atonement by
His blood, *i.e.* an atoning sacrifice which becomes
effectual through faith, with the object of manifesting His righteousness in a way in which it was not
manifested so long as God simply, in His long-
suffering mercy, overlooked sin.   For His righteousness is manifested by an actual putting away of sin,
whether through the death of the sinner or through
an atonement which makes satisfaction for sin; so
long as this was wanting the righteousness of God
had not yet been fully shown; but now through
Christ's atoning death it was to be shown, in both
aspects, as on the one hand condemning sin to death
(Rom. viii. 3) and on the other declaring righteous
the sinner whose sin is atoned for.   The righteousness of which the manifestation is here in view is, it
is true, not simple retributive justice, since, indeed,
instead of punishment, atonement takes place; but
it is not, on the other hand, the same as mercy, for
in that case why should the earlier overlooking of
sins render necessary the present proof of righteousness through a blood-atonement?   That certainly
implies that righteousness as understood by Paul
must involve the idea that sins cannot simply be
overlooked or forgiven without more ado, but only
upon condition of an atonement which makes satisfaction to righteousness.   Therefore this righteousness
is that activity of the Divine will which reacts

against sin, or does away with it, either by punishment or expiation, and which must have its due before the acquittal of sinners can take place. How exactly this corresponds to the assumptions of Jewish theology we shall see later. But when in Rom. v. 8 ff. the death of Christ for us sinners is pointed to as a proof of the love of God and a guarantee of our future salvation from punishment, that does not conflict with the passage just referred to, in which it serves as a proof of righteousness. In both cases it is a question of a compromise between righteousness and love by means of an atonement instituted by the latter, which, by a wiping out of guilt, does away with the cause of the divine wrath and opens up to love the possibility of her activity as saving mercy.

When it is said in verse 10 that we, while we were enemies (of God), were reconciled with God by the death of His Son, and therefore as now reconciled have the more certain hope of being delivered from the (future) wrath through His life, there is here a clear confirmation of what was said above with reference to 2 Cor. v. 19. The reconciliation which we " have received" does not consist in the alteration of the ethical attitude of our will, which could not offer any guarantee of our future deliverance from the wrath of God, but consists in the alteration of our religious consciousness of God's attitude towards us : whereas formerly we knew ourselves objects of the divine wrath, of His enmity which pressed heavily upon us,[1]

[1] That ἐχθροί is to be understood in the passive sense (= deo invisi) is shown by the parallel in Rom. xi. 28, where it forms the antithesis to ἀγαπητοί.

now that our guilt has been wiped out by the death of His Son, we know that His wrath is removed and His love assured to us, and by this there is given to us the guarantee of our salvation at the last judgment.

This fundamental view of the atoning significance of the death of Christ, Paul shared in essentials, apart from his definite dogmatic formulation of it, with the primitive community (1 Cor. xv. 3), but in contra-distinction to the latter he draws from the doctrine further ethical inferences. While his Judaising opponents held that the doctrine of grace when it was made the all in all at the expense of the authority of the law, must necessarily lead to a sinful heathen life (Gal. ii. 17 ; Rom. vi. 1), Paul showed that the same proof of love which God gave in the death of Christ which atoned for the guilt of sin and broke the curse of the law, also broke the power of sin and did away with the tyranny of the law, which was closely bound up with it. That was for him primarily a fact of his religious experience ; the love of God and of Christ which he saw revealed in the death of Christ awakened in him a grateful responsive love, by the power of which he felt himself so overmastered and controlled that his life henceforth belonged only to the Lord who had loved him and given Himself for him (Gal. ii. 20 ; 2 Cor. v. 14 f.). In this complete surrender of himself to the crucified and risen Son of God, he felt that he himself had died as concerns his old man, and risen to a new life. This even now moved so completely in the divine and spiritual element that it was raised as high above the sinful impulses of the flesh as above the tyranny of the written law. It was, however, a characteristic of Paul's thinking to objectify the spiritual experiences of the religious consciousness in a definite act in which the inward and continuous experience was made visible in a single outward event, and thus —as we might perhaps express it—its essential truth received a fixed form. Such an act was baptism, in which the plunge beneath the water not only symbolically represented dying and newness of life, but, for the thought of Paul, and indeed of antiquity generally, was also the mystic cause of these experiences (see further upon this head, below). But since baptism itself was also a representation of Christ's being buried and raised again, it was quite in accordance with this line of thought to see in the death and resurrection of Christ, not merely the prototype but also the mystical commencement and cause of the subsequent dying and renewal of Christians. This mystical view—which is peculiar to and original with Paul—of the death and resurrection of Christ (for the two are in this connection inseparable) appears in Rom. vi.–viii., not indeed in place of his earlier forensic view, but as an essential supplement to it, and in such fashion that the latter is seen beneath it as the abiding foundation.[1]

Starting in Rom. vi. 2 ff. from the principle that Christians in being baptized into Christ are buried with Him, have grown together with Him into the likeness of His death, that their old man is crucified with Him, he is led back, by the inference from this mystical experience of Christians, to Christ Himself, and affirms : " In that Christ died he died

[1] *Cf.* the excellent exposition of Holtzmann, *N.T. Theol.*, ii. 114 ff.

unto sin once for all; in that he lives, he lives to God. Likewise reckon ye yourselves to be dead unto sin but alive to God. Sin shall no longer have dominion over you, for ye are not under the law but under grace" (verses 10 f., 14). By the statement "Christ died to sin once for all" Paul does not mean that He died to it morally, which would of course imply that He had previously lived to it (contrary to 2 Cor. v. 21), but that He by His substitutionary death paid to sin (which Paul, as we saw, thought of as a demonic spiritual being) the tribute which was due, granted to it its right of enforcing the death sentence against the sinful world, but by the very fact of doing so cancelled for ever, on behalf of the sinner whom He represented, all its claims to exercise dominion. Of a "destruction of the flesh" there is here no mention, but the idea of a debt is certainly involved, a debt by reason of which men were sold as slaves into the bondage of sin (vii. 14), until Christ by His vicarious death paid the debt for all and delivered His people from the slavery of sin. It is to be perceived from this that for Paul the ethical effect of the death of Christ, the overcoming of the power of sin, is attached as a simple consequence to the legal payment of the debt and expiation. And the same applies to Rom. viii. 3, " What the law could not do, since it was weak through the flesh, God, sending his Son in the likeness of sinful flesh and because of sin, condemned sin in the flesh," namely, to death, for it is to this only, and not to the sinless life of Christ, that the passage applies. Here, too, the legal view is the basis. God executed judgment in the representative death of Christ, upon (personified) sin and thereby brought all its dominion to an end.[1] The former civil-law analogy of the satisfaction of a creditor by the payment of his due is here exchanged for one drawn from criminal law—the condemnation of a robber or tyrant; yet the former recurs in viii. 12, "So now we are no more debtors to live after the flesh"—a proof that we must not fix these fluctuating modes of representation with pedantic accuracy or nail down the apostle's meaning to one or other of them. If they are for him something more than mere pictures, we may yet fairly see in them merely various pictorial expressions for the one religious experience of feeling himself raised by the inspiration of faith in Christ above the trammels of sin and of the law. How closely these two hang together is clear from vi. 14, "Sin shall no more have dominion over you, for ye are not under the law but under grace." Since the law is the gaoler who holds men in the prison of sin (Gal. iii. 22 f.), liberation from the latter is liberation from the law also. Therefore it is said in vii. 4, "Ye are become dead to the law by the (slain) body of Christ; that ye might belong to another, namely, to Christ who is raised from the dead"; verse 6, "Now we are delivered from the law, having died to its tyranny"; and Gal. ii. 19, "I through the law am dead to the law that I might live unto God; I am crucified with Christ." Since Paul sees in the crucifixion of Christ, which was brought about by the law, the cause of this deliverance from bondage to the law

[1] Simon, *Paulin. Psychol.*, p. 73 : Right was denied to ἁμαρτία —it was condemned in the flesh; the legal claim which it had advanced was denied to it.

which he experienced in himself as the result of his belief in the Crucified, this becomes to him a definite breach with the law, the fulfilment, and at the same time the abrogation, of all its claims upon the humanity which was become new in Christ. Therefore he says in Gal. iv. 4 that the Son of God was under the law in order that He might redeem those who are under the law, in order that we might receive the adoption of sonship. And as we have been redeemed from the tyranny of the law through Christ's vicarious obedience to the law, so we have been delivered from the curse of the law through Christ's vicarious bearing of it in His death. That is stated in Gal. iii. 13 ; Christ has redeemed us from the curse of the law by being made a curse for us (for it is written, " Cursed be everyone who hangeth on a tree "), that the blessing of Abraham might come to the Gentiles in Christ Jesus, in order that we might receive the promise of the Spirit through faith. Paul does not mean that Christ was personally accursed before God, but that He had vicariously taken upon Him the curse of the law which threatens sin with death (*cf.* 2 Cor. v. 21), and by means of this ransom price redeemed us from it; and, moreover, not only from its curse, but also from its binding power, so that henceforth salvation comes by faith without the intervention of the law. The law is here, as in Rom. vi. 10, and like sin in viii. 3, personified as the tyrannic power whose tyranny over Christians is brought to an end by the fact that their representative Head, through His crucifixion, which ideally included theirs also, has given to the law its due. The law has no longer any claim upon

Christians, any more than it has upon the crucified and risen Christ, since they have entered by baptism into mystical union with the death and resurrection of Christ.

In all these passages just referred to the legal idea of representation is extended to that of mystical union. That which took place once *for* us in Christ's death and resurrection, is also the beginning and principle of something which goes on continuously *in* us, who through faith and baptism have become one with Him. In this union His dying to sin and to the law is also our release from both. His resurrection and life for God is also our new life in the Spirit. If we ask how Paul arrived at this doctrine and what was its historically conditioned form, what its abiding truth, we recall first the view current in the Pharisaic theology of the atoning value of the undeserved suffering and death of the righteous, which is imputed to their people in satisfaction for their sins (above, p. 73). Paul has simply applied this general theory to the special case of the death of Jesus. For that very cause—because the fact of the death of Jesus the Messiah on the cross was historically given, and only the religious significance of it was in question—Paul did not touch at all the problem which presents itself to theological thought: Why there was any need of such a means of expiation in order to effect reconciliation, or how far Christ's death was an equivalent sufficing for the redemption of sinners from the curse of the law? Certainly, serious objection can be brought against this theory from the standpoint of the God-consciousness which dwelt in the soul of Jesus, according to which God who is love—an inexhaustibly rich Father-love in giving and forgiving—forgives those who repent and believe out of free grace without first demanding payment of the debt by expiation. But Paul, who was not the personal disciple of Jesus but a disciple of the Pharisees, took as his starting-point for his theory of redemption, not the consciousness of Jesus, but the Pharisaic legal religion, according to which God does not forgive unless payment of the debt is made, any more than an earthly judge, but the payment of the debt may be made by a vicarious service or penance on the part of an innocent person. Through this theory, which rested for him on *a priori* grounds, the interpretation of the crucifixion of Christ as a vicarious ransom and expiation lay so near at hand—was, in fact, one might say, almost forced upon him—that he saw no occasion to think out the premises on which this theory rested, but only to draw the inferences from it in order to give a dogmatic basis to his consciousness of mercy; inferences which, however, went far beyond the presupposed standpoint of the legal religion. Between the fundamental Pharisaic view on the one side—according to which God is the stern judge who does not forgive without demanding payment or expiation, and the law is an absolute tyrant who inexorably insists upon his rights—and, on the other side, the Christian consciousness for which God as the Father of Jesus Christ is the Will of Love, and the law only a "pædagogic" institution of temporary significance—between these two standpoints there is undoubtedly an inconsistency which cannot be logically removed, but only psychologically explained.

From the consciousness of Paul, in which the filial Spirit of Jesus had to struggle with the legal spirit of the Pharisee, there could only spring a theory of redemption which vacillated between the two. But for this very reason — because, namely, it was a compromise between the two, fighting the legal religion with its own forms in order to open up the way for the freedom of the children of God—for this very reason it was from the first and ever afterwards an excellently adapted means of transforming the legal into the evangelical consciousness by elevating the former into the latter.

While the connection of the Pauline doctrine of redemption with the Pharisaic theology is beyond doubt, its relation to the Old Testament sacrificial ritual is very doubtful. A direct reference to the latter is only found in one passage, 1 Cor. v. 7, in which Christ is spoken of as the Passover-sacrifice, but in this passage no dogmatic, but only ethical, inferences are drawn, and therefore it cannot be regarded as authoritative for the Pauline doctrine of redemption. If we remember that the Mosaic law provided sin-offerings and guilt-offerings for lesser offences but not for mortal sins, that there was no sacrifice within the legal order which could make atonement for, and dispense from punishment, one who had incurred sentence of death, we shall find that an application of the Mosaic sacrificial institutions to the saving effects of the death of Christ in Paul's theology is highly improbable.[1] At the same time, it cannot be doubted that the general conception of sacrifice is in no way foreign to Paul's doctrine

[1] *Cf.* Weiss, *Bibl. Theol.*, fifth edition, pp. 305 f., note.

22

of redemption, but in some form or other underlies
all the passages where the blood of Christ is
mentioned.[1] But in this connection we have not to
think of the Mosaic sacrificial theory, but of those
sacrificial ideas which were generally current among
Jews and heathen alike, in which the thought of
vicarious expiation by the carrying out of a legal
sentence, or by free-willed self-sacrifice, and the
thought of a mystic purification which removed
demonic defilement, run into one another. Representations of that kind held their place in the Jewish
mind, in connection with primitive usages, in
complete independence of the Mosaic law. "The
earliest character of the bloody sacrifice carries a hint
of vicarious penalty. The satisfaction is called
Chattah and Asham in Mic. vi. 7 and Isa. liii. 10,
not in the technical sense of the priestly code, but
simply as guilt which is borne by the innocent for
the guilty."[2] According to Robertson Smith[3] the
popular Semitic view (which did not become an
official doctrine) of the public sacrifice was that, on
the one side, it was a substitute for, and spectacular
representation of, an execution, and to a certain
extent serves as a vicarious satisfaction to the
divine righteousness in order to restore the disturbed
relationship between the community and the Deity;
on the other side it serves as an effectual means of
purification, which in virtue of sacred forces which
are concentrated in the body and blood of the sacred
victim, removes the impurity which is a barrier to

---

[1] *Cf.* Holtzmann, *N. Tle. Theol.*, ii. 104 f., note.
[2] Wellhausen, *Prolegomena*, fourth edition, p. 73.
[3] *Religion of the Semites*, pp. 423 f.

intercourse with God. Among the Greeks also the expiatory acts for the reconciliation of the offended gods and spirits, and those of purification for the putting away of demonic influence, often became fused together. In both cases vicarious sacrifices of animals were used, and in special cases even of men, whose death served as an expiatory offering for the purifying of the city.[1] We must suppose that this whole system of ideas belonged to the common stock of the ancient animistic popular religion, which from the most remote antiquity maintained itself beneath all the transformations of the official State-religions, and after their downfall sprang up in renewed strength and here and there gave rise to new and peculiar offshoots. Such, for example, were the manifold mystery-cults in which the most ancient idea of sacrifice as a " sacred communion " or communication of the divine life through the blood of the sacrifice and the sacrificial meal, played the central part. It was otherwise in Israel, where from the popular conception of an expiatory sacrifice there was developed under the influence of the prophetic spirit (Isa. liii.), the above-mentioned theory of the saving power of the martyr-death of the righteous, as is expressed with especial clearness in 4 Maccabees xvii. 21, " By the blood of these righteous men, and by the expiatory sacrifice ($i\lambda a\sigma\tau\eta\rho\iota o\nu$) of their death the divine providence delivered Israel"; and vi. 29, " Make my blood a purifying sacrifice ($\kappa a\theta\acute{a}\rho\sigma\iota o\nu$), and take my soul in substitution for theirs ($\grave{a}\nu\tau\acute{\iota}\psi\nu\chi o\nu$ $a\grave{\upsilon}\tau\hat{\omega}\nu$)."

When Paul transferred these conceptions of

[1] E. Rhode, *Psyche*, pp. 247 f., 366 f.

vicarious expiation and ransom to the death of
Jesus, there entered into the religion of Jesus a
mystical element which is capable of exercising a
disturbing influence on the evangelical God-consciousness if it is fixed down and dogmatised
according to the literal form apart from living
religious experiences. But that is not at all Paul's
intention; it is a misunderstanding and misuse of
his teaching for which he himself cannot fairly be
held responsible. From himself we hear, through
all the formulæ of the forensic and mystic systems
of thought, the ringing note, the genuine heart-
tones, of evangelical piety; which proves that those
theories are only the historically conditioned form
of representation in which the inner truth of his
ethico-religious experience objectified itself. While
we cannot ignore the husk of those forms, we ought
still less to ignore the kernel of deep ethical religion
which is hidden therein. Paul certainly saw in the
death of Christ not merely a legal act—an expiation
which satisfied righteousness and the law—but also,
and essentially, the typical revelation of the holy
love of God which saves sinners, while it judges,
removes, and makes satisfaction for, sins, and has
given the world a pledge and earnest of its saving
purpose in the sending forth and giving up to death
of God's own Son, the image of God and the pattern
of man. Again, in the self-surrender of Jesus to the
divinely ordered death, Paul saw the pattern ethical
act of obedience and love (Rom. v. 19; Gal. ii. 20;
Phil. ii. 8) and the decisive turning-point of history.
By this act the new spiritual man, the second Adam,
made satisfaction for the disobedience of the first

and founded a new era for mankind in which no longer selfishness and slavish fear, but that very Christ-spirit of free, filial obedience and heartfelt, self-sacrificing brotherly love, inspires and impels all who unite themselves in faith with their pattern and first-born brother and thus become one in spirit with Him. Thus, beneath the harsh dogmatic form of a vicarious expiation, there shows itself as the true kernel, the profound thought of a *re-birth of mankind through the inspiring and renewing power of a divine-human deed of love*. The death and resurrection of Christ appear, regarded from this point of view, not merely as single outward events of mystical significance, but also as typical symbols of the eternal order of salvation, according to which the death of the flesh, of the sinful selfish nature, leads to the life of the Spirit, of the God-like personality. As the person of Christ embodies, in Paul's view, the pattern of the Divine Sonship, so the death and resurrection of Christ embodies the fundamental principle of the kingdom of God which Jesus formulated in the saying, "He who loses his life for the sake of the gospel, the same shall save it."

In the thought of Paul the resurrection of Christ is inseparably bound up with His death. Since it is produced by the omnipotence of God, it is the divine seal upon the work of redemption, the reward for the loyal obedience of the Son of God, His appointment to the dignity and influence of the Son of God with power (Rom. i. 4), His elevation to be Lord of living and dead, whose Lordship shall be acknowledged by all who are in heaven, upon earth, or under the earth (Rom. xiv. 9; Phil. ii. 9 ff.). He has now become

"the Lord who is the Spirit," "the Lord of glory,"
whose body is of heavenly radiance (2 Cor. iii. 17;
1 Cor. ii. 8; Phil. iii. 21). No longer suffering
through the sin of the world, He lives henceforth
to God, to maintain the honour of God, and overcomes with kingly might all the enemies of God
(Rom. vi. 10; Phil. ii. 11; 1 Cor. xv. 25). But with
all this God-like and regal splendour of the exalted
Christ, His subordination to the Father is strongly
maintained by Paul; He is and remains only the
instrument of the Father's will, and will therefore
one day, when the victory over the world is completed, render up His authority into the hands of the
Father, and step back into the ranks of those who
are subject to God, the sole ruler of all (1 Cor. xv. 28).
Apart from the significance of the resurrection for
Christ Himself, it has, according to Paul, high
significance for the salvation of the Church also.
As Paul himself was converted by beholding the
risen Christ, he accordingly regarded the resurrection
as the mainstay of our faith in the redeeming work
of Christ. As he says in 1 Cor. xv. 17: "If Christ
is not raised, then is your faith vain; ye are yet in
your sins," i.e. you have in that case no guarantee
that His death really effected your redemption for
sin. Rom. iv. 25, too, is best understood from the
same point of view; the delivering up of Christ
for our sins is the counterpart of His resurrection
for our justification, inasmuch as the justification
assumes faith in the atoning significance of the death
of Christ, but this faith could only arise on the
ground of the resurrection of the crucified. But
Paul sees in the resurrection not only the pledge of

our reconciliation through Christ's death; the hope of our future salvation also is based upon the certainty of the life and work of the risen Christ in and for His Church. For since "the Lord is the Spirit," He works in His Church as the power which interpenetrates the whole organism and every one of its limbs, and inspires a new and higher life which has its source in heaven. In union with Him Christians feel themselves to be also closely united to the Father, whose love is guaranteed and ever newly assured to them in the Lord Jesus Christ, since He ever represents, and intercedes for, those who believe in Him, before the Father (Rom. viii. 34-39). On this rests the Christians' hope that they also will be made alive again in Christ, that they will be made like Him who is the first-fruits of the resurrection, and in communion with His life will share in the final salvation and blessedness (1 Cor. xv. 22, 57; Rom. v. 10, viii. 10 f.); thus the raising of Christ to the heavenly life of glory is the cause and pattern both of our present new life in the Spirit and also of our future new life in glory. In the former aspect, it is the motive and norm of ethical exhortation; in the latter, the ground and pledge of our religious hope (Rom. vi. 4 ff., viii. 11).

CHAPTER XVI

Justification by Faith

THE reconciliation which was accomplished by Christ comes into force by means of faith in those who receive the announcement of it, and accept the offer to let themselves be reconciled (Rom. iii. 25; 2 Cor. v. 20). Faith is therefore the appropriation of the salvation offered in Christ Jesus as a personal and conscious possession of salvation, or as a condition of righteousness before God, a condition of "peace."

According to its common literal significance faith is the confident conviction of the truth of the divine message, whether in the form of promises of future blessings, or of the report of historical revelations of God—a conviction grounded upon trust in God, whose word is believed. Thus the faith of Abraham (Rom. iv. 3) was trust in God that He could and would make His promise come true in spite of all appearance to the contrary. To this faith of Abraham the specific Christian faith is, according to Paul, essentially similar, as being trust in the God who raised Christ from the dead and thereby announced His purpose of justifying the ungodly (Rom. iv. 5, 24). Even when faith appears

344

as primarily purely theoretical belief—*e.g.* of the truth of the announcement that God has raised His Son from the dead (Rom. x. 9)—the specific religious element in it does not consist in the theoretic acceptance of the fact, but in the trust in the divine saving purpose which is revealed in that event. This trust is not so much an act of the intellect as an affection of the heart, a mode or attitude of feeling, as, indeed, Paul says, " With the heart man believeth." This feeling is, it is true, awakened by the involuntary impression made by the proclamation of the gospel message, which forces itself upon the receptive soul through " the demonstration of the Spirit and of power " as divine truth ; and, in so far, faith is an effect produced by God through His word. The believer is laid hold of by Christ, is surrendered to the teaching of the Gospel. God causes the light of the knowledge of the glory of God to shine into our hearts (2 Cor. iv. 6 ; Rom. vi. 17 ; Phil. iii. 12). But through all this, faith is still a human action of self-determination with reference to God and Christ, a will-act of obedience towards the higher truth of the Gospel, of submission to the way of justification which is offered by God, a laying hold upon Christ on the ground of being laid hold of by Christ (Rom. i. 5, vi. 17, x. 3, 16 ; Phil. iii. 12). Only, in all this it is to be observed that faith is not an act of obedience in the sense of a good work or a meritorious service which might have a righteousness of its own ; it consists, on the contrary, in a renunciation of all glorying in oneself, of all achievements, actions and capacities of one's own, in order to have instead all

given to one as God's gift of grace. Faith is therefore humble and trustful self-surrender to the
Divine will, revealed through the gospel as a will
of mercy offering its gifts to men, not as a will of
law demanding service from men. This contrast is
characteristic of the specifically Pauline conception
of faith; faith stands in direct contrast to a man's
own works, his legal acts of obedience, which, as
merits, put forth a claim to reward, in contrast to
boasting of one's own advantages or virtues of
whatsoever kind (Rom. iii. 27, iv. 4 f., x. 3 ff.;
Phil. iii. 4 ff.). It is precisely the recognition of the
worthlessness from the religious point of view of all
such advantages, of the powerlessness of man to
attain righteousness by his own strength, which
forms the starting-point. But on the basis of this
humble valuation of self, the believer rises to a
confident trust in God's mercy, gratefully accepts
His free gift, finds in the gospel a power of God to
inspire the heart which labours miserably under
the yoke of the law, and thus he becomes filled with
grateful love to the mediator of this gift who has
purchased it by the offering of His own life upon the
cross (Rom. vii. 25–viii. 2; Gal. ii. 20 f., iii. 22 ff.;
Phil. iii. 8 ff.).

On this, again, rests a further peculiarity of the
Pauline conception of faith. As the message of
salvation is concentrated for him in the word of the
cross of Christ, faith, too, acquires this specific
reference to Christ as the crucified. While the
primitive Christian faith of the Palestinian church
directed itself rather to Christ as the Messiah-King
who was to come again, and was therefore, in so far,

rather an eschatological hope, the emphasis of the Pauline faith lies more on the personal surrender to the "Son of God who loved me and gave himself for me" (Gal. ii. 20). Thus, there is here united with the firm trust the still more intimate feeling of grateful love to the loving Saviour, in which the believer feels himself bound up with his Saviour in the closest union of life to a moral and spiritual personal unity. This *mystical union with Christ*, this self-identification with Christ in a fellowship of life and death, is the new and significant peculiarity in Paul's conception of faith. In this unreserved, self-forgetting surrender of the whole man to the Saviour, in which the revelation of the divine love, as well as the embodiment of the ideal for man, is beheld as a personal life, the believer feels himself to be "a new creature." The old ego with its inner disharmony, its vacillation between defiance and apprehension, between selfish disobedience and slavish fear, has disappeared, and a new ego has come to life, in which selfless, trustful love to the highest personal ideal has become the ruling affection, the centre of the personal life, and the spring of all religious feeling and moral effort. The ideal of the Son of God has been taken up by love into the heart and has become in immediate experience the power of a life of sonship to God. That is expressed in the fine saying: "It is no longer I that live but Christ that liveth in me, and the life that I now live in the flesh, I live in the faith of the Son of God who loved me and gave himself for me" (Gal. ii. 20). It is evident that here life in the faith means the same as "Christ liveth in me." In that saying Paul

has given the authentic explanation of what faith
in Christ, in the full sense, means to him: it is
the mystic union with Christ, the surrender of the
whole ego to Christ to be made one in life with him.
The expression to be "in Christ" was coined by
Paul as the standing formula for the conception of
faith in Christ; he is a Christian who is in Christ,
or, what comes to the same thing, who has Christ
dwelling in him.   Only where this is actually the
case as a fact of experience is true faith present, as
clearly appears from 2 Cor. xiii. 5: "Prove yourselves whether ye be in the faith.   Or know ye not
that Christ is in you?"   And the same is expressed
negatively in Rom. viii. 9: "He who hath not the
spirit of Christ is none of his."   This specifically
Pauline expression, to be "in Christ," is without
doubt formed in imitation of the generally current
expression to be "in the Spirit," which,[1] according to
the animistic use of language, means the same as
to be in a condition of being filled, seized on,
possessed, by a higher spiritual being, a conception
which the Greeks express by "enthusiasmos"
($\dot{\epsilon}\nu\ \theta\epsilon\hat{\omega}\ \epsilon\hat{\iota}\nu\alpha\iota$).   But what others understood as an
extraordinary condition of ecstasy Paul thought of
as the permanent condition of Spirit-filled Christians;
and as he directly identified the exalted Christ with
the Spirit (2 Cor. iii. 17) it followed as a logical
consequence that the faith which unites men with
Christ in a community of life can be described as a
being in the Spirit or in Christ.   Faith is therefore
not yet present in the full sense where it is mere

---

[1] *Cf.* Gunkel, *Die Wirkungen des hl. Geistes*, p. 92; Deissmann,
Die neutestl. Formel "in Christo Jesu."

subjective consciousness in relation to an external object, whether it be a future good, expected from heaven, or the history of a past event—a miraculous occurrence, for example; it is, rather, the actual union of the heart with the object of its devotion and love, whether God Himself as He reveals Himself in human persons and actions, or the Saviour as the focus of God's revelation of love; it is the union of the soul with Christ into one Spirit (1 Cor. vi. 17), the being filled and impelled by the holy Spirit of the Son of God (Gal. iii. 26; Rom. viii. 14).

Since it is thus a union of life with God and Christ, faith manifests itself as a living motive-power in all the various aspects of the personal life: as a feeling of peace and joy, of hope and patience, as clearness and certainty of religious and moral conviction, as incentive and strength for free self-determination to the good, especially as an impulse of love to the brethren, in which faith displays its loving energy (Gal. v. 6). Everything in which the new inspiration of the man by the Spirit of Christ comes to expression, everything that belongs to his "life in the Spirit," belongs therefore to the content of the life of faith. This latter is therefore not practically distinguished from the life in the Spirit; both are the same, but from different points of view. That which is passively experienced by the man as the influence of the Spirit and received as a supernatural gift is at the same time, as the content of faith, his own consciousness and living activity. The Spirit, although in Himself a supernatural Being and Power, enters into the man in such a fashion that he is, in a measure at least, one with the man's own ego. We shall see below that from the point of view of the popular animistic metaphysic, with which the Pauline teaching of the Spirit is closely bound up, this presents no difficulty. Here, however, we must also notice that this naïve supernaturalistic theory has for its basis the simplest facts of the soul's experience; the inspiration of faith and love is a " pathos " in which the human ego feels itself laid hold upon, impelled and dominated by a higher power, and yet the proper life of the ego feels that its own strength is not paralysed by this " pathos " but intensified, and recognises the actions which spring from this impulse as its own. For this reason Paul can speak of love as a fruit of the Spirit not less than as a mighty proof of faith (Gal. v. 6 and 22); since faith receives and consciously feels the divine love, the latter becomes for it the motive to the activity of ethical love. In this mysticism of faith, as Paul understands it, lie the roots of new ethical power as well as of a deeper knowledge of God; and therefore both of practical and theoretical Christianity.

As faith includes the whole of the Christian life, it is capable of various gradations of strength and weakness, as well as of increase and decrease. Religious uncertainty and unfreedom of conscience are described by Paul as a " being weak in faith," freedom and confident conviction as a being strong in faith. Moreover, the extraordinary and heroic strength of faith which makes possible miraculous healings is one of the special " charisms " or gifts of grace (1 Cor. xii. 9 f.). But, in general, growth in Christian perfection is described as growing in faith, the strengthening of the ethico-religious character is described as standing fast, becoming manly and strong, in faith (1 Cor. xvi. 13). On the other hand, the falling back from freedom into the sensuous trammels of the ritual and legal system is a falling from grace and therefore from faith. In all such passages the comprehensive conceptions of faith as the whole Christian attitude and direction of life is assumed, for only on a very forced interpretation could the narrower conception of trust be maintained throughout.

If faith is this intimate union of a man with Christ in which he becomes one soul with Him, it is quite natural that the believer should come to stand in the same relation to God in which Christ stands; i.e. that he should enter into the relation of sonship in which Christ stands towards God. Therefore, Paul says to the Galatians (iii. 26): "Ye are all sons of God through faith in Christ Jesus." As, in general, surrender to an ideal implies also that one is elevated to it and made like it, so the surrender of faith to the personal pattern of the Son of God is at the same time the realisation of our personal consciousness of sonship to God. We feel ourselves to be, in Christ, the objects of the fatherly love of God and impelled by the holy spirit of sonship. Now, since this new state of consciousness forms a strongly marked contrast to the former condition of bondage and fear, it is natural that the termination of the old condition and commencement of the new should be marked by a divine judgment in which the sinner is acquitted of his guilt and received as a child of God. This is the "justification" of the believer (δικαίωσις, δικαιοῦν).

By this term Paul understands, in conformity with the uniform linguistic usage of the Septuagint and of Jewish theology, the judicial act of acquittal or declaring righteous. It is in this sense that the word must be understood in Rom. iii. 4, where it is said of God, with reference to whom there can be no question of a "making righteous," that "He shall be justified in his words," *i.e.* shall be seen to be right, shall be recognised as righteous, in His judgments. So too, in Rom. ii. 13, "the doers of the law shall be justified," the meaning "declared righteous" is required not merely by the antithesis with the previous "condemned" (verse 12) but also by the connection of thought, since the doers of the law do not need to be "made righteous," but only to be recognised and declared so. In the classic passage Rom. iv. 3–8, where Paul directly lays the foundation of this teaching, the term "justify" is paraphrased by the formula "impute righteousness to," or "count faith for righteousness to," or "not impute sin to"; formulæ which obviously express a judicial judgment. But the basis on which this judgment of justification rests is not contained in the word itself; it can equally express a pronouncement of justification upon a man who has fulfilled the law on the ground of his own work-righteousness (so Rom. iii. 13), or a justification apart from this on some other basis. The first justification on the ground of a man's own legal works or meritorious services, was the regular use in Jewish theology [1]; for Paul, however, this way of

---

[1] It must, however, be noticed in this connection that Jewish theology was acquainted with a justification which was based, not on one's own merit, but upon the imputation of the merits

justification remains a mere abstract possibility, the non-attainment of which was certain upon many grounds. In the first place, because experience convinced him of the universal sinfulness of men (Rom. iii. 23); in the second, because he recognised in this fact of experience the natural consequence of the fleshly nature of man, through which man became the impotent slave of sin which ruled irresistibly in the flesh; finally, however, and especially, because his justification on the ground of his own works stood in contradiction with the essential character of grace, which imparts righteousness, not as a merited reward, but as a free gift (Rom. iv. 4 f., iii. 24). It was therefore here, in his doctrine of redemption, that there lay for Paul the decisive grounds of his doctrine of justification, as appears with especial clearness in

(righteousness) of others—of patriarchs, teachers, martyrs, and notable righteous men of that kind; only this righteousness which was imputed on the ground of the vicarious services of others did not take the place of the individual righteousness in fulfilling of the law, but *merely supplemented it.* In this sense it is said, for example, in Apoc. Baruch. lxxxiv. 10 f., after an exhortation to the fulfilment of the law, "pray that the Almighty may be merciful towards you and not impute to you your many sins, but remember the righteousness of your fathers; for if He did not judge us according to His great mercy then woe to all the sons of earth!" *Ibid.* liv. 16, 21, it is said, "He who believes, receives reward for it." "Thou dost glorify the believers [at the judgment] according to their faith." So too in 2 Esdras ix. 7: "All who are saved for their works' sake or for the sake of the faith which they have kept, shall see my salvation." xiii. 23 : "The afflicted shall be preserved if they have works and faith in the Highest." From this it would appear that in the Jewish theology faith ranked equally with works in fulfilment of the law, and the imputation of the righteousness of the Fathers, as a means of salvation alongside of one's own merits.

Gal. ii. 21 : "I do not frustrate the grace of God ; for if righteousness come by the law, then Christ is dead in vain." The death of Christ, he means, would have been purposeless if it had not had the significance of an act of mercy on the part of God by means of which a new way to righteousness apart from the works of the law is opened up to man. But as the death of the Messiah and Son of God could not possibly be held purposeless, it follows that by means of it a righteousness was instituted which does not come from the law but from Christ's atoning death and from man's faith in him.

We find the negative and positive grounds of justification contained in Rom. iii. 20 ff. Since by works of the law no flesh is justified before God, a righteousness of God apart from the law has been revealed through faith in Christ, of such a kind that all believers are justified freely by God's grace by means of the redemption which has been accomplished in Jesus Christ, by God's setting Him forth as a sacrifice of atonement in His blood, to the end that He might exhibit His righteousness, and be both just and the justifier of him that believeth in Jesus. According to this the ultimate cause of justification is the grace of God, the mediate cause is the death of Christ, in which God has effected a general expiation to make atonement for the sins of the whole world, which then is individually appropriated by all who accept the gift of righteousness (Rom. v. 17), personally appropriating by faith the offered reconciliation. Justification and reconciliation are therefore essentially the same (Rom. v. 1, 9, 10), namely, the being acquitted of guilt by a judgment of divine mercy, which has its objective ground in the blood, *i.e.* the sacrificial death, of Jesus, and is subjectively mediated through faith which has "accepted" the reconciliation (verse 11). As being thus an appropriation of the gift of grace offered by God through Christ, the faith which is the medium of justification forms a contrast to one's own works, to the "works of the law," *i.e.* not only to the performance of ceremonies but even to the performance in one's own strength of moral actions which might claim a reward. In order to mark strongly this unmerited character of the justification of the believer, Paul in Rom. iv. 5 chooses the paradoxical expression "To him that worketh not, but believeth on God who justifieth the ungodly, his faith is counted for righteousness." The expression is without doubt chosen in allusion to the Old Testament passages in which the justification of the ungodly by (corrupt) judges is reprobated in a similar expression as wickedness (Ex. xxiii. 6; Isa. v. 23). But that which is impossible for the human judge, who must judge according to the law, can be effected by a merciful judgment of God, namely, acquittal of the guilty and cancellation of their guilt. Nevertheless the question obtrudes itself at this point: Does not a judgment of God which justifies the godless conflict with righteousness and truth? This appearance of arbitrariness, which is naturally suggested by the paradoxical expression, is removed when we observe that the object of the divine sentence of justification is, after all, not the ungodly as such—that is, man in so far as he is, and desires to remain, ungodly, but a man who in spite

of all his previous guilt is now a believer, and as
such does not desire to remain ungodly any longer.
That Paul does not understand by the faith which
is the medium of justification a passive attitude, an
ethically empty and idle reliance upon mercy
resulting in a serious inconsistency between religion
and morality, may be clearly understood. Even the
example of Abraham's faith is itself instructive on
this point. Why was Abraham's faith reckoned to
him for righteousness? Because in firm confidence,
unmoved by any doubt of the divine promise, he
" gave glory to God " (Rom. iv. 19–22). Therefore
even Old Testament faith, inasmuch as it was a
humble and trustful surrender to the divine purpose
of salvation, has the value of a pious attitude well-
pleasing to God—more valuable than any outward
works. How much more must that be the case in
regard to Christian faith, which according to Paul is
a divine influence manifesting itself in man. For it
results from the preaching of the Gospel through
which God calls those who are destined to salvation
(Rom. x. 17, viii. 30 ; 1 Cor. i. 9), since it demonstrated itself to them as the Spirit and Power of God
unto salvation (Rom. i. 16, 1 Cor. ii. 4 f.). The
confession of Jesus as Lord, and, therefore, faith
in Him, is, according to 1 Cor. xii. 3, only possible
through the Holy Spirit. According to Phil. i. 6,
ii. 13, it is God who begins and completes in us the
good work, who works in us both to will and to do,
who gives us to believe in Christ as well as to
suffer for His sake (i. 29). As the gospel was
preached to the Thessalonians, not in word only,
but in the power of the Spirit and in much assurance,

so it was accepted by them "with the joy which the Holy Spirit gives" (1 Thess. i. 5 f.); therefore the apostle saw in the impression of joyful enthusiasm of faith which his preaching called forth, the influence of the Divine Spirit on and in the hearers. Indeed, he sees in the arising of faith the influence of the very same inspiring power of God which raised Jesus from the dead, and therefore the inner reproduction and continuation of the revelation of God's saving work which was begun in the resurrection of Christ (Col. ii. 12). As, according to this, faith is the new life produced by God in those who are in union with Christ, it is clear that the justification of the believer is not a causeless caprice, for it is available for the sinner, not in so far as he is, and remains, godless, but in so far as he is become new "in Christ." It has indeed been held that faith, as the means of justification, is not to be understood with this fulness of ethical meaning, but simply as the organ by which the merits of Christ are received. But the ascription to the apostle of an abstraction which so artificially separates ethics from religion, has no inherent probability, and is contradicted by many unambiguous statements. According to Phil. iii. 9 the apostle's desire is to attain Christ and be found in Him, not having his own righteousness but the righteousness which is of God by faith.

This shows that justification rests on faith in so far as it appropriates Christ and is a being in Him, a mystical union of life with Him, which is subsequently described (verse 10) as a practical recognition of the power of His resurrection and the fellowship of His suffering in being conformed unto

His death. The same thought is expressed in the
earlier letters also. According to Gal. ii. 17 we seek
to be justified in Christ; according to 2 Cor. v. 21
we are to be made "the righteousness of God in
Christ"; according to Rom. viii. 1 ff. there is no
condemnation to those who are "in Christ," whom
"the law of the Spirit of life in Christ has made free
from the law of sin and death," so that they walk no
longer after the flesh but after the Spirit. Especially
instructive is 1 Cor. vi. 11, in which Paul reminds
the Corinthians of the fact which in baptism lay at the
basis of their standing as Christians, "And such [i.e.
gross sinners] were some of you; but ye are washed,
ye are sanctified, ye are justified, in the name of the
Lord Jesus and in the Spirit of our God." Here,
"being justified" is evidently only a particular
expression for the same religious experience of the
Corinthians which is expressed by being washed
(purified from guilt and sin) and being sanctified
(dedicated and consecrated to the service of God), i.e.
for the saving action of God on which their standing
of grace is founded and which was conveyed to them
in the sacrament of baptism by the naming of the
name of Jesus Christ, that is, by confessing Him, and
by the Spirit of our God which called forth (1 Cor.
xii. 13) this confession. In view of this the dogmatic
abstraction of a special (forensic) act of justification
really distinguished from the inner renewal and
inspiration, can hardly be ascribed to Paul. Justification is for him only a special expression which is
natural from a particular point of view for one and
the same religious experience which from the human
side is called faith, and from the divine side the

gracious gift of righteousness, of the Spirit, of the sonship. In regard to the last expression we shall find
further confirmation of this later ; here we have only
to add that, in view of the foregoing, the dogmatic
distinction between "righteousness of faith" and
"righteousness of life," if supposed to refer to really
different conditions, does not correspond to Paul's use
of the word. He knows only one righteousness of
the believer which is produced by God, which from
one point of view appears as freedom from guilt and
from fear, from another as consecration to the divine
will in obedience and love (Rom. vi. 15–23), but even
this logical distinction cannot be carried through in
the majority of passages.[1]

By recent writers strong emphasis has been laid
on the eschatological character of the thought of
justification ; and this is so far right that the conception of justification had originally, from its
Jewish *provenance*, a reference to the final judgment, which is also frequently perceptible in Paul's
use of it.[2] But that does not justify the statement
that the conception of justification in Paul is solely
or even predominantly eschatological. What is new
in the Pauline thought lies precisely in this, that the
justification which the Jew expected only at the
final judgment, and of which he could therefore
never be assured in this life, is conceived by him as
a gift of divine grace already given and known in

---

[1] *Cf.* the excellent remarks of Cremer, *Paulin. Rechtfertigungs-
lehre*, pp. 336, 366, 424; and Titius, *Paulinismus unter dem Gesichtspunkt
der Seligkeit*, pp. 195, 199 f.

[2] *Cf.* Rom. ii. 13, iii. 20, v. 17, 19 ; perhaps also Gal. v. 5, if here
the ἐλπὶς δικαιοσύνης means the hoped-for righteousness and not,
rather, the hope which attaches to righteousness.

experience through faith in Christ. "Now that we are justified by faith we have peace with God." "There is now no condemnation for those who are in Christ Jesus." "Whom he hath called, them he hath also justified." "Who shall lay anything to the charge of God's elect? It is God who justifies them." "Ye were sinners, but ye are washed, sanctified, justified" (Rom. v. 1, viii. 1, 30, 33; 1 Cor. vi. 11). Justification is therefore the establishment of the permanent condition in which the Christian, standing no longer under the condemning law, but under the grace of God, feels himself assured also of the future attainment of eternal life. Justification is, it is true, not yet identical with the final deliverance, but it warrants the hope and expectation of it (Rom. v. 2 f., 9 f., viii. 10 f., 24, 35 ff.). Is this hope, then, unconditionally certain? On this point the statements of the apostle vary according to whether it is the enthusiasm of religious faith which prevails at the moment, or the thought of the ethical conditionality of the final deliverance and of the defects and fluctuations of the Christian life as shown by experience. The passages cited above, according to which the consciousness of justification, or of present standing under grace, seems to carry with it the certainty of final salvation, stand in contrast with others in which the final deliverance still seems problematical, since it is conditioned by the further conduct of the Christian, the value of which is even said to be determined by a judgment of God which rewards men according to their works (1 Cor. iii. 17, iv. 4, vi. 9 f.; 2 Cor. v. 10, xi. 15; Gal. v. 21, vi. 7; Rom. ii. 6, vi. 21, viii. 13, xi.

21 f. ; Phil. iii. 11 f., 19).   That this expectation
of a judgment according to the individual works
is derived from a different system of thought from
the doctrine of justification by grace and cannot be
directly united with this doctrine, can hardly be
contested.   " The incompatibility of the two representations " (Holtzmann) results from the fact
that, while in both cases the form of a judicial pronouncement, which is unsuitable to the evangelical
standpoint, is the basis, yet the standard of judgment
in the two cases is quite different.   If the form is
discarded there remains on the one side the religious
conception of the divine grace as the unconditional
ground of salvation, and on the other the ethical
conception of human freedom as the always relative
medium of salvation.   That these two sides are
both true and both have their rights is certain ; their
combination—theoretically an insoluble problem—is
always effected in practice by precisely this duality
in the way of looking at it which we see in the case
of the apostle : in so far as faith looks to God it
knows its salvation as fully assured at every time
by the supra-temporal unconditionedness of His
gracious will ; in so far as it looks on itself and on
others, even its hope of salvation is subject to the
conditionality and relativity of the whole temporal
life of man.

That God justifies the believer is a revelation of
the " righteousness of God."   This conception is used
by Paul in connection with his doctrines of reconciliation and justification in a special sense, which is
so far ambiguous that in it, as in the conception
" kingdom of God," a divine activity is thought of

along with the resultant condition. It is only the latter that is in view in 2 Cor. v. 21 ; we are to be " made the righteousness of God "—a rhetorical " breviloquence" which is to be explained as the counterpart of the preceding paradox: " God made the sinless to be sin for us " (*cf.* above, 326 f.). On the other hand, in other passages, like Rom. i. 17, iii. 21 ff., x. 3, where the righteousness of God appears as the subject of the revelation in Christ and in the gospel, and of reception by faith on the part of men, we have to understand by it that will-activity of God which, along with the removal and wiping out of sin, has in view at the same time the deliverance and acquittal of sinners ; a double aim which was attained by the setting forth of the sacrifice of atonement in Christ's death (Rom. iii. 26). Of this righteousness of God, Paul says, on the one hand, that it is witnessed to by the law and the prophets; on the other, that the Jews do not recognise it (Rom. iii. 21, x. 3). In support of the former statement he appeals, in addition to the standing example of Abraham, to the word of Hab. ii. 4, "the just shall live by faith," and to the passage in the Psalms according to which sin is not imputed, or righteousness is imputed, apart from works (Rom. i. 17, iv. 3-8) ; also from Deut. xxx. 11–14, he is able by bold allegorising to extract a proof for the thesis of justification by faith (x. 5–8). In all these passages there is, it is true, no direct mention of the righteousness of God; and for this reason we might have expected rather a reference to Deutero-Isaiah, who often refers to the divine righteousness as the ground of the salvation and the glory of Israel ; in particular, too, of the wiping out of its guilt and of its justification or vindication by God (Isa. xliii. 25, xlv. 24, xlvi. 13, l. 8, liv. 17). That Paul did not appeal to these and similar passages is to be explained from the fact that for him the emphasis lay, not on the conception of the justifying righteousness of God in general, which his opponents did not indeed contest, but upon the particular point that God's justifying sentence was wholly a result of faith, without reference to fulfilment of the law by works. That was the point of which the Jews were ignorant (Rom. x. 3), for they had narrowed the righteousness of God, which for Isaiah was one with His merciful grace and truth, to a judging and retributive righteousness which justifies only the righteous on the ground of his legal works, whereas for the sinner whose own righteousness was defective the divine mercy certainly came into view as to some extent a help, but always only in the sense that the scope of this alternative to the retributive righteousness remained problematical and allowed no confidence of salvation to arise. In this respect it may certainly be said that the Pauline doctrine of the justifying righteousness of God is "a reaching back to the highest intuitions of the prophetic religion across the intervening lower levels of the Jewish legalism" (Holtzmann). Yet we must not overlook a distinction between the two. The believing confidence of the Old Testament saints was directed immediately to the forgiving mercy of God or to His righteousness which vindicated the God-fearing ; for the Pauline faith, however, the justifying righteousness of God is mediated by means of a foregoing cancelling of guilt, by the atoning sacrifice of the death of Christ. That such an atonement for guilt appears needful in order that the divine righteousness may have henceforth not a condemnatory but a justifying action, is obviously a concession to the Pharisaic legalism, for which it was an axiom that with God, the just Judge, there can be no forgiveness without satisfaction. Accordingly, what is to be said is that the Pauline doctrine of the righteousness of God, which, on the ground of the expiation which has been made, justifies the believer, was a compromise between the prophetic and the Pharisaic theories. Paul taught, with the former, the justification of the believer apart from merit of his own; with the latter, justification on the ground of vicarious atonement and expiation. Whereas in the Jewish theology, justification on the ground of meritorious works of one's own and on the ground of vicarious atonement always go together as complementaries, and for that very reason neither makes possible the certainty of salvation; according to Paul the judicial righteousness received its rights and satisfaction once for all in the representative death of the Head of mankind, in order that henceforth the righteousness which justifies the believer out of mercy may alone come into operation. Thus Paul overcame the Jewish legal religion by means of its own presuppositions—"through the law he became dead to the law" (Gal. ii. 19). But this very character of compromise, which made it an effective weapon against legalism and self-righteousness, makes its value as a positive expression of the Christian consciousness of salvation appear very problematical. It is too heavily burdened with the forensic associations of the Jewish legal religion which it was intended to overcome, to be suitable as a simple and positive form of presentation for the religion of the grace of God and the sonship of man.

While setting free the believer from his sin and guilt, God makes him at the same time the object of His fatherly love. The adoption of sonship (υἱοθεσία) is essentially identical with justification, the one being the positive, the other the negative, expression for the transference of the believer into the same position of sonship to God in which Christ, as the first-born among many brethren, stands (Gal. iii. 26 ; Rom. viii. 29). Since, according to the latter passage, God from the beginning destined His elect to be con-formed to the image of His Son, they were essentially, according to the divine predestination, already sons, even while they knew nothing about it, but were still in the position of hired servants under the tutelage of the law and the world-powers. But since God has sent His Son in the flesh to deliver those who were in the thrall of the law, and since He has sent the Spirit of His Son into our hearts, who by crying " Abba, Father ! " testifies to our sonship, we are now (in consequence, that is, of this mission of the Spirit) no longer servants but sons and heirs. According to this interpretation of Gal. iv. 6, which is suggested by the context, the adoption of sonship does not, as a definite act, precede the sending of the Spirit, but in those who were previously sons only ideally and in the counsel of God, the sonship is realised through this gift of the Spirit, in consequence of which the previous consciousness of servitude and

feeling of fear ceases and gives place to the joyful
consciousness of sonship.   Similarly, according to
Rom. viii. 14 ff., those only are true children of God
who are led by the Spirit and obtain the witness of
their sonship.   The enthusiasm of faith which breaks
out in prayer with the cry of Abba, Father! is held
to be due to the influence of the "Spirit of sonship,"
which is called so for the very reason that by testify-
ing to our sonship he assures us of the love of God
(Rom. v. 5), and works in us childlike trust in God.

It is only another form of the same thought when
in Gal. iii. 26 f. it is said that our sonship rests upon
the living union with Christ which is brought about
by faith and baptism ; for to be in Christ is the same
thing as to be in the Spirit, or to have in one the
Spirit of Christ; therefore the bestowal of the Spirit
is practically identical with the transference into the
fellowship of Christ, or the putting on of Christ,
which is mediated by faith and baptism.   If we
observe further that there, too, the statement, " Ye
are all sons of God through faith in Christ," has for
its foundation the preceding statement, " The law
is our paidagogos to bring us to Christ in order
that we might be justified by faith, but since faith
has come we are no longer under the paidagogos," it
is clear that " to be justified " and " to be sons of
God " are interchangeable terms for the same condition of being freed from the law by the faith in
Christ.   This gives further confirmation to the conclusion which we have already drawn from a number
of other passages, such as Phil. iii. 9 ff. ; 2 Cor. v. 21 ;
Rom. viii. 1 f. ; 1 Cor. vi. 11 ; that justification,
adoption, and bestowal of the Spirit are not essentially

different acts of which each forms only a part of the
divine saving work, but that these terms are only
formulæ embodying different aspects of one and the
same indivisible experience of Christians through
faith, in which they recognised the saving work of
God which is mediated through the preaching of
Christ and baptism.[1] For a Christian converted from
Judaism it was natural to represent his feeling of
freedom from the damning curse and burdensome
yoke of the letter of the law as a being acquitted or
justified by God, while for the converted heathen the
childlike feeling of trust in the fatherly will of God
presented itself rather under the aspect of an adoption
by God to which the Spirit bore witness. For all,
however, it was certain that this new religious life
which now warmed the heart with the calm feelings
of peace, joy, hope, and love, now manifested itself in
passionate enthusiasm, in abnormal conditions and
marvellous achievements, was produced by the
influence of the supernatural power of the Spirit of
God's Son which He sent into their hearts, and which
even now gives them assurance of their rights as
children and the future obtaining of the inheritance
of sons. For although, in one sense, a present
certainty, in another aspect the sonship of the Christians is still an object of hope ; for as Christ Himself,
although always the Spirit of Holiness, yet became
" the Son of God with power " only at the resurrection
(Rom. i. 4), in the same way the sonship to God of

---

[1] *Cf.* Titius, *Der Paulinismus*, etc., p. 266. The system of thought
connected with the Spirit is not to be added to justification as
something supplementary ; but is a parallel line of thought which
equally presents the whole of salvation, but under different aspects.

those who believe in Him will not be perfected until
the redemption of the body, that is, at the resurrection, by means of which the disharmony which
still obtains between the inner life of the Spirit and
the mortality of the body shall be done away with
by our being made partakers of Christ's glory
(Rom. viii. 10, 17, 23).

CHAPTER XVII

LIFE IN THE SPIRIT

As the Pauline doctrine of reconciliation arose from the application of the Jewish ideas of atonement to the special case of the death of Jesus, so his doctrine of the Spirit—the other main root of his theology—arose out of the application of the popular metaphysic which is usually called animism to the special case of the enthusiastic experiences of a Christian Church. In both cases the original church had anticipated Paul in the interpretation of those special experiences which marked its history by means of the theories which were universally current; but in both cases Paul deepened in an original fashion the interpretations which he found already in the field, and drew inferences from them which led far beyond the views of the original church and proved remarkably fruitful for Christian theology. Thus he found in the field, on the one hand, the facts of the enthusiastic phenomena, which from the day of Pentecost on recurred again and again in the Christian Church and in individual churches, such as, *e.g.*, the Corinthian, were of daily occurrence, and played an important part; on the other hand, the

24

interpretation of these occurrences according to the
presuppositions of the popular animistic theory of
spirits which was common to the Jews and heathen
of his time, and in general may be considered to
belong to the common stock of popular belief in all
lands and times.

According to this theory all extraordinary
phenomena in the life of nature and of man are due
to the influence of spirits or living creatures of a
character at once supersensible and sensible, which are
not indeed bound by the limits of the gross, visible,
corporeal world, but are not, on that account, wholly
immaterial, but possess a finer, usually invisible,
aërial corporeity, as is, indeed, suggested by the fact
that the word for spirit in Hebrew, Greek, and Latin
is identical with, or closely related to, the word for
wind and breath. As the subjects from which
proceed forces and influences, these spirits are active
beings; and as their activity is conceived after the
analogy of human conscious and deliberate actions,
they are, in so far, personal beings—yet only in a
certain measure; for our modern strictly defined
conception of personality was unknown to antiquity
in general, and for that reason it found no difficulty
in thinking of the same beings sometimes as personally
active subjects, sometimes as objective and passive
bodies. Thus we find both conceptions set naïvely
side by side even in the Biblical representations; the
spirits take possession of a man, dwell in him, make
him their basis of speech and action, the divine Spirit
distributes his gifts as he will; and alongside of this,
the Spirit is an aërial element in which man
temporarily or permanently lives, it can be poured

out, and drunk in, like water, manifests itself visibly
like tongues of flame, makes itself heard as a storm-
wind, and is conveyed from one man to another by
insufflation or by bodily contact (laying on of hands).
It is further connected with this that the spirits are
not individuals strictly differentiated from one another
but interpenetrate one another; a number of spirits
can be fused into a unity, and draw asunder from a
unity into a plurality; indeed a spiritual being can
work at the same time as a unity and as a plurality,
like one breeze amid many breezes, or one flame amid
many flames.   Therefore the momentous question
among exegetes whether the spirits of the prophets,
and the spirits of the several wonder-working powers,
are different from the Spirit of God or of Christ, or
no; and whether the Spirit of God and of Christ are
different, or whether the Spirit is a third Subject, in
addition to both, never presented themselves to the
naïve view of the popular belief.   Finally, the spirits
as active beings are of various ethical quality, which
becomes apparent in their manifestations.   If they
cause disorder in nature, strike men with sickness or
delusion, drive them to reckless action or blasphemous
speech, they are impure spirits belonging to the dark
world of death, to the kingdom of Satan: if, on the
contrary, there proceeds from the Spirit a wholesome
influence upon the body or soul of man, if man feels
himself raised by the wonder-working power of the
Spirit above the limitation of the senses into a higher
world of freedom and light, so that he is able to look
into the depths of the Deity, to discover the secrets
of the heart, penetrate the obscurity of the future, or,
in the rush of pious enthusiasm, to give stammering

expression in strange sounds to his joyful feelings; that can only be due to the influence of a good spirit derived from the higher divine world. If, again, in the Christian Church, in consequence of the enthusiastic preaching of the approaching destruction of the present world and the arising of a new world, and in connection with the confession of faith in the heavenly Lord Christ, enthusiastic phenomena of the kind just described presented themselves, it was entirely natural for men to see therein the workings of a supernatural spiritual being, which, going forth from the heavenly Christ-Spirit, wrought signs and wonders in the believers, which were in a sense harbingers and pledges of the wonderful world which was soon to come into being.

The heathen were accustomed to have similar experiences in their mystery-cults, and they also referred their transports and ecstasies and orgiastic frenzy to their being laid hold of, and filled with, the god in whose honour the feast was held, and therefore called the condition "enthusiasmos," that is, being in God. The character of these experiences was essentially the same at that time as they have been at all periods of great religious excitement, and as those which frequently occur in certain neuropathic states and are known by the psychology of to-day under the terms hypnotism, auto-suggestion, psychological automatism, and the like. " Where such phenomena present themselves to minds which are filled with religious presuppositions of a spiritualistic character, they necessarily find an explanation in accordance with these presuppositions. The appearance of an intelligent will in a man unwilled and unmarked by

the personality which customarily rules in this man,
is apprehended as the entrance into the man of a
spirit from without, or the thrusting out of the man's
own soul by a demonic psychic guest. And as
nothing has been more common among all peoples
and at all times than the spiritualistic (animistic)
presuppositions which give rise to this explanation,
those affected with "duplication of personality"
have from the earliest times to the present day explained these mysterious experiences, in accordance
with their non-scientific environment, by that which
the Greeks call ecstasy or being possessed by God
(κατέχεσθαι ἐκ θεοῦ). It is not that experiences of
this kind do not occur; the arbitrariness lies in the
explanation of them. To the Greeks the pythoness
remained the best known example of the "possession"
of a person by another will and spirit which was
very different in character and knowledge from the
medium when in a state of full consciousness, and
therefore seemed to have forced its way in from
without. The sybils, bacchantes, and seers were
further examples of the soaring of the soul into the
divine, or the entrance of God into the soul. It was
inevitable that there should grow up, on the ground
of these experiences, a belief in an immediate connection of the soul with the divine—in its possessing
the divine nature—and that this belief should feel
itself more strongly confirmed by these experiences
than by anything else. It was not only in Greece
that this occurred." [1]

Even the Orphic theology drew from these enthusiastic phenomena the conclusion that there was a

[1] Rhode, *Psyche*, p. 392.

divine germ in the soul of man which needed only
to be quickened and strengthened by the sacred
initiations. And this thought was further developed
in many directions by the Socratic-Platonic and
Stoic philosophies, all of which aim at purifying the
enthusiasm associated with these mystic experiences
to a divine and spiritual principle of ethico-religious
elevation of conduct permanently indwelling in a man,
thus ethicising and rationalising it. Socrates spoke
of his "demon" which he apprehended in his inner
man, not in a condition of ecstasy, but in clear and
waking consciousness, as a voice of warning and
exhortation which guided and urged him on in the
right way. And in Plato's Symposium the bacchic
frenzy is exalted as a friendly demon of that Eros
which is the constant mediator between God and
man, that is to say, orgiasm "has become a clear
and calm, but for that reason a more abiding, warmth
of ideal enthusiasm for all that is beautiful, true
and good."[1] The Porch had from the first described
the human spirit as a portion and effluence of the
divine world-spirit, and this metaphysical conception
acquired in the later Stoics a religious application
bordering on supernaturalism, the close affinity of
which with the Pauline doctrine is very striking.
According to Seneca[2] there dwells in every good
man a god, a holy spirit, who marks and watches
over our evil and good, who treats us as he is treated
by us, who is so far distinguished from our ego that
he is a separate subject; and the more the contrast
of this good principle in us with the weakness of our

---

[1] E. Pfleiderer, *Socrates and Plato*, pp. 547, 561, 567.
[2] Ep. 41, 73; *cf.* p. 53 ff. *sup.*

sensuous nature is emphasised, the more the former
appears as a divine power given to us from above, a
holy spirit sent down from the Deity to our aid,
through whom we can learn to know the divine
more fully, who indeed has intercourse with us, but
as a guest whose home is in a higher world. God
stretches out His hand to him who strives upwards ;
comes to us ; yea, enters into us ; no heart is good
without God. According to Epictetus, God has
given to each man a demon (good genius) of his own
to be by his side as a guardian who never sleeps nor
allows himself to be deceived : he who withdraws
into his inner man is not alone, he finds God and
his demon there.[1] Naturally, from another point of
view the indwelling demon or god is the man's own
spirit ; thus Seneca[2] says : " How else canst thou
name this righteous, good and great spirit (of the
virtuous man) than as a god dwelling as a guest
in the human body ? " The Alexandrian-Jewish
religious philosophy moves in the same circle of ideas.
According to Wisdom and to Philo, man's knowledge
of truth and man's virtue is a work of God in him,
mediated by the divine wisdom or the Logos or
other intermediate powers, which, at the command
of the Heavenly Father, descend into the human
soul, as the temple of God, in order to purify and
sanctify and bless us. It would be impious to ascribe
good to our own powers, since it is only God who
implants it in the soul. The Logos is sent by God
to the aid of our weakness ; he is the food of the
soul, the producer of good thoughts, the leader in the

[1] Epictet., *Diss.*, i. 14, 12 ff.
[2] Ep. 31, 11.

right way, the ally who helps us to strive victoriously
against the passions; in short, he is the supernatural
divine power which is imparted by God to men;
who unites himself with man's own spirit, but is not
identical with it.[1] We shall see later that precisely
this Philonian conception of the Logos as partly a
supernatural mediator of revelation, partly a natural
immanent principle of reason, was of special service
in solving the problem which confronted Philo in
common with his whole period—that of bringing the
enthusiasm of the religious mystic into the service,
and under the control, of the practical reason.

The relationship of these theories with the Pauline
doctrine of the Spirit is so striking that one might
feel tempted to suppose dependence on one side or
the other. And yet that would not be true. Philo
and Seneca are as little dependent on Paul as he on
them. Their affinity is merely due to the fact that
these ideas were then in the air, and answered to a
religious need which was felt at the same time in
different quarters, to a tone of thought which was
widely prevalent in that period of active religious
ferment. Moreover, the distinction is not to be
overlooked that those philosophic theories resulted
from a speculation, which was, indeed, partially determined by an ethico-religious motive, but yet rested
mainly on abstract ideas of a metaphysical and anthropological character, and therefore always included
something abstract and indefinite; Paul's doctrine of
the Spirit, on the other hand, arose out of a concrete
religious experience, an inspiration or "intuition" in

---

[1] Cf. Gfrörer, *Philo*, pp. 200–212. Cf. also, in a later chapter,
my more detailed description of the Philonian religious philosophy.

which that wonderful enthusiastic ecstatic experience of his conversion objectified itself. Through this, his first, " pneumatic " experience which he interpreted as a manifestation of the glorified Christ, a being laid hold of by Him, he felt his whole being so transformed that it seemed to him as if it was no longer he that lived, his old ego, but only Christ who now lived in him ; he seemed to himself a perpetual miracle. It was no longer merely special abnormal conditions but his life as a whole, with the new content of his thoughts, the new tone of his feelings, the new direction and energy of his willing and doing, that appeared to him as the permanent effect of the same supernatural power at whose first impact upon him the crisis of his spiritual dying and rising to newness of life had taken place, and therefore as due to the influence of the Lord, who, as the absolute Spirit, is the one source of all spiritual influences. In this connection it must remain a moot point whether this strikingly original view of the apostle was formed immediately upon his conversion, or only gradually became clear and definite ; and whether external influences contributed to the process, such as recol- lections of the Hellenistic-Jewish theology, or the Stoic-Cynic popular philosophy which was preached upon the streets of Tarsus. Even in this case the brilliant intuition of the apostle would remain the principal factor, which transformed the elements which he had taken over, under the influence and in the light of a wonderful personal experience, into an original system of thought. We can, however, know nothing further of the way in which this arose, and instead of uselessly contending about it, we prefer to keep to what is given, and to endeavour to understand the Pauline doctrine of the Spirit with its important consequences.

It included two related factors, each of them of great significance—

(1) The equation: the Lord is the Spirit (2 Cor. iii. 17).

(2) The attribution of the whole Christian life, including its ethical features, to this Lord and Spirit as efficient cause.

"The Lord is the Spirit," not merely one of the many and various spiritual beings; the whole, the containing medium, of the spiritual powers which, issuing from God, are imparted to the Church, is comprehended in Christ, and communicated by Him to the believers. That is precisely the same relationship which Philo sees between the one Logos and the many powers of which he is the epitome, but which yet go out from him with a certain independence, and independently exercise influence. The difficulty of conceiving this, which seems to us to lie in the idea of a plurality of spirits which is yet at the same time only one spirit, was not present for the ancient animistic way of thought, according to which spirits interpenetrate each other without fixed boundaries of substance. And we must not conceal from ourselves, either, that alongside of his equating of the Lord with the Spirit, a certain distinction is maintained between the Spirit of the Lord and the Lord Himself who possesses him. This only emphasises, what even apart from this would necessarily be understood, that the personal individuality of the Lord Jesus Christ is not, so to speak, sunk in the general system of spiritual exist-ences, but remains permanently as the ruling ego of the system. And if the Spirit of Christ is not merely identified with Christ but also with the Spirit of God, as happens, very instructively, in Rom. viii. 9 ff., that is not to be understood as a kind of Pantheistic resolution of Christ into God; but that, as the Son of God, Christ has the being of His Father, which is His Spirit, as His own being also. But the religious significance of that cardinal equation, "The Lord is the Spirit," does not lie in these abstract relationships, but in the practical inferences drawn from them. Above all, it lies in the fact that by means of it the manifold spirits which exercise influence in the Church are made subordinate as mere forms of appearance, powers and methods of working of the one Spirit of Christ, not, indeed, according to their substance—it is not merely pictorially that Paul speaks of the spirits of the prophets which are subject to the prophets—but according to their quality, *i.e.* the character and value of their activity. The ethically worthless or even harmful spiritual activity which presented itself not only in the orgiasm of the heathen, but also occasionally in the enthusiasm of the early Christians, was thus consistently condemned. If the Lord is the Spirit, then in the Lord's Church no spirit could claim a place which was foreign, or antagonistic, to the ethical character of the Lord.

In the personal character of Jesus Christ as that of the ideal of the sons of God, the character of the second Adam who had made satisfaction for the disobedience of the first Adam by His own obedience and love, there was thus a principle of the highest authority and of universal intelligibility for the

estimation and regulation of the early Christian
enthusiasm. Only what was in harmony with the
character of the Lord, what was consistent with the
confession of His name, could be recognised in
the Christian Church as due to the influence of the
Christian, Holy, Divine Spirit; all turbulent, un-
disciplined, disorderly conduct was consequently condemned as un-Christian (1 Cor. xii. 3, xiv. 32 f., 39).
Thus through the Pauline equation which combined
the historical personality of the Lord Jesus Christ
with the Spirit, *i.e.* the principle of religious enthusiasm, the result was attained which the best
thinkers since Plato, which a Seneca and a Philo
had striven after: the ".pathos" of religious enthusiasm was brought into the service and under the
control of the ethical ideal. But that the ideal
which formed the standard here was the historical
figure of Jesus and not a mere creation of the
speculative reason—this gave to the Pauline doctrine
of the Spirit its immense advantage, its over-
whelmingly victorious power; it satisfied equally the
two needs of that age, its mystical longing for
revelation and self-surrender, and its effort after a
rational ethical ideal.

It is true that in the identification of the ethical
ideal with a definite historical person there lay a
danger of limiting it in a one-sided way. The fact
that this did not result was again due to the Pauline
synthesis of the Lord and the Spirit, which carries
with it a further consequence besides that first
mentioned. If the emphasis be laid upon the subject
" *The Lord* is the Spirit," that gives an antithesis to
all unethical spiritual excitement, to all orgiastic,

naturalistic, in short, to all heathen enthusiasm. But if the emphasis be laid upon the predicate "the Lord is *the Spirit*," that gives an antithesis to all unspiritual worship of the letter, the form, the tradition, in short, to all the limitations of Judaism. And that this was intended as the primary sense of the apostle's words is shown by the context of the passage (2 Cor. iii. 17), where the words immediately follow, "but where the Spirit of the Lord is, there is liberty." In order to understand this meaning of the primary axiom, we must remind ourselves that the object of the Pauline faith was not Christ after the flesh, not the Jewish Messiah born of David's seed, not the Jew born of a woman and subject to the Mosaic law; of him Paul says expressly, "If we have known Christ after the flesh, yet now we know him no more." And accordingly, "If any is in Christ he is a new creation; the old has passed away; behold, it has become new" (2 Cor. v. 16 f.). That it was the death of Jesus which caused this passing away of the old, has been said before. The earthly life of Jesus was, according to Paul, only an episodic appearance of the Heavenly Man in our fleshly body; as this body was derived from David's seed the earthly Jesus belonged to the Jewish people and was also, in so far, subjected to the Jewish law. But this existence in earthly flesh was not the true and proper mode of being of the Son of God, but only a form of outward manifestation foreign to His heavenly spiritual existence, which He again laid aside in death in order to become, at His resurrection, a pure Spirit (free from earthliness) with a heavenly body of glory appropriate to it. As pure Spirit He stripped off,

along with the limitations of His earthly existence
in general, also the limitation of nationality: the
heavenly Christ, the Lord, who is the Spirit, is no
longer a Jew, but archetypal man, the first-born of
all the sons of God who are called to freedom. And
as He has cast off, for Himself, the limitations of
earth, of nationality, of the Mosaic law, He works
henceforth on those who are His as a liberating spirit
who frees them from all those fleshly fetters and
unites them into one new spiritual body. This
liberating and renewing work of the Spirit of the
Lord is not, however, conceived by Paul merely in
the moral sense, current among us, of a continued
influence of the moral character of Jesus, but in a
mystical sense resting upon popular animistic metaphysics, namely, that the individual person of Jesus,
now existing in heaven clothed with a body of glory,
is at the same time, as a substance or source of power,
free from the limitations of space (" omnipresent "),
present in all his churches, entering into believers, and
as an ethico-religious power producing in them supernatural effects, indeed, a completely new being (a
" new creation "). Upon this extension of the individual person of Jesus—which is, it must be
admitted, easier to picture by the imagination than
to think out conceptually—rests the equivalence of
the two representations mentioned above, " to be in
the Spirit " and " to be in Christ," or to have Christ
dwelling in one. As among the heathen the enthusiasm of the Mysteries was interpreted as a being
rapt away into, or filled with, the being of the special
god of the particular cult, so Paul gave to the less
definite " being in the Spirit " or " being filled with

the Spirit," when used in regard to Christians, the more definite and comprehensive significance of the believer's being in Christ, or Christ in the believer. The animistic background of this form of representation must not indeed be quite overlooked—it explains, as will be shown, certain difficulties in the mystical ethic of Paul—but still less must it be overlooked that this mode of representation is only the clothing in a garb which lay ready to his hand, of a practical religious experience of Paul—the experience of the inspiring and transforming power of his Christian faith and Christian love. We, too, use similar pictorial expressions—a person whom we love dwells in our hearts, takes possession of us, urges us on in our undertakings ; that Paul when he used expressions of this kind in regard to Christ, meant them not only pictorially but literally, is perfectly intelligible in view of the animistic presuppositions which were prevalent in his age, that, namely, spiritual beings enter into men, take possession of them, and work sometimes alongside of a man's own self, and sometimes in opposition to or in union with it. Instead of taking offence at that, we ought rather to endeavour to understand the practical significance of this mystical mode of representation.

This practical significance is that Paul no longer, like the first Christians, holds only extraordinary, momentary, enthusiastic phenomena to be the work of the Spirit, but the whole regular life of the Christian, especially his ethical attitude and conduct. That was doubtless, in the first place, undeniably a heightening of the supernaturalism in which the believers lived and moved from the first. The

miracle was no longer merely confined to certain
individual exceptional circumstances of the present,
corresponding to exceptional individual events in
the past and future (resurrection and Parousia of
Christ); it was declared to be relatively permanent,
it became the rule, the normal condition, of Christians
as such, in which the "old man" is crucified and the
body of sin destroyed, so that he is no longer in
the flesh, but in the Spirit, and can say of himself,
" It is no longer I that live, but Christ liveth in me "
(Gal. ii. 20 ; Rom. vi. 6, vii. 5 f. viii. 9). But in the
very fact of becoming the rule, the miracle changes
its nature, and ceases, in a certain sense, to be a
miracle. The sudden and ecstatic element in early
Christian enthusiasm does not, it is true, wholly
disappear, but it is forced into the background,
becomes an unessential and incidental phenomenon ;
and, as the fact of primary importance, there now
comes into prominence the new Christian life as a
whole in which the pathic state of enthusiasm is
refined into a constant basis of thought and feeling—
of love, joy, peace, gentleness, temperance (Gal. v. 22).
All these virtues are the fruit of the Spirit produced
by the supernatural living power of the Spirit of
the Lord in the Christian, but at the same time
virtues of his own personal being, disposition, and
character. This made room for, and laid the
foundation of, a permanent ethical ordering of life
by the Christian Church, such as would not have
been possible to the earlier heated apocalyptic
mood, which was constantly looking for the
catastrophe of the end of the world and the coming
of Messiah's kingdom, and finding a foretaste of

its blessedness in the rapture of ecstasy. Not as
though the eschatological interest had disappeared
in Paul's case—it finds vigorous expression in all
his epistles — but it is no longer the whole of
Christianity; the unnatural feverish tension which
expected salvation only as a result of a future
miraculous catastrophe is done away with when it
is recognised that the " new creation " is not merely
to come in the future, but is already present in
everyone who is in Christ (2 Cor. v. 17 ; Gal. vi. 15).
Thus Paul's doctrine of the Spirit guided the
transition of Christianity from the apocalyptic
enthusiasm of its earliest childhood, which could
not have given rise to any ethical system of life,
and therefore not to any historical permanence of the
Church, and set it on the path of a regular historical
development. Meantime the boldest spiritualistic
eschatological supernaturalism remains constant in
the background, but its practical dangers are avoided,
its volcanic and revolutionary insistence on the
transiency of the world is softened down, for the
supramundane spirit manifests its miraculous power
even within the boundaries of the present world by
creating a new spiritual race of men and binding
them into a new community, attaching them to
" the body of Christ," the " reasonable service " of
which consists in the doing of the Divine will, in
pure and noble morality (Rom. xii. 1 f.).

The life in the Spirit, as Paul describes it, offers
therefore two aspects for consideration, according
as we look at the supernatural character of the
being and origin of the Spirit, or his natural
manifestation in the life of Christians, his moral
25

activity in the form of faith. Although now one, and now the other, side comes into prominence, they form only two correlated ways of looking at the same Christian truth which Paul had experienced in himself, and ought not therefore to be taken by his expositors in one-sided abstraction. As regards the first arising of the life in the Spirit, so much is clear—that it does not proceed by way of mere development from the natural life of man; the Spirit, who is life and holiness, stands in strict antithesis to the flesh of sin and body of death, and even the reason (*nous*) of the "soulish man" is so far removed from the being of the Spirit (pneuma) that it is unable either to discern spiritual things or to do that which is good (Rom. vii. 23; 1 Cor. ii. 14). As, according to the large supernaturalism of Paul, the second Adam, Christ the Son of God, did not grow out of the human race but was sent down from heaven to earth as a stranger guest, so God has also sent down the Spirit of His Son into the hearts of those whom He has destined for His sons (Gal. iv. 6 compared with 4). The Spirit therefore comes into the heart from above as a being foreign to, nay, standing in opposition to, the old man, in order to take up his abode at this centre of the personal life: man's attitude in this operation is purely passive; he "receives the Spirit" as an emissary from God, or (in a more material form of representation) as a gift presented by God (Rom. v. 5; 2 Cor. v. 5).

It is less clear how, according to Paul, we are to conceive the bestowal of the Spirit as effected. According to Gal. iii. 2 and 5, Christians have received the Spirit, not by works of the law, but by the preaching of faith (from that proclamation of the Gospel which demands and produces faith), just as they are also all sons of God through faith (verse 26). According to this, the means by which the Spirit is imparted seems to be the word of the Gospel, which addresses its call to faith, and causes faith, and which is also spoken of as a demonstration of the Spirit and of power (1 Cor. ii. 4), is preached in power and in the Holy Spirit, and accordingly is also received with joy of the Holy Spirit (1 Thess. i. 5 f.).

On the other hand, in 1 Cor. xii. 13 it is baptism by which all are baptized into one body (become members of one Church) and made to drink of one Spirit; similarly the reference is to baptism in 1 Cor. vi. 11: "Ye have been washed, sanctified, justified, in the name of the Lord Jesus and in the Spirit of our God." In these two passages baptism appears as the foundation of the life in the Spirit, and at the same time as the means by which he is communicated. That is confirmed by those passages in which the mystical union with Christ, which is practically identical with possession of the Spirit, is connected with the mystical ceremony of baptism (Rom. vi. 3 ff.; Gal. iii. 27). Whether we do justice to Paul's view in harmonising the two representations of the communication of the Spirit through the word and through baptism by saying that, since in baptism the faith which is wrought by the word first comes to maturity and completion, it is in baptism that the appropriation of the Spirit as the content and the power of faith is first brought to completion, must remain a problem. It is perhaps better to let these two views stand side by side without mutually connecting them, as in the Pauline description of life in the Spirit the supernatural-mystical and the psychological-ethical aspects (to which these two methods of communication of the Spirit correspond) go side by side but unconnected.

That appears with especial clearness when we consider, further, the relation of the communicated divine Spirit with the natural human spirit or ego. That the two do not coincide may be concluded at the outset from the complete dissimilarity of their character and origin, and this conclusion is confirmed by a series of expressions in which the communicated divine Spirit sometimes appears alongside of, or in contrast with, the human spirit as a second subject, and sometimes seems to stand in the place of the latter. He witnesses to our spirit our sonship to God (Rom. viii. 16); he graciously takes on him the burden of our weakness, representing us before God with groanings that cannot be uttered (Rom. viii. 26); he teaches the apostle words of divine wisdom (1 Cor. ii. 13), urges us on and strengthens us to overcome and keep in subjection the sensuous impulses (Rom. viii. 13 f.); he is the law and the norm of our conduct (viii. 2, 4); makes us feel the love of God in our hearts (v. 5); cries in us " Abba, Father," as we " in Him " make the same appeal (Rom. viii. 15; Gal. iv. 6). He prays in the ecstatic " speakers with tongues " while their reason is unfruitful (is suspended) (1 Cor. xiv. 14), and, conversely, the speaker with tongues himself prays in the Spirit (*ib.* 15). But in many passages the distinction between

the divine and the human spirit in the Christian
cannot be maintained; the divine seems so to have
entered into the human, and so to have become one
with him, that they are related like form and content.
In the "spiritual man" the divine Spirit has become
the proper energy and norm of his thought, feeling,
and will; the personality, so far from being suppressed by him, is raised to the highest freedom and
autonomy, "the law of the Spirit of life in Christ
Jesus has made me free from the law of sin and
death" (Rom. viii. 2); "the spiritual man judges all
things and is judged by no man" (1 Cor. ii. 15);
"whereas I am free as regards all men, I have made
myself the servant of all" (1 Cor. ix. 19).   The
whole faith-life of the Christian is the manifestation
under the conditions of human life of the divine
Spirit which is given to him; he knows this Spirit—
even if he occasionally sets him in contrast to himself
as another subject—to be as a rule his own possession,
his inwardly appropriated power, by which his ego is
made capable of divine knowledge, volition, and action.
Therefore the Christian virtues are fruits of the Spirit
not less than active manifestations of faith (*cf.* Gal.
v. 22 with v. 6, etc.), the apostle serves God in his
spirit and in newness of the Spirit, and his conscience
bears him witness in the Holy Spirit (Rom. i. 9, vii. 6,
ix. 1); his religious activity as well as his ethical self-
estimate is therefore accomplished in the strength
and according to the norm of the divine Spirit, who,
however, has become his own new or divine-human
spirit.   It cannot be denied that this whole form of
conception is to our present-day thinking somewhat
strange.   That a divine spiritual being should be

sent down from heaven into the heart of a man and should there sometimes stand as an independently acting subject in antithesis to the personal ego, sometimes again fuse itself with the latter and become the content and motive-power of the man's consciousness—these are representations which can no doubt be readily explained from the animistic standpoint of antiquity, which was shared by Paul, but which for us have only the significance of pictorial expressions. We are therefore justified in interpreting them in the terms of our present-day psychology; the more so as we cannot conceal from ourselves that animistic supernaturalism is attended by difficulties which are not merely logical but practical. When the Christian life is referred back to a spiritual being of supernatural power coming into man from without, the ethical self-determination of the human ego threatens to be suppressed, and the transformation seems to be effected in the inevitable fashion of a process of nature, in which, along with human freedom, guilt and sin would be excluded—inferences to which Paul does, as a matter of fact, in his ideal picture of the spiritual life under grace, seem to make a near approach (Rom. vi. and viii.); but as he is practical enough to recognise fully the continuance of sin even in Christians, he attributes this to a principle of sin in the flesh which brings the ego into captivity. Over against the abstract ideal of the spiritual man who cannot sin, he sets directly the equally abstract caricature of the carnal man who can do nothing but sin (Rom. vii. 14 ff.), two abstractions which are doubtless meant as the opposite sides of the same

condition (vii. 25 ; *cf.* p. 234 f.), but which are in fact
mutually exclusive, and which, in their opposition,
split the unity of the personal life in a dualistic
fashion.   This difficulty is solved if we translate the
animistic representation into modern psychology and
interpret these spiritual beings as psychic conditions,
motives, directions of the will, which, as they are
developed out of the unity of human nature, are
always held together by the unity of the personal
consciousness in such a way that they form its proper
content, the manifold factors of its life-activity.   The
religious truth of the Pauline doctrine of the Spirit
will, moreover, remain the same on this interpretation, and will shine forth yet more clearly.

The new life in the Spirit manifests itself variously
in accordance with the diverse aspects of human
personality—in the emotion of the heart as well as
in the cognitive and voluntative activities of the
mind.   First, in the heart " the love of God is poured
out " by the Holy Spirit so that it becomes an object
of personal emotional experience (Rom. v. 5).
Therefore " peace and joy in the Holy Spirit " form
the ground-tone of the Christian's consciousness
(Rom. v. 1, xiv. 17).   The consciousness of reconciliation with God which faith gives, removes the fearful-
ness of the bad conscience and produces childlike
trust in God as the loving Father (Rom. viii. 15) ;
peace with God makes the heart calm and removes
its inner disharmony, its indecision between obedience
and self-will, between defiance and apprehension.   It
is this inner calm and contentment which Paul is
accustomed to desire for his converts as the effect of
the grace of Christ in the frequent formula of greet-

ing, "Grace be with you, and peace from God." It
involves, however, not merely the removal of the
previous state of division, fear, and unblessedness,
but also a positive elevation and enhancement of the
self-consciousness—the joy of the Christian, which
rises even to jubilant boasting, to a boasting in
God on the ground of the grateful certainty of His
rich mercy, to which the child of God has free access,
so that it can constantly gain renewed assurance of
it by childlike intercourse with God in prayer
(Rom. v. 2). Even when we do not ourselves know
how and for what we should pray in a fashion pleasing
to God, the Spirit himself intercedes for us with
unspeakable groanings, and the Searcher of hearts
understands the inner movements of the spirit and
knows its devout intent (Rom. viii. 26). Among
these workings of the Spirit, which belong to the
obscure life of feeling, is to be numbered also that
"speaking with tongues" which is peculiar to the
earliest Christianity, and which Paul in 1 Cor. xiv.
13 ff. sets in contrast as a "praying with the Spirit" to
"praying with the understanding," doubtless because
it consisted in ecstatic utterance of feeling without
clear thought and intelligible speech (cf. p. 168).
But though Paul was far from undervaluing this
ecstatic condition of intensity of feeling, he was
equally far from seeing in it a specifically higher
working of the divine Spirit than is found in the quiet
and conscious mood of peace and joy, which manifests
itself in constant strength amid all weaknesses, in
patience and hope amid all afflictions—in short, in
the overcoming of the world. For afflictions are so
powerless to restrain the joyfulness of the Christian,

founded, as it is, in the certainty of the love of God,
that, on the contrary, he is able to glory in them, being
persuaded that they, like all other things, are destined
to contribute to his true good and to be helpful
to him.   Indeed, all the hostile attacks of the world
are unable to break down the joyful confidence of the
Christian ; whatever dangers may meet or threaten
him, he overcomes in all things through Him whom
he has believed. " If God be for us, who can be against
us ?   I am persuaded that nought can separate us
from the love of God which is in Christ Jesus.   Yea,
though our outer man perish, yet the inner man is
renewed from day to day.   We are as sorrowing, and
yet alway rejoicing ; as dying, and behold we live "
(Rom. v. 3 ; viii. 18, 28, 31–39 ; 2 Cor. iv. 16 ff., vi. 4–10).
Of thoughts such as these the writings of the apostle
are full, especially the Second Epistle to the Corinthians, written amid much affliction, and the eighth
chapter of Romans, that hymn of the Christian joy
which overcomes the world and death.   And this
joyful courage of hope is maintained even in the
Epistle to the Philippians, in face of imminent death,
alike in the expectation of deliverance and further
work on earth, and in hope and yearning to be at
home with the Lord (Phil. i. 20–26).   It is in grateful joy over the inwardly experienced salvation, and
in courageous hope of God's victory in the world and
of one's own blessedness with the Lord, that the
Christian attitude, as the apostle exemplifies it for us
in his own person, essentially consists.

The Spirit calls into being, however, not only
emotional experience, but also clear mental knowledge
of the blessings of the divine salvation.   " What

God hath prepared for them that love him, God
hath revealed unto us by his Spirit, for the Spirit
searcheth all things, yea, the deep things of God.
For what man knoweth what is in man save the
spirit of man which is in him ?   Even so none knoweth
what is in God save only the Spirit of God.   We
have not received the spirit of the world, but the
Spirit which is of God, in order that we may be able
to understand what hath been given to us by God"
(1 Cor. ii. 9 ff.).   So intimate does Paul conceive
the Christian's union with God to be, that the
Christian's self-consciousness of the higher divinely
wrought life which is present in himself is at the
same time a consciousness of what God is, of God's
will of love.   It is the same Spirit who searches the
deeps of the Godhead, even God's own knowledge of
Himself, and who works in the Christian the knowledge of the life given him by God.   The spiritual
or spirit-filled man is for that very reason able to
judge all things, because he possesses the judgment,
the understanding, of Christ (*ibid.* 15 f.) ; that is, the
intimate knowledge of God which belongs to the
Son of God is also disclosed to the Christian in
virtue of his spiritual union with Christ.   Therefore
he possesses in all matters of religious truth an
independent judgment, from the scope of which
nothing is withdrawn, and which must not place
itself in subjection to any other.   But in spite of
being, in ideal, perfect, this knowledge is still in
individuals fragmentary, a seeing as in a mirror, in
dim and uncertain outlines, while we wait for the
full immediate vision of pure truth (1 Cor. xiii. 12).
For this reason—because, namely, the possibility of a

true knowledge of God is disclosed to the Christian in the Spirit of Christ, while the full knowledge is not yet realised—for that reason he can and ought to increase in the knowledge of God, to be filled with the knowledge of His will in all wisdom and spiritual insight, and constantly strive to get beyond the childish condition of imperfect understanding and become perfect in knowledge (1 Cor. xiv. 20; Col. i. 9 ff.). As a part of his whole inner transformation, his thought also is to renew itself in such a way that he is able in any given case to examine and decide what is the "good, acceptable and perfect will of God" (Rom. xii. 2; Phil. i. 9 f.). Thus spiritual knowledge, the more it grows out of the fulness of religious experience, sets up an increasingly high standard as the goal of ethical advance.

While the Spirit gives blessedness in heart and enlightens the understanding, it imparts at the same time to the will impulse and strength for new, morally good, will and action. Paul was led to emphasise this point with the more decisiveness because his teaching of justification by faith and the abrogation of the law has been often understood, by friend and foe alike, in an antinomian and libertine sense (Rom. vi. 1, 14). In opposition to this it was important to show that the same spirit of sonship which removes us from the legal standing into that of grace, carries with it also the obligation and the capacity to walk in newness of life, in which the will of God is fulfilled much more truly and purely than it ever was under the law. What the written law had not been able to bring to pass, is accomplished through the law of the Spirit of life in Christ—not

merely the removal of the guilt of sin, but also real
righteousness of life.   Grace not only pronounces a
judgment of acquittal from guilt and penalty ; it also
actually frees from sin, changing the will itself into a
force which makes for holiness of life (Rom. viii. 1
compared with 4).   The connection of this ethical
renewal with the foundation of the new religious
condition is found by Paul in baptism as the decisive
act of faith.   Since in being baptized into Christ's
death we have died with Him, we have been freed
from the dominion of the powers which tyrannised
over our old man, from sin and from the law which
provoked and increased sin, and have entered into
the new life of the reconciled children of God who
stand under His grace (Rom. vi. 2–14).   But this
new and blessed existence is not our free possession
to use according to our own or another's caprice ; it
belongs to Him who has bought it at the costly price
of His death.   For He died for all, that they which
live might no longer live unto themselves but unto
Him who died and rose again for their sakes (2 Cor.
v. 15).   It is therefore the simple motive of grateful
love towards the Saviour, to whose offering of love
we are indebted for our happiness, which binds us to
Him, dedicates us to Him as His possession and—as
He Himself lives only to God—dedicates us to God
as His possession.   It is because they are the dear-
bought possession of Christ and God that Christians
are called by Paul " holy."   The designation implies,
as little as does the like designation of the Old
Testament People of God, the ethical conception of
actual sinlessness.   In this ethical sense Paul could
certainly not have described the churches in which

such grave moral defects were still present as "holy."
He could, however, perfectly well do so in the
religious sense, inasmuch as they, having been called
through the Gospel, had become, through faith in
Christ, God's own people, sharing His Spirit and
holding intimate converse with Him in prayer.   In
this religious holiness, which is involved in justification and sonship, there lies the obligation to ethical
holiness or to living in harmony with the Spirit of
God, to practical service of God in the doing of good.
But it involves not only the obligation but also the
capacity, the power, to fulfil the Divine will.   This
power the law cannot give, because the contrary
impulses of the natural man stand in unconquered
opposition to its precepts.   Only where a higher
living impulse opposes the sinful impulses of nature
with superior strength can they be really conquered,
or the good become the ruling power in men's hearts
and lives.   This is the case with the Christian, since
he is not under the law but under grace.   Over him
sin is no longer lord (Rom. vi. 14), since the consciousness of God's grace arouses in him love to God
and Christ, which, as a holy living impulse, overcomes
the sinful impulses of the natural man ; "the love of
Christ constraineth us" (2 Cor. v. 14).   In this feeling
which the Holy Spirit awakens in the heart there lies
the incentive to all good, for love is the fulfilling of
the law (Rom. xiii. 10).   Here the will of God is no
longer a dead and deadening letter, which by its
commands and prohibitions provokes the opposition
of self-will ; it has become man's own living will, the
free and joyous impulse of the heart, which freely,
from the motive of childlike love, fulfils the will of

the Father.   It is therefore the same spirit of sonship
which makes us free from the law of the letter and
from sin, and which, as the new law of life in Christ,
binds us to God and His service (Rom. viii. 2, 4 ff.).
In this "law of the Spirit" there was set up a
new ethical principle of the widest application, a principle which is equally high above the legal bondage
of Judaism and the capricious lawlessness of the
heathen : both are overcome in the Christian " law of
the Spirit," in which good becomes the free inner
impulse of love.

The effect of this new principle upon the course
of the Christian life is sanctification, *i.e.* a becoming
ethically holy or like God by reason of the religious
obligation to God and holiness.   As the practical
proof of faith, sanctification is the duty and task
of the Christian ; as the effect of the influence of
the Holy Spirit, it is the gift and work of God in
a man.   In the former aspect we have such sayings
as " Let us purify ourselves from all pollution of the
flesh and of the Spirit "; " present your bodies an
offering holy and acceptable unto God, which is your
reasonable service "; " this is the will of God, even
your sanctification " (2 Cor. vii. 1 ; Rom. xii. 1 ;
1 Thess. iv. 3).   To the other aspect refer : " The
God of peace sanctify you wholly "; " He that called
you is true, who will also bring it to pass "; " He that
hath begun a good work in you will also perfect it "
(1 Thess. v. 23 ; Phil. i. 5).   The two aspects are
closely united in Phil. ii. 12 f. : " Work out your
salvation with fear and trembling, for it is God that
worketh in you both to will and to do."   Sanctification
consists, further, in the progressive carrying out of

the same two sides of the saving process which has
its beginning in baptism, the anti-type of the dying
and rising again of Christ; we may name them
the negative and positive, or the fighting and the
formative, aspects of morality. Since the Christian
has died and been buried with Christ in baptism and
has crucified the flesh, so he must continually slay
the movements of his nature which are antagonistic
to the Spirit, his "members which are of the earth,"
laying aside all evil-doing (cf. Gal. v. 24 with 25;
Rom. vi. 2 ff. with 13; viii. 10 with 13; Col. ii. 11 ff.,
20, with iii. 5–9). Again, since in baptism he has
been raised with Christ and become a new creature,
has put on Christ, has been sanctified by the Spirit
of God, he must continually put on Christ, or the
new man who is being renewed in the image of
Christ, must change and transform himself into the
image of Christ, put on the Christian virtues, walk
in the Spirit, and offer his members as instruments
of righteousness unto God, present his body as an
offering dedicated to God (cf. Gal. iii. 27 with
Rom. xiii. 14; Col. ii. 12, iii. 1 with iii. 10, 12;
2 Cor. v. 17 with iii. 18 and Phil. iii. 10; 1 Cor.
vi. 11 with 20 and Rom. vi. 13, 19, xii. 1). In
short, "if we live in the Spirit, let us also walk in
the Spirit" (Gal. v. 25). We must guide our conduct in the consciousness that we are spiritual men;
the divine spiritual life which has been in principle
awakened in us should prove itself the determining
power and norm of an ethical activity in accordance with the will, and for the purposes, of God.
Thus Paul has made the doctrine of the Spirit
the principle of a new ethic, all the demands of

which can be summed up in one: "Be what thou art."

It is the negative, ascetic side of sanctification which is for Paul the first and most important. As the Spirit stands in direct opposition to the sinful flesh, the latter must be constantly morally slain in the Christian by the suppression of the sensuous impulses, as in Christ it was really slain upon the cross. Since, in baptism into Christ, the old man, the flesh with its lusts, has been crucified with Christ—that is, not wholly annihilated, but broken in its power and the free expression of its life, paralysed and delivered over to sentence of death (Rom. vi. 6; Gal. v. 24), therefore the Christian must continually mortify the "deeds of the body" as those "members which are upon earth," that is, no longer allow the sensual, selfish life of impulse to hold sway over them (Rom. vi. 12, viii. 12; Col. iii. 5). Similarly, Paul says that he himself, like a boxer, plies his body with blows of the fist and makes it a slave, that he may not, while preaching to others, himself become a castaway (1 Cor. ix. 27). At the same time Paul did not draw the extreme inference of dualism, complete contempt for the body. On the contrary, he recognises that there is a sense in which the body should be honoured—as the temple of the Holy Spirit (1 Cor. vi. 19). Since the body is destined to be raised up and glorified together with Christ, it ought to be even now dedicated to God as a holy offering, in the rational service of a moral life, and its members should be offered to God as "instruments of righteousness" (Rom. xii. 2 f., vi. 13, 19). It was the healthy realism of the Old Testament which preserved the apostle from the excessive spiritualism and asceticism of Hellenistic ethics. Even in regard to worldly matters the inner freedom of his Christian self-consciousness preserved him from a petty ascetic rigorism; he tells the anxious Christians who scrupled to use meat and wine, that the kingdom of God consists as little in not eating and not drinking as in eating and drinking, that the earth and that which is therein is the Lord's, and nothing is in itself impure (Rom. xiv. 14–20; 1 Cor. viii. 8 ff.). The Christian may therefore, according to Paul, have and use earthly things; only, he must not abuse his freedom in regard to them, should use the world as if he needed it not, shall know himself lord over all, and not allow it to become lord over him (1 Cor. vii. 29 ff., vi. 12). Only in one point does this sound principle undergo a limitation in an ascetic direction—as regards the question of marriage, to which we shall return later. Instead of arbitrary ascetic self-severity, Paul sees the best proof of ascetic self-discipline in patient endurance under the unsought afflictions of the earthly life, which he looks at from the teleological point of view as a divinely appointed means of education and salvation, through which the outer man, it is true, is worn away, but the inner, on the contrary, renewed. While we "carry about" the dying of Jesus in our body, that is, patiently bear the sufferings which come to us as His followers, His life is also manifested in our body, namely, by the consolation and strengthening which proceed from Him, which sustains even the weak earthen vessel of the body, and gives it a wonderful power of endurance

26

(2 Cor. iv. 7–16). To suffer with Christ is the condition and means of being glorified with Him (Rom. viii. 17).

On its positive side, sanctification is the being conformed to the life of Christ, not so much in its earthly aspect, however, to which Paul does not give much attention, because he is not acquainted with it, but rather to the heavenly life of the exalted Lord of the Church. "Sanctification may be regarded as the constant reproduction of himself by the new Head of humanity in those who belong to him, in contrast with the reproduction of the first Adam in his posterity according to the flesh" (Holtzmann). As Christ, dead to sin once for all, is henceforth alive unto God (Rom. vi. 10), so the Christian, who in baptism has not only died with Christ but has also been raised with Him and made alive with Him (Col. ii. 12 f.), must regard himself as one who is dead to sin but alive to God in Christ; though dead to the literal law, he is yet not without law, but must "fulfil the law of Christ" and serve God in newness of the Spirit (Rom. vi. 11, vii. 6; Gal. vi. 2). The same act of becoming a Christian which freed him from his former bondage to sin and the yoke of the law, at the same time placed him on a footing of grace and in the service of righteousness, so that he is now under obligation to be obedient to righteousness (Rom. vi. 15–18). Instead of the old works of the flesh, in which the sinful impulse was active in the members, there now appear the fruits of the Spirit: love, joy, peace, longsuffering, gentleness, goodness, faith, meekness, temperance (Gal. v. 22 f.; Col. iii. 12 ff.). Love either stands at the head as the cardinal virtue (Gal.), or at the close as the "bond of perfectness" which gathers together all the other virtues into the unity of the virtuous character (Col.). As the love of God which is poured into the heart by the Holy Spirit is the fulfilment of the gospel promises of blessing and the highest happiness of the Christian, so love to one's neighbour, which is similarly wrought by the Spirit as the highest gift of his grace, is the fulfilling of the law and the highest power in the Christian, by which faith proves its vitality and energy (1 Cor. xiii. ; Gal. v. 6, 13 f. ; Rom. xiii. 8–10). Love, therefore, does not in Paul's view come in merely as an external supplement to faith ; it is derived from faith by an inner necessity, since in it faith converts the good received from God into the power of doing good ; it is the manifestation of faith in a godly life which arises out of the divine power. In love is realised the reconciliation of freedom and law which neither Judaism nor heathenism could attain. As the inner living impulse of the heart, it gives man perfect freedom, enables him to act by pure self-determination, with the pleasure of self-approval, and with the strength of inspiration ; as the impulse of the Holy Spirit it is at once the norm and limit to the use of freedom ; a self-determination, not by selfish self-will, but by the will of God, which is at one with the good, proceeding from the mind of the Son of God ; it seeks therefore not its own but the good of all, and desires to fulfil, so far as possible, the purposes of God's love. It therefore forms the criterion for the decision of questions regarding things morally indifferent ; even that which is allowable in itself may be abstained

from out of loving consideration if it is likely to
injure or offend one's neighbour. While faith frees
us from all outer compulsion of law, love binds itself
through the law of Christ and voluntarily makes
itself the servant of all (1 Cor. ix. 19; Rom. xiv.).

A lofty idealism appears in this description of the
Christian life. The Christian is no longer in the flesh
but in the Spirit; he has crucified the flesh with its
lusts; the world is crucified to him and he to the
world; he is risen with Christ, lives in the Spirit,
possesses the Spirit of Christ. Christ Himself lives in
him instead of his former ego; he is a new creation;
his life is hid with Christ in God; he has become a
spiritual man; he is like Christ. That over such a
being sin can no longer hold sway is self-evident;
that is what makes it so difficult to grasp the fact
that nevertheless in the actual Christian life sin is
still present. The Christian, as Paul describes his
character, ought properly no longer to be able to sin,
since the divine Spirit is the ruling ego in him, and
the sinful flesh is conquered, abolished. Yet Paul is
far from drawing this obvious inference from his
doctrine of the Spirit. On the contrary, all his epistles
testify with what prudence and care he estimates the
actual ethical condition of his churches, censures their
weaknesses and sins, and exhorts them to lay aside all
evil and contend unremittingly against sin. Spirit
and flesh stand in constant strife with one another,
and the victory of the Spirit does not come to pass
by itself with the unfailing certainty of the laws of
nature, but depends on whether the Christian
endeavours to walk according to the standard set up
by the Spirit, and mortify the deeds of the body, or

allows sin again to have dominion over him ; whether he sows to the flesh or to the Spirit. On the conduct of the Christian, now that he is free, depends his fate at the last judgment. Regarded from this point of view, the ultimate salvation of the Christian appears, in spite of his justification and his possession of the spirit of sonship, as by no means unconditionally assured ; the possibility of his falling away and being lost always remains open, and is used to give force to the exhortation to watchfulness and earnest self-discipline (Gal. vi. 7 f. ; Rom. viii. 13 ; 1 Cor. x. 1–12 ; 2 Cor. v. 10) ; indeed, the apostle thinks of his own ultimate salvation as conditional on the faithfulness of his efforts and struggles (1 Cor. ix. 27 ; Phil. iii. 11 f.). Yet that is not to be understood in the sense that salvation is lost through individual failures ; these are rather to be made good by the godly sorrow of repentance which causes a change of self-recollection (μετάνοια), a turning from the way of error to the right way, and therefore a renewed hope of salvation (2 Cor. vii. 10). To help the erring by brotherly reproof to take up this attitude, is represented by Paul in Gal. vi. 1 f. as the duty of the church. He did not, therefore, ignore the sins of Christians, but made them the subject of his ethical exhortations, and regarded the avoidance and the cure of them as the duty both of self-discipline and of pastoral work.

Now, it is certainly not to be overlooked that between this ethical estimate of the empirical Christian life and the religious ideal of the Christian man there is a wide divergence : on the one side the new life is still in process of becoming, relative,

hampered by, and struggling with, the old, conditional
on the indeterminate conduct of men, the attainment
of the goal not unconditionally secured ; on the other
side, the new life is an inevitable effect of the divine
wonder-working power, the actual existence of a new
creature in contrast to all the past, a spiritual life
which has no longer anything in common with this
world of sin and death, but already belongs to the
coming Messianic world, and therefore is already
assured of ultimate deliverance.　We are accustomed
to conceal or soften this discrepancy by bringing in
our modern idea of development ; the new life is
really present, but only as yet in principle, as a
potency which only gradually develops into actuality.
That is quite correct, too, on the assumption that the
new life is thought of as a new content of human
consciousness, as a new way of feeling, and direction
of mind and will, brought about by specific experiences,
the influence of which can only gradually transform
the old content of consciousness—a process which is
carried out, not by a natural necessity but by the self-
conscious ego ; that is to say, through ethical activity.
But we must not conceal from ourselves that we are
not justified in importing, without more ado, this
modern thought of psychological development into
Paul's doctrine of the Spirit.　In him, as we saw
above (p. 386), "the Spirit" is not a content of
human consciousness, which could only develop and
define itself by a process of consciousness, but a
super-human personified spiritual being, who is sent
down from heaven and enters into the man and
takes possession of him, subjugates his spiritual and
bodily powers and makes them instruments, urges, or

"drives," him on to actions, speaks, prays, cries, groans and rejoices in and through him. How then, in relation to this overmastering divine being, is there room for the free self-determination of the human will? Is not the new man, on this assumption, at bottom a will-less slave of the holy spiritual being in his heart, as the old man was a slave of the demonic sinful being in his flesh? (Rom. vi. 16 f.). Is he the active and responsible subject of sanctification, or is he only the passive object for the possession of which the two hostile powers, the holy spiritual, and the fleshly sinful, contend? (Gal. v. 17). This would indeed be the logical consequence of the Pauline doctrine of the Spirit, as it could not but be in view of the animistic conceptions of his time. But, happily for the ethical value of his teaching, Paul did not consistently carry through that conception of "the Spirit," but allowed man's ethical self-determination its rights; but in virtue of the presuppositions of his theory, he can only do so by alternating between the mystic and the ethical view of the Christian life, and applying both side by side, and in the closest connection, without attempting to unite them inwardly. Sometimes the Spirit is a power which overmasters the man and coerces his free ego, a supernatural wonder-working power which therefore works with automatic certainty, and which by its sole agency makes all things new; sometimes it is the man himself who feels himself urged on by the moral impulse of the Spirit but without feeling compelled to follow it, and who is therefore himself responsible for his spiritual or unspiritual will and action. This vacillation between the religious and the ethical point of view is undeniably a difficulty which is involved in the Pauline doctrine of salvation. The explanation of it is to be found, however, not in eschatological enthusiasm or Rabbinic dogmatism, but simply in the fact that the apostle had no other forms at command for the expression of his Christian experience than the animistic conceptions of ancient supernaturalism, which hypostatised extraordinary phenomena of consciousness as spiritual beings, and believed men to be "possessed" by these. When we have once recognised that the ground of this difficulty lies in the form of representation which was inevitable at that period, we can the more easily, abstracting from this, grasp and rejoice in the abiding kernel of the Pauline ethic. Its fundamental thoughts—Die to live! Be what thou art!—contain the deepest truth for all ages, and were, more especially for his own age, an excellently adapted means of leading Christianity out of the Apocalyptic ecstatic excitement of its early period into the path of a steady historical development. Faith in the perfect ideal of man remains the central motive, an incentive to unremitting striving and struggling directed to the lofty aim of a personal and general salvation which remains ever in the future, to be toilsomely won by conflict and renunciation, and waited for with patience and hope. But yet, on the other hand, the ideal is not a merely transcendental one, but is the completion and manifestation of that reality of the spiritual life which we can even now experience, though it is still in a sense hidden (Col. iii. 3). This reality is the earnest of, as well as the temporary

substitute for, that ideal condition which is to come,
the ideal in which all our striving and struggling
finds its incentive and its restraint, its point of
support and point of rest, its motive and its mitiga-
tion.   It is just this combination of a faith which is
self-sustained, and rejoices in the present and inward
salvation, with a hope and effort which unweariedly
reach out beyond themselves towards the high goal
of perfection, which is the fundamental characteristic
of the ethico-religious attitude of the Christian, as
Paul, out of his own experience, has pictured it.

It is certain that Paul by his teaching laid the
theological foundation of a new ethical system,
which conceived the whole of the ethical life as a
consistent development of one central motive which
has its roots in the religious frame of mind.   The
faith " which worketh by love," while binding our
personality to God, sets it on a basis of its own,
makes it independent of the fears and cares of the
world, and thus lays the foundation of an autonomy
and an inner resoluteness of personal character which
is in no wise inferior to the Stoic freedom.   But
the very same faith binds us at the same time by
the strongest affection, namely, through love, to
human society ; in the first place, to the community
of Christian brethren, and in the next place to
humanity at large, and therefore does not permit
the personality in selfish αὐτάρκεια and unfeeling
ἀπάθεια, in proud self-sufficiency and indifference to
the good of others, to withdraw itself from its social
duties ; it does not dissolve society into isolated
individuals, as Stoicism set its " wise men " in lofty
isolation above the society of struggling and

suffering humanity. Instead it gives men the strongest bond of union, of solidarity, of moral order—love, which, taking root in the pious heart, draws ever new nourishment from religious faith and hope, and finds the norm which it must seek to realise in the highest ideal, in God and His Son. For this reason Paul's ethical principle had a very different measure of success from the principle of Stoic philosophy which is in certain aspects related to it, and was able to work with animating and regenerating, healing and sanctifying, power upon evil and distracted humanity. Whereas Stoic cosmopolitanism merely made men indifferent towards the natural bonds and limitations of society, Christian love, on the other hand, wove new bonds around the divided nations and classes of mankind and made Jew and Greek, bond and free, man and wife, one in Christ (Gal. iii. 28).

CHAPTER XVIII

CHURCH AND WORLD

At the outset, Paul confined the moulding power of the new ethical principle to the religious community; its application to the various departments of ethical life he left to the future. The unity of the Spirit which inspires the believers in Christ binds them one to another into the unity of the body of Christ, *i.e.* the Christian Church. By "ecclesia" Paul understands primarily and habitually — in conformity with Greek usage, in which the word means the popular assembly—the single church in a given locality (Gal. i. 2; 1 Thess. i. 1; 1 Cor. i. 2; Rom. xvi. 1). In the second place, he uses the word in reference to the whole Christian Church, not only to the mother-church, which might still be regarded as a single local church (Gal. i. 13; 1 Cor. xv. 9), but also of the whole of contemporary Christendom. It is in this latter sense that he writes, for example, to the Corinthians (1 Cor. x. 32) "Give no offence neither to the Jews nor to the Greeks, nor to the church of God" or (xii. 28), "God hath in the church set some to be apostles, others to be prophets," etc. But whereas

411

the social conception of the ecclesia widens from
below upwards, rising into the comprehensive conception of the union of believers or "the Church,"
the doctrinal conception of the "Body of Christ"
has as its point of departure the ideal whole, which
has its special manifestations in the individual
churches, and further, in the individual believers, in
whom it manifests its one being in multiple form.
The body of Christ is not constructed out of the
individual churches any more than the body proper
is constructed out of its various members : it is the
logical prius of these, the one life of the Spirit, which
proceeds from Christ as the Head, and unites the
many members to itself. But this unity is still an
ideal (the "invisible Church" of dogmatic theology),
to which corresponds no outward form of unity of
the Church as a whole, no organised federation of
the various individual churches : of this Paul knows
nothing. That which binds the believers to unity
is the one Lord, who, as a person, is the head of
the body, from whom proceeds all life, to whom all
are united, and who as Spirit is the soul of the
body, who fills all, and binds them as members
to one another. This unity of the Spirit finds
expression in the common faith and confession
that Jesus is Lord, and in the fellowship of the
love with which all mutually serve and help one
another in doing and suffering, like the various
members in the bodily organism (1 Cor. xii. ;
Rom. xii.). If, therefore, the body of Christ is
primarily a dogmatic conception—the comprehensive
effect of the Christ-Spirit in the unity of the
believers whom He inspires, a macrocosmic Christ,

so to speak—yet it is immediately connected with
the ethical conception of the fellowship of all
believers in a brotherhood which reaches across
the dividing barriers of race and rank and sex, and,
through the free personal bond of a common faith
and life, makes "all one in Christ Jesus" (Gal. iii. 28).
Paul also compares the Church to a field belonging
to God, in which one works in sowing, and another
in watering (1 Cor. iii. 9); or with a building, or,
more specifically, the temple of God, the foundation
of which is laid in Christ, upon which foundation
Christ's servants continue to build (*ib.* 10–17; *cf.*
vi. 19, where the body of each individual Christian
is called a temple of God).   Once, too, there is found
the picture which later (especially in Ephesians)
receives further development, of the Church as the
bride of Christ, whom it is the apostle's duty to
present as a pure virgin to be led home by Christ
at the Parousia (2 Cor. xi. 2).   The purity of the
Church here spoken of consists in her simple loyalty
to Christ, that is, her complete devotion to Him,
from which the Judaising teachers desired to seduce
her.   The holiness of the Church rests on the same
foundation as its unity—its mystical union with
Christ, and its being filled by the Holy Spirit.

This connection is effected, according to Paul, not
merely by the spiritual act of faith, but also by outward ceremonies, by means of which fellowship with
Christ and the Church is not only represented, but
mystically established and constantly renewed.   As
ceremonies of this kind, Baptism and the Lord's
Supper appear in Paul's teaching with a prominence
which was to have a significant influence in the

ensuing period. " It is not by accident that in later
ecclesiastical linguistic usage the name ' mysteries '
continued to cleave to these acts. For in the transformation and development which these original
Christian usages underwent at the hands of Paul,
they have characteristic points of contact with
certain forms of the general religious life of society,
forms in which the religious spirit of Hellenism,
and indeed of antiquity in general, found manifold
expression, namely, with the ' Mystery ' systems "
(Holtzmann). That whole system of representation,
which may be called *a parte potiori* Hellenistic, or,
more exactly, animistic, since it has its roots in the
fundamental religious conceptions of antiquity as a
whole, did not first make its way into Christianity
in the post-apostolic time, but pervades the whole
Pauline theology, and betrays itself most clearly
in his view of the sacramental acts of the Church.
It is impossible to understand it without thinking
oneself into his completely supernaturalistic mode
of representation.

Baptism was, among the disciples of John the
Baptist, an act of penitence by which are sought
purification and dedication in preparation for the
coming kingdom of God. In the community
founded by Jesus as Messiah it had at first the
same function, but, in addition, it was an act of
confession of faith in Jesus as Messiah, without,
however, any mystical reference to His death. It
was Paul who first attributed this new significance
to baptism and thereby made it a Christian mystery
or ritual of initiation into the mystical union with
the crucified and risen Lord. He sees in the im-

mersion of the candidate, not only a symbol, but a
mystical reproduction of the burial and resurrection
of Christ, whereby the baptized person becomes
partaker of both in such a way that so far as concerns
his "old man," or sinful body, he is buried with
Christ, and as a " new man " is raised up with Him and
made partaker of His new heavenly and spiritual life.
This, it is true, is at first hidden in the Christian,
as his life in the Holy Spirit, but in the future
will be also manifested by the re-animation of the
outward body in a glorified condition (Rom. vi. 2–8).
The same thought receives, in the Epistle to the
Colossians, a new application, baptism being not
merely represented as a being buried with Christ,
but also called a " circumcision of Christ not made
with hands, namely, the putting off of the body of
flesh " (Col. ii. 11). It is therefore the anti-type of
Old Testament circumcision in so far that what in
the former was literally done as regards a part of
the body, was, in the latter, accomplished in a supersensuous mystical sense in regard to the whole
fleshly body, viz., the putting of it off. The reverse,
positive, side of this initiation into Christ's death is
there described as " being raised together with Christ,"
and in Gal. iii. 27 as " putting on Christ." For the
understanding of this peculiar mode of expression it
is necessary to recall a practice which was widely
prevalent in antiquity (and is still found among
primitive peoples) : the practice, in certain acts of
cultus, of the putting on by the celebrants of the
garments, and even, in many cases, of the mask of
their god, in order thereby to indicate and to induce
a feeling of self-identification with the god, by an

incarnation or indwelling in them of his supernatural spiritual being. It is precisely this idea of an identification with Christ effected by means of baptism which Paul seems to have desired to express by "putting on Christ."[1] As, however, the Spirit of Christ has his sphere of operation, his "body" in the Christian Church, it follows logically that it is one and the same mystical act by which a man is placed in spiritual union with Christ and at the same time incorporated into the Church as one of its members. Therefore we have in 1 Cor. xii. 13 the words, "We are all baptized in *one* Spirit into *one* body, and have all been made to drink of *one* Spirit"; both effects are referred to the same act of baptism, in which, therefore, the union of all as members one of another is represented under the figure of being "given to drink of the same Spirit" as of a super-sensible beverage, by which is meant being filled with the Spirit. According to this, there can be no doubt that Paul thought of the reception of the Spirit as being connected with baptism. That, according to other passages, the Spirit is also received by the preaching of faith we have seen above, p. 387. On the presuppositions of the Pauline anthropology and pneumatology it is quite intelligible that the revolution from the natural life of the flesh to the supernatural life of the Spirit "demands as its appropriate representation a mysterious act which not only sets forth and symbolises but also mediates and effects it" (Holtzmann). The combination, too, of the three completed facts which Paul recalls to the memory of the Corinthians (1 Cor. vi. 11), "Ye have been

---

[1] A similar expression is met with in Seneca (*sup.* p. 57).

washed, sanctified, justified, in the name of the Lord
Jesus Christ and in the Spirit of our God "—shows
us that for the apostle purification from the stains
of sin, and endowment with the sanctifying spirit,
and justification or acquittal from guilt, coincide
with the decisive moment which marks the beginning
of the Christian life, with the act of baptism, to
which the being "washed" clearly points. How
closely in the Corinthian church the guarantee of
eternal life was thought of as bound up with the
sacramental operation of baptism, working in a
purely objective manner, is shown in a very instructive way by the usage, which Paul mentions, and
does not censure as being without validity, of letting
oneself be baptized as the representative of relatives
or friends who were already dead, in order to ensure
their resurrection (1 Cor. xv. 29). This so clearly
suggests an analogy with the rites and ideas of the
mystery-cults that an influence from this direction
is probable. In the Eleusinian mysteries of Greece,
as in the Mithras mysteries, which at that time were
familiar in Asia, the main object was to put men in
possession, through mystical ceremonies of initiation,
of a supernatural and immortal life, so that the
initiate knew himself "born again for ever." At
the least it was the same psychological presuppositions and motives which there, as in Paul's Christian
churches, led to similar theories of the sacramental
significance of the sacred ceremonies.

With baptism the Lord's Supper is coupled even
by Paul as a second mysterious act, which similarly
had its prototype in the experiences of the Israelites :
baptism is the passing through the Red Sea; the Lord's

27

Supper is the being fed with spiritual food (manna), and given to drink from the spiritual rock, which was Christ. Paul speaks of the Lord's Supper more in detail, first in 1 Cor. x. 16–22, with reference to the question as to the partaking by Christians in the heathen sacrificial feasts, and then again in xi. 17–34 with reference to the abuses which had grown up in connection with the celebrations of the meal of love. In the former passage he speaks of the "cup of blessing" (ποτήριον τῆς εὐλογίας ; this was the name given to the last cup at the paschal meal, which, after a dedicatory prayer of thanksgiving, was drunk of by all) as the "fellowship of the blood of Christ"; and of "the bread which we break" as "the fellowship of the body of Christ"; and adds, "As it is one loaf, so are we all one body, for we all partake of the one loaf." The exact sense of this mystical mode of speech is not easy to determine. If we argue from verse 17, it seems as if we were to understand by the body of Christ, not the actual body but the mystical body, i.e. the Church, the unity of which is symbolised by the one loaf. According to this, the significance of the observance would be that through the eating of the one loaf the union of individual Christians with the Church, which is instituted in baptism, is constantly renewed and confirmed. But how are we to understand it when in verse 16 the cup and the bread are said to be "the fellowship (κοινωνία) of the blood and body of Christ"? Standing thus in connection with the blood, the body of Christ cannot well signify the Church but only the actual body of the personal Jesus Christ; but the context forbids us to think of the earthly flesh-and-blood body of Christ; are

we then, perhaps, to think of the heavenly body of
the exalted Jesus Christ, in the sense that the
eating of the consecrated bread places the believer in
mystical union with the " body of glory," *i.e.* with
the heavenly mode of existence of the personal
Christ ? But what has the heavenly life of Christ
in common with the blood, since " flesh and blood
cannot inherit the kingdom of God " ? If the
blood is to be thought of as that which was shed in
the death of Christ, then the cup can be a " fellowship
of the blood " only in the symbolic sense that he who
partakes of it appropriates to himself the effects of
this death ; but in that case there is no parallel here
to the " fellowship of the body of Christ." If the
parallel is to be maintained, the blood cannot be
thought of as the symbol of death, but only as the
symbol of life, as is the case in the symbolism of
the Old Testament, and indeed of antiquity in general.
In that case blood and body form only a twofold
expression for the personal life of Christ with which
the partaking of the Lord's Supper places us in a
mystical relation. And since it is now the same life
of the Christ-Spirit, which is present both in personal
form in the heavenly Head and extends itself also to
His earthly body, namely, the Church, therefore the
same act of partaking of the mystic symbols of this
life is capable of effecting and strengthening a holy
communion both with Christ the personal Head and
with His Church ; and thus the ambiguity in the conception of the body of Christ in verse 16 and verse
17 finds its explanation. This interpretation of the
passage seems to me to be strongly favoured by the
circumstance that, if it be accepted, the significance

which Paul ascribes to the Lord's Supper stands in exact analogy to the meaning of the sacrificial meal, which, according to the ancient view, was essentially the means of a "holy communion" between the celebrants and their divinity as well as between individuals and the whole community which was associated in the cultus.[1]

The reference to the death, and, moreover, specifically to the atoning death, becomes the central point of the interpretation which Paul gives in the second passage, xi. 23–27: "I have received from the Lord that which also I delivered unto you, how that the Lord Jesus in the night in which he was betrayed took bread, gave thanks, brake it, and said, This

---

[1] I may refer, in this connection, to the presentation of the sacrificial theory given by Robertson Smith, *Religion of the Semites*, p. 312 ff. According to him, the sacrificial meal served originally as the sacred "cement" by which a bond of living union between the worshippers and their God was created, or maintained in strength. "This cement is nothing else than the actual life of the sacred and kindred animal, which is conceived as residing in its flesh, but especially in its blood, and so, in the sacred meal, is actually distributed among all the participants. . . . The notion that by eating the flesh, or particularly by drinking the blood of another living being, a man absorbs its nature or life into his own, is one which appears among primitive peoples in many forms." In more civilised ages the place of the real flesh and blood was taken by a substitute for these in the form of dedicated food and drink in general, the partaking of which has the same effect of mystical communion. Hence comes the widespread ritual of blood-brotherhood which is sealed by eating and drinking in common. This primitive idea underlies the mystery-cults, in which the partaking of consecrated substances (in the Mysteries of Mithras, bread, with a cup of water or wine) served to make the celebrants partakers in the supernatural and immortal life of their divine Saviour (κοινωνοὺς τῶν δαιμονίων, as Paul says in the above passage, v. 20).

is my body which is broken for you; this do in remembrance of me. After the same manner also he took the cup when they had supped, saying, This cup is the new covenant in my blood; this do as often as ye drink it in remembrance of me. For as often as ye eat this bread and drink this cup, ye do show the Lord's death till he come. Wherefore, whosoever shall eat this bread or drink this cup of the Lord unworthily, sins against the body and blood of the Lord." According to this, the Lord's Supper is a feast in memory of the death of Jesus, in which He gave His life for us, that is, for the expiation of our sins, and poured forth His blood as the means of founding a new covenant in contrast with the first founding of the covenant at Sinai (Ex. xxiv. 5–8), when Moses sprinkled the blood of the sacrifice partly on the altar and partly on the people with the words, "Behold this is the blood of the covenant which Jahve makes with you concerning all these commandments." The thought that Christ's death as the vicarious atoning sacrifice is the foundation of the new covenant, in which no longer the outward law, but justifying grace and the life-giving spirit, are the ruling features, is, as we saw before, the fundamental and original thought of the Pauline doctrine of salvation, and Paul was also the first to give to the "breaking of bread," to the primitive Christian love-feast, this sacramental reference to the central point of his faith. This is the source of the corresponding words in the gospel narrative, as will be shown later. As a feast commemorating the atoning death of the Lord, the Lord's Supper is an act of confession in which the celebrants show the Lord's death—show it, of course, according to its religious significance as the means by which the new covenant is concluded, in such a way that they also in this act of confession acknowledge themselves to be parties to this covenant, and ever confirm it anew until the coming of the Lord, who shall make the partakers of His death to be partakers of His glory.   In this act of confession the bread and the cup [1] serve in the first place simply as symbols of that to which the whole act refers—of the body offered up in death and the poured forth blood ; to sin against the body and blood of Christ by unworthily partaking may consist even in indifference to the significance of the symbols. Yet that can scarcely exhaust the apostle's meaning ; he seems also to suggest a mystical character as belonging to the bread and cup, inasmuch as he describes the occurrence among the Corinthians of numerous cases of sickness and death as a consequence of unworthy partaking of the Lord's Supper.   This probably implies the idea of a substance charged with supernatural powers, improper use of which is visited with serious physical consequences (the idea of a "taboo ").   Paul has thus given to the ethical and social use of the primitive Christian love-feast the

---

[1] The question forces itself upon us in this connection, why Paul always speaks of the cup and never directly of the wine ? Was it perhaps because at the breaking of bread of the first Christians it was not wine but only water that was drunk, and that it was first in wealthier Gentile-Christian circles that the use of wine came into vogue—here, too, not without opposition from Christians of ascetic tendency ? (Rom. xiv. 21).   Paul may have admitted the use of wine the more readily because it serves better as a symbol of blood ; but because the use of wine was a new thing and not generally approved, he avoided the word and spoke only of the " cup," leaving the nature of its contents undefined.

significance of a sacramental act of worship in a twofold sense :—

(1) As a feast commemorating the atoning death of Christ, the Lord's Supper is an act of confession by means of which all confess themselves members of the new covenant founded by that death.

(2) As a partaking of the mystical symbols of the life of Christ it is a " holy communion " which, on the analogy of the sacrificial meal, seals and gives living power to the union of the celebrants with Christ and with one another as the " body of Christ." The sacramental significance of the Lord's Supper was received by Paul, not from tradition but *directly* from the Lord [1] by one of those inspirations which he looked upon as revelations of the Spirit of Christ, and in which we recognise the intuitions of his religious genius, which by means of new combinations of existing ideas constructed an original expression for new and unique experiences.

The religious sanctification which the church receives through its union with Christ and its being filled with the Spirit, it has also to maintain and manifest by the exercise of moral discipline upon its members. The occasional utterances of Paul with reference to this point are conceived from very various points of view. To the Galatians he writes in vi. 11 : " Brethren, if a man be overtaken by a fault, do ye who are spiritual admonish such an one in the spirit of meekness, and take heed to thyself that thou be not also led astray; bear ye one another's burden, and so shall ye fulfil the law of Christ." According to this, sins of weakness and

[1] This is, without doubt, the force of the expression, 1 Cor. xi. 23 : ἐγὼ παρέλαβον ἀπὸ τοῦ κυρίου.

unwariness are to be dealt with by helpful pastoral
oversight, which by gentle exhortation seeks to bring
the erring to a better mind, the fight against sin is to
be the common task of the church, associated
together in a corporate life, in which each feels the
fault of the other as a "burden," *i.e.* must bear it
patiently as a hindrance which causes trouble and
anxiety, and must give him brotherly support in the
ethical duty of overcoming it.   The apostle rightly
sees in this the fulfilment of the law of Christ, for it
is just this bearing and helping love that has been
made by the example of Jesus the principle of the
common life of those who accept His gospel.   On
the other hand, in 1 Cor. v. 9 ff. he writes to the
Corinthians that they must break off all intercourse
with those who call themselves brethren and yet
persist in their old sinful life, and especially that they
must not eat with them, that is, at the holy Supper
of the Lord; here the word of the law applies:
"Put away the wicked person from among you."
Now, it is certainly obvious that this act of judgment (verse 13) exercised upon the members of the
church has in view a different set of circumstances
from that of the helping and bearing of Gal. vi. 1 f. ;
there the reference is to sins of unwariness in which
good will, readiness to let oneself be admonished
and improved, is to be assumed ; here, on the other
hand, to habitual servants of sin who resist discipline.
But if one considers how difficult it is as a matter of
fact to draw the line between the one case and the
other, and that it is just habitual sinners in whom,
in consequence of their evil past, vice has become
a habitual moral weakness, who most need patient

educative love, the question must arise whether the
judicial procedure here demanded—which by isolating
the sinner cuts off all chance of exercising moral
influence upon him—is quite on the same level as
that of Gal. vi. Still greater difficulties surround
the immediately preceding case of the excommunica-
tion of the incestuous person who had his stepmother
as his wife (whether in marriage or not remains
uncertain). By a solemn pronouncement, spoken in
the name of Jesus and of the church, Paul delivered
him to Satan "for the destruction of the flesh in
order that the [his] spirit might be saved in the day
of the Lord" (1 Cor. v. 1–5); that is, he not only
excommunicated him but sentenced him to death,
in the expectation that the sentence would be
executed by Satan as the angel of death and the
instrument of God's punitive justice. By the death
of the body, brought about in this way, the spirit of
the sinner would be saved from the corrupting
infection of his sinful flesh, somewhat as the surgeon
seeks to save the threatened life by the amputation
of the mortifying limb. This passage gives us an
instructive glimpse into the animistic background of
the Pauline theology. Sin inheres like a demonic
poison in the flesh and threatens by its infection to
rob even the spirit, or inner man, of the supernatural
living power communicated to it by baptism; the
means taken to obviate this danger is not, for
example, the ethical means of a helpful influence for
the conversion of the sinner, but the physical means
of the separation of the threatened spirit from the
sinful poison of the flesh by the death of the body,
which is to be caused by Satan. Truly a curious

mixture of animistic magical ideas with the
"jealousy" of the Old Testament prophets! It is
no injustice to the apostle if we come to the conclusion that he is not here on the level of the
evangelical principles to which he gave so beautiful
an expression in Gal. vi. 1, but at the legal standpoint of the old prophets who "had at call the
punitive hand of God."[1] Unfortunately, in this the
Catholic Church followed him only too closely by
transforming the discipline of penitence into a legal
procedure, and in treating sinners and heretics from
the point of view of criminal jurisprudence.

Within the church, God has distributed various
spiritual gifts, calculated to contribute to the edification or religious advancement of the church life, and
therefore involving for those endowed with them the
duty of rendering personal service to the church
(1 Cor. 12). Other offices than those which rest
upon charismatic endowment and voluntary service
(διακονίαι) are unknown to Paul; there was as yet
no organised official status with clearly defined rights
and duties. The charisms or gifts of grace served
partly for religious edification in the church-meeting,
partly the other needs of the church. To the former
belonged especially the gift of prophecy, that is, of an
inspired intuition and declaration of the mysteries
of faith and hope, which, differing in different
individuals, had for its content sometimes wisdom
and knowledge of a doctrinal kind, or interpretation
of the deeper allegorical meaning of scripture, sometimes practical exhortation. There were also many
who could use poetic language for the edification of the

[1] Jakoby, *Neutestamentliche Ethik*, p. 343.

church, inditing psalms and hymns for the common use. Of the special "speaking with tongues," which consisted more in rapt monologues than in edifying discourses addressed to the church, we have spoken above. Other charisms had reference to the direction of the church, to the management of its affairs, to the care of the poor and the sick. The gift of healing of the sick seems to have consisted in an especially heroic faith, which awakened the trust of the sick person and, in conjunction with prayer and the laying on of hands, exercised a salutary influence upon his condition.

An organisation of the church, in the sense of an ecclesiastical constitution, was not merely not given by Paul but not even contemplated by him, for the simple reason that he expected the "Parousia" of Christ in the near future. The same expectation prevented him from devoting his attention to the application of the ethical principles of Christianity to the ethical aspects of social life in the present world. In the spheres of political, social, and family life, his aims were limited to inducing the Christians to recognise, and not contravene, the authority of "the powers that be," desiring the Christians to accord these powers a passive submission but to have as little active association with them as they could, that they might not thereby be hindered in their Christian readiness for the Parousia. The Christian idealism of the apostle has primarily a negative, indifferent, and passive relation to the earthly life, tolerating the existing order of things, while preserving his personal freedom in regard to it; a positive relation of interest in the social order, and effort for the ethical reform of society, lay outside his range of vision.

As regards the State, the Roman Christians are exhorted (Rom. xiii.) to render obedience to every constituted authority as to a divine ordinance. As this ordinance has been set up by God for the defence of the good and the punishment of the evil, the Christian is to submit to it not merely from fear but for conscience sake, to show respect to it, to pay its taxes, and, in short, behave as a quiet and peaceable citizen. "Since the government directly protects legal right, and indirectly serves the interests of the moral law, he who submits to it contributes to the general advancement of the good. To this extent it may even be said that the State has been raised to an object of faith, in that general sense of the word in which the order of the world may be said to be so. This connection of the State with the supersensuous world of moral life could not be made clearer than it is when, in presence of Nero's rule, the demand is set up that Christians should honour the government as a mighty ally of all right conduct and the avenger of all unrighteousness" (Holtzmann). But it is hard to reconcile with this theoretic exaltation of the legal order of the State Paul's warning to the Corinthians (1 Cor. vi. 1–8) not to have recourse to the civil courts, on the ground that it was unworthy of Christians, who should one day judge the world and the angels, to allow unbelievers to pronounce judgment upon them; they are not to seek their rights from the unrighteous, but rather to put up with wrong. This view clearly implies as its consequence the denial of the independent divine dignity and authority of the

civil order; and the Catholic Church has, as a matter
of fact, drawn this inference. Paul only applies it,
however, so far as it is a question of the voluntary
and active use of the civil order, not with respect to
passive obedience to it—an obviously inconsistent and
not permanently tenable position.

Even slavery was to be recognised by the Christian
as an existing condition of service, as one of the
various forms of earthly " calling," which was not
to be altered in consequence of the call to enter
Christ's Church. " Let every man abide in the
same calling wherein he was called [to Christianity];
wast thou called as a slave? care not for it; but even
if thou mightest be made free, rather remain a slave.
The slave who is called in the Lord is the Lord's
freeman; conversely, he who is called, being free, is
Christ's slave. Ye are bought with a price; do not
become servants of men. In whatsoever calling a
man is called, therein let him abide with God," *i.e.*
in his Christian relation to God (1 Cor. vii. 20–24).
This argument is as characteristic of Paul as it is
paradoxical to us. We should rather conclude that
Christians being the dearly - bought property of
Christ ought therefore to be the property of no
human being, and that therefore the Christian view
of the dignity of the personality, which rests upon
the Christian's being the property of God, excludes
the condition of slavery as in opposition to this
dignity. But Paul draws the opposite inference:
since the Christian slave knows himself in his
religious consciousness to be free, it is indifferent
to him whether he is, in his outward position in
life, slave or freeman. Only religious bondage or

subjection to men in matters of religious conviction
are irreconcilable with belonging to the Lord Christ;
not outward or social servitude, which has nothing to
do with faith or with being the property of Christ
from the religious point of view. Anyone who is
able to form an unprejudiced historical judgment will
certainly find this limitation to religious idealism and
this refusal to draw the practical consequences for
the social life easily explicable and excusable—for
what would have become of Christianity if at the
outset it had come forward as the representative
of revolutionary social tendencies? But the unprejudiced observer will also at the same time recognise
therein an abstract dualism between inner and
outer, which must as certainly be overcome in
process of time, as it was certain that it was the
vocation of Christianity to transform the outward
life of the world into conformity with moral ideas,
and to realise God's kingdom and righteousness in
the actual world. And Paul made a beginning in
this direction as regards slavery, when, without
calling into question the legitimacy of the institution, he sought to mitigate its hardness within the
Christian Church. He calls on Philemon to treat his
runaway slave, Onesimus, who had been converted
and sent back by Paul, no longer as a slave but
as a "brother beloved" (verse 16), and the Colossian
masters are exhorted to show justice and equity,
mindful of the fact that they themselves had also
a Master in heaven; while the slaves were to be
obedient to their masters in simplicity of heart and
in the fear of God. They are to do their work as
a service not rendered to men but to the Lord, from

whom they may hope to receive the reward of their faithfulness (Col. iii. 22–iv. 1). Thus Paul seeks to ethicise the existing social relation by the influence of the spirit of Christianity, as the Stoics of the same period sought to do in the spirit of their enlightened humanism.

For the true Christian honouring of marriage and family life the Pauline ethic contains most fruitful principles—in the first place, in the central significance which it ascribes to love; in the second, in the principle that in Christ man and wife were one : and the wife, therefore, in the highest religious relationship, of equal personal dignity with her husband. But here again the consequences of this principle are not drawn.

Paul holds (1 Cor. vii. 1 f., 26–40) that marriage is permitted, and is indeed in some cases necessary as a protection from sexual aberrations; but apart from this relative usefulness as a preventive of something worse, he seems to attribute to it no inherent ethical value, for he declares the unmarried life to be the more advantageous, on the assumption that one possesses the gift of continence, because the unmarried can devote themselves more exclusively than the married to the service of the Lord; the unmarried woman cares for the things of the Lord, that she may be holy in body and spirit; the married, on the other hand, only for the things of this world, that she may please her husband. Paul sees, therefore, in the duties and cares of the married life something worldly which hinders men from complete surrender to the Lord, and something impure which hinders complete holiness in body and spirit — a

judgment in which there are unmistakable traces of
that dualistic ascetic view of the sensible as the
opposing contrary of the spiritual which at that
time was widely prevalent among both Greeks and
Jews. A further reason in his case, even if not
the predominant motive, was the conviction of the
approaching end of the world; in view of the great
affliction which was to precede this he desires to see
the Christians as little as possible entangled with the
cares of the world, and therefore utters the bold
wish that they were all as he was, namely, unmarried
and continent. His eschatological preoccupation no
doubt contributed much to his preference for the
unmarried state; but the principal reason lay deeper:
Paul shared the ancient naturalistic conception of
marriage as a legally ordained method of satisfying
a sensuous need which appeared to him something
unexalted and unclean. Our modern Protestant
ideal conception of marriage as a fellowship of life,
physical, mental, and spiritual, for the mutual completion and perfecting of the two personalities, was
still unknown to him and could not be known,
because he was still trammelled by the ancient
prejudice regarding the inferiority of woman, in
spite of his recognition of the religious equality of
man and wife (Gal. iii. 28). That is clearly shown
in 1 Cor. xi. 7 ff. It is the man only who is the
image and forth-shining of God: the woman is the
forth-shining of the man, and he was not made for
the sake of the woman, but the woman for the sake
of the man; therefore (verse 3) the man is the head
of the woman as Christ is the head of the man.
The man stands therefore nearer to the divine

prototype than the woman: he is a higher creation
than she. As a token of this subordinate position, and also as a protection from the wantonness
of the angels, women are to veil themselves when
they come forward to preach and prophesy in the
meetings of the church. In xiv. 34 f., indeed, they
are even forbidden to speak in public as something
unseemly, something unsuitable to their position
of subjection; this, however, contradicts the former
passage in so remarkable a fashion that there is
reason to suspect this verse as a later interpolation.
In this connection, too, we have to notice the manner
in which Paul speaks, in 1 Cor. vii. 36 f., of the
marrying or remaining unmarried of the young
women as depending exclusively on the pleasure of
their fathers, without consideration of the inclination
of the daughters themselves. That is quite in
accordance with the way of looking at things which
was general in antiquity, but it must be admitted
that in all this the consequences of the principle of
Christian freedom have not been drawn.[1] That
remained for future development, of which Paul had
indeed laid the foundations, but which he had not
himself conceived.

In one very important point Paul decidedly
rejected the ethico-social excesses connected with
the "other worldliness" of early Christianity—the
contempt for work and for property, and the over-
estimation of poverty and almsgiving, which he
constantly opposed. He earnestly enjoined upon the
Thessalonians (1 Thess. iv. 11 f.) to work quietly and
eat their own bread, that, namely, which they had

[1] *Cf.* Jakoby, *Neutestamentliche Ethik,* pp. 355, 393.

earned by honourable work, not obtained by begging, in order that they might not be dependent on any one and might share what was their own with others. From the early Christian ideal of community of goods he was so far removed that his epistles constantly assume the possession by his readers of private property gained by work, and imply that the acquirement of property is not only permitted but obligatory, as a condition of the honourable independence of one's own personality, and of kindly sharing with, and helping of, the needy (1 Cor. vi. 10, vii. 30, ix. 7 ; 2 Cor. viii. 13 f., ix. 7 f.). It is true that in this no theoretic ethical value is as yet allotted to work; the Protestant idea that the application of one's personal capacities to the production of wealth for the general advantage belongs essentially to the ethical ideal, was as foreign to Paul's thought as to that of antiquity in general. In this, as in his estimate of marriage, the monastic morals of Catholicism maintained the early Christian way of thought which was opposed to nature and to the progress of civilisation, whereas Protestantism, with a clearer insight, has corrected it.

CHAPTER XIX

THE METHODS AND AIMS OF THE PLAN
OF SALVATION

THE theology of Paul issues in a religious philosophy of history, which regards the past and the future from the teleological point of view as a connected divine plan of salvation. The impulse to this theodicy was given by the objections brought by Jewish Christians against the Pauline Christianity, which centred about two points. One was the annulling of the Jewish law by the Pauline gospel of faith-righteousness, which seemed to conflict with the character of the law as a revelation. The second, and no less serious, objection, had reference to the actual success of the Pauline mission to the Gentiles, which had indeed at the outset been greeted with joy (Gal. i. 24), but later became more and more suspect to the Jewish mind in proportion as the multitude of the Gentile brethren began to outnumber the Jewish believers in the Messiah. That seemed to make the Messianic kingdom the heritage of the Gentiles, whereas it had been promised to Abraham and to his seed, and ought therefore to belong, if not exclusively, at least primarily, to the people of the promise, namely, the Jews. The practical consequences of the Pauline mission to the Gentiles seemed therefore to lead to the abrogation of the promises made to the Fathers, as his doctrine of faith seemed to lead to the abrogation of the law. It is especially in the Epistle to the Romans that Paul sets himself to meet these two objections. After having defended, in the first eight chapters, his doctrine of justification by faith against the objections taken from the law, and proved its consistency with the divine revelation of the law, he turns, in chaps. ix.–xi., to the solution of the other main question: How was the more rapid increase of Gentile as compared with Jewish Christians in the kingdom of Christ to be reconciled with the promises which God, according to the scriptures, had given to the Patriarchs of Israel?

The offence caused to the Jewish Christians by the actual course of events was based on the impression which had long been deeply rooted in the Jewish mind, that the Chosen People, in virtue of their legal covenant, could make good a documentary claim to hold the prerogative in the kingdom of Christ. In view of this self-righteous claim, Paul reminds them of the truth which was fundamental in his own as in every true, religious life—of the unconditional dependence of man upon the free grace of God, with whom none may litigate and bargain, since He owes no man anything. This unconditional character of the gracious will of God he proves to the Jew from his own history. Even in the history of the Patriarchs, God proved the sovereign freedom of His will in that, without any regard to human worth or unworthiness, He chose one before another, as in the choice of Isaac before Ishmael, in the preferring of Jacob before Esau, and in the showing of mercy to Moses and the rejection of Pharaoh. From these examples the principle of the divine choice is evident: He "has mercy upon whom he will, and whom he will he hardeneth. So then it is not of him that willeth, or of him that runneth, but of God that showeth mercy" (ix. 16, 18). But does not this absence of limitation of the Divine will destroy all human responsibility? Paul himself anticipates this objection, but he does not allow it to embarrass him at all, merely striking it out of the way with the reminder that the creature has no right whatever to litigate with the Creator and to question "Why hast thou made me thus?" As the potter, from one and the same material, makes one vessel to an honourable, and another to a less honourable, destiny, so God, out of the same material of human nature, makes some individuals vessels of wrath, destined to destruction, some vessels of mercy destined to glory. In doing so He willed to exhibit, in the former His wrath, *i.e.* His holiness which must unconditionally destroy evil, and His power, *i.e.* His unconditioned self-determination as creative will; at the same time, however, they were also to serve Him as means—and for that reason He bore with them with great long-suffering, instead of at once delivering them over to destruction—in order to exhibit in the vessels of mercy the riches of His glory which, in contrast with those to whom He does not accord mercy, is manifested the more

gloriously as unconditional free grace (verse 22 f.).[1]
Thus the final aim of all divine fore-ordination is the
revelation of grace, to which the revelation of wrath
served only as a means. That, in itself, indicates that
love, the exaltation of which is the final aim, is also
the highest motive of the divine pre-ordination, and
that the will of wrath is not opposed to it as equally
essential in such a way that they mutually limit each
other and hold each other in check, but that the ex-
hibition of wrath serves only as the temporary means
towards the eternal aims of love—a thought which
is applied to the destiny of Israel in chap. xi., where
Paul consolingly holds out a prospect of the final
acceptance even of those who are now apparently
rejected, but who are in reality only temporarily
put back.

But before he gives his doctrine of predestination
this conciliatory conclusion, he seeks to mitigate its
apparent hardness by another method of regarding it.
He descends from the height of the absolute divine
decree to the historical level, and shows how the

---

[1] In this argument, ix. 19–23, passages from the Book of Wisdom,
xii. 8–22 and xv. 7, have unmistakably been present to the apostle's
mind. From the latter he took the picture of the potter, which
is, however, used there in a different connection. But in the
former passage we find essentially the same thoughts of the divine
patience in sparing the reprobate, which serves to enhance the
glory of the avenging power of the sovereign Lord against His
enemies, and at the same time to exhibit His mercy towards His
chosen children. The author of the Book of Wisdom, not behind
the Pharisees in Jewish self-satisfaction, naturally understands by
the chosen the Jews, and by the rejected the heathen. Paul has
simply reversed this teaching. His doctrine of predestination,
like his doctrine of the law, is simply Pharisaism turned the other
way round.

sad fate of Israel, which he had first referred to as
a determination of the Divine will, can also be
fully understood from the standpoint of human
judgment, as a natural consequence of natural causes.
That Israel is in an inferior position to the Gentiles
in the kingdom of Christ is the quite comprehensible
consequence of the very thing in which Israel
conceived itself to have a ground of boasting as
against the Gentiles. The Gentiles have obtained
righteousness by faith, for the very reason that they
did not seek it by works of the law, because, therefore, they were ready to accept that which is, and can
only be, a free gift of the divine grace as a free
gift ; Israel, on the contrary, while striving after
the law of righteousness, did not attain unto (such)
a law. Why ? Because it did not seek it by faith
but by works ; therefore it fell by the stone of
stumbling, which was precisely this gracious character of the true righteousness, which as such must
be received by men in faith and not earned by
their own works. Israel has shown zeal about God,
about the fulfilling of His will, but it has failed to
understand the true sense of the Divine will, which
has been revealed in Christ as a will of grace. So
Israel's zeal for God, since it was lacking in the
knowledge of what God really wanted of them,
became the natural ground of their misfortune (x. 2 f.).
In this self-willed resistance to God's revelation they
manifested once more the same character of head-
strong obstinacy, of a tenacious clinging to outward
historical forms and resistance to the higher spiritual
truth, of which the prophets had so often had to
complain, and which from of old had been the fatal

character of this people (x. 19 ff.). In so far, therefore, their present rejection is self-inflicted, because it is the natural consequence of their obstinate national character. By this, then, the preceding explanation of Israel's rejection as the result of a free divine act of will is supplemented by a historical causal explanation, but not in the sense that the first is superseded, or even limited, by the second. That which results as a consequence of the historical character of a nation is not accidental and indeterminate—something that might just as well have been otherwise—but rests upon an inner necessity of its individual disposition and character which can with equal truth be regarded as its guilt or its misfortune. Everyone who looks at the history of a nation, as the apostle here does, in its large historical connection, is always obliged to combine both points of view, and does not thereby make himself guilty of a contradiction ; for that which from the historical point of view is character, therefore self-determination, is from the transcendental or religious point of view divine fore-ordination. The two are so far from being mutually exclusive that they are, rather, merely the two complementary sides of the same truth. Moreover, we must also bear in mind that the historical judgment of Israel's attitude which prevails in chap. x., finally, in xi. 7–10, merges itself again into the religious predestination view, inasmuch as the resistance of Israel is ascribed again to a divine " hardening " and " blinding " of the unhappy people. It is so far from being the apostle's intention to annul or withdraw the other that for him they obviously coincide : Israel's character is as much its guilt as its misfortune, Israel's fate is as much the consequence of its own self-determination as of the divine pre-destination.

But, by the very fact that he brings the opposition of Israel to the gospel under the point of view of a sentence ordained by God, Paul opens the way for the solution of the riddle. As God in the earlier history of Israel, amid the gravest transgression and the severest chastenings of the mass of the people, always preserved a remnant of loyal and saved men as harbingers and pledges of a better future, so it is again now. Israel has stumbled, but its fall shall not be for ever. It has suffered loss in the holding back of the greater part of the nation from the kingdom of Christ, but it will not always be excluded from that kingdom. Its transgression was designed to be, in the first place, a means to the salvation of the heathen, its loss was to bring riches to the heathen ; the natural branches of the noble olive-tree of the historical people of God had been cut off to make room for the ingrafting of branches from the wild olive-tree of heathenism. But for this very reason—because this putting of Israel in an inferior place was intended in the divine plan of salvation merely to serve the purpose of passing on salvation to the Gentiles—when this purpose has been attained their temporary rejection will be at an end, and precedence of reception will return to the people of the promise who were the first to be called, though now for a season temporarily rejected. " Hardening in part has come upon Israel, until the time when the full number of the Gentiles shall have entered in (to the kingdom of Christ), and then all Israel shall

be saved" (xi. 25 f.). The entering in of the full
number of the Gentiles will, however, not only
mark the term and limit of the hardening of Israel,
but also serve as the means of putting an end to
it. For as the number of the converted heathen
approaches completion, Israel will be provoked to
emulation, so that even those who have now gone
astray through their disobedience to the gospel of
mercy will then be shamed and won over by the
mercy shown to the Gentiles into becoming capable
of receiving it. Therefore the present disobedience
of the Jews must now serve to apply to the Gentiles,
who before were disobedient, the mercy of God in
Christ; then the precedence of the heathen shall
serve to overcome the disobedience of the Jews, and
to bring to them also their share in salvation; for
if the failure and rejection of the Jews signified the
riches of the heathen, so shall finally the fulness of
the converted Jews cause the full life of completed
salvation to be introduced to the world (xi. 12, 15).
Thus every stage in this historical development becomes the means to the next higher, and finally
reaches the apex in the fulfilment of purpose of the
Divine will of mercy; God has shut up all unto
disobedience, that He might have mercy upon all
(xi. 32). However obscure the divine decrees, however unfathomable the methods of His administration
in the present may appear, they all aim at the one
final purpose of the all-embracing plan of salvation.
If at first a glance directed upon the empirical
history reflected back its oppositions upon God, and
therefore suggested that it saw in God a twofold
determination of will—rejecting wrath alongside of

electing grace—from the vantage ground of the final purpose, this opposition proves to be a means, belonging to its temporal manifestation, for the fulfilment of the eternal and universal purpose, transcending all temporal opposition, of the all-wise love.

This applies, at all events, to the great historical groups of peoples such as the Jews and Gentiles, to whom the whole discussion in Rom. ix.–xi. exclusively refers. As regards individuals, we shall return later to the question whether Paul also contemplated a final reconciliation and restoration of those who were for the present excluded. That he believed in a decree of rejection as regards individuals, as the Calvinistic doctrine represents him as teaching, is at least incapable of proof, since the only passage which can be advanced in support of the position, Rom. ix. 22, is to be referred, in accordance with the context of the whole chapter, to the Jews as a nation, the present rejection of which does not exclude its final acceptance, as we saw above. On the other hand, Paul certainly did teach a decree of election as regards believers. The classic passage for this is Rom. viii. 28–30 : " We know that God causes all things to work together for good to those who love him, to those who are called according to his purpose. For whom he did foreknow, he also did predestinate to be conformed to the image of his Son, that he might be the first-born among many brethren. Moreover, whom he did predestinate, them he also called, and whom he called, them he also justified, and whom he justified, them he also glorified." The Christian knows himself

called on the ground of his love to God to reproduce
in himself the likeness of the Son of God or to share
in the relationship of full sonship to God, of which
Christ is the prototype, with all its glorious consequences. That this divine intention, of which he
has been given assurance when he received the call
of the gospel to believe in the gospel, will ultimately
be fulfilled—this is the hope which is supported by
the conviction that his becoming a believer through
the call of the gospel was not an accident, which
might be contravened and rendered ineffectual by
hostile circumstances, powers, or events, but that it
is a consequence of the divine " purpose " which had
marked out in advance those who should be called,
i.e. chosen them out of the mass [1] and predestinated
them to their lofty destiny as children of God.
This purpose, which in advance, that is, from the
very beginning, had in view the future believers and
destined them beforehand for their status of sonship,
subsequently comes to fulfilment through a series of
temporal acts ; through the call to faith which Paul
thinks of as always effectual or as actually producing
faith ; secondly, through justification by faith ; finally,
through the glorification of the justified. This last
act is, of course, not completed in the temporal life,
but, in the communication of the Spirit, there is
given to believers the pledge of their future glorifica-

---

[1] That προέγνω implies, not the mere foreknowledge of future
belief, but the will-act of Him who chooses those who shall believe,
is made certain by the connection with πρόθεσις (v. 28), which in
ix. 11 is more closely defined as ἡ κατ' ἐκλογὴν πρόθεσις. Besides,
the parallels in Rom. xi. 2 and 1 Peter i. 20, where the people of
Israel and Christ are the object of the προγιγνώσκειν, make the
meaning " foreknown " quite impossible.

tion, so that what remains incomplete in this respect is nevertheless as good as given. The point of the passage, then, lies in this—that for the believer his present status as a justified and loving child of God represents a link in the firmly riveted chain of divine acts of grace, which reaches back into the eternity of the fore-ordaining purpose or decree of grace, and forward into the eternity of the fulfilled purpose, to the glorious goal of union with Christ, and which, since it depends on the free-willed act of divine election, no temporal or earthly power can avail to break or annul. We can see in this quite clearly the psychological motive of the doctrine of election, and it is on that that its religious significance rests. The doctrine does not spring from theoretic speculation upon divine causality and human freedom—that problem first arises in the course of theological reflection upon the doctrine, but the latter itself grew simply out of the practical need of making firm for all futurity the certainty of salvation which the believer already possesses, by founding it on the supra-temporal will of the divine love, and thereby removing it above all chances and changes of the temporal life. The doctrine of election simply expresses the certainty of the religious consciousness that its loving relation to God was willed and caused by God Himself, and therefore that it is a reality resting on unshakable foundations, and not to be destroyed by any finite power. " If any man love God, the same is known of him " (1 Cor. viii. 3); and " I am persuaded that nothing can separate us from the love of God which is in Christ Jesus " (Rom. viii. 39) — this is the simplest explanation of the doctrine of election—if we understand it in its original religious kernel which has been the seed of all further theological reflection.

The certainty of a salvation which cannot be lost, secured by the bonds of love to God and by the imitation of the first-born Son of God, forms the specifically Christian kernel of Paul's hope of the future. There are, it is true, certain peculiar features in the details of his picture of the future, but he attaches himself here more nearly than elsewhere to the conception which prevailed in the primitive Church.

In the foreground of the Pauline eschatology there stands the expectation of the early return of Christ to set up His kingdom in visible glory. According to 1 Thess. iv. 15 ff. and 1 Cor. xv. 51 f., Paul himself hoped to be still alive at this event. It is, it must be admitted, difficult to say how the expectation expressed in Rom. xi., that before the Parousia the fulness of the heathen, as well as of the Jews, must be converted, is to be reconciled with this. But Paul had, as we shall soon see, as early as the time of writing Second Corinthians, given up the expectation of personally surviving till the Parousia, and therefore the interval before the completion of the work of evangelisation might well seem to him likely to be of somewhat longer extent. The Parousia itself he imagined as a visible descent of Christ from heaven accompanied by all His saints (1 Thess. iii. 13), by which we are to understand either angels, or, what is more probable, the Old Testament saints like Elijah and Moses and the patriarchs who had been translated

to God [1]—in any case not Christians, who are to
meet the Lord, and therefore will not descend with
Him from heaven. For, at the command of God,
the voice of the archangel and the sound of the
trumpet, there shall follow first the resurrection of
the Christians who had "fallen asleep," and then the
surviving Christians shall be rapt away to meet the
Lord in the air, and to be with Him evermore.
That in view of this they shall first be "changed," that
is, their gross earthly corporeity be changed into something more ethereal, is not expressly said in 1 Thess.
iv. 17, but it is distinctly stated in 1 Cor. xv. 51 ff.,
where the reason given for this transformation is
that the corruptible must put on incorruption.
Whether the same idea is to be taken as implied in
1 Thess. iv., or whether it is to be understood as a
further development of the Pauline view, may be left
an open question. Even the purpose of this trans-
porting of the Christians into the air is not clear; are
those who are thus raised from the dead and changed,
to remain with Christ in the air between heaven
and earth, or to enter into heaven? But Christ has
just come from heaven in order to hold judgment
upon earth; therefore, it is more probable that they
only go to meet Him in order to form an escort upon
His further descent.

With the Parousia is closely connected, in Pauline,
as in Jewish, eschatology, the judgment. The "day
of the Lord" (1 Thess. v. 2; 1 Cor. i. 8, iii. 13, v. 5;
2 Cor. i. 14; Rom. ii. 16; Phil. i. 6, 10, ii. 16) is

---

[1] Kabisch, *Eschatologie des Paulus*, p. 238, refers to Enoch lxx. 4:
"There saw I the first fathers and the righteous of old dwelling in
that place (heaven)."

from Old Testament times the solemn phrase for
the Great Day of Judgment. As Judge appears, in
some passages, Christ (1 Cor. iv. 4; 2 Cor. v. 10);
in some, God Himself (Rom. ii. 3 ff., xiv. 10); in
some, "God through Christ" (Rom. ii. 16; 1 Cor.
iv. 5). According to 1 Cor. vi. 2, the saints, that is,
Christians, will act as assessors at the judgment:
they shall judge the world and the angels. The
mode in which the judgment proceeds is also represented, quite in traditional fashion, as a judicial
allotment of reward or punishment according to the
measure of each one's works (Rom. ii. 6; 2 Cor. v. 10).
As in the latter passage the reference is to the
judgment held upon Christians, the difficult question
arises, how such a judgment can be reconciled with
the Pauline doctrine that Christians are justified by
faith in such a way that there is for them no condemnation? (Rom. viii. 1). Many seek the reconciliation in the thought that in the judgment held
upon Christians it is not a question of blessedness or
the reverse, but only of degrees of blessedness which
are to be allotted according to the work of each.
And in support of this the passage 1 Cor. iii. 12 ff.
may certainly be adduced, according to which the
life-work of every Christian worker shall be tested
with regard to its soundness, by the fire of the day
of judgment. "If any man's work shall be burned,
he shall suffer loss; but he himself shall be saved,
yet so as by fire." According to 2 Cor. ix. 6, too,
the quantity of the harvest is regulated by the
sowing: that is, by the greater or less degree of
well-doing. But that explanation is not universally
applicable. In Gal. vi. 7 f., which is closely con-

nected with the passage just cited, the Galatian
Christians are warned of the severity of the divine
judgment, "for he that soweth to the flesh shall of
the flesh reap corruption." Similarly Paul exhorts
the Corinthians "Let him that thinketh he standeth
take heed lest he fall," pointing to the warning
example of the Israelites, of whom many were
destroyed although they had all partaken sacra-
mentally of the spiritual food and drink (1 Cor. x.
1-12). To the Romans he says: "If ye live after
the flesh, ye shall die" (viii. 13), and "Take heed lest
he spare not thee" (the Gentile Christian), xi. 21. In
Phil. iii. 19 the destruction of certain Judaising Christians is distinctly contemplated. Indeed, according
to numerous indications Paul seems to be not yet
certain of his own salvation. According to 1 Cor.
ix. 27 he buffets himself that he may not, while
preaching to others, himself become a castaway;
according to 1 Cor. iv. 4 the witness of his conscience
gives him no certain guarantee as to what judgment
the Lord will some day pronounce over him; in
Phil. iii. 11 he expresses only an uncertain hope "If
perchance he might attain to the resurrection of the
dead." In all these passages it is not a question
of a lower degree of blessedness, but frankly of a
possible rejection of those Christians whose moral
conduct cannot stand the judgment of God. Now
what is the relation between these passages and the
assertion that for the justified and reconciled (and
that means all Christians) there is now no condemnation, but the certainty of being saved "from
wrath"? (Rom. v. 1, 9, viii. 1). Is it possible that
justification is to be only a provisional and hypo-

29

thetical thing which does not involve final salvation,
but leaves open the possibility of being lost through
subsequent guilt? But according to Rom. viii. 30
the justified are, as such, also at the same time the
elect, for whom through God's gracious purpose even
the future glory, and therefore certainly the final
salvation, is assured. It is certainly quite clear that
between the unconditional religious consciousness of
present possession of salvation and the ethically
conditioned hope of the future completion of salvation, no reconciliation can be found in Paul's
teaching; the two proceed on parallel lines, and
Paul does not attempt to bring them together. It
is no doubt possible to combine them by means
of the modern conception of a development from
within of an ethico-religious principle of life given
in the personal consciousness, and to be realised in
active life. Paul has at least hinted at this thought
in the picture of the seed and the harvest (Gal. vi. 7),
according to which the final result is the natural
fruit of human conduct, not an award dependent
on a judicial decision. But he was hindered from
carrying it through, and thereby solving the above
controversy, by the supernatural form which was
taken from the first by his representation of the
beginning and end of the life of salvation—at the
beginning, a judgment of justification on the believer
on the ground of the atoning death of Christ; at
the end, a judgment expressive of retributive justice
founded on man's own acts; these are representations
which obviously are mutually exclusive.

From the historical point of view it is not permissible to get rid of difficulties of this kind by a

harmonising reconciliation of the different passages, in which constraint would always need to be put upon one or the other. The task of the historical investigator is rather to discover the various sources and motives of the diverse lines of thought which run through the whole of the Pauline theology and appear with especial clearness in his eschatology. The eschatological representations hitherto mentioned —the Parousia, which is at once the resurrection of the dead and transformation of the living, a solemn judgment, and a judicial sentence in which service and reward are weighed against each other in an outward equivalence which is impossible in the ethical region — all these belong to the Pharisaic side of his theology. Alongside of this there appears in the later epistles an entirely different view, the Hellenistic, as we may describe it for brevity,[1] the implications of which point to an eschatology widely different from the former, and nearly related to the Johannine. The new inclination

---

[1] This description is justified at least *à parte potiori*, though with a twofold reservation : first, that this view was not exclusively limited to the Hellenised races, but was also found among genuine Jews (Essenes and "Apocalyptics") ; secondly, that its earliest roots are not to be found in the Greek philosophy but in the primitive animistic religion, the psychical and supernaturalistic beliefs of which had been developed since the time of the Orphics under the impression and motive of ecstatic orgiasm and enthusiasm, receiving an extension and elevation which had found manifold expression, first in the widely prevalent system of religious ideas associated with the mysteries, and afterwards in the philosophical theories of Plato, of the Neo-Pythagoreans and the religious philosophers of Alexandria, and had passed into the general consciousness of the religiously-minded men of the time as a popular belief in immortality. *Cf.* Rhode, *Psyche.*

towards the Hellenistic eschatology first appears in
2 Cor. v. 1–8. Whereas earlier (First Thessalonians
and First Corinthians) Paul still hoped to survive
till the Parousia of Christ, he there says that he
would fain depart from the body and be present
with the Lord (verse 8), and he knows that we,
when our earthly tabernacle is dissolved, *i.e.* after
the death of the earthly body, have a house of God,
eternal in the heavens, that is, a new heavenly body,
which stands ready at once to replace the earthly
one, to be put upon us as a new garment, so that we
need not fear ever to be in a condition of nakedness,
i.e. in a disembodied state. From this it appears
that Paul expected in the case of his dying before
the Parousia—which now appeared to him probable
—to be immediately clothed with a new heavenly
body, and at the same moment to enter into the
blessed condition of being " at home with the Lord,"
which is obviously something quite different from
the condition of being " asleep " ($\kappa o\iota\mu\hat{a}\sigma\theta a\iota$) in which,
according to the former view, the Christians who
had died before the Parousia were to continue until
the general resurrection at the Parousia. For this
intermediate state of sleep would be exactly what
he now says he need no longer fear—the state of
being naked and far from the Lord, since those who
rise from the graves and the under-world shall go
up from beneath to meet the Lord coming down
from above, and are therefore previously not yet
with Him, but as far from Him as Hades is from
Heaven. This is therefore the new point in the
later view of Paul, that he now no longer believes
that he will be obliged to experience the miserable

intermediate state of disembodied souls in Hades, but hopes for an *immediate* transference after death to a new body and to be in the closest union with the Lord, Phil. i. 23, " I desire to depart and be with Christ " ; " For to me to live is Christ, and to die is gain " (verse 21). That he cherished this hope as a personal privilege for himself alone is quite improbable, for there is not a word to indicate such a limitation ; he speaks quite generally in the plural, including here, as elsewhere, all Christians along with himself. His eschatological view must therefore have undergone an alteration, the immediate impulse to which is presumably to be sought in a personal experience. Paul had, between the writing of First and Second Corinthians, been in grave danger of death, in which he had even given his life up for lost (2 Cor. i. 8). By this his hope of surviving till the Parousia was shattered and the thought of Hades came fearfully near to him. This prospect of separation from the Lord, even though only temporary, was felt by him as so unbearable that he now *postulated* on the ground of his strong sense of mystical union with the Lord, the hope that this union could not be broken off by the death of the body (*cf.* Rom. viii. 38). And this postulate found strong support in his doctrine of the Spirit. If the Spirit of Christ has been communicated through baptism to the believer as a permanent possession, and the Spirit's life-giving power is now manifested in him, not only in the daily renewal of the inner man but also in the sustaining of the outward man amid all the wearing afflictions and trials of the present (2 Cor. iv. 10 ff.), then there can be no reason why this life-giving activity of the Spirit should be broken off by the death of the body, and not rather completed. This thought is clearly expressed by Paul in Rom. viii. 11 : " If the Spirit of him who raised Jesus from the dead dwelleth in you, then shall he who raised Christ Jesus quicken also your mortal bodies through his Spirit which dwelleth in you " ; or according to another reading, " for the sake of his Spirit which dwelleth in you." According to both readings, the Spirit which dwells in the Christian is the pledge of a " quickening," extending to the body, or of the bestowal of a new heavenly body for which God has prepared us by the very act of giving us the earnest of the Spirit (2 Cor. v. 5).

As this new conviction of Paul has its sufficient ground in his theology and his personal experiences, we need not seek its source in the Alexandrian religious philosophy. It is true that 2 Cor. v. 1–5 has such close affinities with Wisd. ix. 15, that the conjecture is legitimate that this passage may have hovered before his mind and perhaps even suggested the choice of his words.[1] But this close affinity by no means proves a direct borrowing of the Pauline doctrine from the Alexandrian Book of Wisdom. Here again the remark is applicable which we have several times had occasion to make, that the analogy

---

[1] Cf. E. Pfleiderer, The Philosophy of Heraclitus, p. 296, note. From the proof offered there that the author of the Book of Wisdom has here followed verbally a passage in Plato's Phædo, 81 C, the conclusion is drawn that "there is a well-grounded possibility that through the link of the Sophia, the most beautiful writing of classical antiquity, the immortal Phædo, has left traces in our New Testament not only of its thoughts but also in two verbal forms (ἐπίγειος and βαρούμενοι)."

of the Pauline with the Hellenistic teaching has its
ground in the fact that both sprang from a common
root and grew up in a similar way. The common
root is, as we saw before, the animistic popular
metaphysic ; from this arose the Hellenistic doctrine
of immortality, not originally through philosophic
reflection, but on the ground of those religious experiences associated with the mystery-cults which
were usually described as " enthusiasm " and considered to be a filling of the man with the divine
Spirit and life. From these grew up, first the Orphic,
and later the Platonic, Neo-Pythagorean, and Alexandrian doctrines of immortality. The part played
in this case by the enthusiasm engendered in the
mysteries, was taken in Paul's case by the enthusiasm
which arose from the mystical union with Christ,
which, to complete the parallel, was connected with
mystical cultus-acts (Baptism and the Lord's Supper).
From this resulted, in the first place, his original
doctrine of the Spirit, and, as a further consequence
of that, his original eschatology, the close relationship
of which to the Hellenistic doctrine of immortality is
therefore quite intelligible. Moreover, the relationship is not one of full identity. Whereas the Greeks
thought of the future life as a disembodied existence of
pure deified souls or spirits, Paul always held fast to the
Jewish belief in a reanimation of the body also, without which he was not able to think of a complete life
of the spirit ; but in distinction from the Pharisees,
again, he thought of the new body as not simply
consisting of flesh or earthly material of any kind
but as a spiritual body—that is, one which consisted,
appropriately to the nature of the heavenly spirit,

of a heavenly substance like light (æther), and which will be the image of the body of the risen Christ (1 Cor. xv. 42 ff., 49 ff.; Rom. viii. 29 ; Phil. iii. 21). In this point his earlier doctrine of the resurrection and his later doctrine of immortality remained the same, and therefore the one view could the more easily pass into the other ; for if the new body is a heavenly body of light which has only, so to speak, the form but not the material in common with the old, there is nothing to prevent this body from being, immediately after the death of the old, at the disposal of the soul as a new habitation or garment, as Paul expects in 2 Cor. v. 1 ff.

The consequences of this new eschatology are not indeed drawn by Paul himself, but they could not fail to be drawn in course of time. The putting forward of the reanimation to the moment of death does away with the future general resurrection, and in view of the immediate entry of the soul of the Christian, separated from the earthly body, into the closest union with Christ, the return of Christ from heaven becomes superfluous; for if Christians at death go to Christ in heaven, it is impossible to see why Christ should come down to earth to the Christians. But along with the Parousia goes also the solemn day of judgment and the establishment of a visible kingdom of Christ upon earth. All these conceptions, which have their roots in the Jewish eschatology, are replaced later by the simple "eternal life" in the Johannine sense as the "unio mystica" with Christ the Son of God, which, while it begins in the present, is to be completed in the Father's house in heaven. The importance of this

Hellenistic direction imparted by Paul to the early Christian eschatology can hardly be rated too highly, for we must consider that the religious aspiration of contemporary heathenism was not, like the Pharisaic realism, directed to the restoration of the flesh, but to liberation from the sensuous and to immortality of the soul in a higher, supernal state of existence; and further, that the more the hope of the general resurrection at the Parousia had to be put back into the indefinite future because of the delay of the Parousia, the more it lost power as an incentive, and a substitute for it became necessary in the Hellenistic hope of the blessedness of individuals in the other world— such as first meets us in Paul's teaching. It is true Paul does not seem to have thought of working out the consequences of the hope which had newly dawned upon himself, for even in the later letters we find, constantly recurring, the conceptions which he had adopted from the Jewish-Christian eschatology— the Parousia, resurrection and judgment (2 Cor. iv. 14, v. 10; Phil. iii. 11, 20), without any indication as to how they are to be reconciled with the new ideal of the future. Yet something of this kind may perhaps be found in Col. iii. 3 f. : " Ye are dead, and your life is hid with Christ in God ; when Christ who is your life shall appear, then shall ye also appear with him in glory." What is here expected as a consequence of the Parousia of Christ is not properly a resurrection of those who till then have been asleep to a new life, which is then first beginning, but only the manifestation in glory, in visible appearance, of the same heavenly life which Christians in their union with the risen Christ already possess in a hidden invisible fashion, and which, self-evidently, cannot be taken from them or impeded by bodily death; it is not, according to this, in the future that they are to be raised up, but because they are already risen and their life and work belongs to the heavenly world of Christ (verse 1); that life which is now hid with Christ in God shall survive victoriously beyond the bodily death, and at the Parousia shall cause its imperishable essence visibly to appear in glory. The Parousia, according to this, does not properly bring about anything new; it only causes the new life of the children of God, which is already present, to be gloriously and victoriously manifested free from the fetters of earthly existence, so that thereby the curse which lies upon the groaning creation shall be broken and its hope of redemption fulfilled (Rom. viii. 21).

In view of this characteristic of the Pauline eschatology, this chaotic medley of old and new ideas of the most diverse kinds, it is not merely impossible to reduce them to a systematic unity, but even in detail much remains problematical. Such questions as the following can hardly be answered with certainty: Did Paul hold that there was more than one resurrection? Did he expect a universal resurrection of mankind? Or, if not, how did he conceive of the fate of those men who were not to rise again? Did he hold that there would be an earthly kingdom of Christ between the resurrection and the final end? How did he conceive of the position of Christ in the final condition of all things? In this last question the point at issue is the exposition of the difficult passage

in 1 Cor. xv. 22–28 : " As in Adam all die, so in
Christ shall all be made alive ; but each in his own
order : first Christ, then those who are Christ's, at
His Parousia. Then cometh the end, when He giveth
up the kingship to God the Father, when He shall
have destroyed all rule and power and might. For
He must reign until He hath put all enemies under
His feet. The last enemy that shall be destroyed is
death. For ' He hath put all things under His feet '
(Ps. viii. 7), but when it is said that all has been
made subject unto Him, it is evident that He is
excepted who hath subjected all things unto Him.
But when all things shall have been subjected to
Him, then will also the Son Himself subject Himself
to Him who has put all things under Him, that
God may be all in all." The question arises whether
in v. 23 f. three stages in the resurrection are
to be distinguished : (1) The resurrection of Christ ;
(2) that of Christians ; (3) that of the remainder of
mankind. In favour of this are the words " each in
his own order" (τάγματι), by which a series seems
to be indicated, and this is not intelligible without
the third member of the series. Verse 22, also, may
be alleged in favour of a general resurrection, since
in it the making alive of all in Christ is the converse
of the dying of all in Adam, and therefore the " all "
in the two members of the sentence is naturally
understood in an equally absolute sense. But, as a
counterpoise to that, only those can be made alive
in Christ who are really in Christ ; but that is
only Christians, who have the Spirit of Christ.
Only, the possession of the Spirit is the pledge and
earnest of the resurrection (2 Cor. v. 5 ; Rom. viii.

11, 29), which, for that very reason, is described as a being conformed to the image of Christ (1 Cor. xv. 48; Phil. iii. 21). By this a resurrection of the godless to judgment is excluded. If Paul, nevertheless, held that there was a final resurrection of all men, that would necessarily imply that he also held a general conversion to Christ of all men, including all former generations. But how that could be possible is difficult to imagine, since faith comes by preaching, and the possession of the Spirit by baptism. Besides, he speaks often of the "lost" alongside of the saved, and even, as we saw (p. 448 f.), leaves open for Christians the possibility of going astray, and with that the holding of a general conversion and deliverance of all men can hardly be united. But if the universality of the resurrection stands or falls with the universality of conversion— since there is only a resurrection *in Christ*—it is hard to say what remains over in verse 23 f. for a third stage of the resurrection, after that of Christians. Yet if there is no third stage, the "end," when Christ gives up the rule to God, seems to coincide in point of time with the Parousia (verse 23), and therefore seems to leave no room between for a kingdom of Christ. Against this it may in turn be urged that the statement in verse 25, that Christ must reign until all enemies and, as the last enemy, death, have been put under His feet, seems to point to an exercise of His Lordship during a certain interval after the Parousia. But if, on the other hand, with the resurrection of Christ at the Parousia, the victory over death and Hades is already won (xv. 54 ff.), and in the judgment which follows immediately thereon all powers inimical to God are already condemned — how can there be any enemies left, whose subjugation might be the task of a continued exercise of Christ's Lordship after His Parousia? Or should we be justified in regarding the judgment, not as a unique act and decisive world-catastrophe, but as a lengthy process, and the gradual conquest of the powers which are hostile to God?[1] To decide what answer Paul gave to these questions is so difficult that it is perhaps best to leave it as an open problem.

The end of all things will consist, according to Paul, in Christ's giving up His Lordship and subjecting Himself to the Father; and then God shall be all in all. This subjection of Christ has always been found extraordinary, and it is indeed really so, not merely from the ecclesiastical and Trinitarian standpoint, but also from that of Paul. Passages like Rom. xiv. 9, Phil. ii. 10 f. (not to mention Col. i. 15 ff.), speak of Christ's Lordship in so unconditional a fashion that no one would ever suspect that its importance was only temporary. There intersect here the divergent interests of a strict monotheism and of the lofty doctrine of Christ which was already rising above its historical foundations—two interests the reconciliation of which led to the Church's doctrine of the Trinity. That God shall be "all in all" is not easy to understand on the assumption that besides the blessed there are also the lost who are objects of the divine wrath; for although God might be fully Lord over these finally vanquished enemies, it could not well be said that He was all

[1] So Kabisch, *Paulinische Eschatologie*, p. 260 ff.

" in " them. That could only be the case if they were inwardly conquered, that is, converted. But Paul speaks of the destruction and death of the ungodly in so uncompromising a fashion that we cannot well attribute to him the thought of a general restoration of all. It would be easier to suppose that the reprobate undergo death in the absolute sense, that they entirely cease to exist, and that thenceforth there were only the good and the blessed in whom God was the all-ruling principle of life. That could no doubt be reconciled with Rom. ii. 8 f., if we could understand by tribulation and anguish only the elements in the execution of judgment, but as, according to the foregoing verse 7, eternal life is given by the retributive justice of God to those who strive after noble ends, we must suppose in the parallel case an enduring condition of misery. That brings us again to a group of antinomies which is scarcely to be solved. How, we are compelled to ask, is a continued state of damnation to be reconciled with the principle that God at the last shall be all in all? And how, again, is the damnation of a portion of humanity to be reconciled with the assertion, in which the Pauline theodicy reached its climax, that God has shut up all unto disobedience, in order that He might have mercy upon all? (Rom. xi. 32). And how, on the other hand, is the assertion that all ethically noble effort among Jews and Greeks is rewarded with eternal life to be reconciled with the dogmatic presupposition that eternal life is only for those who are made alive in Christ, namely, Christians? But this difficulty—which arises from the collision of universal human morals with the positive dogmatic, based on historical means of salvation—is shared by the Pauline theology with that of the Church in general; and it must be admitted that inconsequence on this point does Paul more honour than the logical " extra ecclesiam nulla salus " does to the Augustinian churchly theology.

In all this we have found confirmed the expectations to which the Jewish-Greek education of Saul-Paul the Hellenist and Pharisee naturally gave rise: the Pharisaic and the Hellenistic ways of thinking form the two currents which in Paulinism flow through one channel, yet without being really united. The two disparate lines of thought run alongside one another, sometimes mutually complementary, sometimes contradictory or mutually exclusive. This state of matters may, from the logical point of view, appear a defect, and it is certainly a "crux" for such theologians as believe themselves under obligation to construct a Pauline "system of doctrine." The historical investigator, however, will not only find the situation psychologically quite intelligible, but must also recognise that it is precisely this characteristic of the Pauline theology on which its great historical significance was based, and which enabled it to guide Christianity in its expansion beyond the narrow framework of a Jewish - Messianic community into a world-religion. The link of transition could only be a theology which, like the Pauline, shows two faces, and which, to change the metaphor, planting one foot upon the specifically Jewish or Pharisaic system of thought, .set the other well within the circle of thought which

was common to the religiously disposed heathen of
the time, and to the Jews of the Diaspora who had
had a Greek education,—into the circle of thought
of Hellenism, and which thus united the two
highest achievements of the religious spirit of pre-
Christian mankind, the Jewish belief in God, and
the Platonic belief in immortality. This religious
philosophy of Hellenism, with its yearning for
freedom from the sensuous, for the supremacy of
the spirit, for exaltation above the world and
communion with the divine life, received from
Paul's gospel of the heavenly Son of God and
exalted "Lord who is the Spirit," a firm centre
and a historical background, by means of which its
abstract world of ideas became a concrete world of
beliefs which laid hold upon the imagination, was
capable of serving as a motive force, and included in
itself a power of uniting men in religious fellowship.
The Pharisaic elements of Paulinism, however, served
to free the new Christian Hellenism from the fetters
of legal Judaism which the Jewish Hellenism had
never been able to break and cast off (cf. Philo),
because a mind fettered by legalistic prejudices could
not allow itself to be overcome by speculations presenting themselves to it from without, but could only
be overcome by arguments which were governed by
its own point of view as to the authority of revelation.
Only Paul the Pharisee could break the spell of the
Jewish legal system and get rid of the drag which
had hitherto always impeded the universal extension
of the Jewish belief in God. And only Paul the
Christian, the apostle of the risen Christ, could
overcome the dualism of the Hellenistic system of

thought, and point out to it the fulfilment of its
unsatisfied yearning after an ideal world in Christ,
the heavenly Lord, and in the Spirit which inspires
His Church and is the pledge of our own heavenly
perfection.

Paul became, as he himself says, a Jew to the Jews
and a Greek to the Greeks, in order that he might
win both for the Gospel and bind them together into
a new fellowship, the Church of Christ. This aim he
could only attain by combining Jesus' gospel of sonship to God and of the kingdom of God with various
ideas of Jewish and Greek origin, which might seem
to obscure its simple ethico-religious kernel and to
make turbid its pure truth by foreign admixtures.
But to reproach Paul on that account would be very
unreasonable, and would imply a failure to perceive
the necessity involved in the historical circumstances.
How could Christianity have forced its way out
of the narrow bonds of the Jewish Messianic church
and taken the form of a world-religion, unless it
had cast off the limitations of Jewish nationalism,
of Jewish legalism, and of Messianic hopes of an
earthly and eudæmonistic, of a social and political,
apocalyptic and revolutionary, character? However
high Jesus' own mind was exalted above these
Jewish limitations, they had by no means been
surmounted by the community of His immediate
disciples. To surmount them was the work of Paul.
It was he who freed the kernel of religious truth
which had been given in Jesus' personality, life and
death, from the husk of Jewish nationalism, legalism,
and politico-Messianic hopes, and made it a living
principle of development for the whole world. That

30

could only be effected, however, by separating this new religious principle from its first historical manifestation and distinguishing the spirit of evangelical sonship to God from the person of its first representative and herald, who, as a Jew, was still subject to the law of his people and shared their hopes. But, in accordance with the ideas of the time, this distinction could only take place by the evangelical principle, the spirit of sonship, clothing itself, for Paul's thought, in the form of a concrete spiritual Being who pre-existed in heaven as anti-typal man and Son of God, and came down to earth in order by His obedience to atone for the disobedience of Adam, and by His sacrificial death to break the curse of the law and the power of death, and by His resurrection to inaugurate the new life of freedom for the sons of God. Only by the symbolism of this divine-human drama could the spiritual truth of the gospel of sonship to God be freed from the husk of Judaism and made intelligible to, and serviceable for, the needs of the heathen world. Now it is obviously incontestable that this drama of the Pauline doctrine of redemption has affinities of form with the heathen legends of gods and sons of God. But instead of being disturbed by that, we ought to consider, in the first place, how great, in spite of all affinity of form, was the distinction and superiority of contents of the Pauline symbols as compared with the heathen myths. The swarm of gods and heroes of the nature-religion which were only ideal projections of natural, sensuous and selfish humanity, was forced to vacate the field in favour of the one Lord and Son of God who is the ideal of ethical humanity, of free obedience and love. The saviour-gods of the mysteries, to whom the piety of the declining heathenism attached itself, were imaginary figures without ethical content, and therefore without any truth ; the Stoic ideals of virtue in which the philosophers sought support and strength were abstractions of the reason without visibility, life or reality ; the Son of God of the Pauline gospel was the ethical ideal made visible in the historical figure of Jesus, the sufferer of Golgotha, but also the risen, the heavenly Lord, and the pledge of salvation to those who are His. Here were united what the thought of the wise and the heart of the simple was seeking, the highest truth in the most visible, intelligible, heart-moving form. What harm was it that this truth also clothed itself in the robe of symbol woven by fancy—namely, in myth ? Did this garment obscure the essence of the truth of the Gospel ? Did it not make its light more acceptable and better adapted to the weak vision of humanity ? Can religion ever—popular, Church religion—dispense with the veil of symbol ? If no one will venture to maintain that it can, should we not rather praise than blame him who was able to clothe its contents in the fairest, most appropriate, and most generally intelligible symbols ? And what is true of the symbols of the doctrine of salvation, applies also to those of the cultus, in the mystical ceremonies of which the supersensible is objectified in pictorial form for the apprehension of the Church. It is quite true that Paul introduced the sacraments into Christianity, and also that these bear, in point of form, a close analogy to those of the heathen mysteries. But Paul is not

to be blamed for that either. Rather, it is to be
recognised that he created for the growing Christian
Church the elements of its ceremonial, without which
no Church religion could arise or maintain itself.
In estimating the ceremonies of worship, the paramount consideration always is, what ideal content
they express, and whether they make an ethically
elevating impression. Is not that the case with
baptism and the Lord's Supper as conceived by
Paul? The former is the symbolical expression
of the fundamental principle of evangelical ethics :
" Die to live ! " The latter is a memorial feast
commemorating the death of Jesus, and a pledge
of divine-human love which unites in holy communion the members with the Head and with one
another. How incomparably higher is the value of
these mysteries as compared with all those of the
heathen ! Spirits of demons, orgiastic frenzy,
naturalistic unchastity, blind superstition, gave way
before the Spirit of the Lord, who is freedom and
love. But Paul's doctrine of the Spirit, in particular,
which is the root of all this mysticism, has incurred
the reproach of introducing an unhealthy enthusiastic
element into Christianity and troubling the purity
of evangelical piety. This is a curious reversal of the
actual historical position. Enthusiasm was, at the
beginning, the very breath of primitive Christianity.
The glowing expectation of a near and miraculous
catastrophe which should bring the present age of
the world to a close, transform all existing circumstances, and lay the foundations of a new order of
the world and of society, produced a feverish tension of mind which expressed itself in ecstasies and

wonders of all kinds, which, while it gave the impulse
to heroic asceticism in the form of voluntary poverty
and renunciation of the world, also made men
indifferent to the present world and weakened the
sense of obligation to orderly work. This unbridled
enthusiasm, which tended to throw human society
into confusion, was overcome by means of the
Pauline doctrine of the Spirit, and Pauline ethics.
Without letting go of the apocalyptic prospect, he
transferred the emphasis of the belief in redemption
from the future to the present, to a new life which
was not first to begin at the end of the world, but
is already present in the hearts of those who have
the spirit of sonship and thereby peace with God,
freedom from the world, love to the brethren.
Thus it was by his doctrine of the Spirit that he
restrained and ethicised the primitive Christian
enthusiasm, moderated the unhealthy other-worldliness, and prepared the soil for a "reasonable service"
of God in the loyal fulfilment of social duties; to
the State, to marriage, property, and work, he gave
their due places, and barred out the communistic
tendencies to idleness and mendicity which had
manifested themselves in the earliest Messianic
churches. In short, he led Christianity past the
critical years of its enthusiastic childhood and into
the path of an orderly church life, and by so doing
he saved its historical future and made possible its
development into a world-religion.

It is true there is in the history of the world no
progress or gain which is not purchased at a certain
cost, and this was the case with the vast gain for
which Christianity is indebted to the apostle Paul.

Its emancipation from the bonds of Judaism, and introduction into the Græco-Roman world, were only made possible by means of the distinction of the Spirit of Christ from the historical manifestation of the Person of Jesus. That was an abstraction which did not indeed destroy the ethico-religious value of the person of Jesus—that constitutes indeed the content of the Christ-Spirit—but nevertheless exposed it to the danger that the definiteness of its historical character might be sublimated into an abstract idea. And this danger became so much the greater, the more the tendency grew up in the Gentile-Christian world to regard the Spirit of Christ as a metaphysical being similar to the gods of mythology, or made these philosophical hypostatised conceptions the object of further speculation which took leave of the historical ground altogether, like that of the Gnostics in the second century. Against this danger of a complete dissipation of its religious content, and of its definite historical character, into vague Gnostic theories and phantasies, Christianity was not sufficiently protected by the Pauline theology, because this itself rested on an abstraction, and contained gnosticising elements. It needed, therefore, to have this defect supplied from the historical side. This end was met by the Gospel narratives, in which the historical picture of the life and teaching of Jesus was definitely fixed, on the basis of the recollections of the primitive community, and handed over to the Church as its priceless bequest. In the realism of the Gospel history, Christianity possesses the indispensable counterpoise to the idealism of the Pauline theology. As Christianity needed, and continues to need, Paul to free it from every kind of Jewish narrowness and limitation, so it needed, and still needs, the Gospels to give it its historical orientation, and to enable it to maintain itself against the manifold forms of heathenising error.